RE-COVERING MODERNISM

To My Parents
For Filling My Life with Books
And Love

Re-Covering Modernism
Pulps, Paperbacks, and the Prejudice of Form

DAVID M. EARLE
University of West Florida, USA

ASHGATE

© David M. Earle 2009

All rights reserved. No part of this publication may be reproduced, stored in a retrieval system or transmitted in any form or by any means, electronic, mechanical, photocopying, recording or otherwise without the prior permission of the publisher.

David M. Earle has asserted his moral right under the Copyright, Designs and Patents Act, 1988, to be identified as the author of this work.

Published by
Ashgate Publishing Limited
Wey Court East
Union Road
Farnham
Surrey, GU9 7PT
England

Ashgate Publishing Company
Suite 420
101 Cherry Street
Burlington
VT 05401-4405
USA

www.ashgate.com

British Library Cataloguing in Publication Data
Earle, David M.
Re-covering modernism: pulps, paperbacks, and the prejudice of form
   1. Modernism (Literature)
   I. Title
   809.9'112

Library of Congress Cataloging-in-Publication Data
Earle, David M.
   Re-covering modernism: pulps, paperbacks, and the prejudice of form / by David M. Earle.
       p. cm.
   Includes bibliographical references.
   ISBN 978-0-7546-6154-2 (alk. paper)
    1. Modernism (Literature) I. Title.

PN56.M54E27 2009
809'.9112—dc22

2008033888

ISBN: 978-0-7546-6154-2

Printed and bound in Great Britain by
TJ International Ltd, Padstow, Cornwall

Contents

List of Figures   *vi*
Acknowledgments   *viii*

Introduction   1

1   *The Smart Set*, Modernism, and the Expanded Field of Magazine Production   17

2   Pulp Modernism   71

3   Lurid Paperbacks and the Re-Covering of Modernism   151

Bibliography   *219*
Index   *235*

List of Figures

I.1	*Man's Magazine*, Oct. 1961 © 1961 Almat Publishing Corporation	2
1.1	*Smart Set*, June 1914 © 1914 John Adams Thayer Corporation	19
1.2	*Smart Set*, Sept. 1915 © 1915 Smart Set Company, Inc.	43
1.3	*Smart Set*, April 1923 © 1923 Smart Set Company, Inc.	44
1.4	*Smart Set*, Sept. 1923 © 1923 Smart Set Company, Inc.	46
1.5	*Saucy Stories*, Nov. 1919 © 1919 The Inter-Continental Publishing Corporation	47
1.6	*Snappy Stories*, Dec. 1, 1925 © 1924 New Fiction Publishing Corporation	53
1.7	*Flapper*, May 1923 © 1923 The Flapper Publishing Company	55
1.8	*Smart Set*, July 1927 © 1927 Magus Magazine Corporation	57
1.9	*Golden Book*, Dec. 1925 © The Review of Reviews Corporation	67
2.1	*Courtroom Stories*, Aug.–Sept. 1931 © 1931 Good Story Magazine Company, image supplied by Adventure House	76
2.2	*All Story Love Stories*, Sept. 21, 1935 © 1935 The Frank A. Munsey Company	81
2.3	*The Plot Genie*, 1931 © Ernest F. Gagnon Company. Copyright never renewed	96
2.4	*Film Fun*, April 1930 © 1930 Dell Publishing Company	99
2.5	*Black Mask*, Feb. 1922 © 1922 Pro-Distributers	108
2.6	*Operator #5*, Dec. 1934 © 1934 Popular Publications, image supplied by Girasol Collectibles	117

2.7	Ad, Nuxated Iron from *Parisienne*, May 1919 inside back cover	133
2.8	Ad, International Correspondence School, *Argosy*, Aug. 7, 1937. Pg. 1	134
2.9	*Illustrated World*, Dec. 1916 © 1916 Illustrated World	138
2.10	Keeler Graph, *The Author and Journalist*, April 1928. Pgs. 18–19. Copyright never renewed	143
2.11	*The Author and Journalist*, April 1928 © 1925 The Author and Journalist	144
3.1	*Bubu of Montparnasse*. Berkley Publishing Corporation, 1957	152
3.2	*Against the Grain*. Albert and Charles Boni, 1930	156
3.3	*Portrait of the Artist as a Young Man*. Penguin Signet, 1948	163
3.4	*Nana*. Pocket Books, 1945	170
3.5	*The Great Gatsby*. Bantam Books, 1946	171
3.6	*Women in Love*. Avon, 1951	181
3.7	*Aaron's Rod*. Avon, 1956	182
3.8	*Snappy Magazine*, Sept. 1935 © 1935 D.M. Publishing Company	191
3.9	Ad, Uthaid from *Ulysses*, A Collectors Publication (pirated) n.d.	192
3.10	*Pylon*. Signet, 1951	199
3.11	*Wild Palms*. Penguin; 1948; Signet, 1950	207
3.12	*Across the River and Into the Trees*. Dell, 1953	211
3.13	*One Lonely Night*. Signet, 1952	212
3.14	*The Damned*. Lion Library, 1956	216

Acknowledgments

The idea of this book started, I must believe, long ago with me lying on the carpet in my father's library, leafing through the pages of Tony Goodstone's book on the pulps. I couldn't have been more than eight or nine years old, but I remember the fascination that the sensational, colorful, often gruesome but always exciting cover illustrations held for me. I was soon voracious for Edgar Rice Burroughs, Robert E. Howard, H.P Lovecraft; I collected their paperbacks, early Grosset and Dunlap reprints, and eventually their pulp magazines. And as I grew older I ranged wider, into Hemingway, Fitzgerald, and eventually Joyce—all under the quiet influence of my father's library and my mother's indulgence. Hence it is for them that I must dedicate this book for instilling in me the passion for reading, the academic hunger, and the somewhat maddening fetishes of a true collector. But most of all, for the unceasing love and support and faith that allowed them to never dictate, but let my passion lead. And I am of course indebted to the rest of my family: my sister and brother; to my grandparents who are sorely missed; to Brisa Roche; Scott Bakoss, Jamie DiPietro, and Luca. And Monica.

Early on, Patrick McCarthy, Zack Bowen, Anthony Barthelemy, and Brandy Kershner were all invaluable due to their insight, their patient and particular readings, and their enthusiasm. Ann Ardis also gave me wonderful advice and suggestions. Ira Nadel, Jane Lewty, Robert Scholes, Ron Corthell, Robert Trogdon, Adam McKible, Suzanne Churchill, Bill Brockman, Mary Chapman, Sharon Hamilton, Jim LeBlanc, and Cheryl Hindrichs all helped along the way by sharing academic insight or a drink or both. Alison Kelly helped with some photos and quite a bit more. For support and understanding I must thank Bridget Haas and Rochelle Verchick, Johnny Evers and Marilyn Herschman, and, of course, Emily Vera who has remained a steadfast friend through it all. And thanks go to the great bookman and friend, Mike Zubal (www.zubalbooks.com), whose generosity with books and a fine meal or two inspired quite a bit of literary insight. Thank you all.

In the pulp world, I would like to thank John Gunnison, Doug Ellis, Alfred Jan, and the late, great Sheldon Jaffery. The UCLA Special Collections was fruitful during the early stages of research. I am indebted to Allen Hemlock at Else Fine Books for the scan of the Bantam *Gatsby* dust jacket.

Introduction

Man's Magazine is a typical example of the mid-century men's adventure magazine, a genre known for sensational color covers that usually featured men or scantily clad women being attacked by baboons, Nazis, or more scantily clad women. The December 1961 issue is no exception (see Figure I.1). A portrait painting of Field Marshall Kesselring, "The Nazi Butcher of Rome," glares from its cover, complete with warts and beads of sweat. In the background shirtless male prisoners are being gunned down by Nazi guards. The headline reads "10 Italians Must Die For Every German." The rest of the magazine substantiates the cover's sensationalism. Besides the usual ads for stag films, correspondence schools, and hair tonics, there are stories on jungle survival, Brigitte Bardot, ways to improve one's sex life, and hidden among these is James Joyce's short story "Two Gallants," replete with suggestive illustration and the tagline: "She made love willingly, but he – and his pal – wanted more."

The sensational connotations of this version of "Two Gallants" might surprise those familiar with the canonized reading of the story as being more about economics and Dublin homo-social behavior rather than risqué sexuality. Considering Joyce's reputation as the flagship of modernism, it is surprising that he is appearing in such a venue at all. In actuality, Joyce's appearance here was really not so strange for he made numerous appearances in similar magazines throughout the 1950s. The first issue of *Nugget* magazine (Dec. 1955) republished "The Boarding House." There were articles about him in magazines such as *Debonair* (Feb. 1961), or about *Ulysses* such as *Modern Man's* "Classic Battle over a Sex Classic" (March 1957). The example of "Two Gallants" is a bit more extreme since *Man's Magazine* is lower on the cultural scale from such pseudo-literary *Playboy* knockoffs, but Joyce wasn't the only "highbrow" author to appear in these magazines; they were liberally peppered with stories by modernists: *Gent Magazine* featured Faulkner, John O'Hara, Huysman, and even Jean Paul Sartre; *Escapade* featured S.J. Perelman, William Soroyan, Somerset Maugham, and Jack Kerouac; *The Dude* featured D.H. Lawrence, Farrell, Faulkner, Budd Schulberg, and Robert Lowry; *High* featured Farrell and Pierre Louys; the list goes on. Other authors that appeared regularly were Nelson Algren, Norman Mailer, Erskine Caldwell, Ben Hecht, and Paul Bowles. Many magazines also featured articles *about* famous literary figures: not only Joyce, but Faulkner, Henry Miller, DeMaupassant, Lawrence, and Oscar Wilde as well.

These stories and articles are interspersed with pictorial features that tie into the innate risqué nature of modernist art, such as the premiere issue of *Nugget*'s articles "The Eternal Idol," about famous erotic sculptures like Rodin's "The Kiss," and "Modern Art for the Modern Man," which counterpoints nude pinups with paintings by Renoir and Modigliani. These articles rely upon, or at least belie, a certain fascination with the dynamics of modernism. This use of highbrow art and

Fig. I.1   *Man's Magazine*, Oct. 1961 © 1961 Almat Publishing Corporation

authors was pragmatic, giving such magazines cultural capital to fight censorship, but it also parallels how modernist works often relied and profited by notoriety and sensationalism—the popularity and canonization of *Ulysses* and *Lady Chatterly's Lover* are the obvious examples. Furthermore, modernist pieces in this context, like "Two Gallants" and "The Boarding House," recapture the innate risqué nature they held at their original publication, lost in their usual sanctioned surroundings of academic anthologies or editions—indeed, *Man's Magazine*'s marketing (taglines and illustrations) of "Two Gallants" relies upon the same ambiguity that Joyce uses to make the story's climax so effective.

These men's magazines of the 1950s and 1960s are the final apotheosis, the death throes of the Pulp Magazine, and apparitions of modernism under these hyper-masculine connotations can even be seen as the culmination of Pound and company's reaction to a popular literature that they defined as too effeminate. Such instances of "Pulp Modernism" don't mark colonization of the movement by the sensational mass market, but actually divulge an alternate populist history of modernism that can be traced back to its very beginnings, one that has been studiously ignored. This book is an overview of that history of popular modernism.

I chose to begin with Joyce in the 1950s not only because he is the archmodernist, but because his largely overlooked *popular* publishing career spans, encapsulates, and bookends populist modernism. This is especially true in America where he started his publishing career more than 40 years earlier in the middlebrow *Smart Set*, which published "Eveline" and "A Little Cloud" in 1915 alongside authors such as Achmed Abdullah, the author of the pulpish *Buccaneer in Spats* and *The Thief of Baghdad*. Joyce also appeared throughout the 1920s and 1930s in mass reprint magazines such as *Golden Book*, *Two Worlds*, and *Fiction Parade*, and in the 1940s and 1950s in popular men's magazines and paperback editions and anthologies. Poetry of his from *Chamber Music* even appeared in *American Girl* (May 1933), the magazine for the Girl Scouts of America.

These overlooked, popular manifestations of modernism involve a series of submerged tensions and dichotomies that are emblematic—and problematic—to a reified idea of modernism as a canonized, defined movement. The idea of a popular, alternate, or shadow history of modernism singular with its inception and rise (but not canonization) troubles the idea of the continuous absorption of the avant-garde into mass-culture; rather, it forwards the idea of a popular avant-garde. That Joyce appeared alongside established pulp authors in *The Smart Set*, or that the magazine's editors, H.L. Mencken and George Jean Nathan, were also publishers of the lowbrow pulps *Parisienne*, *Saucy Stories*, and *Black Mask* is enough to warrant critical attention. The overlooked *Smart Set*—just one of the many ignored outlets for modernism considered in this study—illuminates how slanted our history of the movement is in regard to the *forms* of modernism; our increasingly sophisticated understanding of modernism is still reductively based upon the material forms that those early literary historians thought worthy of archiving: the little magazine, manuscripts, and first editions, rather than reprint magazines and literary digests, reprint and circulating library hardback editions, pulp magazines, and paperbacks—all forms that evince a modernist (yet unsanctioned, ignored) heritage. *Re-Covering Modernism*, an exploration and illumination of modernism's popular genealogy, establishes a relationship far from antagonistic between modernism and the most popular and ephemeral literary forms of the time; it does so by focusing on the forms of popular literary production in the twentieth century: early fiction and reprint magazines, interwar pulp magazines, and popular paperbacks.

This portrait of modernism is admittedly controversial, though less so than it would have been thirty years ago when the concept of modernism was still built upon exclusion and elitism, constructed as a singular coterie avant-garde movement based on stylistic experimentation and difficulty, and defined by its "great divide" from popular culture. Artists and critics have been attempting to define modernism as a cohesive movement since its inception; indeed, the date of its inception has been a point of contention, whether Woolf's 1910 or the "men of 1914" of Eliot and Pound. Such an attempt for concrete dates and, more importantly, definition is obviously counterintuitive to the multivalence of modernism. Certain books, like Michael Levenson's *A Genealogy of Modernism* (1984), attempt to sidestep problematic definitions by seeing the term "modernism" as a necessary evil: as Levin puts it, "Vague terms still signify," and "As a rough way of locating our attention, 'modernism' will do."[1] Yet such flippant motioning to perhaps the most problematic labeling in English studies history is indicative of the deeper reductivism in both Levenson's book and pre-revisionary modernist studies. Though a sophisticated study of the criticism of Arnold, Eliot, Pound, and Hulme, Levenson's book just propagates the Monolithic and Elite definitions of modernism: Monolithic because he does not take into consideration the rich histories of women, homosexuals, and minorities working within (and against) the movement; Elite because he never takes into account how modernism was working within the marketplace or even that there were popular forms and aspects of the movement. This latter is more forgivable than the former, for the feminist revision of the modernist canon was well under way when Levenson was writing in the mid-1980s; the attention paid to women writers in his book is confined to three passing references to Woolf—a gross injustice even by 1984 standards. But the latter—the debunking of modernism's elite coterie—has only now come into full revisionist momentum.

But this still leaves the problem of definition. Invariably, the more attempts there are, the more modernism becomes difficult to pin down. The problem or "paradox" (as Robert Scholes has labeled it) of modernism's resistance to categorization and reduction is in actuality the problem of the academy, of the codifying mindset.[2] At its very heart, modernism defies borders, it is anomalous, anti-structural. The shortcomings innate in applying such a necessarily reductive codifying ethos to a multivariate, multivalent, and ultimately noncohesive movement become evident in those many contrasting dates that critics and artists have assigned to the beginning and end of modernism, and more so in the revisionists' charges of reductivism aimed at the idea that modernism was solely the realm of white males.[3] The worrying of the term and definition of modernism has been one

---

[1] Michael Levenson, *A Genealogy of Modernism* (NY: Cambridge U P, 1984), vii.

[2] See Scholes, *Paradoxy of Modernism* (New Haven: Yale U P, 2006).

[3] See Bonnie Kime Scott, *Refiguring Modernism: The Women of 1928* (Bloomington: Indiana U P, 1995), 80–83.

with the expansion (or explosion) of the traditional modernist canon through the recovery of lost authors, forgotten texts, overlooked little magazines, and media such as film, jazz, and radio. Feminist, postcolonial, and African-Americanist critics have justly revealed the omissions of the predominately white, male model of the artistic avant-garde forwarded by largely male and new critical literary historians. Feminist critics were the pioneers of this and continue to be so, ranging from such innovative works as Bonnie Kime Scott's *Refiguring Modernism* (1996) and Shari Benstock's *Women of the Left Bank* (1987) that forwarded the female role in the modernist agenda, to the rediscovery of female authors such as Mary Butts, to the recent and promising studies of print and periodical culture, such as Francesca Sawaya's *Modern Women, Modern Work,* Jean Lutes's *Front Page Girls: Women Journalists in American Culture and Fiction* (2006), and Sharon Harris and Ellen Gruber Garvey's *Blue Pencils and Hidden Hands* (2004). Riding this wave of expansion, academic societies and journals, such as the Modernist Studies Association, *Modernism/Modernity*, and *Cultures of Modernism*, have taken to using "Modernisms" as indicator of the movement(s)'s plurality.[4]

This revisionist momentum has brought modernist studies to a moment of both crisis and fertility: as Jennifer Wicke pointed out at the initial meeting of the Modernist Studies Association and in an ensuing article for *Modernism/Modernity*, the multitude of modernisms and modernist re-envisioning threaten to undermine our own critical project.[5] For Wicke, our reinvention of modernism into "new modernisms" involves a "purifying" agenda without acknowledgment of our own implication with Modernism's "brand name" or market dynamic. This, and the ensuing debates about what *is* (or should be) modernism only encapsulates or highlights the pluralist agenda of modernism that was simplified by the monolithic definition of the movement constructed in the mid-century by new critical canonization and by critics such as Malcolm Cowley. It is this plurality that Wicke appreciates in her suggestion to see ourselves—the critics and historians of modernism—in terms of colportage, displaying a simultaneity of plurality, a richness of product not so much without value judgment but heavily invested with a plurality of values. In this sense, *Re-Covering Modernism*, organized around fiction and reprint magazines of the teens and 1920s, interwar pulp magazines, and '40s and '50s paperbacks, is critical colportage on a massive scale concerned with forms of publishing that consisted of dozens of genres, hundreds of subgenres, thousands of titles, and millions of readers, all seen in relation to, implicated within the traditions of modernism. And like colporteur in its true sense—a traveling hawker of books and newspapers—this study is innately about and organized around the material product, modernism in the marketplace, as found on the newsstand, in the drugstore, over the counter.

---

[4] See also Richard Shepherd's "The Problematics of European Modernism," in Giles' *Theorizing Modernism* (NY: Routledge, 1993).

[5] Jennifer Wicke, "Appreciation, Depreciation: Modernism's Speculative Bubble," *Modernism / Modernity*, Vol. 8, No. 3, 389–403.

Likewise, it might be useful to define the age of modernism materially—like the Iron Age or Bronze Age—as the Paper Age, as a way to broaden the definition of the movement, or at least to spark thinking about it in terms of material production. In the latter half of the nineteenth century, technology made possible affordable paper, printing, graphic reproduction, and large-scale means of distribution. The birth of national magazines and newspapers, modern advertising and circulation, mass publications, mass entertainment created the first media-influenced mass culture, where an entire nation had simultaneous access to the same titles, authors, articles, news, and opinions. As Mathew Schneirov points out, "Popular magazines, forerunners of modern mass communications, were central in the development of the new social order of corporate capitalism."[6] These things—mass culture, popular magazines, advertising, corporate capitalism—are exactly what modernism is traditionally said to be a reaction against, to be separated from by a "great divide." Hence it is the little magazines, (small, privately produced, noncommercial avant-garde periodicals) that are seen as the forms and propagators of the movement. But if, as divulged by popular material manifestations of modernism, this great divide is illusory, more of a posture for self-marketing, then modernism is just another aspect of this age of production, of the paper age. In Andreas Huyssen's influential but hotly contested study of the Great Divide, mass culture has always been the hidden counterpoint of modernism.[7] In *Re-Covering Modernism* though, modernism has always been an available aspect of mass culture.

My title, *Re-Covering Modernism*, not only plays off of my focus on the visual material aspects of marketing modernism (covers, dustwrappers, the physical properties of book production), but also my return and rediscovery of aspects of modernism that have been overlooked exactly due to their very mass appeal, marketability, and sensationalism. If we consider the outward aspects of a text, such as cover, font, price paid, and venue as integral to a book's overall "aura," then the marketing of a book is an important text in its own right, necessary to study. The construction of elite modernism would have it that literature is above monetary concerns, and the corresponding forms that have been archived by the academy have been collected as rare products of the pure production of art. The forms of the all-fiction wood-pulp magazines and the mass paperback examined here are oppositional to this idea. They epitomize literary ephemera in the mass marketplace: the pulps, for example, were seen as disposable literature produced cheaply on disposable (almost instantly disintegrating) paper. Likewise, modernist reprints in popular digests and magazines, cheap circulating library editions and paperbacks are uncollected and unexamined despite the fact that they had circulations in the tens or even hundreds of thousands. There has been no academic capturing in amber of what has always been considered and remains the literary trash of the early twentieth century. Instead, pulp magazines and paperbacks have

---

[6] Matthew Schneirov, *The Dream of a New Social Order: Popular Magazines in America 1893–1914* (NY: Columbia U P), 1994.

[7] Huyssen, *After the Great Divide: Modernism, Mass Culture, Postmodernism* (Bloomington: Indiana U P, 1986).

existed solely in the hands of collectors and in an (ironically, given the popular nature of the pulps) increasingly rarified and subculture marketplace. Literary reprint magazines are even less scrutinized, uncollected since the literature therein is usually available in more desirable, earlier editions.

This trashy and ephemeral aura helps explain the long-standing academic ignorance of these forms, for academia, especially as concerning literature and the avant-garde, establishes its reputation in opposition to material, economic, or physical dynamics. Yet there is another element of irony in the long purportedly antagonistic relationship between the pulp forms and modernism, for modernism has always been fascinated with, even reliant upon, capturing and translating the ephemeral and common, which, in literary terms, is embodied in the pulp form. We can easily find traces of this modernist agenda as early as 1863, when Baudelaire stated that "Modernity is the transitory, the ephemeral, the contingent, one half of art, the other half being the eternal and immutable" and follow it through, at least, to *Finnegans Wake*'s nexus of contemporary allusions.

Re-Covering Modernism takes as its point of impetus the symbolic reliance upon such popular paper ephemera by modernists such as Joyce, Flaubert, Woolf, and Faulkner in whose fiction flies the paper debris of twentieth-century culture: Joyce's use of pamphlets, throwaways, advertising, and popular novels in *Ulysses*; Flaubert's use of romance novels in *Madame Bovary*; Woolf's use of the newspaper in *Between the Acts*; Faulkner's use of the popular magazine in *Light in August*, *Pylon*, and *Wild Palms*. These authors used paper ephemera, often imbued with cultural and symbolic resonance, as a means to flesh out their realistic world portrait. Only recently have the critics of modernism started to examine advertising, newspapers, and popular periodicals within the work of modernists, either as overt allusions or subtle influences. Brandy Kershner, for example, has examined such diverse Joycean allusions as the pamphlets of physical culturist Eugene Sandow as a means to look at Bloom's masculinity, and Victorian funeral and spirit photography to look at the unseen presence of Bloom's dead son Rudy.[8] Jennifer Wicke has likewise looked to popular magazines and advertising in relation to both Bloom and Gerty.[9] More recently, Patrick Collier has examined the relationship between newspaper journalism as an outlet for modernism, as well as its role within modernist fiction.[10] Such materialist criticism is revisionist, nontraditional since it embeds modernism in the marketplace; it sees modernist literature as involved with and influenced by material production. This is at odds with the construction of modernism as being above the dynamics of consumerism, despite the fact that this is itself a topic, often paradoxically treated, within modernist fiction.

---

[8] Kershner, "The Strongest Man in the World: Joyce or Sandow?" *James Joyce Quarterly*, Vol. 30, No. 4 (Summer/Fall 1993), 667–694; "Framing Rudy and Photography," *Journal of Modern Literature*, Vol. 22, No. 2 (Winter 1998/99), 265–292.

[9] Wicke, *Advertising Fictions* (NY: Columbia U P, 1988).

[10] Patrick Collier, *Modernism on Fleet Street* (Hampshire: Ashgate, 2006).

Seeing modernism in the marketplace or, in Wicke's case, as a brand name, is a fertile trend for critics: books such as Cherniak, Gould, and Warwick's *Modernist Writers and the Marketplace*; Dettmar and Watt's *Marketing Modernisms*; Lawrence Rainey's *Institutions of Modernism*, Katherine Turner's *Marketing Modernism Between the Two World Wars*, and Loren Glass's *Authors Inc.* all come to mind as notable explorations of the business side of modernism. In *Modernism and the Culture of Market Society,* John Xiros Cooper goes even further by contending that the coterie aspects of modernism paved the way for modern corporate society. There are also numerous single-author studies that examine closely the economics of writing and publishing, such as Schwartz's *Creating Faulkner's Reputation*, Garry Leonard's *Advertizing and Commodity Culture in Joyce*, and Robert Trogdon's *The Lousy Racket: Hemingway, Scribners and the Business of Literature*. Such explorations fly in the face of the construction on the part of both modernist entrepreneurs, like Pound and Eliot, and the subsequent academics of the avant-garde being unconcerned with economics and salability, a stance that certainly evokes a certain cultural capital that translated into the marketplace: the *Little Review*'s masthead of "Making No Compromise with Public Taste" is an obvious example.

Similarly, *Re-Covering Modernism* sees commercialism as an aspect of modernism, and modernism itself, especially pulp modernism, as a result of hyper-production in the age of capitalism. Wicke's analogy of Modernism as brand name is helpful in illustrating the self-marketing aspects of the movement: its elitism, newness, and innate cultural betterment—ideas integral to this book's agenda. Yet this study is certainly—exuberantly so—guilty of Wicke's warnings about "devaluing" the brand, not of "purging" or "purifying" modernism but of sullying it, pulling it down from a cultural height and putting it in the hands of immigrants and the working class. To a certain extent, this book's agenda is playing devil's advocate in regard to modernism by comparing it to an extremity of production, a sensational form, as means to both "burst modernism's speculative bubble" and to make obvious the elephant in the parlor which is early-twentieth-century mass publishing. I am not trying so much to raise pulp fiction to canonical heights as much as to broaden our scope of study, or, more exact, to show the limitations innate to our historical scope of study; as Michael Coyle points out in his rejoinder to Wicke, the issue "is less about canon-busting than it is about changing the criteria of canon formation," in this case, to step outside of canonicity and examine its dynamics for innate prejudice.[11] In other words, whereas *Re-Covering Modernism* stands upon the shoulders of recent works that have resubmerged modernism into the marketplace, it contends that there is still further to go in seeing modernism as a product in the *popular* marketplace. The trail for this has been paved by recent works that have expanded the study of modernist periodicals, broadening the old portrait of the movement beyond those sanctioned and archived forms of the little magazines: small coterie magazines produced by and for the artistic

---

[11] See Coyle, "With a Plural Vengeance: Modernism as (Flaming) Brand," *Modernist Cultures*, Vol. 1, No. 1., 16.

elite. Mark Morrison's *The Public Face of Modernism* and Lawrence Rainey's *Institutions of Modernism*, two of the more influential examinations, work to expose modernism's involvement in the marketplace, such as the influence of mass periodicals on the *Masses'* marketing techniques, Pound and Eliot's pandering to *Vanity Fair* as an outlet for *The Wasteland*, and Joyce's involvement with the rare book trade as a form of patronage. These studies have been influential through their consideration of modernism's "market dynamics." *Re-Covering Modernism* looks beyond modernism's traditional, elite, and restrictive forms by considering a truly popular modernism. When considering the overall scene of publishing, which I do at the end of Chapter 1, such venues as the *Masses* and *Vanity Fair* are such a slight market percentage as to be inconsistent with the overall influence and spread of modernism, especially as our concept of modernism deconstructs into a myriad of modernisms. Modernism therefore must have been available through other formats such as *The Golden Book,* just one popular reprint magazine, which flourished throughout the 1920s, and which had a monthly distribution in 1925 of 175,000 copies (i.e., a circulation of over half a million).[12]

The interwar wood pulp magazine was another such venue but one that, in its extremity of production, reflected all aspects of culture: critical, formulaic, prejudiced, modernist alike. The pulps lasted for decades, with hundreds of titles and millions of readers; they were the meat and potatoes of the American reading public and rode the wave of globalization to Europe and as far as Australia. Yet the pulp form is missing from any focused study of modernism and most academic studies of twentieth-century American publishing, despite the fact that they made up a huge percentage of the American public's reading material—one contemporary study averaged the pulp audience as upward of 3,000,000 readers in the early 1930s. The pulps are the glaring omission in the history of American readership. This is all the more surprising because the pulp magazine as a symbol or allusion appears within many important modernist works from Joyce to Faulkner, and many modernists, such as Djuna Barnes and Bob Brown, got their start in the pulp magazines.

Yet the pulp magazines are scarcely mentioned in modernist criticism: among the rare exceptions are an essay on the subject by Joseph Blotner in Abadie and Fowlers' *Faulkner and Popular Culture,* it is a subcurrent in Greg Foster's *Murdering Masculinities*, and in a few scattered footnotes from general works regarding Hammett or Chandler—all of which concern themselves with the dynamics of hard-boiled fiction. This, in general, parallels the overall neglect of the pulp magazines in magazine and publishing histories, though this seems to be changing as the sensational covers for pulps move into the realm of popular kitsch. Modernist literary studies comes closest to acknowledging the pulps in works that examine hard-boiled fiction, which, due to its cynicism, proletariat heroes, and urban setting, offers an excellent albeit obvious parallel to modernism. There are a handful of such books of literary criticism on pulps, the most important of which are Sean McCann's *Gumshoe America*, Erin Smith's *Hardboiled: Working Class Readers and Pulp Magazines* (influenced by Michael Denning's important

---

[12] Obviously, the newspaper was another outlet for modernism. See Collier, cited above.

book about Dime Novels and the nineteenth-century working class, *Mechanical Accents*), Christopher Breu's *Hard-Boiled Masculinities*, and Woody Haut's books about 1950s noir paperbacks. Because all of these studies concern themselves solely with hard-boiled fiction, however, their portrait is narrow and slanted. Smith's book in particular falls short in its construction of the pulp audience in that there were a myriad of other genres and pulp audiences: Romance Pulps, Spicy Pulps, True Confession Pulps, Science Fiction, etc. And almost without exception, the romance pulps outsold any other genre (see circulation information in Chapter 2 [p. 78–9]) Breu's book, a study of iconographic pulp masculinity, continues this trend. With the exception of hard-boiled, pulps have been uniformly written off by literary historians and cultural critics alike even though pulp titles existed by the hundreds at newsstands during the heyday of modernism, and despite the fact that by their very mass they emitted a gravitational pull, economic and stylistic, on the publishing world. Though narrow in scope, the above mentioned works prove the expanding field of pulp study, but an exploration of the relationship between modernism and the large body of popular literature—either in comparative or adversarial terms—is sorely needed.

The need for such a study of 20th century popular periodicals is all the more necessary given the growing popularity of periodical studies in the critical canon—already a well-established trend in Victorian Studies, yet a relatively recent one in modernist studies. This lag is due, I believe, to the prejudice against popular material forms innate to the canonization of modernism and missing from Victorian Studies; the dynamics of elitism innate to, say, the publishing history of Joyce are missing from the publishing history of Dickens. The publishing history of Joyce though was not entirely coterie or elite, as I have already pointed out, but the idea that it was has been handed down to us and militantly protected: consider the legal battle against Samuel Roth for pirating *Ulysses* in the innately popular *Two Worlds* magazine. Such a popular version of *Ulysses* undermined the book's marketing strategy as a rare commodity, as an investment worthy of smuggling out of Paris. Hence the portrait of Victorian literary production is much healthier, much more fleshed out than that of Modernism.[13]

As Laurel Brake points out in "On Print Culture: The State We're In," the robust health of periodical studies is due to the rise of technology that expands the manner and site of archival study; rare and ephemeral periodicals are available to more readers in much more reader-friendly ways.[14] Modernist studies is also benefitting from this moment, as illustrated by Robert Scholes and Sean Latham's Modernist Journals Project (MJP), a digital archive of important pre-1922 modernist periodicals. This infinitely promising project makes such rare little magazines as Lewis's *Blast* available for the student, critic, and common reader alike. The need

---

[13] See Latham and Scholes, "The Rise of Periodical Studies," *PMLA* (Vol. 121, No. 2), March 2006, 517–531.

[14] "On Print Culture: The State We're In," *Journal of Victorian Culture* (Spring 2001, Vol. 6, Issue 1), as well as her *Print in Transition, 1850–1910* (NY: Palgrave, 2001) and *Encounters in the Victorian Press* (NY: Palgrave, 2005) edited with Julie Codell.

for expanding our idea of the archive has quickly become obvious just since the MJP's inception. Whereas it was initially concerned only with little magazines, it has quickly expanded its scope to popular magazines as well, illustrated by their current aim to digitalize *Scribner's Magazine*. There is still much farther to go before the idea is accepted that modernism was available through mass-distributed reprint magazines, news magazines, or popular fiction magazines.

Recent books such as Ann Ardis's *Modernism and Cultural Conflict* (2002), Adam McKible's *The Space and Place of Modernism: The Russian Revolution, Little Magazines, and New York* (2002), Suzanne Churchill's *The Little Magazine Others and the Renovation of American Poetry* (2006), Dean Irvine's *Editing Modernism: Women and Little Magazine Cultures in Canada* (2007), and McKible and Churchill's *Little Magazines and Modernism: New Approaches* (2008) are all important and groundbreaking in their pushing the boundaries of the scene and production of modernism. I offer a broader view of the larger scene of magazine publishing and the availability of modernism via popular periodicals—two aspects integral to *Re-Covering Modernism*.

Luckily, the popular sphere of the pulp and genre fiction fan have kept the pulps alive in republications, fanzines, conventions, and histories.[15] The amount and quality of ground-level research on pulp publishers, authors, and illustrators is worthy of notice and respect from academic critics; whereas it is rare for a modernist critic to hunt out the surviving publishers, compatriots, and participants in the original scene of modernism, pulp collectors have amassed a daunting archive of original sources though these are mostly regulated to hard-to-find pulp fanzines that are not collected in academic archives (and generally hard to find). The true history of pulp production (publishing records, author bios, and the pulps themselves) are in danger of slipping into oblivion—though that is where they've always resided for academic study.

As the subtitle of this book points out, the prejudice in academia is one against form, namely the popular forms of modernism that have been ignored for two broad reasons: 1) they were forms of mass publishing with all their unavoidable commercial trappings, forms produced cheaply for quick consumption and disposal;

---

[15] John Gunnison's Adventure House is an excellent example of the type of publishing house that keeps the pulps alive. Over the last few years, Gunnison has published overviews, often with lovingly reproduced illustrations, of different genres of pulps or illustrators, such as Doug Ellis's *Uncovered: The Hidden Art of the Girlie Pulps* (Silver Spring, MD: Adventure House, 2003); *Pulp Fictioneers: Adventures in the Storytelling Business* (Silver Spring, MD: Adventure House, 2004); and *Belarski, Pulp Art Masters* (Silver Spring, MD: 2003). Gunnison also publishes individual pulp magazine reprints and *High Adventure*, a pulp fanzine. Off Trail Publications, whose Pulpwood Days series is an excellent insider view of the pulps. Volume 1, *Editors You Want To Know* (Castroville, CA: Off-Trail Publications, 2007), for example, uses long-out-of-print articles from hard-to-find trade journals such as *The Author and Journalist* and *Writer's Digest*, both of which are primary sources for info on the pulp industry. Girasol Collectables is also worth mention for their wonderfully faithful reproduction of hard-to-find (and usually extremely expensive) pulps.

2) because they were irrevocably linked to the mass public and working class in the intellectual's mind, as blatantly illustrated by the eugenic anti-pulp and anti-paperback diatribes of critics such as H.W. Van Loon and Malcolm Cowley, which I discuss in the second and third chapters. There are a few other critical works that forward a working-class modernism: most comprehensive is Jonathan Rose's *The Intellectual Life of the British Working Class*, which convincingly builds the case of a formidable intellectual avant-garde active in the lower classes of British society, familiar and versed in modernism. Other works, such as Patrick Collier's *Modernism on Fleet Street* demonstrate that modernists relied upon and were available in mass-circulated newspapers. *Re-Covering Modernism* is similar to both of these studies in that it proposes both a working-class modernism and canonical figures of modernism available to the working class, but initially uses the United States as its location.

Collier's study is exceptional in that it looks beyond little magazines for a venue of modernism, important because (as I've already mentioned) the forms of popular modernism have been eclipsed by forms such as the little magazine and small press publications, which were much more obviously artistic and conducive to the manner of elite marketing pioneered by high modernism. This has been substantiated in the reciprocal relationship between the academy and the literary archives, that is, what is archived is that which is worth studying and what academia deems worth studying is that which is in the archives. Little magazines are the perfect example of this. Along these same lines, written forms of popular modernism have been ignored by academia in lieu of other media; critics are willing to examine modernism as manifest in popular films, for example, but not in books or magazines. Paula Rabinowitz's *Black and White and Noir: America's Pulp Modernism* (2002), for example, looks to film noir and populist documentary photography rather than the actual pulp magazines, which she only mentions a few times in passing, despite her subtitle. Again, the studied neglect of the popular literary form/venue is glaring. We can expand this to visual studies in general, which usually opt to look at other media than the book, which was innately visual especially when considering dust-wrappers and newsstands. Seemingly, in literary criticism, it is safer to examine nonprinted forms rather than popular, obviously economically driven literary forms. Likewise, Smith's, McCann's, and Rabinowitz's books, all of which deal (at least nominally) with the pulps, are confined by their focus only on hard-boiled or noir. This, in and of itself, illustrates the academic prejudice of form since it is hard-boiled, with its patois and urban cynicism, that most obviously approaches the dynamics of modernism. We would benefit from looking beyond this (often masculine-driven genre) to less obvious pulp forms such as the romance and science fiction.

On a pragmatic level, the "exclusion" of the popular pulp form is symptomatic of the problem that pulp magazines just do not exist in the libraries and archives. Hopefully, this project shall in some way illustrate the need to preserve this important yet quickly disintegrating historical and literary form. No Benjaminian reconstruction of the twentieth century could ever be complete without the *detritus* of pulp magazines.

Throughout the book, I follow such critics as Chris Baldick, Terry Eagleton, Astrudar Eysteinsson, Leonard Diepeveen, and John Guillory in seeing the relationship between modernist authors and the nascent industry of academic English studies as self-propagating and mutually beneficial, which together form an institution akin to Michel Foucault's power structure. Innate in this model is the idea that the pulp form is a type of subjugated knowledge, disregarded, excluded not only from the canon but from the institutional archives and academic accounts of twentieth-century literary history.[16] "Pulp modernism," a seeming oxymoron, obviously conflicts with many of the traditional definitions of modernism— modernism's inscrutability, stylistic experimentation, resistance to or disavowal of the marketplace—and purposefully so, for where and when modernism and popular literature do overlap, it illustrates the shortcomings of the traditional definition of modernism. If, as Foucault believes, it is at the extremities of society (i.e., prison or madhouse) that the machinations of the power mechanism are most readily apparent, then the pulp phenomenon (by both its very vastness and the vast body of critical derision aimed at it by critics and intellectuals) is an excellent place to look for institutionally sanctified subjugation.

Furthermore, my focus on book history likewise hopes to bridge the gap that has existed at least since the 1970s rise of poststructuralism between criticism and scholarship (i.e., bibliographic or textual studies), what Wim Van Mierlo sees as a generationally based resistance to theory by traditional archivists and a resistance to scholarship that is "endemic to the profession as a whole. Archival studies are rarely thought of as an end in itself."[17] What is needed to bridge the gap between a traditional textual scholarship, which is increasingly seen as archaic, and modern criticism is the simultaneous expansion in scope of both in regards to the material form—an extension of genetic criticism to the reception of a work beyond initial publication, and a return to the physicality of the book through the removing of the shellac of literary elitism that is an echo of new criticism.

My approach therefore is revisionist, pluralist, and materialist. Since revisionist, it will be necessary to refer to the different aspects of the historical construction of modernism. Throughout this study, then, I'll use three different modifiers in order to side-step the reductivism innate in that history: by "Monolithic" modernism, I mean the traditional idea that modernism was produced by and for a single coterie that consisted mostly of male authors and publishers, in other words, the "usual suspects" of Eliot, Joyce, Pound, Lewis, Hemingway, exclusionary of other genders and races; by "Elite" modernism I refer to the idea that modernism was seen as an avant-garde movement unconcerned with material, economic, or mundane matters; finally, I will use "traditional modernism" and/or "the traditional definition of modernism" to refer to the general reductive idea of modernism, of which these two

---

[16] There are individual exceptions, such as Dashiell Hammett who has been included into the canon—included exactly because of his modernist attributes. I am writing of the pulp genre as a large and relatively cohesive (yet kaleidoscopic) form.

[17] "Reading Joyce In and Out of the Archive," *Joyce Studies Annual* (2002).

former concepts are a part, that was largely constructed—or at least propagated—roughly from the 1930s to the 1970s (but with earlier and later manifestation) at the hands of the ensuing academic canonization of the movement.

The trajectory of this book is historical, material, and moves from concrete to increasingly abstract: the first chapter initially follows a more traditional model of periodical study by considering a single magazine, *The Smart Set*, as a neglected venue for modernism. Edited by H.L. Mencken and George Jean Nathan from the mid-teens to the early 1920s, *The Smart Set* is an odd conglomeration of modernists, little magazine–like attitudes, middle-brow and pulpish authors. And whereas the neglected history of the magazine and Mencken's waning reputation in literary studies points to the stress placed upon the rise of the expatriate school of Pound and Hemingway, it also offers an entry into popular magazine publishing for Mencken and Nathan edited a series of pulp magazines, often trading authors between them and *The Smart Set*. I see *The Smart Set* as the launching point (literally) for numerous such all-fiction magazines: early pulps that existed as venues of modernism before (or contemporary to) any schism or self-construction of elitism. Examples of populist modernism to be found in these magazines are the milieu of Left Bank Paris and the popularity of the Flapper as challenging restrictive American morals. With the history of such mass-circulation magazine in mind, I consider the overall scene of magazine publishing to put into perspective the disproportionate attention paid to little magazine as the only venue for modernism. Finally, I look to popular reprint magazines as an example of the "fallacy of first appearance," that is, that we need to look beyond the initial publication of modernist works and at subsequent publications, which invariably reached tens or even hundreds of thousands more readers than the initial often-restricted appearances.

Whereas the first chapter looks at actual appearances of canonical modernists in popular venues, the second chapter examines ways in which the dynamics and tensions that fascinated, were propounded, or were navigated by modernists appeared in similar ways in the interwar pulp magazines. In the chapter's first part, I outline pulp production, the breadth of the pulp audience and the form's cultural status, including the role of women both as readers and producers of pulp magazines, the pulp's relation to race, and the antagonistic relationship between the pulps and modernists or cultural critics—that is, the ways in which the pulps seemed diametrically opposed to modernism. I establish this antagonist relationship so that in the chapter's latter half I can deconstruct it by making obvious a pulp/modernist nexus: the existence of a pulp working-class modernism that ranged from cultural criticism to stylistic experimentation. If the first chapter moves down the cultural scale by showing modernist authors' shadow careers in pulp magazines, this chapter attempts the opposite by illuminating dynamics of modernism within a disregarded popular form. For example, I look to the science fiction form (on both sides of the great divide) to show how a traditional pulp form lent itself to experimentation and astute cultural commentary; I examine Robert Coates' Dadaist *Eater of Darkness* in relation to pulp author Stanley Weinbaum and

Harlem author George Schuyler. On a more abstract level, I look at the dual pulp/modernist fascination with technology, speed, and the masculine body. Finally, I look at how pulp hyper-production lent itself to Joycean-like avant-garde stylistics in the fiction of Harry Stephen Keeler.

In the third chapter, I examine the innate sensationalism of high-modernism as an entry point for a popular audience. To do this, I look at the ways in which modernist authors were presented/marketed during the paperback phenomenon of the late-1940s and 1950s. By doing so, I retroactively return to the earlier scene of modernism and the ways in which modernist literature relied upon elements of sensationalism in the marketplace. There was in fact a history of authors such as Lawrence and Joyce appearing in paperbacks even in the late 1920s. The gap between the sensational paperback covers of modernist works and the works' reputations as staid highbrow literature is the illusory divide between the academic and common reader or between canonized and genre literature (encapsulated by the gap in style of Conrad's *Lord Jim*) constructed by ensuing criticism in order to reorient reception away from sensational (and erotic) elements innate to modernism. Some of this elite construction was actually done at the hands of the authors themselves as an attempt to control the reception of this work: D.H. Lawrence's limited edition of *Lady Chatterley's Lover* is the obvious example, as is Joyce's *Ulysses*, but in both cases the instabilities of the text and of reception won out: Lawrence published a popular edition to counteract the numerous pirated editions, and Joyce's work was bought and persecuted, smuggled and read as erotic literature. This of course bothered Lawrence, with his somewhat tortured class issues, much more than Joyce who reveled in textual instability. But what this points out is the innate and important materiality of text, how reception is controlled (often unsuccessfully) by publishing aspects. Again, I argue in this chapter for the need to resist the fallacy of first appearance and extend genetic, bibliographic criticism to a book's afterlife of reprints and popular reception.

At the end of the third chapter I forward this idea by offering "case studies" of Faulkner and Hemingway in order to examine elements of violent and sexual sensationalism, economic patronage, commercial pandering, and intrinsic visuality. Whereas throughout the book I look to non-canonical authors and the popular and pulpish aspects of established modernist figures, this section's concentration upon the usual suspects of male-oriented, monolithic modernism stresses how the same dynamics of androcentric canonization undergirded both the academy and the paperback revolution of the 1940s; therefore a portrait of paperback modernism, like the portrait of 1950s men's magazines that started this introduction, illustrates again that popular culmination of popular dynamics not resisted but initiated by figures of high-modernism, a culmination that wouldn't have been made possible without the aid of the patriarchal cultural designators of critics and academia. Ironically, these are the same dynamics, which, in the process of institutionalization, wrote popular modernism out of history in lieu of a history based upon difficulty and rarified forms. This study recovers that lost history.

Chapter 1
The Smart Set, Modernism, and the Expanded Field of Magazine Production

How to Appear Sophisticated
1. Express yourself in free verse, the crazier and the more meaningless the better.
2. Refer familiarly to H.L. Mencken, Theodore Dreiser, D.H. Lawrence, the intelligentsia, and your bootlegger.
3. Interlard your stuff with French phrases, such as may be found in any First French book.
4. Allude often to Freud and play up his jargon.
5. Emit an occasional cynicism about books, jakes, yokels, morons, etc.
—*Oakland Tribune*, 13 April 1924.[1]

MODERNISM is sweeping the intelligent world. You find it in music, in the arts, in literature. You can't ignore it. Yet, what do you know about it? What do you *think* about it?
You won't always understand modernism. But you should at least be able to appreciate it.
There is a way, an easy way, to know and enjoy the newest schools of modern thought and art … . A forum where the most brilliant minds of two continents exchange their ideas.
This forum is the magazine Vanity Fair […]
Vanity Fair always presents the modern point of view … the sketchy, sophisticated, half gay, half serious outlook on life …
It is, in a true sense, the mirror of modernity.
Subscribe Now and assure yourself a fresh and modern point of view for all of 1929 …
1 Year Vanity Fair $4.00
—Subscription Ad, *Vanity Fair Magazine*, 1927

Academic criticism is grounded firmly upon the doctrine that all literary values may be established scientifically and beyond cavil, as the values of hog fodders, say, may be established – in other words, that criticism is an exact science, like thermo-dynamics or urinalysis.
—H.L. Mencken. *The Chicago Tribune*, January 3, 1925.[2]

By September 1915 the prospects of H.L. Mencken and George Jean Nathan were on the up-swing. The two young journalists were quickly becoming the darlings

---

[1] Quoted in Robert F. Nardini, "Mencken and the 'Cult of Smartness,'" *Menckeniana*, Vol. 84 Nos. 1–12 (Winter 1984), 8.

[2] Quoted in Mayo DuBasky, *The Gist of Mencken: Quotations from America's Critic* (Metuchen, NJ: Scarecrow Press, 1990), 541.

of the literati, their reputations resting on years of no-holds-barred criticism in the pages of *The Smart Set* magazine, most of which decried the stagnant state of American culture and the arts. But now, after a long series of difficult editors and cantankerous owners, *The Smart Set* had been sold for debts owed to Eugene Crowe, paper manufacturer and publisher of *Field and Stream*—and Mencken and Nathan had been appointed joint editors with carte-blanche to turn *The Smart Set* from its position as a light hodgepodge of clever fiction with high-society trappings into a sophisticated forum of artistic fiction and criticism. And for the first time the two editors were actually making money. Hence Mencken, writing book reviews in his Baltimore home, was unprepared for the late night, frantic phone call from Nathan summoning him immediately to the magazine's New York offices.

It seems that that day an agent of the local vice society, working undercover, had walked into the office at 331 Fourth Avenue and talked the advertising manager Irving T. Myers into giving him a copy of the magazine that Nathan and Mencken edited. This in turn quickly resulted in a raid upon the offices by John Saxton Sumner, confirmed Son of the American Revolution, member of the Founders and Patriots of America, and the newly appointed secretary of the New York Society for the Suppression of Vice. Sumner, implementing the Federal Anti-Obscenity Postal Statutes, had Myers, as well as the magazine's publisher, Eltinge F. Warner, arrested on obscenity charges.

The vice societies—or "Comstocks," as Mencken had labeled them in honor of Anthony Comstock, Sumner's predecessor and author of the postal laws that sported his name—were a powerful force in the first few decades of the twentieth century, again and again browbeating publishers to withdraw questionable books from circulation. 1915 was just the beginning of Sumner's career, and within six months he would succeed in suppressing Stanislaw Przybskewski's *Homo Sapiens* and more notably Theodore Dreiser's *The "Genius."*

Nathan and Mencken were worried for their publication, but were in no danger of prosecution since, even though they edited the magazine in question, their relationship to it was not made public, for it was not *The Smart Set* that had been the object of the raid but the *Parisienne*—a tawdry pulp rag that Mencken and Nathan had started solely to support themselves and the floundering—yet more serious—*Smart Set* (see Figure 1.1). According to Mencken, the French name and continental milieu of the *Parisienne* had been chosen simply to cash in on the Francophilia that proliferated in the States in the early days of World War I, and, unstated by Mencken yet obvious, for the promise of risqué bohemianism and romance that France held for a provincial country where Comstockian Puritanism held so much sway. Instead of using their own names, Mencken and Nathan signed all *Parisienne* correspondence with a series of French-sounding *noms-de-plume* because the last thing that the editors wanted anyone to know was that they, the high priests of American culture, were responsible for putting together a magazine that overtly pandered to popular taste.

In his memoirs, Mencken notes that "the pulp magazines were just then beginning to make money and we resolved to set one up. If the broken down hacks who were operating some of the most successful of them could get away

Fig. 1.1   *Smart Set*, June 1914 © 1914 John Adams Thayer Corporation

with it, then why not such smart fellows as Warner, Nathan and me…even if our proposed pulp failed, the net loss would not be large, and if it made a hit with the morons it would not only pay well in itself, but also further reduce the overhead on *The Smart Set*."[3] And the morons came through. From the very first issue,

---

[3]   H.L. Mencken, *My Life as Author and Editor* (NY: Vintage, 1995), 72–73.

the *Parisienne* proved to be an assured moneymaker, netting the two editors, as well as publisher Warner and owner Crowe, a considerable profit.

The obscenity charge was indeed worrisome. If they were indicted, it would soon put an end to this lucrative venture as well as damage the social standings of Crowe, Warner, and Myers. Although Mencken and Nathan found considerable glee in the idea of Myers and Warner sweating it out for a magazine they really had no responsibility for, they were leery of upsetting Crowe who could easily curtail their plan for turning *The Smart Set* into a trail-blazing literary review.

But Crowe, an old-time magazine mogul with influence reaching to Tammany Hall, made sure that nothing would happen to his cash cow. According to Mencken, at the trial the charges were dropped due to Crowe's influence and $500 cash slipped to one of the three presiding judges. It was a lesson for Sumner, and one that he must have taken to heart—he would rarely lose such cases over the next few years. This was also the first in a series of confrontations between Mencken and the vice societies, and Mencken would rarely pass up the chance to bad-mouth the Puritanism that plagued American arts over the next decade.

At work in the preceding interaction are a series of submerged tensions and dichotomies that would become emblematic—and problematic—to the growth and reification of modernism as a canonized, defined movement. These tensions concern the dynamics of cultural stance and definition, of hidden economics and patronage, of marketing schemes, sensationalism, and audience reception. The fact that Charles Sumner approached both modernist and pulp fiction alike—he would soon be instrumental in censoring the serialization of James Joyce's *Ulysses* in *The Little Review*—or that a magazine like *The Smart Set*, which introduced thousands of American readers to Ezra Pound and Joyce, shared authors with a series of Mencken and Nathan–edited pulp magazines, hints at popular aspects of elite literature that have long been ignored. It also divulges a multilayered prejudice regarding the *form* of literature by forcing the question of why certain media and formats have lended themselves to canonization while others have been kept out of the archives. *The Little Review*, for example, has been reprinted and digitized, collected and studied while *The Smart Set* has barely been more than a footnote in the history of literature despite an impressive list of authors and editors. And the *Parisienne* has been wholly neglected.

The Smart Set as Modernist Venue

What are we to do with *The Smart Set*? Over the course of its 30-year run it was a high-society fiction and gossip magazine, a general fiction magazine, a forum for daring and modernist fiction, and a women's true confession magazine. Critics have categorized it as both an avant-garde little magazine and a pulp magazine. Ezra Pound considered it "frivolous," yet he constantly submitted manuscripts and introduced authors to its editors. The magazine's composition even during its most critically acclaimed period was uneven, publishing highbrow fiction as well as authors who were famous in the all-fiction pulp magazines. For decades, *The Smart Set* lay forgotten. As the definition of modernist literature became canonized and unified, *The Smart Set* fell under the radar of critics and cultural historians. With the recent revitalized interest in both print culture and the expanded portrait of modernism, there seems to be revitalized interest in the magazine: the Modernist Journals Project has given it high priority for digitization, there will be a chapter dedicated to it in Oxford University Press's forthcoming three volume *Oxford Critical and Cultural History of Modernist Magazines*, and there is at least one unpublished dissertation on it.[4] The small body of existing work on the magazine provides a tempered but still partial portrait by privileging the modernist and elite authors or only Mencken's and Nathan's role, rather than the larger percentage of popular, overlooked, or noncanonized authors and fiction. This dynamic of exclusion, which involves an entire matrix of substantiation—economic, social, political—can be seen in Frederic Hoffman's influential study of little magazines (1947), which includes *The Smart Set*—though few critics have expanded upon or questioned this definition. The little magazines are traditionally thought of as *the* venue for modernism. They were usually short-lived, poorly financed, even more poorly circulated, small run magazines put out by and for the intellectual and artistic avant-garde; they were often politically left magazines with culturally radical overtones or culturally radical magazines with politically left overtones. Circulation rarely went over a few thousand and, in most cases, over a few hundred. Being a "pure" product of the avant-garde, they are traditionally defined as beyond the taint of commercialism—a defining trait that even influenced their very form and physicality (though this definition has come under revision in recent years as critics have looked to expand the venues of modernism to newspapers, trade journals, film, and radio, and popular magazines).

Such historians of *The Smart Set* discount almost entirely the magazine's popular aspects, or simply regulate them to the non-Mencken years, even though it was this very popularity that made the magazine attractive to modernist entrepreneurs like Ezra Pound. It is this same dynamic of exclusion that forced *The Smart Set* under the radar of critics, privileging magazines like *The Little Review* and *The Dial* that were easier to codify and more obviously in keeping with the idea of what an avant-garde periodical should be.

We, as enlightened and politically savvy critics and readers, have come to realize that all those old definitions of modernism, molded by the hands of not only dead white male authors (Joyce, Pound, Lewis, Ford) but dead white male critics (Kenner, Cowley, Wilson), are slanted, partial, and even self-serving. We know this, as current criticism continually attests by uncovering the important modernist voices and roles of women, people of color, lower classes, and other positions that undermine monolithic modernism. Yet our study of the forms and venues of modernism is still restrained to a certain type of publication, excluding those magazines that have a taint of the popular about them. This chapter (and the study in general) considers how *The Smart Set* meets many of the requirements of

---

[4] Sharon Hamilton's unpublished dissertation *The Smart Set Magazine and the Popularization of American Modernism, 1908–1920* (Dalhousie University), 1999.

modernist canonization while simultaneously being an outlet for popular fiction, hence divulging a popular modernism. Establishing *The Smart Set* as an obvious and fluid outlet of modernism is purposefully ungainly, confessedly disingenuous for doing so blatantly ignores the magazine's convoluted history and composition, but attempting to do so also illustrates the ungainly and constricting dynamics of academic definition, of trying to codify an anomalous mass. Rather, *The Smart Set*'s lost legacy, which is as important, if not more so, than its modernist history, is as progenitor of a subgenre of early pulp magazines that forwarded a type of popular modernism dependant upon moral and social change rather than stylistic inscrutability. By establishing this genealogy of popular modernism, my ultimate goal is to show how *The Smart Set* is only a single, obvious (and still semi-elitist) example among many other venues, such as short story reprint magazines and the all-fiction precursors to the pulp magazine, that evinced a modernism friendly to the masses. Indeed, when considering the overall mass of periodical publishing in the first few decades of the twentieth century, modernist little magazines and *The Smart Set* alike are only drops in an ocean of popular periodicals, almost all of which have been excluded by literary and book historians.

The Smart Set was always a commercial venture, even during its years as a modernist venue—roughly 1914 to 1923. This time period can't be separated from its earlier stage, for it likewise always maintained its early mantle and aura as a society magazine—a fact that Mencken eventually (and somewhat mockingly) used to his advantage.

The magazine was the brainchild of Colonel William D'Alton Mann, publisher of the already successful *Town Topics*, which was something of a race-form for New York's upper crust, giving stats and descriptions of their scandals and soirees.[5] Mann was already infamous before the turn of the century due to his uncanny talent for scandal mongering, which relied on a network of informants composed of disgruntled butlers, bookies, and maids, but also due to his polite blackmailing of those who didn't want their names to appear in print. When Mann ran into someone whom he had the goods on, he would delicately hint at the subject and the person in question would, of course, ask that it not appear in the next issue of *Town Topics*. The Colonel would oblige, but sometime later he might happen to need a few thousand-dollars loan from the party in question, a loan that was rarely paid back.

And so *The Smart Set* was financed. It started in 1900 as a literate sister magazine to *Town Topics*, "by, for and about the 400."[6] The early *Smart Set* managed to

---

[5] I have culled the history of *The Smart Set* from a number of major sources: Mencken's own *My Life as Author and Publisher*; Carl R. Dolmetsch, *The Smart Set, A History and Anthology* (NY: Dial Press, 1966); George H. Douglas, *The Smart Magazines* (Hamden: Archon, 1991); and Thomas Quinn Curtis, *The Smart Set: George Jean Nathan and H.L. Mencken* (NY: Applause, 1998). Much of the information on Willard Huntington Wright can be found, in addition to the above, in John Loughery's wonderful biography, *Alias S.S. Van Dine* (NY: Scribners, 1992).

[6] Dolmetsch, 22.

capture the right combination of urbane irreverence, light entertainment, and upper class snobbery to capture the public imagination. By 1902 "the Magazine of Cleverness," as it was known (a term that would later become derogatory in the mouths of modernists), had published early work by O Henry, James Branch Cabell, and Arthur Symons, as well as monthly pieces in French by authors such as Anatole France, but for the most part it consisted of formulaic pieces of light irony and romance by authors such as Van Tassel Sutphen and Prince Vladimir Vaniatsky (real names or not, there was certainly a *tone* achieved). The circulation continued to grow until 1906 when it peaked at 160,000—and then Colonel Mann's reputation caught up with him.[7]

The muckraking journalism so popular in the first decade of the century finally turned its focus upon its own backyard; the flamboyant figure of Colonel William D'Alton Mann, gentleman blackmailer, was too good a target to resist. Mann's scandal mongering for *Town Topics* was taken to task in an editorial for *Collier's* magazine, and his thinly veiled machinations were brought to light in the ensuing defamation trial. Mann was too slippery to ever be charged, but the resulting fallout resulted in plummeting circulation for *The Smart Set*; it was guilt by association.

Despite the additions of Mencken and Nathan as literature and drama critics, in 1908 and 1909 respectively, *The Smart Set* was not much different from popular magazines such as *Ainslee's* and *Everybody's*. By the time Mencken joined the staff, he had already published books on Nietzsche (the first in English) and Shaw (the first book-length treatment), as well as one of his own verse, and he had already made a name for himself as the author of the *Baltimore Sun*'s infamous and barbed editorial column, "The Free Lance." But it would be a few years before either Nathan or Mencken would actually "find their voice" in *The Smart Set*. Perhaps their biggest contribution to the magazine before their own editorships came in 1913 when they convinced the magazine's new owner, John Adams Thayer, that the road to success lay in changing the tone of the magazine to one of modernity and the avant-garde, and they knew the perfect man for the job: Willard Huntington Wright who years later would become famous as mystery writer S.S. Van Dine.

Thayer was admittedly more of a businessman than a literary connoisseur. His ownership resulted in an increase in the number and quality of advertisements, periodic changes in cover art, and less periodic changes in increasingly ineffectual editors. Wright, on the contrary, was one of those impresarios of teens and 1920s modernism, like Gilbert Seldes and Carl Van Vechten, who wrote about European Painting, the American scene, avant-garde writing, and philosophy. Willard Huntington Wright's brother, Stanton Macdonald-Wright, was a cubist artist who moved on the fringes of Gertrude Stein's Paris salon before World War I, where he met Picasso and Matisse; he was the founder of "Synchromism," which has been called the first modernist art movement in America to be

---

[7] Ibid., 15.

represented internationally.[8] Willard was like-minded: a Harvard dropout who became the literary editor for the *Los Angeles Times* when he was 19 years old. By the time he took over the editorship of *The Smart Set* he had books underway on Nietzsche, on literature, on modern art and aesthetics. Wright stated in his first issue that "We want to make *THE SMART SET* not only the best magazine in America, but something entirely new—the sort of magazine that Europe has been able to support, but so far has not yet been attempted in America."[9] He saw the opportunity to create a venue for new fiction, writing that would replace the gilded platitudes and "effeminacy" with realistic fiction, much along the lines of European magazines like *The Yellow Book* and *The English Review*.[10]

Wright's single year of piloting *The Smart Set* was turbulent indeed: he not only charted the future course of the magazine to become one of the most influential American literary magazines, he also almost shipwrecked it economically. As Pound was wont to point out, to Wright and *The Smart Set*'s credit, "I don't scorn the S.Set crowd, for I remember that Wright did his best with the magazine. It reduced the circulation from 70,000 to 20,000. Then they had to quit. No other American magazine of our time has made as gallant an effort. Not that Wright's ideas are mine, but he was going the limit, as he saw it, and he was accepting stuff on its literary value as he understood it, and damning the public's eyes."[11]

Through his editorials Wright stormed the bastions of *The Smart Set* and American literature alike, but as he hopefully pored over the incoming manuscripts, he could not believe the glut of tired, formulaic stories. He had not foreseen the plain lack of good raw material available. Wright managed to cause some slight ripples with his own editorials, with Floyd Dell's "Jessica Screams"—a story about a sexually liberated young girl—and in the fuming columns of "Owen Hatteras," a pen name that Wright, Mencken, and Nathan all wrote under. But there just wasn't enough new material coming in. Wright published an editorial, "A Word for Authors," calling for stories "marked with the fidelity of life" and, in June 1913, he left for a month long, expenses paid, manuscript-buying trip to Europe. There he enlisted the help of Ezra Pound, who became the de facto foreign editor for the magazine.[12]

By 1913 Pound was already well known as a protégé of Yeats, and as one who had his finger on the pulse of European and expatriate literature. Through Pound, as well as his own networking, Wright gathered an impressive list of modernist authors: D.H. Lawrence, Joseph Conrad, Strindberg, Yeats, George Moore. The

---

[8] http://arttech.about.com/library/blreadings_news_wright_lacma.htm.

[9] Quoted in Sharon Hamilton, "The First *New Yorker*? *The Smart Set* Magazine, 1900–1924," *The Serials Librarian*, Vol. 37, No. 2 (1999), 97.

[10] Dolmetsch, 35.

[11] Letter to Margaret Anderson. *Pound/the Little Review: The letters of Ezra Pound to Margaret Anderson: the Little Review Correspondence*, edited by Thomas L. Scott, Melvin J. Friedman, with the assistance of Jackson R. Bryer (NY: New Directions, 1988), 202.

[12] Loughery, 10–11.

extreme nature of some of these writers' works, as well as the high price Wright was willing to pay for quality and reputation, had ramifications upon his relationship with Thayer upon whom it was beginning to dawn that what he had envisioned for *The Smart Set* and what Wright was accomplishing were two very different things. Perhaps the greatest tension between the two came from the pressure put on the company coffers due to the high price Wright paid for quality manuscripts, and the continuous threat of advertisers fleeing from the new, controversial material. Their relationship quickly disintegrated, the break finally coming when Thayer discovered that a mock-up for *The Blue Review*, an avant-garde journal that Wright, Mencken, and Nathan had been kicking around, had been charged to *The Smart Set*'s account.[13] Wright was suddenly out of a job (his ensuing career as S.S. Van Dine is another instance of middlebrow genre literature with modernist trappings that worries traditional hierarchies), and the editorship reverted to former editor Norman Boyer, who immediately turned down a number of stories sent along by Pound, including those of James Joyce. It was just like old times, except for the pile of unpublished quality poems and stories bought by Wright, and the knowledge that he had suddenly raised the bar, if even for a moment.

We can look to the June 1914 issue for an idea of the weird mixture of pap and Wright's leftover quality bits that the year's run featured: for example, Owen Hatteras's formerly acerbic topics were now confined to "The Bridge Game" (the feature story), and the painful new level of literary banality can perhaps best be seen in the "Première Danseuse" by Fanny Hodges Newman, which included the memorable stanzas:

> Call of the boughs asway, asway,
> Call of the bending blades of wheat,
> Drag of the stars away, away;
> Ah, here am I with answering feet!
>
> Dance with me, winds that rock the sea,
> I am the wave across the deep;
> Blow sweet amours and dandle me,
> Far in some glamourous cave, to sleep.

Dandle Indeed. One might be tempted to think that this could be Mencken or Nathan having fun at Boyer's or the magazine's expense, but it is not so: the faint subscription stamp on the copy of *The Smart Set* that I mined this gem from held the San Diego address of the poet herself; besides that, there is mention of a Fanny Hodges Newman poem in Florence Churchill Casebeer's (and if that isn't a Menckian name) *Biographical Sonnets* (Sonnet XXIV, "To my challenged self"), and Newman wrote the lyrics to the 1918 patriotic song "We Are All Americans" ("O, England's full of Englishmen / And France is full of French, / And Italy has sons enough / To fill up ev'ry trench").

---

[13] Not to be confused with John Middleton Murray's *The Blue Review* started in 1913 in England.

Other works in this issue include an O'Henry-type story by Edwin Baird (who would go on to edit *True Detective* and *Weird Tales* magazines) about a rich and rebellious son and a poor but beautiful department store clerk, and "Fate's Luck," a love story about murder, love, and philosophy by Furnley Maurice. What are (most likely) Wright's footprints are also evident: "An African Epic," a story from Donn Byrne, the Irish-American author who would later become most famous for his book *Messr. Marco Polo* (1921); there are poems by Sara Teasdale and Louis Untermeyer; and a realistic novelette about immigrant Italians by Robert Carlton Brown. (At this point Brown was a confessed pulp hack. See the next chapter for a discussion of his life in Paris in the 1930s and relationship with Duchamp, Crosby, Stein, and others.) And there are, of course, Mencken's and Nathan's columns. But the chaff far outweighs the grain.

With the magazine again about as adventuresome and offensive as a taffy-pull, Mencken and Nathan were conspiring to leave its ranks. But salvation came from a strange quarter—the war. Thayer, already wobbly from his battle with Wright and the ensuing loss of subscribers, panicked in the depression following the news of war and sold *The Smart Set* to his largest creditor, Eugene Crowe. Crowe had previously enlisted the help of Eltinge Warner to turn *Field and Stream* from a failing magazine into an established favorite, and he wanted to attempt the same with *The Smart Set* in order to get back as much of the debt owed to him as possible. Warner was an excellent publisher, but he was no editor. Luckily for him, as well as for posterity, he had met George Jean Nathan on a trans-Atlantic crossing and been duly impressed. Warner and Crowe offered Nathan the editorship, which he accepted on the condition that he share the position with Mencken.

As George Douglas has pointed out, by the start of World War I, *The Smart Set*, as well as Mencken and Nathan, were "cherished by the elite and a whole new generation of writers," though it was far from successful or popular in any commercial sense.[14] F. Scott Fitzgerald, another *Smart Set* find, ordered his agent to continue sending short stories to the magazine even though he could get much, much higher wages from bigger magazines, because "I want to keep right in with Nathan and Mencken for they are the most powerful critics in the country."[15] By 1920, both Mencken as a literary critic, and Nathan as a drama critic, were at the top of the game due not only to their work in *The Smart Set*, but also because they published widely in other venues. Both produced numerous books of criticism, much of which had been culled from *The Smart Set*'s pages. Whereas Mencken and the magazine in general stood mute on political issues during the war, he made good use of his newspaper columns. And as cultural commentators, both Nathan and Mencken were outspoken, especially in matters of censorship of the arts—though they were always very careful not to push the boundaries too far. In the pages of *The Smart Set*, they waged war mainly through preaching rather than practice.

And *The Smart Set* helped make Mencken *the* gargantuan figure of American letters. Any American writer who wanted to be of importance had to contend with

---

[14] Douglas, 83.
[15] Curtiss, 209.

Mencken—in the late 1920s the *New York Times* labeled him "the most powerful private citizen in America," and Sherwood Anderson stated in his memoirs about his artistic circle, "Henry Mencken was our great hero."[16] His voice was adopted by a generation of earnest young writers, as Edmund Wilson, James Branch Cabell, and F. Scott Fitzgerald pointed out.[17] Robert Nardini put it concisely by stating that "An entire generation of novices fell into cadence with Mencken and their work spread like the plague."[18]

The Smart Set became an outspoken magazine through its effort to break the hold that provincialism had upon American magazine publishing. Despite all of his later bad-mouthing of Mencken, Hemingway sent a barrage of manuscripts to the *American Mercury* during its first year (1924), and had earlier taken Mencken's *Smart Set* reviews to heart. Pound published in *The Smart Set* and stated that he considered Mencken and Willard Huntington Wright his "American discoverers";[19] he continually introduced new writers and sent manuscripts to *The Smart Set*; he lauded Wright and had a lengthy correspondence with Mencken. These facts are undeniable, even if they were surrounded by a studied indifference, a wariness that is indicative of the elitist tone of the high modernists. In a review of Mencken's *Book of Prefaces* in *The Little Review*, Pound wrote, "The next point is that Mencken is in some circles considered a purely frivolous person…because he edits or half edits a frivolous magazine. In a half baked country one has to use what tools one can lay hold of. I would call one fact to the attention of the cognoscenti, namely that *The Smart Set* is the only magazine in America that has ever reduced a circulation […] in a quixotic attempt to break the parochial [sic] taboo and give America free literature."[20] Such begrudging praise went further; on numerous occasions Pound instructed Margaret Anderson to seek pieces for the *Little Review* by Mencken and Owen Hatteras, which was in fact Mencken and Nathan's pen name in *The Smart Set*; Pound stated that such contributions "would be of no small use."[21]

Throughout the teens and 1920s, Pound carried on a long correspondence with Mencken; these letters, though full of literary gossip and critical discussion, are mostly Pound's campaign to publish authors of his coterie in the magazine.[22]

---

[16] Nolte, *H.L. Mencken's Smart Set Criticism* (Ithica: Cornell U P, 1968), xii; Anderson 369, quoted in Nardini, 6.

[17] See Robert F. Nardini, "Mencken and the 'Cult of Smartness,'" *Menckeniana*, Vol. 84 (Winter 1984), 1–12.

[18] Nardini, 7.

[19] Sutton, Walter, ed. *Pound, Thayer, Watson, and The Dial; A Story in Letters* (Gainesville: U PF, 1994) 157.

[20] Pound, *Pound/Little Review*, 156–157.

[21] Ibid., 106.

[22] See for example Pound's letter to Mencken 18 February 1915, which mentions Joyce, Hueffer, Lawrence, May Sinclair, or his February 1925 letter asking for help in placing Cheever Dunning's *The Four Winds*, both in *The Letters of Ezra Pound* (NY: Harcourt Brace, 1950), see especially 197–198.

That modernists such as Joyce, Lawrence, and Pound sought *The Smart Set* out as a means to reach a larger American public beyond the grasp of magazines such as the *Little Review* illustrates that *The Smart Set* functioned as a modernist outlet. Fitting *The Smart Set* into the rubric of the little magazine forces the issue of what actually constitutes "modernism" and "modernity," especially considering the privileged position that little magazines hold as the singular outlet for the avant-garde.

The modernists's hot/cold relationship to *The Smart Set* was indicative of the somewhat schizophrenic composition of the magazine itself: it was a blend of avant-garde attitude and trappings mixed with admittedly "entertaining fiction." In the normally hierarchical schema of literary publishing (not to mention academia's codified categorizations), *The Smart Set* is a nebulous entity. Mencken and Nathan published work by Ezra Pound, James Joyce, Djuna Barnes, Carl Van Vechten, F. Scott Fitzgerald, Aldous Huxley, Alistair Crowley, Samuel Roth, Padraic Column, Anatole France, Eugene O'Neill, and Joseph Conrad. While they published some works of D.H. Lawrence, they turned down others as too risky. They also turned down work by Robert Frost, Sherwood Anderson (too frank), and T.S. Eliot (too highbrow). *The Smart Set* also filled its pages with stories by popular authors who were simultaneously publishing in the mass-circulated magazines of the day or who would go on to long careers in the pulp magazines: Achmed Abdullah; Harold Hersey, who would go on to be a famous pulp magazine publisher/editor; Harold De Polo; Clark Ashton Smith, who would become an important member of the Lovecraft circle in *Weird Tales*; and Carl Glick, who would write mystery reviews for *Black Mask*.

This cultural montage of authors and styles seems to defy not only *The Smart Set*'s self-construction as a highbrow and high-society magazine, but also Andreas Huyssen's idea of modernism as defining itself against popular- and mass culture. But what Huyssen does not take into consideration with his concept of the "fear of contamination" as modernism's defining trait is that this opposition is itself a type of marketing, a type of posing that informs the relationship between the modernists and *The Smart Set*. Pivotal and vocal figures like Pound and Margaret Anderson (as well as Mencken) often loudly said one thing and then quietly did something quite contradictory. Pound's view that "The influence of a magazine don't depend on the size of its circulation (*Smart Set*, for instance hasn't and couldn't possibly have the faintest influence on anything)" is hypocritical considering that he continually looked to *The Smart Set* for exposure on this side of the Atlantic that *The Little Review* and *Poetry* could not provide.[23]

Almost 80 years after it stopped publication, it is difficult to pinpoint the exact influence and cultural position of *The Smart Set*. Much of this ambiguity results from the use of defining traits of literary modernism as the standard requirement of canonization. Numerous critics have tried to reconstruct the magazine according to this template: Hoffman's *The Little*

---

[23] Timothy Materer, ed. *The Selected Letters of Ezra Pound to John Quinn, 1915–1924,* (Durham, Duke U P, 1991), 47.

Magazine: a History and Bibliography (1947), the cornerstone of "Little Magazine" scholarship, saw *The Smart Set* as spawning an entire school of little magazines, "the eclectics [which were] the spiritual heirs of the commercial *Smart Set*,"—a definition dependent upon the magazine as a modernist venue.[24] Similarly, Sharon Hamilton has written about how *The Smart Set*'s challenged sexual mores through the literature of D.H. Lawrence (among others) and racial stereotypes through the fiction of Joyce, and championed modernist stylistics through the fiction of Conrad—all of which allowed it to function like a commercial little magazine. These studies largely ignore the popular aspects of the magazine (besides perhaps circulation) such as the popular tone, authors, and advertisements. They ignore the fact that there was a double standard in Pound's patronage of *The Smart Set* and statements such as the already noted remark that *The Smart Set*, for instance, hasn't and couldn't possibly have the faintest influence on anything.

The paradoxes innate to *The Smart Set* lay bare the inadequacies of modernist definition and academic pigeon-holing. Concentrating on the dichotomy of *The Smart Set*—the reasons for this simultaneous avowal/disavowal of *The Smart Set* by the modernists—reveals the machinations behind modernist marketing and self-construction, which involve a number of seldom examined tensions of disavowal: first, Mencken's (and *The Smart Set*'s) reputation waned because he advocated American regionalism more militantly than he advocated the European-influenced, expatriate modernism of Pound and Co.; second, *The Smart Set* and Mencken's brand of modernism was anti-academic, so didn't have the bolstering of universities and rising English studies to aid in canonization as did Pound, Eliot, and the high modernists; third, the tone of *The Smart Set* differed from the militant advocacy of the avant-garde in magazines like *The Little Review*. It was more "Clever," meaning light and flippant. This was visible in the evolving look of the magazine itself, which reflected its close relationship with the early pulp magazines of the time. Ultimately, these tensions lead to an alternate history of a modernism advanced through a large body of ignored popular magazines lower on the cultural scale from *The Smart Set*.

Reluctant Bedfellows: Hemingway's Modernism vs. Mencken's Regionalism

In the last issue of *The Smart Set* that H.L. Mencken and George Jean Nathan edited (December 1923), Mencken published something of a coda that summed up the state of American letters. In it he stated:

> Well, then, what of the youngsters? Do they show any sign of seizing their chance? The answer is yes and no. On the one hand there is a group which, revolving 'round the *Bookman*, talks a great deal and accomplishes nothing. On the other hand there is a group which, revolving 'round the *Dial, Broom,* and

---

[24] Charles Allen, Frederick Hoffman, and Carolyn Ulrich. *The Little Magazine, a History and a Bibliography* (Princeton: Princeton U P, 1947), 9.

the *Little Review*, talks even more and does even less. But on the third hand, as it were, there is a group which says little and saws wood. ... There seems to be nothing in concert between them [the authors of the latter group], no sign of a formal movement, with its *blague* and bombast, but all of them have this in common: that they owe their opportunity and their method to the revolution that followed *Sister Carrie*. Most of them are from the Middle West, but they are distinct from the Chicago crowd, now degenerated to posturing and worse. They are sophisticated, disillusioned, free from cant, and yet they have imagination. The raucous protests of the evangelists of American Idealism seem to have no more effect upon them than the advances of the Expressionists, Dadists and other such café-table prophets.[25]

Based on this, it is both hard to believe that Mencken had championed writers like Joyce (albeit *Dubliners* era rather than *Ulysses* era) and Lawrence, and easy to see why modernists like Pound ceased to champion *The Smart Set* and, explicitly, Mencken. Mencken would continue such a stratified advocacy of regionalism while deriding the expats in his new venture, *The American Mercury*, where he published a particularly barbed exposé on the Left Bank's empty bohemianism by Sinclair Lewis. But the criticism was not just one-handed; Pound often criticized Mencken as indicative of the stagnant American scene, but it was Ernest Hemingway, following in Pound's footsteps, who most harshly criticized Mencken and the Midwestern regionalism that he had championed for years in *The Smart Set*.

Hemingway can surely be grouped in with those café-table prophets, especially in light of his earliest published story, "A Divine Gesture," the dada-inspired experiment in the *Double Dealer*. Considering Sherwood Anderson's statement that Mencken was "our great hero," it is telling that Ernest Hemingway burlesqued them both in *The Torrents of Spring*, the 1925 parody of Anderson's *Dark Laughter* that was purportedly written in an effort to break Hemingway's contract with Horace Liveright (also Anderson's publisher).[26] The book was likewise a break with Anderson (which some, including Hemingway's wife Hadley and his friend John Dos Passos, considered backstabbing); Hemingway wanted to put a stop once and for all to any idea of mentorship or influence between himself and the older, established writer.

Long written off as simply satire or as a means to take advantage of a contractual loophole, the book is one of the least scrutinized in Hemingway's oeuvre. Whereas it is highly cutting satire at Anderson's expense, it is also full of submerged tensions between the two literary scenes of American regionalism and modernist expatriation.

The Torrents of Spring takes place in Petoskey, Michigan and tells of short-story writer Scripps O'Neil, recently published in *The Saturday Evening Post* and *The Dial,* who hits the rails after his wife leaves him. The pairing of these publications is itself telling: the *Post*, as the most popular magazine in America,

---

[25] Nolte, *Smart Set Criticism*, 331.
[26] Ernest Hemingway, *The Torrents of Spring* (NY: Scribners, 1998).

was the epitome of middle-class acceptance, whereas *The Dial* was one of the most elite and reputable little magazines. Sherwood Anderson won *The Dial*'s 1921 annual literary award, Eliot 1922's. Hemingway's grouping of these two magazines is a comment on the commercial success of Anderson's *Dark Laughter*, which was a best seller when Hemingway's *In Our Time* hit the stands; these two magazines, the breadth of Anderson's outlets/audience, are a veiled accusation of Anderson's selling out.) Arriving in Petoskey, Scripps spontaneously marries Diana, an elderly British waitress at Brown's Beanery, but he soon falls in love with Mandy, a younger, literary anecdote-reciting waitress. The two women are juxtaposed throughout the story: Diana as an Anderson-like character who reads literary magazines voraciously as an attempt to "hang onto" Scripps, Mandy as an Ezra Pound or Gertrude Stein–like character who has the inside gossip on literary figures. In an effort to impress Scripps, Diana learns empty literary pretension via her magazines' editors and critics such as Glenn Frank, Carl Van Doren, and above all, Mencken; Mandy obviously has lived in literary circles. Thinking about Mandy, Scripps muses, "What a background she must have, that girl! What a fund of anecdotes! A chap could go far with a woman like that to help him!"[27] It is telling that Scripps thinks in terms of advancement, especially if we consider Hemingway's mentorship as moving from Anderson to Pound, since the latter is well known for his Machiavellian promotion for the movement.

In contrast to Mandy, Diana repeatedly tries to pry Scripps away from Mandy by tempting Scripps with literary tidbits she gleaned from her magazines: "Was it doing any good? Was it holding him? At first it seemed to be. Diana learned editorials by John Farrar by heart. Scripps brightened. A little of the old light shining in his eyes now. Then it died. Some little mistake in the wording, some little slip in her understanding of a phrase, some divergence in her attitude, made it all ring false."[28] She tries to impress him with a story by Ruth Suckow, about "a little girl from Iowa...about people on the land. It reminded me a little of my own Lake Country [in England]," but to no avail.

For her final attempt, she pleads:

> "I wish you felt like coming home, Scripps, there's a splendid thing in this [*American*] *Mercury*. Do come home, Scripps ... Oh, won't you come home?'
>
> Scripps looked up. Diana's heart beat faster. Perhaps he was coming. Perhaps she was holding him. Holding him. Holding him.
>
> "Do come, Scripps dear," Diana said softly. "There's a wonderful editorial in it by Mencken about chiropractors."
>
> Scripps looked away.

---

[27] Ibid., 39.
[28] Ibid., 43.

"Won't you come, Scripps?" Diana pleaded.

"No," Scripps said. "I don't give a damn about Mencken any more."

Diana dropped her head. "Oh, Scripps," she said. "Oh, Scripps." This was the end. She had her answer now. She had lost him. Lost him. Lost him.[29]

Whereas Mencken saw the regionalism of authors like Suckow, whom he discovered and championed in *The Smart Set*, as being the means of developing an intrinsically American voice, Hemingway saw authors such as Suckow as under the yoke of English literary tradition and stylistics (i.e., Iowa like the English lake country), hence Diana's call for Scripps to come home could very well be the call for the expatriates not to turn their backs on their homeland. But Hemingway seemingly had no need to return to the actual scene of his fiction; America was stagnant, as were the ideas of its number one critic and literary power, Mencken. Hemingway didn't give a damn for Mencken. This rejection is more than an early example of what would become Hemingway's infamously barbed attacks against critics. Rather, it is illustrative of the rift between two emerging schools of modernism: the American regionalism of the Mencken/Anderson school and the expatriate modernism of the Pound school.

That Anderson was considered a "modern" during his day is undeniable; for example, John Drewry's *Some Magazines and Magazine Makers* (1924) describes *Winesburg, Ohio* as "everywhere praised by critics as one of the best creations of the school of the moderns."[30] Yet considering *Torrents*' caustic criticism of Anderson and Mencken, Hemingway is seemingly of another school entirely. Much of the satire in the book stems from the incongruities of Left Bank Paris culture transplanted to rural Michigan, a criticism of what Hemingway saw as Anderson's waffling between American regionalism and modernist stylistics. Such criticism is ironic, even puzzling, as these two types of modernism had a complex and in no way oppositional relationship; it discounts how influential and "new" Anderson's experimentation and characterization was (as well as Hemingway's own regional Nick Adams stories), yet it is in keeping with Pound's 1913 claim to Harriet Monroe that "'England' is dead as mutton. *If* Chicago (or the U.S.A. or whatever) will slough off its provincialism, if it will be aware of Paris (or of any other centre save London) ... there is no reason for Chicago or *Poetry* or whatever not being the standard. [...] All I want is that the 'American artist' presuming that he exist shall not use merely London, but Paris, London, Prague or wherever, as a pace-maker."[31] Judging by *Torrents*, the attitude was pretty much the same a decade later when Hemingway came under Pound's influence.

These diverging attitudes between creating a purely American literary aristocracy for Mencken and breaking entirely from an English influenced

---

[29] Ibid.
[30] John Drewry, *Some Magazines and Magazine Makers* (Boston: Stratford, 1924), 158.
[31] Pound, *Letters*, 24–25.

American voice for Pound are indicative of the multivalent aspects of modernism *as it existed* at the time. What has been constructed since as a cohesive and monolithic movement was in fact a myriad of different sites, styles, and schools of modernism. The monolithic construction of 'high' modernism has disintegrated over the last few decades of revisionist criticism, therefore (my argument here) what these early tensions evince are overlapping aspects of modernism and the illusory nature of modernist cohesion, created initially for self-marketing and later adopted for academic ease of definition.

Therefore *Torrents* is not only Hemingway's break with American (particularly Midwestern) regionalism, but his pledge of allegiance to the expats, the school of the "boys of 1914": Pound, Lewis, and Joyce. By deriding Mencken, Anderson, and the American scene, *The Torrents of Spring* was a vehicle for Hemingway to cement his reputation as part of another cultural movement. Throughout the book, Hemingway breaks narrative in order to describe the author's place of writing—the literary Left Bank of Paris—and includes anecdotes about F. Scott Fitzgerald, John Dos Passos, H.G. Wells, and Ford Madox Ford. He states, for example, "If any of the readers would care to send me anything they ever wrote, for criticism or advice, I am always at the Café du Dôme any afternoon, talking about art with Harold Stearn and Sinclair Lewis," a blatant jab at Lewis's recent attack on the Left Bank crowd.[32] Such anecdotes illustrate Hemingway's place and familiarity with an elite movement, just as his jabs at Mencken in *The Sun Also Rises* deflates America's most influential critic's power and literary insight, effectively (and cleverly) setting the book above Mencken's consideration. About Robert Cohn's inability to understand irony, Jake Barnes wonders "where Cohn got the incapacity to enjoy Paris. Possibly from Mencken. Mencken hates Paris, I believe. So many young men get their likes and dislikes from Mencken." Likewise, Harvey Stone—the Harold Stearn character in the book—sums up the expats' feelings toward Mencken, stating, "'He's through now … He's written about all he knows, and now he's on all the things he doesn't know … nobody reads him now.'"[33]

Hemingway quickly established himself as part of the "new," taking on many of their methods of self-promotion and attitudes toward the American scene, including their self-definition against American regionalists. Such statements as that above, even in fiction, are ipso-facto advertisements for both the author and the expatriate movement—upon publication of *The Sun Also Rises* reviewers saw Hemingway as "undeniably one of the 'moderns.'"[34] Hemingway's statement (via Stone) was also quite Poundian in nature; both Timothy Materer and Lawrence Rainey have written about Pound's astute advertising for modernism, specifically in the use of brand name recognition (e.g., Imagismé, Vorticism) and the use of

---

[32] Hemingway, *Torrents*, 47.
[33] Hemingway, *The Sun Also Rises* (NY: Scribners, 1926), 42, 43.
[34] *Times Literary Supplement* (Nov. 4, 1926), 766. Quoted in Volume 1 of Audre Hanneman's *Ernest Hemingway: A Comprehensive Bibliography* (Princeton: Princeton U P, 1967), 351.

bombast and spectacle à la Lewis (*Blast*). Each of these aspects depends upon separation and disavowal of what has come before, both are propagandistic, as even Pound referred to them: "My propaganda for what some may consider 'novelty in excess' is a necessity."[35] This use of "advertising" to explain the modernist's stance of elitism and disavowal is based upon advertising as creating a "want" or lack in the consumer, a cultural inferiority to be filled by X product, in this case modernism (this, as we'll see, becomes all the more explicit in the marketing of little magazines such as the *Little Review*).

In retrospect we can now understand that there was a multitude of modernisms: regional, racial (i.e., the New Negro movement), socialist and proletariat, gendered, etc., but during the 1920s and '30s there were efforts at both self-definition and self-marketing, often with these various movements defining themselves against each other: the Midwestern regionalists against the Greenwich Village crowd, the Left Bank enclave against the regionalists. Many of these groups depended upon the same venues as what would become defined as a monolithic modernism even though they aren't often thought of in those terms. For example, American regionalists had their own little magazines, such as Iowan Frederick Hoffman's *The Midlands*, started in 1915.[36] This is despite Mencken's statement that there is no "formal movement" or "concert" between them. Of course, all these categories now seem counterproductive and have been impinged on by subsequent criticism, but these divisions were a seemingly valid debate in the mid-1920s and one that, according to literary history, the expatriates won. Today Mencken is not thought of as a proponent of the early twentieth-century avant-garde, nor does *The Smart Set* hold anything but a peripheral position in the history of modernism.

The Academy and Cultural Production

In 1915, Ezra Pound wrote that "Scholarship is but a hand-maid to the arts," an idea that he relied upon again and again as he tried to promote movements like Imagismé and Vorticism and authors like Joyce and Eliot.[37] Mencken, on the other hand, evinced a strong anti-academic attitude, often lambasting the state of higher education. Modernists like Pound and Eliot courted and were adopted by

---

[35] See Materer, "Make it Sell! Ezra Pound Advertises Modernism." *Marketing Modernism*. Kevin Dettmar and Stephen Watt, eds. Ann Arbor: U of MP, 1996; see Rainey's *Institutions of Modernism* (New Haven: Yale U P, 1998). Pound, *Letters*, 48. I see this related to but distinct from Sean Latham's label of snobbery. Rather than an aesthetically based cultural position, I see it closer related to a veiled commercial marketing scheme, Pound's "Make it New" as "Now, New and Improved." See Latham's *Am I a Snob? Modernism and the Novel* (Ithaca: Cornell U P, 2003).

[36] See Tom Lutz, *Cosmopolitan Vistas: American Regionalism and Literary Value* (Ithaca: Cornell U P, 2004), 129–136. In this same section Lutz also sees a strong anti-academic strain to Midwest regionalism.

[37] Pound, *Letters*, 48.

academia while Mencken's stance outside of the disciplinization of literature (both within and outside of the academy), and specifically Pound's brand of modernism, resulted in the eventual decline of his reputation. As Leonard Diepeveen has substantiated, professionalization, as the discourse of difficulty, was central in the arguments that high, monolithic modernism was built upon.[38] Malcolm Cowley, who was instrumental through his memoirs and edited anthologies in giving expatriate modernism a cohesive feel and definition, waged a particularly barbed war against Mencken.[39] In Cowley's *After the Genteel Tradition* (1937), Louis Kronberger states that Mencken's single contribution to American letters "was his fight to purge our literature of its puritanism and gentility"; besides that, Mencken was "utter inadequacy," he lacked "esthetic judgment," and "indulged in much disingenuous thinking, much cleverness"—with no acknowledgment for his introducing modernist fiction to the U.S. in *The Smart Set*.[40]

Mencken's reputation in the academy suffered at the hands of proponents of modernism such as Kronberger and Cowley, for the upswing of modernism as an academically defined aesthetic and cultural movement led to the descent in Mencken's reputation. Mencken, as a self-taught scholar, often scorned the university system in print, and one of the ongoing series published in *The Smart Set* under Mencken and Nathan's editorship was aimed at criticizing the nation's foremost universities. He was arguably the last of the cultural critics working outside the academy that modernists such as Pound and Eliot were helping to create as a means to further the cultural standing of their art. Mencken would have loudly refuted Eliot's statement that "poets in our civilization, as it exists at present, must be difficult."[41] Critics such as Terry Eagleton, Astrudar Eysteinsson, Leonard Diepeveen, and John Carey have commented that the formation of modernism as a canonical movement was symbiotic with the formation of modern English studies in academia—a reciprocal relationship built upon the difficulty of the text.[42] Look, for example, at Eliot's introduction and inclusion of notes in *The Waste Land*—a move that instantly demanded erudition on the part of the reader as well as gave the poem a mantle of intellectual worth. We can therefore consider Eliot's own influential criticism, with its redefinition/refocusing of the canon upon pre-romantic poetry, a brilliant marketing move. Eagleton states, Eliot's literary tradition is based upon "not so much which works of the past are eternally valuable, as which will help to write his own poetry"—and, we could easily add, to sell it.[43]

---

[38] Leonard Diepeveen, *The Difficulties of Modernism* (NY: Routledge, 2003), 96–97, 1.

[39] M.K. Singleton, *H.L. Mencken and the American Mercury Adventure* (Durham: Duke U P, 1962), 7.

[40] Cowley, *After the Genteel Tradition* (NY: Norton, 1937), 89, 90.

[41] Quoted in John Carey, *The Intellectuals and the Masses* (Chicago: Academy, 2002), 17.

[42] See Eagleton, *Literary Theory, an Introduction* (Minnesota: U of Minnesota P, 1983), 31–40, Astrudur Eysteinsson's *The Concept of Modernism* (Ithaca: Cornell U P, 1990), 76–78, Diepeveen, esp. 226–227, as well as Carey.

[43] Eagleton, 39.

Joyce likewise saw the importance of such educational cultural capital, stating that his many ambiguities and puzzles in *Ulysses* would ensure his reputation because it would keep professors busy for years to come. Difficulty, as the litmus of good art, is not only self-propagating on the part of the artist, advancing his/her reputation, but on the part of the academy as well, for it teaches one how to read critically and establishes a need for academic priests to decode the sacred texts.[44] This institutionalization of language that occurred via modernism in the academy helps explain the hypocritical disavowal of *The Smart Set* by modernists.

Astradur Eysteinssen, writing about the symbiotic canonization/definition of modernism and fomentation of literary studies, which occurred during the 1920s and 1930s, states that:

> The critical attempts ... to isolate and elevate the literary uses of language [as a modernist trope is related to] the vested professional interests of those whose careers are felt to be dependent upon literature as an autonomous field of study. By securing the autonomy of literature, preventing it from being overly 'polluted' or even swallowed up by 'other' modes of social discourse, literary criticism is also protecting its vulnerable specificity and justifying its existence as an area of significant cultural inquiry.[45]

Hence the construction of "Modernism" has to do with the propagation of a mode of reading, a profession and an intellectual elitism, just as the original modernists drew cultural borders between their work and popular literature. Gail McDonald, speaking specifically about Pound and Eliot, states that they "set out consciously to turn the creation and criticism of poetry into an occupation equal in rigour, precision, and importance to the work of medical diagnosticians and research scientists with whom they often compared themselves."[46]

And it was this academy that Mencken was working against. It is understandable then if his past criticism met with disavowal and resistance by the modernists, for Mencken's criticism didn't advocate lingual difficulty but accessibility. What Mencken did advocate was social and cultural complexity and portrayal as means to social uplift.

The idea of a nondifficult modernism, or a modernism that is not dependant upon stylistic inscrutability flies in the face of Pound, Joyce, Barnes, Woolf, and Eliot (or at least their accepted reputation, since each of these authors have popular gateways into their work, which I'll discuss in Chapter 3), but not in the face of Hemingway, Nathanael West, Lawrence, Anderson, Mary Butts, Fitzgerald, Huxley, and a whole range of minor modernists. Hemingway, for example, sent a barrage of manuscripts to Mencken for publication, and he earlier took Mencken's luke-warm

---

[44] To push this analogy a bit farther, notice how the discipline has adopted formerly religious terms such as exegesis and hermeneutics to describe its practice.

[45] Eysteinsson, 77.

[46] Gail McDonald, *Learning To Be Modern: Pound, Eliot, and the American University* (Oxford: Clarendon Press, 1993), 75.

review of *In Our Time* to heart. The pattern of tutelage and disassociation informs our reading of modernism's general relationship with Mencken and *The Smart Set*. According to Pierre Bourdieu, such distancing substantiates the artist's expertise in the coded dynamics of cultural competence within the field of restricted cultural production. The hierarchization in the modernist's disavowal of Mencken is highly ironic, for both Mencken and the modernists' parallel positions in regard to each other as well as the masses in general ultimately undermine the idea of autonomous cultural production. Bourdieu substantiates the elite role of the artist by claiming that the "duality of the principles of hierarchization [between heteronomous and autonomous cultural production] means that there are few fields (other than the field of power itself) in which the antagonism between the occupants of the polar positions is more total," yet the double standard of modernism reveals a disturbing presence and simultaneity within each sphere, a gravitational presence of not purely symbolic economics in the autonomous sphere.[47]

The case of modernists *in* the academy (Eliot, Pound, Faulkner) establishing the accepted critical "language"—Bourdieu's "principle of legitimacy"—self-reflexively blurs the borders between the field of cultural production and the field of power. The disavowal of Mencken by the academy illustrates the disavowal of the heteronomous field (i.e., bourgeois) by the autonomous field of production. This likewise illustrates the difficulty of Bourdieu's call to distinguish the "power which writers and artists possess *qua* writers and artists" from the "heteronomous power they wield *qua* experts or cadres."[48] Yet the distinction between these blurs and the idea of autonomous cultural production of literature falls apart when considering commercial venues, here specifically magazines. Not until recently has the idea of what constitutes a modernist venue been questioned and expanded—for example, that a little magazine *is* commercial at all. The differentiations between "commercial" magazines and little magazines are often dependant upon their actual site of commerce, that is, distributed in book stores or newsstands; on economics, that is, do they pay the authors and what scale; and finally on composition and salability, or in other words on their "commercial" or "noncommercial" aura. This last point is difficult to navigate since a noncommercial aura itself constructs an audience and is negotiable into salability.

Moving beyond Bourdieu's model of cultural production, I turn to Michel Foucault who, in his attempt to illuminate the dynamics of the power structure, describes an archaeology of subjugated knowledge, innate to which is a "historical knowledge of struggles," and he offers a genealogical approach that works under the radar of the privileged and totalizing "theoretical avant-garde"—as in a "scientific" structure of thought.[49] Such an approach is the "combined product of an erudite knowledge and a popular knowledge." For Foucault, it is at the power structure's extremities of control where subjugation is most apparent, in the prison,

---

[47] Pierre Bourdieu, *The Field of Cultural Consumption* (NY: Columbia U P, 1993), 46.
[48] Ibid., 273n13.
[49] See Foucault, *Power/Knowledge* (NY: Pantheon, 1980), 83.

the asylum, where liminality is regulated and locked out of sight. If we consider the rise of English studies in the academy as the scientification/reification of literary knowledge, the academy as a manifestation of the power structure (which it undoubtedly is), then it is in the acts of canonization and exclusion where the dynamics of control become most evident.

Therefore, the scientific hierarchization of English studies, from which the category of modernism, with all its lingual, cultural, and thematic connotations, enacts the "aim to inscribe knowledges in the hierarchical order of power associated with science."[50] In the traditional model of modernism, with its establishment of the marketplace and popular as antipode, the study of that which is noncanonized offers an opportunity to examine academia's own "self-identification," its own self-propagating and similarly subjugated motivations. The venues of modernist production in the 1920s and 1930s, for example, magazine production, offer an ideal opportunity for a genealogical effort to "emancipate historical knowledges from the subjection, to render them, that is capable of opposition and of struggle against the theoretical, unitary, formal and scientific knowledge."[51] The library archive, with its reciprocal relationship to cultural worthiness (i.e., we constitute and study what is archived and what is archived is that which is deemed worth studying) becomes the site of sanction and disavowal. *The Smart Set*, as a hybrid form of realism, elite modernism, and popular literature, illustrates the tip of the iceberg of a subjugated form or literary venue, neither archived nor studied.

The Smart Set and *The Little Review*

Margaret Anderson's *The Little Review*, on the other hand, has been championed by academia—reprinted and archived. It is telling to compare the first few years of *The Little Review* with the contemporary *Smart Set*. *The Little Review* is seen as, arguably, the most influential modernist little magazine, much of its renown stemming from publishing *Ulysses* and its ensuing suppression. The similarities between the early years of the *Little Review* and *The Smart Set* of the same time are remarkable. The first issue of the *Little Review* was March of 1914, two months after Willard Huntington Wright was fired from his year of editing of *The Smart Set*. Over the next few years, both magazines relied upon Pound as a foreign editor (though much more overtly with *The Little Review*), and there is a large overlap of authors and themes: Floyd Dell, Sara Teasdale, Vachel Lindsey, Ezra Pound, essays on Nietzsche, laudatory essays on Dreiser, etc. There is even overlap in terms of how the two magazines were marketed: *The Little Review* carried the subtitle, "The Magazine That Is Read By Those Who Write The Others," and *The Smart Set* stated "The Magazine That Other Magazine Editors Read." At one point the *Little Review* proudly flouted "Making No Compromise with the Public Taste" under the

---

[50] Ibid., 85.
[51] Ibid., 85.

masthead, which can be compared to *The Smart Set*'s tag "One Civilized Reader is Worth a Thousand Boneheads." It is evident in the similarities of these slogans that both magazines were catering to a certain audience, were trying to cater to, even create, a sense of cultural superiority. Though such tactics are commonplace today, in the early decades of twentieth-century magazine publishing, which catered to the masses (*Everybody's Magazine, Popular Magazine*—the titles speak for themselves), this was revolutionary, and a technique that would later reach its pinnacle with Condé Nast's stylish *Vanity Fair*.

A difference in tone becomes apparent when scrutinizing these slogans, which is indicative of the differences of the magazines as a whole. Look, for example, at the use of the word "bonehead," which denotes flippancy and humor blatantly missing from the *Little Review*. There is a degree of seriousness, a sense of mission to the little magazines, what Mark Morrisson calls a "militant advocacy" that is missing from *The Smart Set*.

Mencken's stance in the pages of his magazine fluctuated between calls to arms for innovative young writers and statements that his goal with *The Smart Set* was not to educate, but to entertain. *The Smart Set* never broke out of the mold of "cleverness" that had been its trademark for years, another element that worked against the magazine in relation to the literary elite. And considering the marketing value that flippancy had in privileging the reader, the editors did not especially want to change their tone. The term "cleverness" is another complex idea of modernism. In the mouth of modernists it has negative connotations of empty posturing, especially when applied to Mencken and *The Smart Set*; for example, Kronenberger's claim that Mencken indulged in "much cleverness," and that this was a "blemish."[52] It was smartness for the sake of smartness, rather than for the sake of social or cultural depiction or upheaval.

In *The Public Face of Modernism*, Morrisson contends that the scene of modernist little magazines was in fact greatly influenced by mass-marketing publishing techniques and relied upon them in order to gain and influence a popular audience. He looks specifically at Ford Madox Ford's cultivation of a tone of "disinterest" in his *English Review*, a tone used effectively in the *Mercure de France*—the inspiration for both coming from the rise of aesthetic discourse in the eighteenth-century enlightenment. Such a stance was the result of Ford's professed nonpartisan aim to redeem the splintered public sphere through the unbiased exploration of avant-garde art.[53] It is possible to see Mencken and Nathan's mission with *The Smart Set* in this light, but rather than using the popular Edwardian form of the critical review magazine, they kept their existing form of mass-market periodical, and rather than a professed tone of "disinterestedness," they cultivated a tone of self-mocking "cleverness" and insouciance in keeping with the history of the magazine (and perhaps did so with tongue firmly in cheek).

---

[52] Cowley, *Tradition*, 90.
[53] See Morrisson, *The Public Face of Modernism: Little Magazines, Audiences, Reception* (Madison: U Wisconsin P, 2000), 17–53, and especially 18.

The air of irreverent intellectual and cultural superiority that marked (marketed) *The Smart Set* and *Little Review* alike gave the reader a sense of elitism, but the audience that this appealed to, the same audience that enjoyed stories that took to task provincialism, Puritanism, and tradition, wasn't seemingly large enough to make these magazines self-sufficient. Even though *The Smart Set* gained an audience of irreverent youth, which, as Morrisson has shown, was also the *Little Review*'s target audience, it never profited in the same way that *The American Mercury* later would.[54]

Mencken's own relationship to his audience is similar to the dynamics of disavowal and patronage of the modernists; the magazine's growing popularity with collegiate groupies, or Menckenoids, to borrow James Branch Cabell's phrase, made Mencken's audience those that he constantly derided—the clever young men of the newly literate bourgeoisie that Mencken had always referred to as "Shoe-Drummers," the same audience that numerous modernists from Wells to Eliot portrayed and looked down upon as "clerks," symbols of empty bourgeoisie neo-intellectualism.[55] In reality though, as Jonathan Rose has shown, the clerks and day laborers led a rich intellectual life, often self-educated and with more than a nodding familiarity to Eliot and the moderns.[56] The same was true in America—Mencken's outspoken attitudes in the teens and early 1920s became the norm for rising intellectuals, as illustrated by the success of the *American Mercury* (Mencken and Nathan's magazine after *The Smart Set*), the first issue of which, in 1924, sold 15,000 copies, and became an instant collector's item, which recalls Jake Barnes's line in *The Sun Also Rises* that "So many young men get their likes and dislikes from Mencken."[57] Referring to *The Smart Set* in the *Little Review*, Pound stated "I may reserve my opinion that literature is not a commodity, that literature emphatically does not lie on a counter where it can be snatched up at once by a straw-hatted young man in a hurry."[58] It seems that for the literary elite, Mencken, as well as his *Smart Set*, became an emblem for middlebrow culture.

Joan Shelley Rubin, in *Making Middle Brow Culture*, has noted academia's neglect of the middlebrow, stating that, in general, "students of American literature – loyal ... to the avant-garde – have ordinarily focused on figures who have viewed themselves as alienated: expatriates, writers for the 'Little Magazines,' modernists."[59] Rubin, writing as a means to expose the role of long-ignored middlebrow critics,

---

[54] See Morrisson's chapter "Youth in Public," 133–166.

[55] See Carey 46–70, as well as Nardini's description of the rise and fall of Mencken's reputation.

[56] See, for example, his discussion of Richard Burke and A.E. Coppard, 414–421, *The Intellectual Life of the British Working Class* (New Haven: Yale U P, 2001).

[57] Singleton, 53; Hemingway, *Sun*, 42.

[58] Pound *Pound/Little Review*, 156–157. There is a photo reprinted in Mencken's *My Life as Author and Editor* of Mencken from this time, showing him in the midst of a sea of adoring young men, illustrates wryly Pound's quote.

[59] *The Making of Middlebrow Culture* (Chapel Hill: U North Carolina P, 1992), xv.

places Mencken on the side of the literary elite—which is somewhat ironic seeing as the modernists saw him aligned closer to the middlebrow. It is more feasible that Mencken has fallen into the illusory gap between the two. But Rubin's claim that literary history has long overlooked the middlebrow substantiates the neglect of *The Smart Set* due to that magazine's mix of authors. Likewise, that modernist critics such as Gilbert Seldes championed middlebrow art, or that artists such as Joyce and Eliot had an affinity for the middlebrow music hall, has long been ignored until the recent rise of cultural studies with its accompanying goals for the revision of modernism.[60]

Mencken's own tirade against restrictive cultural values went hand in hand with the social realism in *The Smart Set's* fiction about immigrants and the working class, stories that would have fit in with socialist little magazines such as *The Masses* (Joyce and Robert Carleton Brown are two examples).[61] This was seemingly in direct opposition to the magazine's "smart" tone—which was both a remnant of the magazine's beginnings and nurtured by Mencken. For example, in 1915 Mencken asked a writer: "Which brings me to a commercial matter. Have you an idea for a novelette of 30,000 words, dealing with well to do people and lively in tone?"[62] Such stories did not sit well with Theodore Dreiser, who had long been a *Smart Set* contributor, Mencken's cause célèbre, and Comstock's poster child for literary decadence. Dreiser was sorely disappointed that the magazine didn't lose its studied *insouciance* with the new editors. Mencken answered:

> I am sorry to say that *The Smart Set* doesn't please you. As it stands, of course, it represents a compromise between what we'd like to do and what the difficulties that we face allow us to do. …We haven't enough money to take long chances. We have to give them, to some extent at least, what they seem to like, and more particularly what we are able to get… But the light touch you protest against is what we want. *The Smart Set*—consider the title! —is no place [for] revolutionary fustian…. But let it go! We are not trying to shock 'em, but to entertain 'em![63]

Mencken's quote, which readily admits the magazine's popular tone ("Consider the Title!"), also identifies both the magazine's artistic compromise (unlike the *Little Review*'s "Making no Compromise with Public Taste") and need for economic support. Early on, *The Little Review* experimented with popular magazine marketing techniques, such as lowered cover price and advertisements from popular publishers, but since it didn't posses sufficient ad or subscription revenue

---

[60] For Eliot and the Music Hall, see Faulk, "Modernism and the Popular: Eliot's Music Halls," *Modernism/Modernity*, Vol. 8.4 (2001), 603–621; for Joyce, see Herr, *Joyce's Anatomy of Culture* (Urbana: Illinois U P, 1986).

[61] See, for example, Sharon Hamilton's dissertation chapter on "*The Smart Set* and Nativism: The Example of Joyce's *Dubliners*, 1915."

[62] Guy Forgue, ed., *Letters of H.L. Mencken* (Boston: Northeastern U P, 1981), 60.

[63] Dolmetsch, 49–50.

it turned to patrons and gifts.[64] *The Smart Set* likewise turned to patronage, but an entirely different kind; rather than actual patrons, the editors started their series of "louse" pulp magazines, as Mencken was wont to call them. Just as Anderson was willing to eschew rent and camp out on the shores of Lake Michigan when necessary so as to keep her magazine alive, her use of private investors and patrons (similar to that of Pound, Eliot, and Joyce) illustrates the type of militant advocacy of the avant-garde and the extent that she was willing to go to in order to avoid involving her magazine in commercial pandering that would curtail her editorial choices. In Mencken and Nathan's system, they used *Saucy Stories*, *Parisienne*, and *Black Mask* both for economic support and as an outlet for the hundreds of manuscripts they received for *The Smart Set,* delegating the more popular stories to the unabashedly popular outlets and freeing up *The Smart Set* for more serious submissions.

Yet we cannot overlook the dynamics of patronage even with this odd system. My use of the word patronage in this situation relies upon its involvement with the marketplace. Even in the high modernist practice of private patronage there resides the specter of control and tension. As Lawrence Rainey states, patronage was a "capricious institution," which could be "arbitrary in its choices and operations" and "lacking in the reliability and rationality that secures trust in the functioning of an institution."[65] Rainey has discussed the taint of patronage as going against the "work ethic" in the ever heightening pace of capitalist society, and T.W. Heyck has discussed the rise of Literary Guilds in order for the profession to avoid the taint of both the marketplace and, conversely, the taint of charity. Pound's revival of patronage somewhat goes against the mid-Victorian author's pride in market success, as T.W. Heyck asserts, "most Victorian men of letters valued their independence from patronage, and took pride in honest production for the market."[66] This move on Pound's part again underlines the marketing of modernism as autonomous, as opposed to the marketplace. Yet more than this, the tensions between the artist and the marketplace—the sin that is "selling out"—also exist in the relationship between artist and patron, albeit often unstated. The threat of pandering to or displeasing the patron, of the cash-cow drying up, looms over the history of Zora Neale Hurston and Langston Hughes's relationship with their patrons, and, less evident, over Harriet Shaw Weaver's reaction to *Work in Progress*.[67] With *The Smart Set*, there is even the sense of an influence (some would say contamination), both in terms of marketing and appearance, from their pulps.

---

[64] Morrisson, 136.

[65] Rainey, 108.

[66] T.W. Heyck, *The Transformation of Intellectual Life in Victorian England* (NY: St. Martin's Press, 1982), 32.

[67] See, for example, the accounts of Hurston's "fooling" her patrons, and of Hughes's break with his patron in Nathan Irvin Huggins' *Harlem Renaissance* (London: U P of Oxford, 1973), 129–136.

The Smart Set, *Modernism, and the Expanded Field of Magazine Production*   43

Fig. 1.2   *Smart Set*, Sept. 1915 © 1915 Smart Set Company, Inc.

By 1922, the *Smart Set* shared paper and ads with the other magazines of the advertisement and distribution service the "Newsstand Group," which included *Action Stories, Lariet Stories, North-West Stories, Ace High, Black Mask,* and *Saucy Stories*. Its design, double-column blocks of print with no illustration, was the same as other fiction magazines. Over the course of Mencken and Nathan's editorship, the physical connotations of *The Smart Set* became undeniably "pulpish" as its paper quality declined in order to save money; one critic described it as

Fig. 1.3   *Smart Set*, April 1923 © 1923 Smart Set Company, Inc.

resembling "a glorified pulp magazine."[68] In a letter dated June 20, 1923, written as Mencken was preparing to leave *The Smart Set* and start the *American Mercury*, he stated: "Confidentially, I am making plans to start a serious review—gaudiest and damnedest ever seen in the republic. I am sick of *The Smart Set* after nine years of it, and eager to get rid of its title, history, advertising, bad paper, worse

---

[68]   Douglas, 89; see the next chapter for a thorough definition of "pulp."

printing, etc."⁶⁹ *The Smart Set* now resembled, at least physically, the same type of magazines that it was trying to differentiate itself from, those same magazines that were paying its bills.

Over the course of Mencken and Nathan's first year of editorship, *The Smart Set*'s covers evolved from uniform and decidedly high-tone (and Edwardian) black-and-white pen drawings of a man and woman—the man in tuxedo, hat in hand, standing above a young lady playing coyly with a fan (see Figure 1.1 again)—to covers that depicted the same scene but mimicked in decidedly flapperish style by John Held (see Figure 1.2), whose cartoons would become synonymous with the Jazz Age. By 1918, the magazine lost this vignette totally, featuring cover girl portraits. From then until Mencken and Nathan left, the covers turned abstract, often depicting high-society cultural themes such as a couple looking at abstract art (see Figure 1.3). Others were more gritty or impressionistic such as that of September 1923 (see Figure 1.4), which portrays four hunched figures trudging through a gray urban landscape, under their arms are four placards or magazines upon which is written the magazine's current logo: "Life, Literature, Criticism, Wit." These figures, possibly a self-mocking depiction of bohemian *Smart Set* readers, illustrate the whimsical abstraction of the avant-garde that could be found between the magazine's covers—Modernism Lite, as it were. Other covers, especially the early pinup or "cover girl" portrait type, were exactly the same in appearance as dozens of other all fiction titles, such as *All-Story* and early *Blue Book*. Even the later, more whimsical covers resembled closely those of *The Smart Set*'s sister magazine *Saucy Stories* (see Figure 1.5).

What these covers illustrate is not only how the defining line between these magazines was fine indeed, but how *The Smart Set*'s physicality allowed it to gesture toward cultural elitism yet to remain entertaining for a wide public; indeed, its attitude of intellectual privilege captured in the later cover illustrations and slogans appealed to readers, giving them edginess by proxy. *The Smart Set* pioneered a flippant modernism, clever in tone and subject matter (if not in appearance) that the later "smart magazines"—*Vanity Fair, New Yorker, Esquire*—eventually perfected through an advocacy of expatriate modernism and economic privilege. But more than this, it also pioneered a lineage of populist modernism in snappy, flapperish pulp magazines.

Smart Magazines and Smart Modernism

The "Smart Magazines" have received some critical attention as popular outlets of modernism; Sharon Hamilton, for example, sees *The Smart Set* as the *New Yorker*'s direct forebearer, stating that it played "no less [a] literary role in the American marketplace than its well-known successor" and it "introduced more American readers than any other magazine of the period to the particular writers, the literary trends, and the critical ideas which would prove to be key

---

⁶⁹ Quoted in, Douglas C. Stenerson, *Critical Essays on H.L. Mencken* (Boston: Hall, 1987), 156–157.

Fig. 1.4   *Smart Set*, Sept. 1923 © 1923 Smart Set Company, Inc.

factors in the development of American modernism."⁷⁰ But it was *Vanity Fair* that fine-tuned *The Smart Set*'s high-tone marketing into its raison d'etre; it was a high-culture Baedeker. It did not come into its own until the mid 1920s, but it started its slow climb in 1914 when Condé Nast hired socialite Frank Crowninshield. Nast, rich from the success of *Vogue* magazine, had recently purchased competitor

---

⁷⁰ See Sharon Hamilton, "The First *New Yorker*? *The Smart Set* Magazine, 1900–1924," 89.

The Smart Set, *Modernism, and the Expanded Field of Magazine Production* 47

Fig. 1.5   *Saucy Stories*, Nov. 1919 © 1919 The Inter-Continental Publishing Corporation

Dress magazine and combined it with the pseudo-socialite rag *Vanity Fair* in order to breathe new life into *Dress*. Crowninshield accepted the editorship on the condition that the magazine drop women's fashion and concentrate upon cultural fashion. Crowninshield, a member of New York society, facilitator and ambassador for the Armory Show, author of *Manners for the Metropolis*, (which was a tongue-in-cheek guide to high society written for those "newer millionaires and plutocrats" who "become utterly helpless and panic-stricken at the mere sight of a gold finger bowl, an alabaster bath, a pronged oyster fork, or the business end of an asparagus,") was the perfect choice for *Vanity Fair*'s editor.[71] The magazine became successful just as *The Smart Set* was bowing out. Ironically, one reason for this was Crowninshield's agenda of highlighting modern art. Nast stated that Crowninshield's "interest in the modern French art movement, at first, did us a certain amount of harm. We were ten years too early (1915) in talking about Van Gogh, Gauguin, Matisse, Picasso, etc. At first people took the ground that we were (presumably) insane."[72] Whereas *The Smart Set* never had the monetary luxury to follow such an edgy agenda, to use photographs and glossy covers, or be printed upon anything other than high-grade pulp paper, *Vanity Fair* had the limitless backing and resources of Nast's publishing empire. More so than any little magazine, *Vanity Fair* advanced the idea that modernism was solely for the privileged; its advertisements pandered to the socialite: the best hotels and resorts, cars, clothes, and jewelers. It was the stylebook for the cutting edge modern consumer—the 1927 *Vanity Fair* subscription ad epigram quoted at this chapter's beginning, for example, states "Modernism is sweeping the intelligent world…you won't always understand modernism. But you should at least be able to appreciate it." This ad, as well as *Vanity Fair*'s whole aura shows how the idea of modernism was highly marketable through the 1920s and early 1930s.

This is important to point out when considering the modernists' own memoirs and reflections about the movement since it explains the peculiar return to the scene of modernism in the early 1930s; Margaret Anderson wrote *My Thirty Year War* in 1930, Norman Douglas wrote *Looking Back* in 1933, Cowley wrote *Exile's Return* in 1934, as did McAlmon his *Being Geniuses Together*. This return again occurred in the 1950s and early 1960s: Sylvia Beach's *Shakespeare and Company* appeared in 1956, Cowley extensively reedited his *Exile's Return* in 1951, Joseph Barry published *Right Bank, Left Bank, Paris and Parisians* in 1951, Caresse Crosby wrote *The Passionate Years* in 1953—these lists are far from complete (especially considering that I have omitted the large number of scholarly examinations appearing at this time). Such texts became, as Marc Dolan puts it, "Lightning rods for subsequent citation" and any aspect of *marketing* contained within them has been carefully overlooked, rarely scrutinized until recently.[73]

At least since the 1960s there has risen a large body of criticism dedicated to identifying the boundaries of autobiography, which involves issues of fiction, fact, and self-invention—especially since, as Paul John Eakin states, "the fictive nature of selfhood is held to be biographical fact."[74] The fictive nature of memoir is most notably and publicly illustrated in the 2006 scandal surrounding James Frey's *A Million Little Pieces*. Yet missing from the large and varied body of

---

[71] Crowninshield, *Manners for the Metropolis* (NY: Arno, 1975), 5.

[72] Quoted in Douglas, 99.

[73] Dolan as well notes the reification of the "lost generation" in memoirs and description in the 1930s and 1950s, 29, 18–26.

[74] Paul John Eakin, *Fictions in Autobiography* (Princeton: Princeton U P, 1985), 182.

autobiographical criticism is any cohesive exploration of self-invention in terms of the marketplace, either of a single author or an entire literary movement, as in the case of modernism, which I believe is another instance of the tenacity of the idea of artistic autonomy in the academy. Despite the identification of the problems innate in memoirs and autobiographies, there has always been little questioning of the academic assumptions and constructions that have been built upon such subjective texts as modernist memoirs, at least until the rise of the feminist rereading of modernism.[75]

Bonnie Kime Scott has pointed out that, "Modernism as we were taught it ... was perhaps halfway to the truth."[76] The gendered slant of modernism has rightly come under revision thanks to such groundbreaking feminist critics of modernism such as Bonnie Kime Scott, Shari Benstock, Gilbert and Gubar, and Jayne Marek who opened the modernist panorama to long overlooked female writers and editors.[77] The endeavor to correct or rewrite modernism has logically involved a return to or retro-construction of that original site of modernism through opening the canon to overlooked works, but also by opening and examining the literary archives in an effort to remove the androcentric neglect innate in the unquestioning acceptance of modernism—a modernism based in part upon memoirs and autobiographies. It is important to consider these in the milieu of the popular marketplace, both cashing in on modernism's popularity and being innate self-publicity.

Hemingway's *A Moveable Feast* offers one instance of such self-construction; little consideration has been given to Hemingway's motive in writing *A Moveable Feast* or of its fictive elements. Even Marc Dolan's otherwise excellent and thorough reading of the book simply glosses over Hemingway's nostalgia "that permeated the author's last two decades of writing" as just being the result of a series of Paris-linked experiences.[78] By 1957, when Hemingway concentrated in earnest upon *A Moveable Feast*, his persona was years and miles away from the bohemian aura of legitimacy that he had built his career upon. He had gone from having his name on the cover of the *Transatlantic Review* and *transition* to being named "America's Number One He Man" on the cover of the cheesecake men's magazine *Modern Man* (June, 1956) or voted "One of ten most sexciting men alive" by Zsa Zsa Gabor in the February 1957 *Show* pinup digest. *A Moveable*

---

[75] There is a large and extremely varied body of criticism dealing with the dynamic and self-construction of autobiography. I have relied upon Paul John Eakin's *Fictions in Autobiography* and Timothy Dow Adams's *Telling Lies in Modern American Autobiography* (Chapel Hill: U of North Carolina P, 1990).

[76] Bonnie Kime Scott, *Refiguring Modernism: The Women of 1928* (Bloomington: Indiana U P, 1995), 2.

[77] Scott's two volume *Refiguring Modernism*, Benstock's seminal *Women of the Left Bank, Paris, 1900–1940* (Austin: U of Texas P, 1986), Sandra Gilbert and Susan Gubar's *No Man's Land: The Place of Women Writers in the Twentieth Century* (New Haven: Yale U P, 1988), and Marek's *Women Editing Modernism: "Little" Magazines and Literary History* (Lexington: U P of Kentucky, 1995).

[78] Dolan, 49.

Feast was written during Hemingway's waning years as an effort to recapture the symbolic capital of his bohemian years. There is little doubt, no matter how bastardized the posthumous manuscript is, that Hemingway is writing about his own issues of having "sold out"—of his loss of artistic integrity which came with success, as well as his movement from private to public figure.[79]

The 1950s popular fascination with modernism, of which Hemingway's overwhelming presence in men's magazines and adventure pulps is just a single example, is not a "co-option," the adoption and use of an artistic or avant-garde aura for marketing purposes or as counterpoint to raunchy, lowbrow elements, but is rather a manifestation of popular modernism. For Josephine Herbst, who was a reader for both *The Smart Set* and a pulp magazine publisher, sees the 1920s as a time before distinct literary categories, when an author could send "one manuscript to *transition* and another to H.L. Mencken" on the same day.[80] Herbst, in her own modernist memoir, "A Year of Disgrace," acknowledges the duplicity innate to memoirs, continually states her intent to give a true portrayal of the 1920s, to avoid nostalgic and academic reductivism, writing that "But is there such a thing as the twenties? The decade simply falls apart upon examination into crumbs and pieces which completely contradict each other in their essences. The twenties was not the museum piece it has since become, where our literary curators have posed on elevated pedestals a few busts of the eminent." It was a time when "literature had not yet been boxed off from life. Nor had a body of critics nominated themselves as 'the elite.' You might write reviews for the literary supplements without having to qualify as a professor."[81]

Unlike many modernist memoirs of the 1950s, Herbst's, written in the early 1960s, is both a product of the rising civil rights and emerging feminist movement, and a reaction against the academic and androcentric crystallization of monolithic modernism.[82] It scolds the totalizing voice and views like those Malcolm Cowley is guilty of in *Exile's Return,* a book that aided in reifying the monolithic and masculine-led idea of modernism. According to Dolan, Cowley "undergird[ed] the so-called American Studies movement of the 1930s, 1940s, and 1950s, which represented, in many ways, the academic digestion, summation, and extension of a century long movement towards national self-analysis and self-conscious

---

[79] See Dolan, 50–54, as well as Jacqueline Tavernier-Courbin's *Ernest Hemingway's A Moveable Feast: the Making of Myth* (Boston: Northeastern U P, 1991). It is possible to see Hemingway constructing his fall from artistic grace in *A Moveable Feast*, symbolized in his leaving his first wife for Pauline Pfeiffer, a writer for *Vogue* and whose moneyed uncle became an ergo patron for the young Hemingway, and so attempting to return to his anti-commercial modernist reputation.

[80] Josephine Herbst, *The Starched Blue Sky of Spain and Other Memoirs* (Boston: Northeaster U P, 1999), 78.

[81] Ibid., 74–75.

[82] On Herbst's memoirs as rising from the civil rights and feminist movement, as well as her awareness of "history and autobiography [as] representative acts," see Elizabeth Francis' introduction in Herbst, vii–x, xvi.

mythologization,"—a project in which Cowley, as critic, obviously had a vested interest.[83] Indeed, whereas the contemporary modernist memoirs of the 1930s can be seen as an effort on the part of modernist facilitators to reconfirm the exclusivity of modernism, or bolster the constructed borders of the movement, it is just as easy to see them as an example of popular modernism, though this goes against the movement's mantle of restriction. Just as Hemingway's later, overblown celebrity was a result of his own early self-marketing, so are the extreme, visual examples of mid-century modernism: *Gent*'s October 1957 issue, which explored the scene of 1920s modernism (with articles on "Lost Bohemia," excerpts from John Dos Passos' *Big Money*, and a nude pictorial of flappers); an interview with Aldous Huxley in *Dude*; articles on Faulkner, Joyce, and Lawrence in other raunchy men's magazines such as *Debonair* and *Jem*—all of these can be considered popular aspects of modernism generally ignored by critics, a culmination of monolithic and masculine/misogynistic modernism's self-marketing similar to Pound and Lewis's blasting of popular literature as "effeminate" or modernists such as Hemingway, Dos Passos, and Fitzgerald's appearances in *Esquire Magazine*. Of course the sensationalization of the movement wasn't new, as we have seen, but this canonized, masculine mid-century modernism ignores earlier feminist aspects of popular modernism.

Mass Modernisms in the Snappy Pulps: Risqué Paris and the New York Flapper

When returning to the scene(s) of modernism, it is important to realize that the milieu of the earlier memoirs such as *Exile's Return*, *My Thirty Year War*, and *Being Geniuses Together* wasn't Joyce's *Ulysses* or Barnes's *Nightwood* as much as popular representations of modernism in books like *This Must Be The Place* (1934) by Jimmy Charters, the barman from the Dingo Bar, *Paris With The Lid Lifted* (1927), by Bruce Reynolds, which promised "The peppy, purplish, palpitating Paris that all true 'joy-seekers' yearn to see" (i.e., a travel guide to the bars and bordellos of Paris), and Sisley Huddleston's *Paris Salons Cafes Studios* (1928), which was popular enough to be republished in a mass edition by Blue Ribbon Books, a cheap reprint house even lower on the culture scale than Grosset and Dunlap. The popularity of such books illustrates the overall fashion for "pop decadent" modernism, to borrow Michael Murphy's phrase, which was likewise encapsulated in the popularity of Fitzgerald and Jazz-age modernism, and which made Hemingway's *The Sun Also Rises* a surprise success.

The Smart Set is just such a manifestation: it initially published many of the stories compiled in Fitzgerald's *Flappers and Philosophers* and *Tales of the Jazz Age;* the 1915 covers by John Held appeared a decade before his covers for *Life* and *The New Yorker*. Yet it not only published Fitzgerald, but a whole pantheon

---

[83] Dolan, 98.

of authors who also appeared in the dozens of all-fiction, early pulp-wood paper magazines of the time. Even before *The Smart Set* joined the Newsstand Group, unsold issues and newsstand returns were rebound with returned *Parisienne* and *Saucy Stories,* recovered and sold as 15 cent pulps on the rural market, entitled *Clever Stories* and *Fascinating Fiction*—hence it is possible that a Joyce story or a Pound poem could have ended up in a popular pulp magazine in a rural train station.[84] If we compare the look, distribution, circulation of *The Smart Set* to the little magazines, then *The Smart Set* offers a popular outlet for modernism. In actuality though, *The Smart Set* doesn't offer as accessible an outlet for popular modernism as do the numerous magazines that it either spawned or inspired—not the smart magazines, but mass-produced fiction magazines like *Saucy Stories, Spicy Stories, The Parisienne, Brief Stories, Telling Tales,* and *Live Stories,* all of which relied upon popular portrayals of modernism.

The Parisienne, for example, which Mencken started in 1915, was full of stories about bohemian Paris, jazz, artist's models, and "peppy" living. The August 1919 issue featured drawings and vignettes about "How Paris Amuses Itself," including "The Famous Bal Tabarin: The First and Greatest of All the World's Jazz Places." This was a year before prohibition, Fitzgerald's *This Side of Paradise* and *Flappers and Philosophers*, and seven years before Hemingway's *The Sun Also Rises* captured the public imagination and sparked an influx of thrill seeking expat Americans. In 1918, *The Parisienne* published the one act play by Djuna Barnes, "Madame Collects Herself," a dada-esque vignette that deals with the fragmentation of the female body, much as *Nightwood* would a decade later.

The French setting of Barnes's play, as with most stories from *Parisienne*, reflects the popular fascination with the artistic life of Paris and the nightlife of Montmarte; this was an ubiquitous theme in such magazines and nowhere better illustrated than in the series "Paris in Profile," written by Robert W. Sneddon for *Snappy Stories* in 1914. In the June installment, the narrator describes his morning rambles through Montmarte with Solange, one of the "ladies who contribute their gaiety to the night restaurants." The sights are filled with off-duty jazz musicians, English dancers from the Bal Tabarin, lingerie and kimono clad coquettes, with artists, poets, authors, composers, and singers. Sneddon was a prolific short story author for many of the general fiction mags and pulps from the teens through the 1930s. He published in *The Smart Set* and Edward O'Brien's *Best Short Stories of 1917* as well as in pulps ranging from *Flynn's Detective Weekly* to *Ghost Story*. His account of Paris is full of the bohemian aura that would only be compounded during World War I and eventually make the Lost Generation a household name, more so due to their risqué reputation than their stylistic experimentation. In 1922, *Snappy* would even publish a story about Kiki, a strong-willed French

---

[84] Again, the rarity of these pulps makes it nearly impossible to know the contents. There is no bibliography for any of Mencken's pulps except for *Black Mask*, see Hagemann, *A Comprehensive Index to Black Mask, 1920–1951* (Bowling Green: Bowling Green U Popular P, 1982).

Fig. 1.6 *Snappy Stories*, Dec. 1, 1925 © 1924 New Fiction Publishing Corporation

model obviously inspired by the real life Kiki, Alice Prin. This was years before Hemingway wrote the foreword to her memoirs, introducing her to the American public (see Figure 1.6).

This popular appeal of sensational bohemian life often forwarded strong and independent female role models, or at least women who wrestled independence away from their male counterparts. Such as in "Preferring Things

Risqué" from the August 1920 issue of *Saucy Stories*. Roger, Emily's husband, reads French novels, tells risqué anecdotes, and takes his wife to shocking social plays; one night he mentions going to a French restaurant. Emily's friend Isabelle warns her that Roger might have a "secret longing" for a bohemian life, and that Emily had better be ready if her husband "comes home wearing a Byron tie, drags you off to a table d'hote, talks free love, and drinks green creme d'menthe, and mentions the super-soul, and declares that he need more self-expression." In order to overcome her "Quaker" appearance, Emily quickly borrows a dress (the maid's *pièce de résistance* with her street-car-conductor sweetheart), makes up gaudily, starts smoking, and memorizes epigrams of Oscar Wilde. Roger is aghast and their marriage quickly cools. The wife's misunderstanding of the difference between the risqué and culturally (i.e., morals, fashion, social convention) challenging nature of bohemianism, illustrated in her empty trappings of modernism (i.e., a cheap dress mistaken for a scandalous one), drives Roger to the flapperesque Isabella, who is well versed in the use of an eyebrow pencil and rouge. Ultimately, Isabella, who has had her fun, negotiates reparation between the two via Emily's evolution to a fashionable coquettetry, with ensuing confidence and control of Roger. Seemingly, performing modernism leads the way to feminism and independence.

This figure of the flapper as a strong, independent woman, thoroughly modern and challenging old-world conventions was a common trope in many of the magazines in the post-war years.[85] Other magazines like *Flapper's Experience* and *Home Brew* were dedicated to challenging gender roles, moral codes, and prohibition; though light in tone and material, they often have a d.i.y. and underground feel about them, sort of like prohibition-inspired little magazines. The May 1923 issue of *The Flapper* (see Figure 1.7) epitomizes the modernity of the Flapper-style new woman: it contains an essay calling for a new, nonreligious-based definition of morals while defending itself from religious campaigns against amoral magazines; a "message to flappers" from Carrie Keeley, champion woman boxer of the world; a photo-article on "How Flappers Keep Fit"; letters from flappers and flippers (their male counterpart); and numerous short stories and "flapper confessions." Other all-fiction magazines like *Snappy Stories* and *Telling Tales* both relied upon and promoted the flapper while pushing the boundaries of popular fiction from safe Edwardian romance to peppy popular fiction. A series of flapper-helmed stories were published in *Telling Tales* in the early 1920s; some, like "The Flapper Fares Forth," just capitalized on the flapper fad to repackage a formulaic adventure yarn, but others, like C.S. Montayne's "The Flapper Husband" and Nancy Lowe's "The Taming of the Flapper" captured the tensions that arose from the disintegration of the prewar values, the challenging old values.

---

[85] It is difficult to express just how ubiquitous these modernism-themed stories are in these magazines. These examples are culled from the dozen or so issues in the author's private collection. A cohesive study of these titles is extremely difficult since extended runs of such magazines are impossible to find. Even the Library of Congress has only limited runs or odd volumes.

Fig. 1.7   *Flapper*, May 1923 © 1923 The Flapper Publishing Company

Stories like "Knees of Clay," published in the February, 1925 *Snappy Stories* asked "Are there fires beneath the sparkling nonsense of the flapper?" Answer: Yes. Such was the real milieu of F. Scott Fitzgerald's "Bernice Bobs Her Hair" (Again, see Figure 1.6).

Just as Fitzgerald built his reputation upon his expertise of the flapper (some reviewers and interviewers even labeled him the "inventor of the flapper"), other authors made a name for themselves in the all-fiction magazines with flapper subject matter. Dawn Powell is one such example. Years before becoming the chronicler of Greenwich Village bohemianism and launching her prolific career as a novelist, she initially published flapperish short stories in magazines like *Breezy Stories* and *Snappy Stories*. "And When She Was Bad--" from August 1921 *Breezy*, for example, is about an annoyingly Puritanical school teacher who attends a convention in New York City, her first trip to the big city. As the story starts, she wakes up in her hotel with no recollection of the night before; over the course of the day she finds out that she had her first alcoholic drink, raised hell, and did something unnamed with Kelsey, a handsome yet staid bachelor. She ensuingly loses her job, but is proposed to by Kelsey. "'Isn't it queer,'" the story ends, "'that all the years I was so awfully good, and everyone *knew* I was awfully good, nothing nice ever happened to me? And now, – when I am bad –' 'You're irresistible!' finished Kelsey, and kissed her on the mouth." Seemingly, good things happen to naughty flappers. Powell's later stories for *Snappy* just further this: a wife recaptures her wandering husband by learning how to flirt with other men; a lonely girl captures a beau by playing the wild society girl; a chorus girl plays the tease to a sugar daddy, but her refusal to deliver the goods leads to the choice for independence and career.[86] These stories forward the image of the modern and independent woman while navigating the formula of the romance story. Most of these issues of *Snappy* are illustrated with vignettes by John Held, such as "How a petting party should end"—*Snappy* is an overlooked playbook of the flapper, as is the post-Mencken *Smart Set*.

After Mencken and Nathan left *The Smart Set* the magazine reinvented itself—not as a literary or even a general all-fiction magazine, but as a slick true confession magazine geared for modern young women (see Figure 1.8). By 1926, it featured an odd combination of first-person stories and diaries by "modern women" about careers, sex, and morals; short romance stories illustrated by photos; articles like "Behind a Family Doctor's Door" were "true" stories where a women learns to schluff off constricting Puritan styles and "vamps," often to recapture an erring husband. There were also pictorials of flappers' (bare knee) beauty pageants. A photograph of the prototypical vamp, Louise Brooks was featured in the October 1929 issue, one of the last, and there is a relatively famous photograph of her reading a copy of *Smart Set,* all of which illustrates the magazine's audience and importance in forwarding the flapper role. Articles like "A Flapper Sets Me Right" outlines—almost in manifesto form—the flapper history and philosophy, how:

> With the passage of the years the boys were given more and yet more liberties, and their pursuit of the lying, pretending girl [i.e. the repressed girl who adhered to unnatural social constraints]. Old maids, frumps and iron jawed she executives were held up to us by our parents as moral patterns. The picture was truly not an interesting one to a young and beautiful girl with a mind already in rebellion against Victorian standards and prejudices. Actually, we came to

---

[86] "Applesauce for the Gander," *Snappy*, Vol. 91, No. 1 (June 1925); "The Primrose Gate," *Snappy*, Vol. 91, No. 3 (July 1925); "Margie and the Men," Vol. 88, No. 2 (Feb. 1925).

Fig. 1.8   *Smart Set*, July 1927 © 1927 Magus Magazine Corporation

associate virtue with ugliness and cotton underthings. [...] The war had much to do with the overturn. Our brothers and sweethearts met and loved the daughters of the French people, the most frank and outspoken people in the world. Then our soldiers returned and found us a collection of moral and mental hypocrites. [...] So we resolved, universally and individually, that we would become honest; that we would meet our men folk on the common ground of their own choosing, taking unto ourselves their privileges and customs. And why not, I ask? The woman puts as identically as much into the home as does the man. Justice demands that her reward in happiness be equal to his. [...] Today we do exactly what our boy friends do, and we defy them to criticize us!"[87]

The article goes on to discuss how the flappers' open attitude about "'flirting' or 'spooning'" has allowed them to differentiate between "real and spurious love." Along the way it advocates women's rights and sex education. Yet other articles, like "I Simply Had to Get Thin Again – to Keep My Husband," are more troublesome, illustrating contentious aspects of 1920s feminism such as male idealism of the body (it is interesting to note that Belasco, author of "A Flapper Sets Me Straight" was a theater producer, confirming the idea that early films gave ascendancy of the flapper as an object of desire).[88] But rather than explore the troubling aspects of the flapper in regard to suffrage or political feminism, I'd like to stress the flapper as a symbol of popular modernism, with all its innate paradoxes of simultaneous misogyny and feminism, implicated in social change and upheaval, as well as stress the innate paradoxes in these magazines, whether high and low or modern and traditional.

Frank Luther Mott, writing of the *Smart Set* in the late 1950s recounts how a former reader, upon seeing the new incarnation of the post-Mencken *Smart Set* stated: "Look at the trollop! Why couldn't she have died before she lost her good name?" Likewise, Mott himself states that the magazine, full of "sex and sensation fiction," was "wallowing in a vulgarity unworthy of past achievements."[89] The sexual overtones of such statements parallel the charges leveled against the sexually and socially liberated flapper. The new *Smart Set* evolved, with its full color flapper cover girls by Henry Clive, to symbolize both the sensation and the rebelliousness of the modern girl. The magazine's evolution also embodied both the magazine's popular strain that had existed since its inception and challenging of American Puritanism that had marked (and marketed) the magazines ethos since the days of Wright, confirming how the earlier manifestation was part of the zeitgeist challenging sexual and social conventions—illustrated by the confrontation between Mencken and Sumner. Tellingly, the circulation of *The Smart Set* went from 31,000 in 1924 when Mencken left to 384,000 in 1926 when it was both marketed by (via covers, ads, and articles) and for the women's flapper youth movement.

But *The Smart Set*'s real contribution to culture was the birth of the subgenre of these snappy magazine; they were spawned by a "pulp war" between it and its former owner, Colonel Mann. After selling *The Smart Set*, Mann, along with future pulp maven W.M. Clayton, immediately established *Snappy Stories* in 1912, an obvious pastiche of his former magazine. Both magazines' logos sported elongated S's in the title, and whereas *The Smart Set* was touted as "The Magazine of Cleverness,"

---

[87] David Belasco, "A Flappers Sets Me Straight," *Smart Set* (July 1927), 90–91.

[88] For some of the issues surrounding both the flapper and 1920s feminism see Angela J. Latham, *Posing a Threat* (Hanover: Wesleyan U P, 2000).

[89] Frank Luther Mott, *A History of American Magazines, Volume V: Sketches of 21 Magazines 1905–1930* (Cambridge, MA: Harvard U P, 1968), 271.

Snappy Stories was "A Magazine of Entertaining Fiction," and the two were often confused. Mencken and Nathan retaliated by starting the *Parisienne* to cash in on the fascination for anything French in America during the early days of World War I. The *Parisienne*'s success resulted in Clayton's appeal to the vice society (through a middleman, of course), even more devious because he knew that Mencken wouldn't retaliate with a vice complaint of his own against the *Snappy Stories* because he didn't want it confused with the similar *Smart Set*. Instead Mencken and Nathan set up *Saucy Stories* in 1916, their own pastiche of *Snappy*. This proved even more popular and more of a moneymaker than *Parisienne*, and launched the genre of peppy pulp mags; by the mid-1920s, Parisian-themed girlie mags like *Paris Life, Paris Nights, French Follies* flourished. But in the early 1920s, *Snappy, Saucy*, and their kind were still general fiction pulp-wood magazines, featuring domestic romance, O'Henry-like stories, and the odd exotic adventure. *The Smart Set* started a whole genre of pulp titles. I consider this *The Smart Set*'s real legacy, as a progenitor of popular modernism rather than elite little magazines or smart magazines.

Beyond Little Magazines: the Larger Scene of Magazine Publishing

In general, there is very little work upon the early all-fiction and pulp-wood magazines—none academic.[90] There is a huge disparity when considering the amount of work devoted to both popular nineteenth-century periodicals and twentieth-century little magazines. In the academy, the study of magazine production in the first half of this century and the role it played in the development of modernism has traditionally been limited to a) the little magazines as *the* elite modernist forum; and, in opposition to the little magazines, b) the "slicks"—mass-market "family" magazines such as *Saturday Evening Post* and *Liberty's*.[91] These two forms have alternately been labeled "elite" and "popular," high- and lowbrow (though, high- and middlebrow would be more appropriate), upper class and bourgeois, avant-garde and commercial. This binary is evident in the earliest academic definitions of "little magazines," such as in Hoffman, Ulrich, and Allen's *The Little Magazine*, the first full-length study and bibliography (1947) and still the cornerstone, which stated that "A Little Magazine is a magazine designed to print artistic work, which for reasons of commercial expediency is not acceptable to

---

[90] Only Doug Ellis's *Uncovered: The Hidden Art of the Girlie Pulps* (Silver Spring, MD: Adventure House, 2003) considers these early snappy pulps, but the books is mostly concerned with the cover art of the later girlie pulps.

[91] The *Saturday Evening Post* is thought to be the epitome of the popular slick magazine. Look for example at the chapter in James Playsted Wood's *Magazines in the United States* (NY: Ronald Press, 1949) entitled "Magazine Reflection of a Nation: The Saturday Evening Post," as well as *Magazines for the Millions:* gender and commerce in the *Ladies' Home Journal* and the *Saturday Evening Post*, 1880–1910 (Albany: State University of NY P, 1994) by Helen Damon-Moore.

the money minded periodicals or presses...The real criteria for the little magazine being the fact that they publish unknown authors"; they are considered the "advance guard," filtering authors for the big "quality" magazines and publishers, which "are the rear guard...because their editors will accept a writer only after the advance guard has proved that he is, or can be made, commercially profitable."[92] Oddly enough, this "real criteria" also defines the all-fiction pulp wood magazines of the day, such as *All-Story, The Cavalier*, and Mencken's pulp series, which were the training ground for writers before they broke into the smooth paper magazines (I'll expand upon this in the following chapter). One of the reasons that these types of magazines—and especially any popular traces of modernism in them—have been ignored is due to that trope of commercialism as the antithesis to modernism (evident in the above quote) propagated via academia and modernist memoirs.

The explosion of national magazines in the last few decades of the nineteenth century was due to numerous factors, not the least of which were technological advances in production and distribution, as well as the growing literacy of the middle and lower classes. It is impossible to gauge exactly how many American magazines existed in 1900, but Peterson estimates that there were around 3,500, with more than 50 of them being nationally distributed—some with a circulation of 100,000, yet most of these popular magazines were aimed at the upper echelons of society, for they were the ones who could afford it.[93] It wasn't until the mid-1890s that the modern newspaper and magazines for the masses evolved.[94] The most popular magazines for the middle and upper class were *Century, Harper's*, and *Scribner's*: the successful and cultured triumvirate. These magazines emulated the ideal of the educated man.[95] Meanwhile magazine entrepreneurs such as S.S. McClure and Frank Munsey were inventing modern magazine marketing by increasing the number of copies, decreasing the cover price to below production cost, aiming the magazine at a mass market, and making revenue via advertising. In 1882 Munsey began *The Golden Argosy*, which, after a rough start, was destined to become one of the best and longest running pulps in history. But it was his other magazine, *Munsey's*, which was the first truly successful and

---

[92] Allen, Charles; Frederick Hoffman; and Carolyn Ulrich, *The Little Magazine, a History and a Bibliography* (Princeton: Princeton U P, 1947), 2–3.

[93] Theodore Peterson, *Magazines in the Twentieth Century* (Urbana: U of Illinois P, 1956), 52.

[94] Between 1893 and 1895 both McClure and Munsey started their cut-rate magazines aimed at the working class and 1896 is the year that Alfred Harmsworth started the *Daily Mail* in England, the "Busy Man's Paper." See Peterson, 10–16, and Carey, 6–10. For more about Dime Novels and Penny Dreadfuls, which were early working- and lower-class reading material, see Denning's *Mechanical Accents* (London: Verso, 1987) as well as Michael Anglo's *Penny Dreadfuls* (London: Jupiter, 1977). Also worth noting is Pendergast's interesting study of the construction of African-American masculinity through popular magazines, *Creating the Modern: American Magazines and Consumer Culture, 1900–1950* (Columbia: U of Missouri P, 2000).

[95] Peterson, 2–3.

modern magazine, hitting a circulation of 500,000 in 1895, its second year of publication. Between 1892 and 1922, the flagship year of modernism, circulation rose from 2,231 to 2,187,024.[96] By mid-century the actual number of magazine titles had grown by at least a thousand. Peterson conservatively estimates that in 1900 there were approximately 2,369 monthly periodicals, by 1920 there were 3,415, and by 1954 there were 7,429.[97] Unfortunately, gauging circulation records for magazines is never exact; they are often based solely on the bigger selling magazines. For example, the overall circulation statistic for a single month in 1914, 18,000,000 issues, is based only on the 54 magazines checked by the Audit Bureau of Circulation (A.B.C.).[98]

Little magazines are not considered by the A.B.C.; Peterson, for example, does not consider the little magazines either in his history or his statistics for they "generally are not published with commercial intent," and Wood's *Magazines in the United States* dedicates barely three pages out of 317, practically as an afterthought.[99] Of course, the obvious reason for this is that little magazines made up such a small percentage of the readership. But this again underlines a disparity when considering how scholarship dedicated to little magazines is a cottage industry. The study of modernist periodicals and little magazines are important aspects of such works as Kevin Dettmar and Stephen Watt's edited *Marketing Modernisms* (1996), Cherniak, Gould, and Willison's *Modernist Writers and the Marketplace* (1996), Lawrence Rainey's *Institutions of Modernism* (1998), Bornstein's *Material Modernism* (2001), and Adam McKible's *The Space and Place of Modernism* (2002), which have all attempted to support Raymond Williams's point that literature is a commodity whose production has all the necessary commercial dynamics. But of these, the most "popular" magazines with traces of modernism are *Vogue* and *Vanity Fair*. Other works, such as Michael North's *Reading 1922* (1999) and Aaron Jaffe's *Modernism and the Culture of Celebrity* (2005), have attempted to break down the great divide by linking aspects of modernism to mass entertainment and celebrity.

North, for example, has looked to Seldes's *The Seven Lively Arts* (1924) in order to expand our conception of the scene of modernism. Seldes's book examines differing types and figures of popular entertainment through the lens and criteria of high art. He covers Mack Sennett, Charlie Chaplin, Ziegfield Follies, jazz and popular song, George M. Cohan, vaudeville, modern dance, comic strips, George Herriman's Krazy Kat, Picasso, etc. And throughout his study, Seldes uses Joyce and Eliot as the litmus of artistic worth. Yet, interestingly enough, of all the popular entertainment he scrutinizes and attempts to raise into highbrow circles, the only fiction or literature is that of Ring Lardner, and even then, he hints that as satire the methodology is wonderful but its sights are set too low. North, following

---

[96] Ibid., 12.
[97] Ibid., 41, 53.
[98] Wood, 198.
[99] Peterson, viii.

in Seldes's footsteps, misses the disproportionate attention paid to nonliterary media rather than popular literature. This has long been a weakness of cultural studies in general. There are numerous volumes looking at modernism in terms of popular film, music, theater, and journalism, but very little that examines it in terms of fiction or its own medium.[100] This would seem to support a fear of contamination, not so much for the artists of modernism, but for academia—a conscious or unconscious prejudice or strengthening of borders when it comes to the same medium, but a willingness to accept interrelationships when it comes to different forms. It is seemingly safe to examine the influence of jazz upon modernism for they are so intrinsically different, but critics stop short when it comes to examining the pull of popular fiction magazines on modernism.

Of the works that do consider the popular magazines, most only examine the relationship between modernist authors and more popular "Slick magazine" such as *Vogue*, *Cosmopolitan*, and *Vanity Fair*. Jane Garrity's "Selling Culture to the 'Civilized': Bloomsbury, British *Vogue* and the Marketing of National Identity" discusses how the Bloomsbury group and particularly Virginia Woolf, "[were] not isolated from the mass culture of the 1920s," due mostly to their publishing articles and cultural reviews in the pages of *Vogue* magazine; Michael Murphy's "'One Hundred Percent Bohemian': Pop Decadence and the Aestheticization of Commodity in the Rise of the Slicks" discusses how *Vanity Fair* acted as a meter of modernism's ironic consciousness of its own consumption and commodification; Lawrence Rainey, in his chapter on *The Waste Land*, in *Institutions of Modernism*, which examines how *Vanity Fair*, as a possible venue for Eliot's seminal poem, denotes "the ease and speed with which a market economy could purchase, assimilate, commodify, and reclaim as its own the works of a literature whose ideological premises were bitterly inimical toward its ethos and cultural operations."[101] And this list of interrelationships between the little magazines and the slicks can be easily expanded—Hemingway's relationship with *Esquire* quickly jumps to mind—but such connections are perhaps too easily made. The magazines that these critics are opposing to modernism—*Vogue, Vanity Fair, Esquire*—are still elitist, even though they reached a larger audience; they marketed themselves through the idea that modernism was for and by the elite, as did many of the little magazines. Elitism, whether a question of intent or of marketing, whether in the little magazines or the slick magazines, was still elitism; it is just a question of scale.

---

[100] There are of course exceptions: Brandon Kershner's *Joyce, Bakhtin and Popular Literature* (Chapel Hill: U of North Carolina P, 1989) as well as his 'Joyce and Popular Literature: The Case of Corelli,' in Diana A. Ben-Merre and Maureen Murphy's *James Joyce and His Contemporaries* (NY: Greenwood, 1989). Other exceptions include a handful of articles on Faulkner and Southern romance and pulp fiction (see Chapter 3, note 37). But such high/low comparative criticism is inordinately rare, especially considering the high amount of criticism produced by the Joyce and Faulkner "industries."

[101] Murphy in Dettmar and Watt, *Marketing Modernisms* (Ann Arbor: U of Michigan P, 1996); Rainey, 91.

Magazines such as *Vanity Fair* were "filter" magazines—ones that adopted an elite mantle, interpreting and defining elite modernism for a large audience, cementing its position in the social hierarchy—in other words, magazines that used the same self-marketing techniques as the moderns. There is little doubt that magazines like *Vogue* and *Vanity Fair* reached a larger audience than *The Dial* and *The Little Review*, but the gap between an avant-garde little magazine for the culturally elite and a polished venue for both the culturally elite and the aspiring culturally elite is somewhat negligible, especially in contrast with the larger reading public and scene of magazine publishing in the 1920s and 1930s. The relationships between key modernists and venues with larger exposure than the little magazines are less simplistic than the traditional binary, but they are still stilted and exclusionary. The number of both little magazines and filter magazines as compared to popular magazines, including pulp magazines, is miniscule in the grand scheme of production. Compare the total circulation of these magazines (*Vogue*, *Vanity Fair*, *The Dial*, *The Little Review*)—about 270,600—to the circulation of a *single* pulp magazine, *Western Story Magazine*, published by Street and Smith, which reached a circulation of half a million in 1921:[102] It is important to remember that the circulations for the elite and little magazines are combined and contrasted to a *single* pulp title, of which there were dozens.

Actually, the term pulp is a bit of a misnomer since it didn't come into use until the 1930s. In the early 1920s magazines like *Western Story* were referred to as either all-fiction magazines or wood-pulp paper magazines. These magazines were often owned and started by magazine conglomerates. Street and Smith was one of the oldest, growing out of the mid-1800s magazine, newspaper, and dime-novel explosion. In 1924, the Street and Smith Combination published *Ainslee's*, *Popular*, *People's*, *Top Notch*, *Detective Story*, *Western Story*, and *Love Story* magazines with a combined monthly distribution of 1,179,449, with an even greater readership when considering the common practice of multiplying the distribution by three to find the actual audience, or circulation. *Vanity Fair*'s circulation for this same period was 81,856; *Scribner's* was 71,414; and *Smart Set* was 31,262, but *Snappy Stories* combined with *Live Stories* was 137,916. Other long-standing titles such as *Argosy* and *Blue Book* were much more popular with circulations around half a million.[103]

Such statistics are often overlooked in magazine histories, especially since organizations such as the Audit Bureau of Circulation only considered a sampling of periodicals (none of which were little mags). To further put this into perspective, of the more respectable magazines the A.B.C. did consider in 1926, there were 25 magazines with a circulation over 1 million, and 6 of those had a circulation over 2 million.[104] In 1925, the aggregate per-issue circulation of all magazines in the United States was over *150 million*. That would make the market percentage of

---

[102] See Quentin Reynolds, *The Fiction Factory* (NY: Random House, 1955). 180.

[103] All circulation statistics from *The Audit Bureau of Circulation, Publisher's Statements, Periodicals. Period Ending June 30th, 1924* [A.B.C.].

[104] Peterson, 62.

little magazines and elite slicks (*Little Review, Dial, Vanity Fair, Vogue, Smart Set*) something like 0.18 percent—and it is that 0.18 percent that literary critics and modernist historians base their definition of modernism upon, what makes up almost entirely the focus of modernist periodical studies. It should be obvious that differentiations between the little magazines and the modernistic filter magazines, traditionally considered "quality," "commercial," and "popular," become moot when placed in the milieu of the general magazine market; the difference between a little magazine and *Vanity Fair* isn't one of elite versus popular but elite versus slightly less elite.[105] The point is that even the most popular of literary magazines were for a small fraction of the audience. If we consider magazine production on the whole as a pyramid, the "modernist" venues—both avant-garde and popular—amount to what is still only the tip of the pyramid, the smallest production and audience, with popular slicks taking up the majority of the pyramid.

The border between elite modernism and popular modernism loses some of its power when we consider the thousands of magazine titles and styles below the miniscule upper cultural strata of little magazines and smart magazines: the slicks like *Saturday Evening Post* and *McCall's*, the trade magazines, the specialty magazines, and, at the lowest end of the spectrum, the all fiction and pulp magazines.[106] Under scrutiny, the differentiation breaks down; it is itself a product of the modernist practices of exclusion on the part of the publishers, academy, and the artists themselves. In "One Hundred Per Cent Bohemian," Michael Murphy states:

> But the very term developed to describe magazines like *Vanity Fair* [...]—which in fact filled such a new market niche that they required the invention of an entirely new publishing category for themselves [i.e., the slicks]—is suggestive of the sort of market savvy normally thought of as anathema to the modernist aesthetic. Of course, in one sense, the term *slicks* said to come into common use around 1930, forms a simple allusion to the newly invented glossy paper upon which the slicks were printed. And yet in another it is difficult to ignore how the term resonates with the marketplace-related connotations of *slickness* [i.e., how it was marketed].[107]

---

[105] If anything, these circulation statistics for the little magazines are generous, for they do not take into consideration the overlap of readership. The scant information on circulation records of little magazines that were produced at this time—*The Double Dealer, Liberator, Secession, Broom,* and *Poetry*—are yet another instance of the definition of the little mags being beyond the concern of the marketplace, that such things as circulation have no place in the production of art.

[106] The specialized magazine, such as the juvenile, farm, religious, company and business publication, the circulation of which amounted to the millions, is another form of publication that has long been overlooked—but one not concerned with fiction per se, hence I don't consider such for this study; I suggest James L.C. Ford's *Magazines for the Millions, the Story of Specialized Publications* (Carbondale: Southern Illinois U P, 1969) to those interested.

[107] Dettmar and Watt, 67.

Murphy defines the "slicks" as elite magazines that marketed themselves through their elite content (constructed an elite audience appeal) as well as their slick appearance, but what he does not consider, in fact passes over quickly, is that the very term "slick" arose in definition against the use of pulp paper and pulp form. Whereas *Vanity Fair* was a "Slick" magazine, so was any popular mass-produced "quality" magazine that wasn't a pulp magazine or popular fiction magazine, including *Saturday Evening Post, Better Homes and Gardens, Life*, as well as cultural magazines such as *Harper's* and *The Atlantic*. Murphy places the slicks in opposition to the little magazines, even though the term he really wants is the more appropriate "Smart." Such attempts as Murphy's to show the Slicks as the diametric opposite to the form of modernism have, as I hope I've shown, succeeded in illustrating a popular, yet still elite, aspect of modernism, but, ultimately, have not gone far enough. It was not the Slicks that were the diametric opposite of modernism on the scale of production, but the early pulp and all-fiction magazines; the very fact that the term "slick" rose is in opposition to a form that we don't even consider anymore is telling of the gap in our history. Perhaps we, as literary historians and the gatekeepers of culture, need to rethink our focus when considering that our current field of modernist study constitutes—to be generous—less than 5 percent of actual literary output.

The above portrait does not even take into account the 1910s before the separation between general all-fiction magazines, pulp magazines, and even literary magazines took place, when mass-circulated magazines were the training ground for the entire spectrum of writers and styles: Ernest Hemingway sent manuscripts to *Red Book*, *The Saturday Evening Post*, and *Adventure*—all of which were turned down; Djuna Barnes published poetry in *All-Story*, *The Cavalier*, and *Pearson's* next to pulp authors like Max Brand and Edgar Rice Burroughs; Edwin Baird published in *The Smart Set* and *All-Story* before going off to edit *Weird Tales* where he discovered H.P. Lovecraft; Robert M. Coates could publish simultaneously in *Telling Tales* and little magazines like *Broom* and *Gargoyle*, Dawn Powell's first publications were in *Snappy Stories*.

And this is not just true in America—consider Conrad's *Heart of Darkness* in the milieu of the other adventure serialization that appeared in *Blackwoods*. Besides *Blackwoods*, Mike Ashley has outlined the history of 144 popular British fiction magazines, such as *The Strand, The Story-Teller*, and *Nash's*.[108] Many American magazines, including *The Smart Set*, jumped the Atlantic to be published in London. Obviously, not all such fiction magazines in either country contained work by established or struggling modernist authors, but there were enough to worry the idea of modernism as a purely restricted arena—despite its ensuing portrait. If modernism was indeed an attempt to restrict literature, plenty of players from the opposing team slipped through the "cultural goalposts," to borrow a phrase from Jonathan Rose.

---

[108] Michael Ashley, *The Age of the Story Tellers* (New Castle, DE: Oak Knoll Press, 2006).

The Fallacy of First Appearance

Finally, I'd like to point out that the incongruity between the influence of modernism (i.e., its monolithic presence as the twentieth-century style) and its limited production or actual slight market percentage points to the fact that the dynamics of modernism must have been available through a larger venue than the sanctioned forms of little magazines and rare or first editions. For example, reprint houses like Grosset and Dunlap, who reprinted modernist authors and distributed to drug stores, five and dimes, and newsstands, reached hundreds of thousands more readers than first editions. It is important to realize that they sometimes used the same dustwrapper illustration, the same plates, and even the unbound leaves of the actual first edition; the only difference was price and distribution.

As literary critics, we privilege a work's initial appearances in first, signed, and limited editions; little magazines, even manuscripts, when in reality the works of modernism were spread through magazine reprints, popular editions, paperbacks, book clubs, in sensational marketing (as in the case of Joyce, Lawrence, Hemingway, Faulkner). I call this "The Fallacy of First Appearance." It is an attempt to keep the book as close to the author and his intent as possible, but as vice trials or popular, pulp, and pirated editions—all subjects of this book's ensuing chapters, all examples of populist modernism—illustrate, authorial intent is often a moot point in the face of the instability of reception.

The reprint magazines that flourished in the 1920s are an excellent example of the fallacy of first appearance. Magazines like *Famous Story*, *Best Stories*, and *Fiction Parade* reprinted short stories and poems by popular authors and modernists alike, but were much closer to pulps in feel, appearance, and distribution than sanctioned fiction magazines such as *Scribner's* or *Poetry*. The most successful of these was the *Golden Book* (see Figure 1.9). Appearing on newsstands late in 1924, the *Golden Book* was an all-fiction magazine started by Henry Wysham Lanier and published by the *Review of Reviews*. The gamut of authors that it featured was truly amazing, as the December 24, 1924, issue of *Time* magazine pointed out:

> Among the Christmas magazines at the news stalls there lay a newcomer, a monthly fiction magazine, a creamy cover, a big golden moon, a golden skirted lady and gold stars. You stared at this magazine, because there, besides the lady's skirt, in big red letters, the list of contributors looked so extraordinary. You had heard all the names before, but for a moment you could in no way connect them with a news-stall. It was like running across a bishop in a saloon or seeing your wife about to play quarterback for Varsity. "Hullo, what are you doing here?" you said, as you read: "Heine, Dumas, Kipling, Gaboriau, Tolstoy, de Alerçon, Anatole France, Robert Louis Stevenson..."[109]

The writer of this review applauds finding a quality fiction pulp paper magazine in a news-stall because the newsstand was traditionally the domain of cheap and sensational fiction weeklies. Literary magazines and little magazines were found in a bookstore, not a bus station.

---

[109] Quoted in Mott, 117.

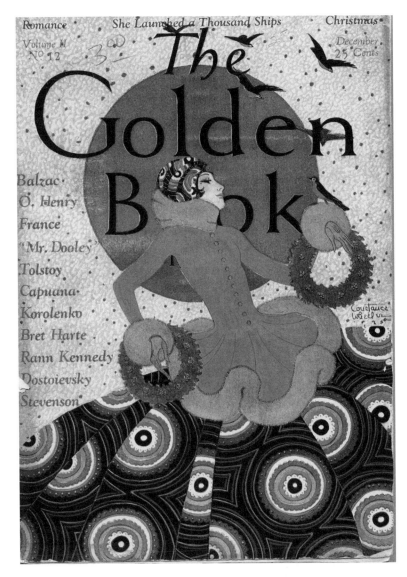

Fig. 1.9   *Golden Book*, Dec. 1925 © The Review of Reviews Corporation

The Golden Book, like *The Smart Set*, offers an instance of pulp slippage, of an outlet for modernist authors aimed at a general reading public. *The Golden Book* was printed on cheap pulp paper, but with truly deco covers, at a time when art deco was just breaking upon the American market and still carried with it an aura of edgy bohemianism. Within its pages could be found Aldous Huxley alongside Robert Louis Stevenson, Swineburne alongside Jack London, Sherwood Anderson next to H. Rider Haggard, James Joyce alongside Achmed Abdullah (again).

Other authors included Conrad, Anatole France, Katherine Mansfield, Eugene O' Neill, Lady Gregory, Dorothy Parker, D.H. Lawrence, and John Millington Synge. The magazine's intended audience can easily be reconstructed through its advertisements; the first 23 pages of its second issue (February 1925) consist of a few ads for investments services and commodities such as furniture, but more numerous and larger are the ads concerned with self-improvement: LaSalle Extension University, the Miller System of Correct English, the *Encyclopedia Americana*, the "history of the world" library, the American School "High School Course in Two Years," The Sherwin Cody School of English ("Is Your English a Handicap? This Test Will Tell You"), the International Correspondence School, the University of Chicago home study course, etc. We can imagine, taking into consideration the magazine's distribution and these ads, that *The Golden Book* appealed to the newly literate, hopefully upward mobile working class; this is further attested to by the fact that the magazine's circulation reached 165,000 by 1926.[110] *Scribner's Magazine* during the same period was only 75,000.[111]

Nor was *The Golden Book* the only such magazine: an article in *Time Magazine* (September 16, 1935) stated that soon after its initial publication, *Golden Book* had four imitators. Among them was *Famous Story*, which copied *Golden Book* down to its deco covers and, if anything, relied more heavily upon the modernists; it reprinted poems by W.B. Yeats and Amy Lowell, and serialized Conrad's "End of the Tether" in 1925 and Fitzgerald's *The Great Gatsby* in 1926. Other similar magazines included *Fiction Parade*, which eventually merged with *Golden Book* in the mid-1930s, and, of course, *Reader's Digest*, which created its own publishing niche. On the other side of the Atlantic there were similar magazines like *Argosy* (not to be confused with America's *Golden Argosy* pulp) and *Hutchinson's Story Magazine*.

If, as Foucault claims, the dynamics of hegemony are more visible at the extremities of exclusion, then establishing such disregarded magazines as the reprint and pulp as the diametric opposite of the academically defined venue of modernism, the little magazine, not only illustrates such cultural exclusion, but finding any interrelationship between the two forms also breaks down such hierarchies. Magazines like *The Golden Book* and, to a lesser degree, *The Smart Set* offer moments of such slippage. Upon scrutiny, the pulp genre in general offers numerous interrelations and reliance between itself and high literature, ones of form, style, and marketing.

Magazines such as *The Smart Set*, *Snappy Stories*, *Golden Book* functioned across cultural and literary hierarchies; their careful exclusion from the annals of modernism occurred not at the time, but in the ensuing construction and canonization of the movement. With the exception of *The Smart Set* (which, as I've stated, is getting some recent critical attention) these magazines are entirely and notably missing from recent critical histories of modernism, a fact that

---

[110] Ibid., 118.

[111] A.B.C.

underlines the continuing subjectivity of Modernist studies. This, as well as critics' (à la Huyssen's, Carey's, and Bourdieu's) preoccupation with simple binaries, is symptomatic of the academic need to distill, to reduce and categorize for consumption. It is symptomatic of the all too simplistic, traditional, and monolithic definition of modernism, though the entire history of modernism intrinsically refutes this. Ironically, that standard construction of modernity that was well cemented by the 1950s and, though under revision, lingers today is ultimately very nonmodernist. Whereas modernism has expanded greatly over the last generation through feminist and multicultural revision, in the area of class-based forms and venues of the movement, there is still an element of reduction, a dependence upon binaries. Its reconstruction of history is incomplete. Whereas modernism hopes to resuscitate the present through the re-creation of history, the construction of its own history is slanted. The popular modernism of these magazines unties modernism's double bind—that tension between the two poles of modernism and populism, which were in reality (and on the newsstand) simultaneous and not exclusive. This is was modernism's "pulp dynamic."

Chapter 2
Pulp Modernism

And who knows what some future historian may say about the relative merits of the forests of pulps that go into the magazines and books of today? After all, the masses throughout the world enjoyed the entertainment of slapstick Charlie Chaplin long before the highbrows discovered that he was an "artist incomparable."
But I should be the last one to think about the verdict of the future. I've got a Western pulp, a detective pulp, and a mystery pulp all going to press. There is a foot and a half of manuscript to be read with their bang-bang and rat-tat-tat, and corpses galore...
—A.A. Wyn, pulp editor. *New York Times*, Aug., 30. 1932.

Books?
Books?
My god! You don't understand.
They were far too busy living first-hand
For books.
Books!

True,
On the table lay a few
Tattered copies of a magazine,
Confessional;
Professional;
That talked of their friends on stage and screen.
—Joseph Moncure March, *The Wild Party*[1]

My god is a machine.
—Frank Lloyd Wright

Part 1

Establishing the Pulp/Modernism Binary

In the October 15, 1938, issue of *The New Yorker*, S.J. Perelman published "Somewhere a Roscoe ...," an ebullient essay about Dan Turner, a recurring protagonist from *Spicy Detective* pulp magazine. One of America's foremost humorists, Perelman recounts how finding a tattered copy of *Spicy* was a turning point in his life, how it saved him from being "almost a character in a

---

[1] *The Wild Party* (London: Picador, 1994).

Russian novel"; now, if the publishers of *Spicy* will have him, he'd marry them because "their prose is so soft and warm."[2] And Perelman supplies us with examples, plenty of them—all from the narrations of Dan Turner, that "apotheosis of all private detectives."

Turner, the creation of Robert Leslie Bellem, represents either the best or the worst in pulp stylistics: "I glued my glams on her blonde loveliness"; "a brunette jane was lying there ... she was as dead as vaudeville"; "I said 'Nerts to you, Confucious,' and gave him a shove on the beezer"; and of course, "From a bedroom a roscoe said: 'Whr-r-rang!' and a lead pill split the ozone past my noggin." These examples (Perelman's) are culled from only a few of the 300-plus Dan Turner stories, which in turn are only a fraction of the 3,000 or so stories that Bellem wrote for the pulps. Dan Turner was popular enough in his day to warrant his own eponymous magazine *Dan Turner, Hollywood Detective*. The "Spicy" line of pulps—*Spicy Western, Spicy Adventure, Spicy Detective, Spicy Mystery*—likewise represent both the high point and the low point of pulp production; they are pulps, already an extreme, at their most unrestrained: misogynistic, xenophobic, violent, yet stylistically exuberant. *Spicy* marks the apex of pulp publishing, a pulp mass-subculture (if such a thing is possible) before the medium was destroyed by pressures of censorship, film and mass-media, and war-time production; pulp production was a type of publishing that both pandered to and relied upon a readership that defined itself against mainstream, slick periodicals. Today, the "Spicy" pulps are among the most sought after by collectors.

In his essay, Perelman's fondness for *Spicy* comes through, but from whence does it stem? Appearing in the popularly erudite *New Yorker*, is it a mocking send-up of extreme working class reading matter? Perelman points out that despite the originality and extremity of the prose, the stories themselves are dreadfully formulaic, secondary to the style. Or is Perelman, who often claimed that his biggest influence was James Joyce and who moved in highbrow and modernist circles (his brother-in-law was Nathanael West), in love with *Spicy* because of the unrestrained originality and slang-rife urbanity of the prose style? This paradox of extremity runs deep; even Bill Pronzini, mystery author and pulp historian, can't decide whether Bellem's style is intentionally funny or not.[3] There is an innate paradox in Perelman's mocking respect for Dan Turner, one that is endemic to the relationship between modernism and the pulp form, for the history of modernism is rife with both a panicked damning of the pulps and a fascination or patronage of them.

For Perelman, the pulps offer a tonic for the trauma of modern life, they are the cure for his being "moody, discontented, restless, [lying] on my bed for days drinking tea out of a glass." The portrait sounds suspiciously like a pretentious modern poet or bohemian—regardless, one who suffers from being

---

[2] S.J. Perelman, "Somewhere a Roscoe...," *The Most of the Most* (NY: Modern Library, 2000), 15.

[3] *Gun in Cheek* (NY: Mysterious Press, 1987).

"introspective," "overstrained," "stale." Once he discovers *Spicy*'s saucy "blend of libido and murder" and juxtaposition of "steely automatic and frilly panty," it is "a turning point," a "story of a mind that found itself." As Perelman goes on to list numerous examples of Bellem's prose ("I don't like dames to be rubbed out while I'm flinging woo at them") there is a sense that it regrounds one, is anathema to too much thinking, is heightened by comfortable formulaic structure of the stories; the reader knows what to expect: "the murders follow an exact rigid pattern almost like the ritual of a bullfight or a classic Chinese play."[4]

Yet for other cultural critics, like Aldous Huxley and Theodore Adorno, it was just this formulaic aspect of the pulps that threatened to destroy American culture, just as for the moral majority it was pulp violence and sex that threatened to destroy American morals. It was common for the pulps to be used as a symbol of cultural degeneration during the first half of the twentieth century. During the 1920s especially, they were a favorite subject of derision and persecution by both the watch and ward societies and by cultural critics and intellectuals; hundreds of readily available pulp titles, such as *Saucy Stories, Parisienne, Breezy Stories, True Confessions*, and *Snappy Stories,* were singled out as being detrimental to America's youth and very moral fiber. Paul Boyer in his history of book censorship in America describes this moral onslaught.[5] In 1928, for example, Arkansas congressman John N. Tillman held up a copy of *Telling Tales*, blaming its ilk for the moral disintegration on college campuses.[6] In 1924, H.W. Van Loon called pulp magazines "a putrid stream of the most despicable, the most iniquitous, and on the whole the most dangerous form of a degraded variety of literature."[7] Boyer sees this witch hunt as alleviating unwanted scrutiny from the publishing of risqué (and more expensive) modernist publications, paving the way for a broader and freer modernist testing of Victorian values; but this wasn't always the case: certain crusaders of purity condemned these lowly mass-entertainment magazines and modernist magazines alike. In his speech proposing a bill for the establishment of a National Board of Magazine Censorship, Congressman Thomas Wilson damned outright not only pulps, but artistic magazines such as *Scribner's, American Mercury*, and *Vanity Fair*.[8]

It may be surprising that pulp magazines and highbrow modernism could ever be grouped together; the pulps are seemingly the diametric opposite of the carefully crafted, rarified, experimental, political, and groundbreaking modernist field of production. They are voluminous, cliché ridden, disposable, ephemeral products of mass-market pandering and production. Even stating that there is a relationship between these two diametrically opposed styles of twentieth-century literary production is contentious, seemingly oxymoronic, but, as the role of modernists in the early pulps (detailed in the last chapter) illustrates, there was a relationship,

---

[4] Ibid., 17.
[5] Paul S. Boyer, *Purity In Print* (Madison: U Wisconsin P, 2002), 154–161.
[6] Boyer, 160.
[7] Quoted in Boyer, 155.
[8] Ibid., 160.

rich and complex. By concentrating on the pulp form itself, this chapter will explore relationships that range from the more traditional (i.e., modernist authors and critics who disavow and define themselves against such mass and popular forms), to surprising (i.e., the shadow careers of modernist authors who published in the pulps), to the unexamined (i.e., a full range of modernist tensions that were navigated within the pulps themselves). Indeed, I contend that the pulp magazine is itself a peculiarly and purely popular form of modernism.

The pulp magazine is so named because it is made of cheap wood pulp; it is the result of a modern, scientific, and technical process that creates a physical and concrete literary form out of a formless mass.[9] By elite modernism's very definition solidified by critics from Malcolm Cowley to Andreas Huyssen, the pulp genre is that which modernism defines itself against; the pulps are fiction for the masses, produced quickly and cheaply for fast distribution, consumption, and disposal. Modern fiction, on the other hand, is painstakingly produced for posterity. The idea of pulp as sensational counterpoint to artistic fiction is best illustrated in the connotations of the word itself; in recent years, the moniker of "pulp" has grown to mean trashy, popular forms and fiction—from the dime novel of the 1800s through the sensational men's magazines of the 1950s and 1960s to the lurid paperbacks and the overtly violent films of the 1960s and '70s. In this study, at least initially, I am using "pulp" to describe the form of popular magazine, the rise and death of which directly parallels that of modernism. On the most basic, literal level, the definition of a pulp magazine is an all-fiction magazine, published on cheap pulpwood paper, priced, marketed, and distributed toward a popular audience. Unlike the popular slick magazines, pulp magazines did not rely upon advertising, but upon newsstand sales. The idea was to keep the production cost as low as possible so that if only a fraction of the run sold, there was still a profit to be made.[10]

The pulp magazine grew out of the same tensions and dynamics of modernization that modernism is a commentary upon. Its history directly mirrors that of literary modernism—the pulp form was perfected just prior to World War I; it reached maturity in the early 1920s, was at its most popular between the wars, and faded during and directly after World War II.[11] Rising from the dime novels of the nineteenth century, the pulp magazine is purely a modern phenomenon. It was a product of technological advances in paper manufacturing and the mass-printing process, of lowered second-class mailing rates, of modern systems of distribution. The story of the pulps is the story of modern marketing. Frank Munsey is generally known as the father of both the modern magazine and the pulps; he pioneered the use of cheap pulp paper and started *The Golden Argosy* (eventually shortened

---

[9] And modernism works similarly, at least according to Eliot, who, in "*Ulysses*, Order and Myth," stated that art imposes order on the formlessness of modern life or "history."

[10] Peterson, 284.

[11] I consider the rise of the Futurists, Imagists, Vorticists, etc., as the formation of the modernist avant-garde, and the rise of the specialized pulp magazine with *Detective Story Magazine* in late 1915 as the coalescence of pulp form, yet both obviously had earlier manifestations.

to simply *Argosy*) in 1882; by going all-fiction in 1896, it became the first (and subsequently longest lived) pulp title. By the first decade of the twentieth century, *Argosy* had a circulation of half a million, closely trailed by other Munsey fiction titles like *All-Story Weekly* (the publisher of *Tarzan of the Apes* in 1912), *Cavalier*, and *Munsey's*.[12] Munsey's successes led other publishers to turn their attention from the declining dime stories to pulps. Street and Smith, the largest producer of dime novels (publishers of *Nick Carter Weekly*, *Buffalo Bill*, *Diamond Dick*, *Frank Merriwell*, and the *Alger Series*), broke into the pulp market with *Popular Magazine* in 1903 and *Top-Notch* in 1910. Other important publishers of early pulps included Doubleday (*Short Stories*, 1910), Butterick (*Adventure*, 1910), Clayton (*Snappy Stories*, 1912), and Warner (*Parisienne* and *Saucy Stories*, 1915 and 1916).

The early pulps were general fiction, a smattering of romance, Western, adventure, historical, detective stories, etc., and not so different from more respectable fiction magazines such as *Colliers* or *Cosmopolitan*, but over time the pulps (d)evolved into their own genre. As the pulps grew in popularity, they became stratified, narrowing their focus to certain genres and distancing themselves from other general fiction magazines. This, in general, set the pattern for pulp production, with publishing companies running numerous titles (sometimes dozens) simultaneously, each with a different slant. Much of this had to do with their reliance upon newsstand sales rather than advertising, which more importantly brought about their method of marketing via subject specificity and audience pandering. During World War I their popularity allowed them to specialize, devoting themselves to one specific genre. It is usually said that *Detective Story Magazine* was the first specialized pulp, starting in October 1915, but Robert Sampson points out that *Railroad Man's Magazine* predated it by almost a decade.[13] Regardless, hundreds of pulps soon appeared devoted to any and every genre and topic imaginable, such as *Courtroom Stories* (the first issue featured a cover story on the Oscar Wilde trials, see Figure 2.1), *Football Action*, *Zeppelin Stories*, and (my favorite) *Gun Molls Magazine*. Such theme magazines started (and often folded) quickly in order to pander to and/or capture the audience's tastes in fads and fancies. The pulps pioneered such shotgun, trial-and-error market saturation. And overall, they were extremities of marketing, with lurid, colorful covers carefully planned to capture the reader's eye at the newsstand even if only a corner of the magazine could be seen from under a pile of other similar pulps.[14] The cost was low, the writing fast and high in action and energy. Writers were paid by the word so income was directly related to how

---

[12] *Argosy* circulation, Goulart *An Informal History of the Pulp Magazine* (NY: Ace, 1972), 12.

[13] Sampson, *VI*, 15.

[14] Harold Hersey, *Pulpwood Editor* (Westport: Greenwood, 1974) 54–58. There is no critical attention to the role of newsstands and book/magazine cover design in the rise of visual culture. The hundreds of racial, nationalistic, and gendered images as they existed on urban street stalls would have offered a flanneuristic and kaleidoscopic panorama of life. The fact that critics consider advertisements and posters but not newsstands again mark that prejudice of form.

Fig. 2.1   *Courtroom Stories*, Aug.–Sept. 1931 © 1931 Good Story Magazine Company, image supplied by Adventure House

quickly one could churn out a story; few could afford to rewrite. The pulps were streamlined for quick consumption by the mass public, and with their low-quality paper and prose they were ultimately produced as disposable literature. And it is exactly this ephemeral quality that has assured the pulp magazine's exclusion, its position beneath the literary critic's radar.

On the material level, due to both their cultural status and their fragile composition, the actual magazines are elusive, especially in comparison to their initial production: today, they are rarely archived and mostly in the hands of collectors.[15] The magazines were either thrown out long ago or have disintegrated. Only a fraction survived in comparison to the number of pulps produced. Even publishing records are scarce; hence it is difficult to gauge the number of pulp titles and almost impossible to gauge their exact circulation. Even so, one contemporary editor in 1935 estimated the American pulp audience at 10,000,000 readers, and I would consider this figure conservative.[16] In 1933, *Vanity Fair* magazine stated the pulp readership for the year 1928 as being 20,000,000, and of individual titles, "Almost any one ... has more circulation than a 'quality' magazine such as *Harper's* or *Forum.*"[17] In a 1935 letter to the *New York Times*, pulp editor A.A. Wyn defended the pulps against a charge that they were a "little known" form in literature, stating that "Certainly the 10,000,000 people who go to their news stands each month to buy pulp magazines know and recognize this publishing world. When you consider that these 10,000,000 buyers, in usual computation, make over 30,000,000 pulp readers, you have an astounding percentage of the entire American reading public. [It is standard practice to calculate a magazine's readership by multiplying circulation by three.]"[18] The Audit Bureau of Circulation (A.B.C.) can give us another idea of the pulps circulation and growing popularity: in 1926, the A.B.C lists roughly 30 pulp magazines (this number is unsure because often companies lumped their titles together) with a total actual circulation of 8,654,102, by 1938, the A.B.C. lists 126 titles with a combined circulation of 10,346,573, hence we see that despite the depression and growing draw of cinema, the pulps were able to maintain and add to their audience.[19] Of course the A.B.C. statistics are limited to only those pulp publishers that participated. There were plenty of small and fly-by-night publishers that didn't, so even these statistics are low. Regardless, the pulps obviously had a huge audience, too big for them to be ignored by literary historians, especially when considering that the usual multiplication of buyer to reader falls short with respect to the pulps: Wyn states that the Salvation Army does a brisk trade in old issues. American pulps flooded the British magazine market as stores such as Woolworth's jumped the Atlantic and sold "remaindered" pulps. A 1936 article in the *New York Times* about the

---

[15] See Jess Nevins *Pulp Magazine Holdings Directory: Library Collections in North America and Europe* (Jefferson, North Carolina: McFarland, 2007) for an idea of library pulp holdings. There is an undeniable rise in the interest of pulp magazines; worth noting is an art exhibition, "Pulp Art: Vamps, Villians and Victors From the Robert Lesser Collection," which took place at the Brooklyn Museum in 2003.

[16] Peterson, 286.

[17] *VF* 6.1933, 26.

[18] A.A. Wyn, "Pulp Magazines," *New York Times* (September 4, 1935), 18.

[19] Statistics from the *Audit Bureau of Circulation Publisher Statements* for 1926, Vol. 2 and 1938, Vol. 1.

recirculation of magazines states: "For many an old magazine the wastebasket is not, by any means, the end of the trail. Janitors and waste-paper dealers conspire to salvage an amazing proportion of all printed matter not given directly to welfare organizations. ... In the second-hand market pulp magazines make up for the earlier stepchild phase of their existence by taking ascendancy, in at least one respect, over quality-group and popular-publications. They are the real nomads of the print world; one dealer annually ships a vast quantity to England, whence they journey to the various British colonies."[20] Such distribution points to the widespread international influence and audience of the pulp form.

It has generally been taken as a given that the pulp audience was mostly masculine, composed of the working class, the barely literate, and the juvenile (in both body and mind). Erin Smith, for example, has attempted to re-create the portrait of the typical pulp reader, based solely on the hard-boiled genre, particularly *Black Mask* magazine. Smith uses contemporary accounts, marketing studies, advertisements, and letters published in the magazines themselves to show that the pulp audience was composed mostly of lower- and lower-middle class, the industrial working class, and adolescent readers. It is the first such modern study of its kind, hence invaluable in drawing attention to the pulps, but it is narrow in scope, completely overlooking the majority of both pulp readers and the larger pulp market. Her concentration upon the hard-boiled genre of pulp as indicative of the pulp market as a whole limits her study and reflects academia's prejudice for hard-boiled since it is the genre that reflects most obviously the canon: for example, she states that pulp fiction "was aimed emphatically at men."[21] There were, in fact, millions of female readers of the "love" and true confession type pulps—Peterson, in *Magazines in the Twentieth Century*, cites that in a single year alone, eighteen "love pulps" (only a small fraction of such titles) sold around three million copies each month.[22] In 1938, for example, *Ranch Romances*, a bi-monthly published by the same company as the monthly *Black Mask* (hence distributed and marketed the same) had a per-issue circulation practically double that of *Black Mask* and it came out twice as often, which also illustrates its greater popularity. And true confession pulps, generally geared at a female audience, were much more popular than male-oriented magazines—in 1926, *True Romances* had a circulation of 544,000 while *Black Mask* was only 66,000. Hard-boiled fiction was not the most prevalent genre: it just happens to be the most "literary," the genre that most approaches the obvious dynamics of modernism. The three most recent academic books to be published on pulp writers—Smith's, Sean McCann's *Gumshoe America*, and Christopher Breu's *Hardboiled Masculinity*—only examine the hard-boiled detective genre, and while these books all examine the construction of masculinity in popular literature, they

---

[20] "Old Magazines Travel Widely," *New York Times* (March 22, 1936), Sunday Magazine, 23.

[21] Erin Smith, *Hard-Boiled: Working Class Readers and Pulp Magazines* (Philadelphia: Temple U P, 2000), 26.

[22] Peterson, 284.

also continue on the long-standing androcentrism of academia, ignoring entirely the huge audience of female pulp readers, not to mention the many female pulp writers and editors. Tellingly, these authors also readily dismiss the fact that the early *Black Mask* published romance stories alongside western and detective.[23]

Pulp Feminism

Case in point: in the last chapter I discussed how early pulps challenged moral and cultural codes via the modernist character of the flapper. Similarly, adventure and romance pulps often featured strong female lead characters who busted feminine stereotypes and made their own way in the world. Stories like Rathburne Case's "The Gun Girl" from the April 1926 *Blue Book* and Victor Maxwell's "A Good, Smart Girl," from July 1935's *Street & Smith's Complete Magazine* feature heroines who are not only not helpless, but who outwit con men and husbands-to-be and generally use the dynamics of the patriarchal sphere against itself. In "The Gun Girl," Miriam Halley bucks convention, secretly supporting herself and her unknowing but proud grandmother by traveling abroad as Mlle. Artheris, World's Champion pistol shot. She returns home to foil the thief of her family's fortune and clear the name of her childhood beau. She is worldly, capable, and confident, not only the heroine of the story but the master of her own fate and that of her family. The heroine of "A Good, Smart Girl" is Maisie Belknap who runs the cigar stand in the lobby of a ritzy hotel. She is depicted as knowing all the angles, she can disarm a leering wolf as easily as she disarms a disguised murderer and jewel thief. Though she is described as attractive, it is her intelligence, worldliness, and professionalism that comes through; the character is not objectified but is a role model for a successful working girl always looking to better herself and her position by mastering and subverting traditionally male (and phallic) objects (i.e., gun and cigars).

In the pulps, such professional women moved the female beyond the figure of the sexually charged flapper. They even encroached upon the traditionally masculine territory of the gangster. Magazines like Harold Hersey's *Gangster Stories* and *Gangland Stories* regularly featured women reporters, mob bosses, and detectives, often written by female authors. C.B. Yorke's character Yola Yates is a female detective who runs her own agency.[24] Introduced in the story "Hot Numbers" in the May 1931 *Gangster Stories*, Yates moves seamlessly

---

[23] Considering this spectrum of pulp publishing, I think that it is time for academia to start looking beyond hard-boiled. I say this despite the fact that I rely steadily upon it throughout this study. This, I think is necessary to both show a comprehensive view of the field, but also to refer to some canonical (however loose that term) material as well as unknown, unread, and hard-to-find primary sources.

[24] Unfortunately there is little or no information about many, many pulp authors. Publishers used house names and authors used pen names. Similarly, many relationships between the publisher and author were through the mail, so we can't know exactly how many women published under men's names or vice versa.

between the masculine sphere of the detective genre and the feminine sphere of high-fashion dress-design; she can be tough (she "twisted forward, freeing the gun in her pocket. 'Mobsters with a Tommy!' she shouted. 'Gun 'em, guys!'") and she just as proficiently uses her feminine knowledge to crack the secret of a counterfeit dress ring. Yorke (and Yates) seem to enjoy busting stereotypes:

> "Why the gun play, Sister? ... What's the idea – busting in here like you owned the place. Who are you?"
> "Just a woman—" she said evenly, and after a brief pause added, "—detective."

Yorke wrote numerous series with such strong female heroes: Velma Dare, a gun moll and ex-con who tries to go straight; Queen Sue, a gang leader; Fay Laurence, a reporter. Author Margie Harris, another Hersey regular, wrote numerous stories about "Ex—Dick, Feminine," another female detective. Such characters were popular enough to deserve their own series, and even their own magazine, *Gun Molls,* which ran for two years starting in 1930.

These characters appealed to both the male and female pulp audience. The popular trope of the working girl, whether reporter or gun moll, grew out of the new urban female work force. By the end of the 1920s more than half of all single women in America were employed.[25] It was to this population that the romance pulps were geared, full of stories about female office workers, servants, shop and counter girls. "In Search of Love" (Dec. 1925, *Cupid's Diary*) is about Janet Lacey who "might have been one of fifty thousand stenographers in the city of New York." Despite her "assured position in a grimy office building, salary that came in regularly every week, and a bank account," she spontaneously quits and books travel for Europe where she, of course, marries her new employer, an American millionaire. Other stories, such as Jane Littell's "On Strike" from September 1935's *All-Stories Love Story* (see Figure 2.2), dealt with the female job market during the depression. The role that such stories, and romance fiction in general, has played in the construction of femininity has been debated in feminist criticism. Whereas romance literature both uses beauty as a means to cement the feminine role as consumer and objectifies the subject, it also establishes a female based sphere of literature outside of the male dominant canon. Carol Wicker-Wilson has pointed out that even canonized female-authored fiction is dependant upon either the male organized new critical (and modernist) values of pessimism and irony, or the negativity of feminism's "literature of need."[26] Romance fiction offers an alternative.

---

[25] See Joshua Zeitz's *Flapper* (NY: Three River's Press, 2006) for a thorough cultural contextualization. Demographics on women's employment from Lynn Dumenhil's *Modern Temper* (NY: Hill and Wang, 1995), cited in Zeitz, 29.

[26] See Carol Wicker-Wilson's "Busting Textual Bodices: Gender, Reading, and the Popular Romance," *The English Journal*, Vol. 88, No. 3 (Jan. 1999), 58–59. And see, of course, Janice Radway's *Reading the Romance* (Chapel Hill, NC: U North Carolina P, 1984).

Fig. 2.2   *All Story Love Stories*, Sept. 21, 1935 © 1935 The Frank A. Munsey Company

The apex of the working girl romance novel is *Girl in Overalls* (1943) by Ellen Ashley, pen name for Elizabeth Seifert. Seifert is better known as the author of more than 80 romance novels between 1938 and 1982; she took to writing after dropping out of medical school when she was told that women didn't belong in the medical profession. The majority of her books concerned doctors: *Young Doctor Galahad* (1938), *Doctor at the Crossroads* (1954), and of course *Hillbilly Doctor* (1940).

Though many of these novels feature career women surviving in a man's world, *Girl in Overalls*, Seifert's only pseudonymous novel, is different. It not only deals with the issues innate to the feminine-mobilized wartime bomber factory, but it features a heroine—Edith "Rusty" Baylis—who is at war with the frivolous world of her high-society family, namely her sister and mother who accuse her of losing her femininity. On the very first page, Rusty joyously asserts herself first by wearing pants and then smoking, "She grinned. Mom did not approve of pants. Certainly not! [and] A nice girl did not smoke as she walked along Lindell Boulevard. A Nice Girl, a nice girl – Rusty hated the connotation Mom put on the phrase. She set a girl on the block, to be inspected, chosen, sold to the highest bidder." By working in a bomber plant Rusty not only takes part in the war effort and captures a saboteur, but she wages her own war against the upper-class propriety of her moneyed background, which negates a woman's independence and dictates marriage. As Rusty tells a reporter, "I am not working for fun. I'm working for my pay check and because I think this war is, to quite a large extent, my war. They won't let me fly a plane, but they will let me help make one. So – I'm doing it." By the end of the novel Rusty discovers that "a women can be feminine, and useful, too. At least, in war times."[27]

The modifier of that line disturbingly places a situational limit on Rusty's usefulness and appears to undermine the innate feminism of the novel. Of course it might be a cynical prescience of the 1950s trauma of gender and hyper-domesticity, but there is little evidence for this. In actuality, it points to a larger paradox within romance fiction. A novel like *Girl in Overalls* can be blatantly feminist yet simultaneously confirm patriarchal patterns. And many romance stories undeniably fall into such patterns without the saving graces of such strong characters as Rusty Baylis or her situation. Romance fiction is far from simplistic. Wicker-Wilson points out, "The popular romance offers one of the richest imaginable repositories for exploring conflicting understandings of gender and sexuality."[28] Similarly, the romance pulps of the 1920s and 1930s often have such conflicting messages as independent heroines who (like Mrs. Dalloway) ultimately are dependent upon traditional gender roles (giving up career for marriage, exactly what Rusty refuses to do). For example, just as the flapper or professional woman sashays through the pages of 1920s romance pulps, displaying fierce independence and open sexuality (riding in cars with boys, sneaking out of windows to jazz clubs, living on her own, drinking, smoking, spooning, etc.), her lifestyle often gets her into trouble where she will be saved by the man she eventually marries. Confessional magazines, like *True Story* and *I Confess* were full of cautionary tales for the independent girl, relating the repercussions of the carefree flapper lifestyle. These stories, previous to the tacked-on moral, still pushed themes of open sexuality and freedom into the daylight and out of the Victorian parlor. As historian Allen Goldberg puts is, "The breakdown of the Victorian code, with its emphasis on feminine purity ... accelerated during the 1920s. There was greater sexual freedom

---

[27] *Girl in Overalls* (NY: Dodd, Mead & Co., 1942), 1, 45, and 274.
[28] Wicker-Wilson, 63.

during the decade, reflecting the influence of Freud, the automobile, and the 'sex and confess' magazines."[29]

Just as overlooked as this female pulp audience is the large number of women authors and editors within the pulp industry, such as Fanny Ellsworth, editor of *Ranch Romances*; Alice Strope, associate editor at Street and Smith in the 1920s, later editor of *Crime Mysteries*; Daisy Bacon, the "Queen of the Woodpulps," who had a long and successful career as editor at Street and Smith, most notably for the highly successful *Love Story Magazine*; Harriet Bradfield, editor of *Love Romances* and the "New York Market Letter" columnist for *Writer's Digest*.[30] There were also plenty of women editors for pulps outside of the Romance field, including Fanny Ellsworth, editor for *Black Mask*. These women are entirely overlooked, even in current revisionist work within periodical studies, exemplified by Ellen Gruber Garvey and Sharon Harris's excellent collection of essays about women editors, *Blue Pencils and Hidden Hands: Women Editing Periodicals*. But this again just illustrates how deep the academic prejudices run against these popular magazines—not that there is any prejudice on the part of, say, Harris or Gruber Garvey. Despite their necessary efforts of rectifying a portrait of literary production, they (as are we all) are just the inheritors of not only an archive of omission, but an innately patriarchal literary history that is equally prejudiced against popular forms. Whereas the pulps get little enough critical attention, this overlooked history illustrates that what does exist is focused on the male pulp reader and masculine focused hard-boiled fiction. Not only does this reflect the patriarchal foundations of English studies, but it is slanted in that it ignores the important and often overlooked role that women played as both consumers and producers of the pulps. Hence female pulp editors and authors are doubly damned for they were working in a field that has been written out of history. The same could be said for ethnic authors and editors, but given the prevailing prejudices of the day it is more than likely that, like so many pulp authors, such authors hid behind pen names and relationships of correspondence.

The Pulp Audience

It is also important to note the diversity of both the general pulp audience and the pulp genres. Smith and (less explicitly) McCann have pointed out that the pulps served as an important force in the "Americanization" of the working-class culture, as illustrated by the many ads for English improvement systems and schools, though the pulps themselves often seemed to strengthen American homogeneity via stereotypical and vilifying portraits of ethnicity, which is especially apparent on the many "Yellow Peril" covers (which were common enough that some pulp enthusiasts collect *only* yellow peril covers) and in stories inspired by Sax Rohmer's

---

[29] Ronald Allen Goldberg, *American in the 20's* (Syracuse: Syracuse U P, 2003), 94.
[30] See John Locke's *Pulpwood Days* (Elkhorn, CA: Off-Trail Publications, 2007) for contemporary profiles of Daisy Bacon and Harriet Bradfield.

Fu Manchu tales (which would later be published in the pulps).[31] It is possible when considering the daily display of pulp covers on every corner newsstand to see the pulp marketplace as a mundane street museum visually reifying social norms by their negative depiction of the racial Other or their objectification of women. Such a display reinforces the social pressures of acculturation, and the fiction contained within pulps like *The Wizard* (a masked hero of Wall Street) and *Fame and Fortune* helped to instill the promise of the American Dream and working-class industry, especially during the bleak years of the depression. In *Black Boy*, Richard Wright tells of reading "tattered copies of *Flynn's Detective Weekly* or the *Argosy All-Story Magazine* ... [and fantasizing] about cities I had never seen and about people I had never met" (133), themes that emerge in *Native Son*. Likewise, the narrator of Joyce's "An Encounter" looks to dime novels as an imaginative means to escape Dublin life, inspiring his actual "adventure."

It is no coincidence that John Fante's characters, about whom always hover the constant tensions and struggles of Italian American acculturation, often read pulp magazines, which become symbols of both promise of escape and class shame. In *Wait Until Spring, Boldrini* (1938), the boy protagonist twice locks himself in the bathroom and covertly reads copies of *Scarlet Crime* or *Horror Crimes*. Both instances accompany attempts to escape shame, not only the shame of his own guilt or dishonesty, or the shame of his disintegrating home life, but shame for his cruelty to his mother who is the scapegoat for his feelings of racial otherness, inadequacy, and poverty. The act of reading the pulp becomes the literary counterpart to Philip Roth's masturbatory adventures in *Portnoy's Complaint*.

The pulps' depictions of the Other were generally far from politically correct. Characterization was in general forsaken because of the stress placed upon simple story structure and fast action; hence villains had to be painted in black and white, or yellow and white or red and white, depending upon whether the story had an African, Oriental, or Western setting. Ethnicity became a quick signifier for evil or wantonness. But this in itself forced authors to find other quick, hard methods of characterization, much like Sherwood Anderson's use of the grotesque in *Winesburg, Ohio*. Hammett's description of Sam Spade in *The Maltese Falcon* offers the prototypical example:

> Samuel Spade's jaw was long and bony, his chin a jutting v under the more flexible v of his mouth. His nostrils curved back to make another, smaller, v. His yellow-grey eyes were horizontal. The v *motif* was picked up again by thickish brows rising outward from twin creases above a hooked nose, and his pale brown hair grew down – from high flat temples—in a point on his forehead. He looked rather pleasantly like a blond satan.[32]

William Marling, in *American Roman Noir*, cites Hammett's use of the "*v motif*" as a metonymic source tied to "one of the first conscious uses of art nouveau

---

[31] On Americanization, see Smith, 23.
[32] Dashiell Hammett, *The Maltese Falcon* (NY: Vintage, 1992), 3.

[*sic,* deco?] in American popular literature [which] epitomizes the complex of technological and economic forces affecting the mass of Americans."[33] While this may be so (see the second half of this section for a different approach to technology and the pulps), it is unquestionable that Hammett was just deftly adhering to the pulp form's need for quick characterization and speedy tone. Similarly, the pulp protagonist's very difference was often used for originality, to set the story apart from its milieu; hence detectives of race, such as Raoul Whitfield's Manilan Detective Jo Gar, or even the physically handicapped heroes of Bruno Fischer, became popular.[34] McCann has examined Hammett's complex (and modernist) portrayal of race that seemingly worked against these stereotypes. But, in general, such examples of humanistic depth are rare in a field that is remarkable for its stereotypical, derogatory, and extreme depictions of Otherness. It would be reductive not to point out that the prejudice of the pulps was just a more extreme, more lurid case of the same exoticism and primitivism that was concurrently at work in high modernism. The stereotypes that filled the pages of the short-lived pulp *Harlem Stories* (1932), for example, capitalized on the fascination for African American exoticism, just as they did in the writing of Stein and Williams, the letters of Pound and Eliot, and the subject matter and popularity of Carl Van Vechten's *Nigger Heaven* and MacKaye's *Home to Harlem*.[35] Interestingly enough, during the early 1920s Mencken and Nathan bandied about the idea of starting an "all negro" pulp magazine but decided against it because they thought the market too narrow. Considering both how influential their other pulps were and how the narrow focus of 1930s pulps (i.e., *Courtroom Stories, Zeppelin Stories*) became an integral aspect of the form, then it is a shame they didn't go through with the venture.

Pulp fiction's relationship to nation and race is complex. It often enunciates both cultural criticism and a strident nationalism, which grew stronger with World War II; besides an obvious jingoism, the pulps were also a site of fierce independence that was often anti-corporate and circumspect in regard to the government, especially during the depression, though they were often (but not always) oppressive in regard to minorities and gender. Pulp genre fiction both reified the fast-paced speed and technological advancement that made America a national power and criticized it. Such dualities mirror those that existed in modernism: for example, the pulps often questioned and mocked the restrictive morals of, say, prohibition and sexual Puritanism through bootlegger heroes and spicy situations.

---

[33] Marlin, William. *The American Roman Noir*, (Athens: U of Georgia P, 1995), 73.

[34] Jo Gar is the protagonist of Whitfield's (writing under the penname Ramon Decolta) "Death in the Pasig," originally published in *Black Mask*, March 1930, republished in Joseph T. Shaw's *The Hard-Boiled Omnibus*. For more on Fischer, see p.111.

[35] See Michael North's *The Dialect of Modernism* (NY: Oxford U P, 1994).

Cultural Criticism in the Pulps

A typical example is "The High Jackers," from an early issue of *Black Mask* magazine.[36] The hero is Cannon Ball Toombs, ex-automobile racer, a "graduate" of the Indianapolis 500, recently turned whiskey runner at the behest of a local judge. The story recounts a single run from Canada for the Judge who is wining and dining a senator and a newspaper baron, both stridently Volsteadian in policy but not practice. Along the way, Coombs is waylaid by three hijackers, but manages to fight them off, sustaining considerable injury but getting the liquor through safely. The author, Harford Powell Jr., returns numerous times to the blurry definition of what a crook is, "This is a crook story," he states early on. "All that puzzles me is to know which of the three people is the crook." The story ends with the Judge, callously unconcerned with Toombs' injuries, interested only in when he can pick up his liquor shipment. The three figures of power—the Judge, the Senator, the newspaper magnate—parallel the three hijackers, and, if anything, are even more harshly vilified for their hypocrisy, since the three criminals are portrayed as products of the times; only Toombs emerges morally, if not physically, unscathed, despite his illegal profession. We can see the similar blurring of hero and nationalism in the fiction of Hemingway or Fitzgerald, in Frederick Henry or Jay Gatsby. Such expatriate authors' own relations to the United States were similarly complex.

Many of the dichotomies that exist in the pulp form have to do with the pulps' audience-based self-definition. It is necessary to question reconstructions of audiences such as Smith's, especially in regard to class, for they do not take into consideration the stigma that has always been associated with reading popular literature of the pulp kind. For all those reasons that inform the construction of modernism as elite, it is similarly undeniable that bourgeois and upper-class readers of pulp magazines—and there are instances of such—would be adverse to admitting an affection for sensational literature, though to what degree they comprised the pulp audience is impossible to tell. In 1937, Harold Hersey, longtime pulp editor, stated, "Neither is it true that only the partly educated and the poor indulge in this national habit. If I were to offer a sweeping generalization, I would say that pulpwood readers are nearer to the unimaginative than the unintelligent, and in average financial condition. As imagination is as rare in one class as in another, it is obvious that they are not a class, but a proportion, and a fairly substantial one at that."[37]

Even though the exact audience of the pulps is impossible to reconstruct, what is apparent is the fact that the pulps, as a form, became the bottom of the cultural hierarchy of the 1920s and 1930s, which is why the pulps frequently felt the need in editorials to define their audience as being economically mobile, reputable,

---

[36] Harford Powell Jr., "The High Jackers," *Black Mask Magazine* (Feb. 25, 1923), 27–32.

[37] Hersey, 3.

and of a high cultural position—all of which illustrates a beleaguered reputation, a bolstering of the defenses against continuous criticism. These contemporary portraits of the pulp audience are complex—many self-descriptive pulp editorials show a hopeful upward mobility, yet are careful not to ostracize the main, working-class readership; the pulps often attempted to hopscotch that line between popular and quality. For example, in 1935 A.A. Wyn wrote:

> We all know that plenty of bankers and brokers, lawyers and doctors, salesmen and Senators are addicted to reading the pulps. How often have we heard them say, 'Pulps? Um, yes – I read them myself once in a while – they help to put me to sleep.' The sly liars! Imagine our blood-and thunder stories, sweated out to provide the utmost in spine-chilling, blood-tingling fiction, being used as a sedative! We disown such faint-hearted friends – give us the honest pulp fan who writes, 'Your man's great! Wish it came out once a week.'[38]

The actual dynamics between the forms of low-, middle-, and highbrow culture were much more complex than Huyssen's model of duality would have us believe.

The Cultural Position of the Pulp Magazine

The pulp debate illustrates tensions that existed between the elite modernists and the bourgeois, between high- and middlebrow. But elite modernism often looked to the lowbrow for inspiration, the proletariat for realistic fodder, as in Joyce's use of mundane ephemera and fondness for Edgar Wallace, Stein's appreciation of Hammett, Faulkner's love for aviation pulps, or, in general, modernism's colonization of primitivism. If the middlebrow had aspirations toward elitism, they were the most vocal in damning the pulps. And for the lowbrow pulps, they damned the "Braham" and elite trappings of the highbrow, but their mark of success was when a writer graduated from the pulps to the popular and respectable middlebrow magazines.

McCann points out that pulp editors, writers, and fans saw the magazines as a subculture, as a democratic brotherhood, and an alternative to the mainstream magazine.[39] Pulp writer Will McMorrow claimed that pulps were unlike "the Brahman type of [magazine] to be found on the library table of every cultured home. With the pages uncut. Wood-pulp magazines are not bought for ornamental purposes. They are read."[40] This self-definition of blue-collar practicality and utilitarianism is offset in the same letter by the proud claim that "Nine out of ten successful smooth-paper writers started out in the wood-pulp." Even though the pulps kept a close relationship with their readers, constantly repeating their allegiance to the working class, they also often kept a weather eye upon the slicks, and lauded any of their own that vaulted the divide, hence reaffirming the pulp's own quality.

---

[38] Wyn, 18.
[39] McCann, 48–52.
[40] *New York Times*, Letters to the Editor (March 18, 1933), 12.

Such defensive claims as McMorrow's (which also cites the great economic and industrial benefit of the pulps during the depression) and Wyn's are understandable for, in middlebrow circles and publications, the pulp form was gazed upon with horror, as the insidious reading matter of the working class. In a 1933 issue of *Vanity Fair*, Marcus Duffield wrote about the pulp magazine, "They swarm over the newsstands, gaudy, blatant, banal: Wild West Weekly, Astounding Stories, Ranch Romances. They are the Pulps. ... Into this underworld of literature most of us never dive unless, like Mr. Hoover's Committee on Recent Social Trends, we are curious about the literary preferences of those who move their lips when they read." There is a tone of hysteria, a fear of literary fecundity in Duffield's description of the swarming masses of underworld readers—yet there is also a trace of fascination, as well, a type of literary slumming akin to the modernist infiltration of Harlem, which was quite conspicuous in *Vanity Fair* as well. Another article, which more explicitly exemplifies that underlying fear, is Margaret MacCullen's "Pulps and Confessions," from a 1937 issue of *Harper's*, which bemoaned, "It is not pleasant to think of the immature minds and mature appetites that feed on such stuff as their staple fodder, but there is no ducking the fact that sensationalism is the age-old need of the uneducated. The steady reader of this kind of fiction is interested in and stirred by the same things that would interest and stir a savage." And again, at the 1936 meeting of the National Council of Teachers of English, Miss Anita P. Forbes, of Hartford, Connecticut, claimed that 90 percent of high school students read pulp magazines and that this "constitutes a menace to the pupil's morals, his English, and his mind."[41]

The pulps emerge as a symbol of degeneration in modernist literature—for example, in the recently "re-discovered" work of John Fante, a later modernist who moved in the intellectual circles of 1930s Los Angeles. In Fante's *Ask the Dust* (1934), the semi-autobiographical sequel to *Wait Until Spring, Bandini*, the adolescent narrator, Arturo Bandini, describes his life as an idealistic writer, struggling to make it in Los Angeles. In his cheap Bunker Hill room, Bandini writes endless letters to his mentor, the mighty magazine editor, J.C. Hackmuth ("J.C."—a Savior figure for "hack"/professional writers, perhaps?), who is obviously Fante's real life mentor H.L. Mencken, describing the romantic western sunsets. Bandini is constantly interrupted though by his neighbor, the alcoholic Mr. Hellfrick, who is described as an "atheist, retired from the army, living on a meager pension, scarcely enough to pay for his liquor bills, even though he purchased the cheapest gin on the market."[42] Tellingly, Hellfrick lies each afternoon with his head out the window to catch the last rays of the setting sun; and his room is "madness, pulp western magazines over the floor, a bed with sheets blackened, clothes strewn everywhere, and clothes-hooks on the wall conspicuously naked, like broken teeth in a skull."[43] If Hackmuth stands for the idealistic pinnacle of literary success, then

---

[41] Marcus Duffield, "The Pulps: Day Dreams for the Masses," *Vanity Fair* (June 1933); *Harpers* (June 1937), 98; also quoted in Smith; *New York Times*, "Pulp Magazines Called A Menace" (November 29, 1936), 27.

[42] John Fante, *Ask the Dust* (Santa Rose: Black Sparrow, 2000), 28.

[43] Ibid., 29.

Hellfrick is the specter of Bandini's literary failure: broke, bitter, debauched. More, he symbolizes the reality of Los Angeles in contrast to both Bandini's letters and the romantic depiction of the lost West depicted in the Western pulp magazines. For Fante, the pulp magazine becomes a marker, not only of shame and escape in the earlier novel, but of the pitfalls of a literary career, the threat of selling out, for the pulp is not only directly opposed to Hackmuth's magazine but it offers literary vacuity, the cheapest literary gin for the mind. In Hellfrick's hands, it also stands for cultural disintegration and depravity.

These examples should give some idea of how the pulp was viewed (at least publicly) by the "educated," by that section of society that looked upon books and literature as integral to social uplift, and "quality" books as integral to social standing. Logically though, the pulps constituted not so much a threat to culture, but instead were, due to their very availability and appeal to immigrants and working class alike, an important building block in literacy, as one letter to the editor of the *New York Times* illustrates: "It is a healthy sign that these magazines flourish. They are constantly recruiting book lovers out of the ranks of the illiterate movie fans, for they foster reading habits which, it is safe to assume, afterward crave better fare. There are many who, never entering libraries, find in the wood-pulp magazine the inevitable blessings of the printed word. The tabloid newspaper and the movie are then found wanting and it needs only the happy chance of reading 'action' classics to make them converts."[44]

Seemingly, the designators of culture thought that there were too many readers already—converts were not wanted. Such a fear of the pulp form, especially evident in MacCullen's analogy of the pulp reader as savage, hides a fear of unchecked production, a fear of cultural degeneration, and a reaction to a quickly growing bourgeois readership. Megan Benton, in her article "'Too Many Books': Book Ownership and Cultural Identity in the 1920s," describes the fall of the book as literary artifact and its rise as a popular, yet empty, symbol of cultural pretence. As Benton puts it, books had formerly been "recognized as both agent and emblem of the cultivated intellect, soul, and life ... [testifying] to one's wealth, education, and leisure."[45] She describes the intellectual elite's fear of the newly literate bourgeoisie, citing, for example, Henry Seidel Canby's article in a 1930 issue of the *Saturday Review of Literature*, where he "even preferred the 'barbarism' of the 'newly housebroken who have moved into living rooms in the recent eras of prosperity'" over that of the frivolous middle-class book consumer, because the former "brought 'no such sacred arks of culture with them, and they have used the shelves for phonograph records, *all story magazines*, and the cat's saucer of milk.'"[46]

---

[44] *New York Times* (March 22, 1933), 16.

[45] Megan Benton, "'Too Many Books': Book Ownership and Cultural Identity in the 1920s," *American Quarterly*, Vol. 49., No. 2 (1997), 268.

[46] Benton, 267 (italics mine).

In other words, Canby prefers readers who know their place; the fact that he prefers a lower class without cultural pretensions or aspirations illustrates the modernist need of a lower-class literary form that supports and reifies the superior cultural position of the highbrow intellectual. This dilemma of middlebrow culture is best illustrated in the decline of the book's standing as cultural marker and artifact. But this, I'd like to argue, isn't so much a trickle-down from the elite to the bourgeoisie, as an upward spread of pulp-like marketing, what was seen as the threat of degeneration rising from the literature of the masses, which resulted in an attitude of literary eugenics on the part of critics.

The pulp magazine, as the most extreme (and pioneering) example of modern marketing and distribution, best exemplifies the popularization and disposability of the book. The mid-1920s saw the rise of the book club, the first paperbacks, the expansion of the book market into newspaper stands, railroad and bus stations, drugstores, and lending libraries—all of which were made possible by the early pulp popular fiction magazines, and all of which constituted a threat to the book as the cultural artifact of the elite. In other words, the pulps are indicative of the incursion of the mass marketplace into the dynamics of overall book production; the pure mass of the pulp market and the extremity of its pioneering marketing techniques had what can be described as a gravitational pull of influence upon the entire book industry. One manifestation of this was the trend on the part of numerous publishers during the early years of the depression to reduce the price of books from two or three dollars to one dollar. This sparked a heated discussion of American cultural disintegration on the part of critics and intellectuals. The reading fad in the years before the depression resulted in not so much the loss of the book's rarified position as marker of cultural and intellectual superiority, but a general diffusion of book availability across classes: books were in danger of becoming a symbol of consumption rather than of discrimination, a commodity rather than a status symbol.

Michael Josephs writes about this trend in his 1926 *The Commercial Side of Literature*, seemingly a writer's guide to publishing with chapters about approaching publishers and overviews of the marketplace, but which is also rife with a scolding tone about the hyper-production of books in America and the resulting low quality of fiction:

> It is a commonplace to say that nowadays everyone thinks he can write a book. It is a book-writing age. Practically everyone of importance has been prevailed upon (one suspects that many of them did not require much persuasion) to write his or her reminiscences. Even people of no conceivable importance have inflicted their reminiscences on the public. Presently we shall have high-school girls unburdening their memoirs, for the craze continues.[47]

One reaction against this was the establishment of a rarified book production, namely an effort by modernist publishers and authors to create books that were

---

[47] Michael Joseph, *The Commercial Side of Literature* (NY: Harper and Brothers, 1926), 2.

instant icons and artifacts of cultural and economic superiority through the rise of limited and fine editions, distribution via subscription—in other words, instant scarcity. As general book distribution moved onto the street and into the drugstore, specialty book dealers bolstered the position of the book. The rise of small press publishers, which limited themselves to modernist works—Harry Crosby's Black Sun Press, Robert McAlmon's Three Mountain Press, Nancy Cunard's Hours Press, Woolf's Hogarth Press, to name a few—catered to limited readership restricted to those either in the know or with money. Sylvia Beach's publication of *Ulysses* is an excellent example with its instant aura and instant rarity.[48] Commercial publishers such as Scribners jumped on the bandwagon by producing limited, fine, autographed first editions of books such as Hemingway's *Farewell To Arms*—510 signed and numbered copies, complete with partial vellum binding and slipcase, and which sold for $10, a high price for 1929. Alfred Knopf's Borzoi press is another example, slightly less commercial than Scribners. Knopf specialized in authors such as Mencken, Thomas Mann, Carl Van Vechten, and Katherine Mansfield, all printed in highly attractive, fine editions. In 1925, Knopf published a 10-year anniversary volume that supplied bios, portraits, and thoughts of many of its authors by other Borzoi authors. The book is, in fact, a beautifully produced advertisement/catalog, that certifies its own coterie and rarity. It also clues us into a double standard: Borzoi's modernity is good marketing. Scribners, likewise, put out limited and small editions of modernist authors while selling the rights for republication to cheap edition specialists like Grosset and Dunlap (*Farewell To Arms* edition was published in 1931 and sold for $1). These economically inspired hierarchies of editions reached their pinnacle, as Lawrence Rainey has pointed out, in the carefully constructed marketing of *Ulysses* by Beach and Joyce. Such instances illustrate not only an overt marketing of modernism that works against its traditional image as independent of the marketplace, but also modernism's reaction to and reliance upon the strategy of pulp-like marketing.

Another aspect of the elite's criticism of empty intellectualism was, ironically in view of modernist attempts at a rarefied book market, denouncing the use of the physical book as an empty, visual signifier of culture and wealth on the part of the bourgeois: buying books by the yard and faux shelves of pasted leather bindings are two examples of bourgeoisie cultural passing, as it were. As Benton states "Ownership of books, which traditionally bestowed a certain elite cultural credential, meant less and less per se as unprecedented numbers of Americans began buying books for a host of reasons, including explicitly for their iconographic powers."[49] Fitzgerald's description of Gatsby's beautiful but unread library is an excellent example of the modernist elite's fear of the loss of its identity as based upon book ownership. Gatsby's library is, Benton states,

---

[48] Akin to this is Laurence Rainey's idea that modernism became even more rarified through the rise of the market for manuscripts and galleys, best illustrated by the relationship between Joyce and Rosenbach, see Ellman, *James Joyce* (Oxford: Oxford U P, 1982), 559, 594, and Rainey, 42–76.

[49] Benton, 269.

"the extravagant culmination of Gatsby's youthful resolve to 'read one improving book or magazine per week,' but with it he achieves only a meaningless cultural illusion."[50] The library symbolizes Gatsby's passing as upper class. Oddly enough, Gatsby's unread library—"'It's a bona-fide piece of written matter. It fooled me. This fella's a regular Belasco. It's a triumph. What thoroughness! What realism! Knew when to stop, too—didn't cut the pages'"—echoes pulp writer McMorrow's sneering description of the unopened "Brahman" magazines on "the library table of every cultured home." The book becomes, for both the pulpster and the highbrow, a symbol of Veblen's conspicuous consumerism.

But the book's diminishing cultural importance is only one episode in the effort to solidify the blurring borders of class and culture in the age of modernity. As I have shown in the previous section, modernist authors were available not just to a rarified coterie, but to the public *en masse* in magazines such as the *Golden Book* and *Smart Set*, not to mention in cheap reprint editions and paperbacks. Ads in the pulps and the smart magazines, which appealed to the upwardly mobile lower- and lower-middle-class readers, evince the preoccupation with reading and self-betterment. Ads for book clubs and classical literature libraries proliferate in *The Golden Book*, for example, as well as less sophisticated pulps. Other instances that pulled the cultural rug from under the feet of the intellectual included *The Little Leather Library*—small, leatherette-bound classics contained in boxes of Whitman's chocolates (books as premiums for consumption, culture as a Cracker Jack prize); Emanuel Haldeman-Julius' successful "Little Blue Books," which sold more than 300,000,000 copies and made modernist and socialist works—both reprints and originals—available for 5 and 10 cents and included authors such as Yeats and Huxley (and which Hammett mocks in *The Thin Man* when Nick receives for Christmas a copy of "Haldeman-Julius Little Blue Book Number 1534 [...] *How to Test Your Urine at Home*"); the increasing number of book clubs and publishing houses like Grosset and Dunlap and A.L. Burt that specialized in cheap reprints and "movie editions" of more expensive, "respectful" books for drugstore, department store, newsstand, and train station distribution; the Modern Library; paperback books.[51] Many of these book forms used the type of scatter-gun-marketing perfected by the pulps' niche specialization. The intellectual saw such modern marketing as commodifying culture, as putting literature on the same level as the pulp magazine.

Hence the pulp debate and the "too many books" scandal were just two parts of a many-sided debate about the position of quality literature, the physical book as a symbol of cultural elitism, and to whom cultural and intellectual superiority (as founded upon literature and discrimination) was made available. Elite publishers, academicians, and modernist critics, such as Mencken, fought such movements

---

[50] Ibid., 288.

[51] See Rubin, 94; Tebbel, *Between Covers* (NY: Oxford U P, 1987), 155 for accounts of the Little Leather Library; Hammett, *The Thin Man* (NY: Knopf, 1934), 52. For a short history and description of the Little Blue Book, see Schick's *The Paperbound Book in America* (NY: Bowker, 1958), 60–61 as well as *The World of Haldeman-Julius* (NY: Twayne, 1960), compiled by Albert Mordell.

as the lowering of book prices by policing the lines of stratification between high, middle, and low culture. In a 1930 issue of *The New Republic* Lewis Mumford, writing about publishers' attempts to expand the reading market, states that "Once the attempt is made to reach this audience, the sort of book produced *en série* will be the exact equivalent of Dream Stories and True Romances [direct references to pulp magazines], and on the whole, violet-ray treatments and vacuum cleaners and cheap motor cars take care of the surplus income of this group quite as satisfactorily as books possibly could, *with a smaller amount of cultural degradation*" (italics mine).[52] Literature has its place, and, according to Mumford, that place certainly isn't with the masses (notice the allusion to "cheap motor cars," which I shall return to below).

The attempt to maintain the cultural gap, apparent in Mumford's article, only serves to illustrate the contemporary blurring of class and social borders and resulting fear of the disintegration of the traditional position of the elite reader and designator of good taste. Throughout anti-pulp diatribes there is a level of prejudice, which is to be expected, but in the language itself there arises a disturbing pattern—the pulp reader as savage, barbarian, a force of cultural disintegration. Such language echoes the semantics of xenophobia and eugenics. The modern/ highbrow fear of cultural disintegration, above and beyond that of literature, often stems from the threat of over-production, the threat of fecundity. Just as the threat of over-population, immigration, growing lower classes, resulted in prejudice and the bolstering of cultural borders, the pulps, as the reading material of the lower classes and immigrant, become the literary Other. And the many diatribes against the form evince a "Yellow Peril"-like literary prejudice—the Pulp Peril if you will.

These ideas of the pulp magazine as a marker of cultural decline and the fear of racial degeneration meet in Faulkner's *Light In August* when Joe Christmas spends the day before murdering Joanna Burden reading "a magazine of that type whose covers bear either pictures of young women in underclothes or pictures of men in the act of shooting one another with pistols."[53] Christmas's pulp is not only in direct contrast to Burden's hopes for him to attend a black college and pursue a career of racial uplift (her last name is a reference to the term "white man's burden"), but the description of its cover foreshadows the scene of murder itself, for the masculine, nightdress-wearing Burden attempts to shoot Christmas before he cuts her throat. At the end of the novel, Christmas's literary black blood echoes that of Madame Bovary, both of which echo a self-conception tainted by, among other things, degenerative popular literature.[54] For Faulkner, Christmas, self-exiled from both the white and black worlds, marks the endpoint of cultural degeneration and miscegenation, like the howling, retarded Jim Bond in *Absalom,*

---

[52] Mumford quoted in Ann Haugland's "Book Propaganda: Edward L. Bernays's 1930 Campaign Against Dollar Books," *Book History*, Vol. 3 (2000), 235.

[53] Faulkner, *Light in August* (NY: Vintage, 1972), 102–103.

[54] André Bleikasten comes to a similar conclusion in "'Cet affreux gout d'encr' Emma Bovary's Ghost in *Sanctuary*" in Gresset and Polk's *Intertextuality in Faulkner* (Jackson: U P of Mississippi, 1985).

Absalom! who will eventually "conquer the western hemisphere," just as the pulps, in Duffield's words, "swarm over the newsstands."

Such racial threats to hegemony that feed Faulkner's racial hysteria also echo throughout the dynamics of modernism from *Heart of Darkness* to Pound's *Cantos*; they are informed by the presence of, reliance upon, and simultaneous fascination with the Other. The fear of literary fecundity, like the economic and cultural threat from racial Otherness, was a by-product of modernization. For critics, the pulps, because of their formulaic pattern and pervasiveness, marked the disintegration of quality, a possible death knell to good literature due to its standardization: as Duffield puts it, "The mass production of day-dreams by the Pulps has been accompanied by a phenomenon unique in literature: the standardization of fiction. Even as Fords and hairpins are standardized, so are the stories. These magazines represent the incursion of the Machine Age into the art of tale-telling."[55] Pulps became the literary embodiment of the excesses of modernity.

Duffield and Mumford all look to the automobile as the epitome of mass-production, as the symbol of standardized and frivolous mass-consumption. It is relatively common to use Henry Ford, or the Ford automobile metonymically as the symbol of modern mass production.[56] Huxley's *Brave New World* best exemplifies the interwar intellectuals' damnation of what happens when Ford's mass production spills over into the realm of culture. Huxley's vision of the future is one irrevocably changed by the production line: procreation has been replaced by mass scientific production of test-tube babies; genetic chemistry predetermines caste; mass entertainment and consumption replace religion and art; Henry Ford is the divine being; and above all, individualism is strictly taboo, if not impossible. *Ends And Means* (1937), written five years after *Brave New World,* is something of a nonfiction counterpart to the novel—a warning siren of the growing militaristic and shallow trend of the modern world. In it, Huxley names the forms of mass entertainment the "psychological equivalents of alcoholism and morphinism," and asserts that "pulp-magazine stories are transcriptions of the commonest and easiest daydreams."[57] Huxley's portrait of the modern culture industry names pulp magazines, which "offer to millions of readers their quota of true confessions, spicy detective stories, hot mysteries" along with tabloids, "imbecile and squalid films," jazz, and political propaganda as the misused products of modernity that are helping to create a non-peace-loving, nonindividualistic society.[58] For Huxley and other intellectuals, the pulps become the literary low point of the modern cultural technocracy.

John Carey, for one, sees Huxley's espousal of high art as symptomatic of a belief in natural intellectual elitism.[59] Huxley saw the benefits of modernity—cultural, technological, scientific—as being potentially beneficial, but in reality

---

[55] Duffield, 27.
[56] See Marling, *The American Roman Noir* (Athens: U of Georgia P, 1995).
[57] Aldous Huxley, *Ends and Means* (NY: Harper, 1937), 245–246, 240.
[58] Ibid., 220–221.
[59] See Carey, 88–89.

dangerous because of misuse. Birth control is one example of this dichotomy: Huxley thought it was one of the most important technological achievements of the twentieth century for the control of overpopulation, yet it could potentially deprive the world of "children who might have contributed to its betterment."[60] As a result, he criticized the misuse of birth control throughout *Brave New World* for its role in making sex and pleasure a totalitarian tool for stupefying the masses.[61] In *Ends and Means*, Huxley sees art lacking catharsis, or when used only for "self-titillation," as "emotional masturbation"— nonproductive in society.[62] It is logical then that Huxley would damn pulp magazines, especially considering their taint of mass fecundity and cultural disintegration, and Fordism alike as potential dangers to individualism.

In *Dance of the Machines*, Edward J. O'Brien, editor of the long-lived "Best Short Story" series likewise decries the state of the popular short story in 1929, citing the mechanization of modern society, comparing the impersonality and destructiveness of the modern military to the magazine trade. This fear of standardization, of Fordism encroaching upon literature, arises again and again in critiques of the pulps, one reason for which was the simplistic formulas that many of the pulp genres adhered to—their plot-by-numbers construction. Frank Gruber, in his memoir *Pulp Jungle* about life as a pulp writer describes such a formulaic plot construction:

> I used to analyze stories. What elements were required? Over a period of time I evolved a formula for mystery stories. It consisted of eleven elements. With these eleven elements in a mystery plot I could not miss. I used to work out each element at a time, concentrating on one until I licked it, then going on to the next…Once I had worked out these eleven elements, the job of coming up with plots for mystery stories was greatly simplified…to this day I claim that this plot formula is foolproof. You can write a perfectly salable mystery story with seven or eight of these elements, but get them all into a story and you cannot miss.[63]

Similarly, Max Brand (the pen name of Frederick Faust) claimed that he wrote 300 Western novels using only a single plot.[64]

But there is no better illustration of the formulaic aspect of the pulps than in the Ernest E. Gagnon Company's Plot Genie system of plot construction (see Figure 2.3). Invented in 1931 by Wycliffe A. Hill, the *Plot Genie* and accompanying

---

[60] Quoted in Jerome Meckier's "Aldous Huxley, Evelyn Waugh, and Birth Control in *Black Mischeif*," *Journal of Modern Literature*, Vol. 23, No. 2 (1999), 278.
[61] See ibid., 277–290.
[62] Huxley, *Ends*, 237.
[63] Frank Gruber, *The Pulp Jungle* (LA: Shelbourne Press, 1967), 179.
[64] Gruber's eleven elements consist of: Colorful hero, Theme, Villain, Background, Murder Method, Motive, Clue, Trick, Action, Climax, Emotion. Faust's plot is: "The good man becomes bad and the bad man becomes good." Quoted in Gruber, 183. Gruber's portrayal of pulp writing is fascinating; his constant effort to find the formula for different genre stories is more like a poker player looking for a winning system than a creative artist.

Fig. 2.3   *The Plot Genie*, 1931 © Ernest F. Gagnon Company. Copyright never renewed

"Plot Robot" was a series of books—a general index and, initially, *Romance without Melodrama*, *Adventure without Love Interest*, *Mystery Stories*, and *Comedy*, soon to be followed by supplements such as the *Short-Short Story*—that aided the popular author in constructing plots for salable short stories. These books listed hundreds of numbered possibilities of all the elements of a story, from protagonist to locale to complications and love interest. All the author had to do was to turn the dial of the cardboard "plot robot," which resulted in a random number that appeared in the plot genie's crystal ball and then find the corresponding element—for example, you need a "predicament or crisis," dial the number and you get 36, "One is about to be attacked by a maniac." Hall stressed both the importance of style in his method and how the randomness of the plot robot fought against cliché.

Cultural and literary critics latched onto this formulaic and standardized aspect of pulp fiction as its most insidious aspect, as can be seen in MacMullen's *Harper's* article, "It [the large pulp readership] is not a happy picture; for sharply as these magazines differ in appeal and emphasis, they are all alike in one thing, a denial of reality"; the *Vanity Fair* article, "By the process of trial and error through the career of the Pulps, definite specifications have been evolved for the various types of stories. The specifications have been formulated into a series of editorial rules, both commands and taboos, which assures the essential sameness of all the stories";[65] and in the statement by the schoolteacher from Connecticut that the pulps were evil because they "require no mental effort from the reader" because of their formulaic composition. Similar criticism was raised against the Book of the Month Club. John Macrae stated that book clubs were the beginning of the "mechanization of the American Mind," and, according to the *Commonweal*, they "standardize American reading."[66]

Whereas mass culture has signified cultural degradation at least since the classical era, as Patrick Brantlinger has established in *Bread and Circuses* by tracing the dynamics of eugenics from Juvenal to Marshall MacLuhan, the standardization of fiction, or (considering the beleaguered social position of the book) the destandardization of reading, added to the bleak outlook of modern culture for the intellectual in the twentieth century. Aldous Huxley's call to arms in *Ends and Means* is surprisingly similar to Theodore Adorno and Max Horkheimer's damning critique of mass culture in "The Culture Industry: Enlightenment as Mass Deception," published a decade later; for them, because of the standardizations of the culture industry, "No independent thinking must be expected from the audience…any logical connection calling for mental effort is painstakingly avoided."[67] For those, like Adorno and Horkheimer, of the Frankfurt School of criticism, the culture industry becomes a force of conformity and complicity under capitalism, quelling individual, critical, and abstract thought through the standardization and homogenization of culture.

Horkheimer and Adorno do not mention the popular pulp magazines, or much fiction in general, choosing instead to concentrate upon film and music, yet the totalizing dynamics that they describe concerning these other media are especially apropos to the pulps. If we consider the standardization of pulp fiction—that "incursion of the Machine Age into the art of tale-telling"—that I have described, and the interdependence of other forms of mass media upon the pulps, it is easy to see how the pulp form is the embodiment of Horkheimer and Adorno's fears.

---

[65] MacMullen, 94, Duffield, 27.
[66] Quoted in Rubin, 97.
[67] Theodore W. Adorno and Max Horkheimer's *Dialect of Enlightenment* (NY: Continuum, 1999), 137.

The pulps' hyper-specialized niche marketing—that idea that whatever a reader's interest, whether travel, romance, Western, boxing, campus life, or zeppelins, there was a corresponding pulp—perfectly describes Adorno's concept of "pseudo-individuality," which is the illusion that individualism exists within the choices made by the consumer. Pseudo-individuality is a beguiling machination of the culture industry, hiding the standardization of output: "Marked differentiations such as those of A and B films, or of stories in magazines in different price ranges, depend not so much on subject matter as on classifying, organizing, and labeling consumers. Something is provided so that none may escape; the distinctions are emphasized and extended."[68]

For Adorno and Horkheimer, one of the symptoms of the culture industry is its homogenizing effect: the blurring of film, music, literature so as to be indistinguishable. Culture becomes interchangeable, depoliticized, stereotypical, predictable. The idea of the interweaving of the arts, again, is perfectly illustrated in the incestuous relationships between film, radio, and the pulps: such characters as the Shadow, Zorro, Buck Rogers, and Tarzan made the transition from the pulps to radio and film into American culture;[69] alternately characters like the Lone Ranger made the jump from radio to the pulps; pulp serials such as Hammett's *Maltese Falcon* made the jump from magazine to novel to film and radio; other pulp-harvested Hollywood subjects include Rafael Sabitini's *The Sea Hawk* and *Captain Blood*, Clarence Mulford's Hopalong Cassidy (first published in *Short Story* in 1921),[70] and A.E. Merrit's *Seven Footprints to Satan*—scripted by Cornell Woolrich, whose own pulp stories were the basis for films such as *Phantom Lady* and *Rear Window* (the latter based on "It Had to be Murder," published in 1942 *Dime Detective*); Max Brand himself had more than 60 movies either based upon his stories (the Dr. Kildare series, *Destry Rides Again*, for example) or that he scripted;[71] pulps, such as *Saucy Movie Tales* and *Film Fun*, were published to capture the movie audience (see Figure 2.4). The pulp writer stables were combed by Hollywood, just as the magazines were combed for film ideas. The list of pulp writers who made the transition to screen writer is extensive: Max Brand, Frank Gruber, Steve Fisher, Dashiell Hammett, Raymond Chandler, Leigh Brackett (science fiction and mystery author, one of the most successful female pulp writers, and also screen writer of *The Big Sleep*, *Rio Bravo*, and *The Empire Strikes Back*), Richard Sale, George Harmon Coxe, Horace McCoy, etc.[72]

---

[68] Ibid., 123.

[69] For a while, Orson Welles voiced the Shadow on radio to raise money for his Mercury Theatre, illustrating another economic patronage of the pulp genre akin to Mencken and Nathan's.

[70] Sampson, *Yesterday's Faces: Volume 6 –Violent Lives* (Bowling Green: Popular Press, 1983), 236.

[71] See Jon Tuska and Vicki Piekarski, eds., *The Max Brand Companion* (Westport, CT: Greenwood Press, 1996), 210–214.

[72] Seeing Hollywood as a site of pulp and modernist amalgamation is thought-provoking, but would take a study all its own. But I would at least like to point out that the economic pull of Hollywood on the modernists and pulp authors alike breaks down both

Fig. 2.4   *Film Fun*, April 1930 © 1930 Dell Publishing Company

The above lists offer just a smattering of examples—to make them exhaustive would be difficult indeed and would constitute a study of its own—but they are sufficient to illustrate not only the great influence of the pulp form on American

---

the hierarchies of modernism and the idea that modernist authors were unconcerned with the marketplace. Hollywood was the common denominator, the "the great salt lick," as the Faulkner character states in the Coen Brother's *Barton Fink*.

popular culture, but the appropriateness of the pulps as a model of Horkheimer and Adorno's culture industry as well. The pulps were the perfect offspring of the marriage between literature and the machine age, seen by modernists as a hideous progeny of unchecked and banal production for the ungoverned masses.

Adorno and Horkheimer state, "Under monopoly all mass culture is identical, and the lines of its artificial framework begin to show through...Movies and radio no longer pretend to be art. The truth that they are just business is made into an ideology in order to justify the rubbish they deliberately produce. They call themselves industries..."[73] There is little doubt that the pulps were an industry. There is little sign of pretensions of uplift or art. Not many authors, editors, or artists involved in the pulps seemingly thought that they were producing more than dreams for mass consumption. The consciousness of their role in the "dream industry" reaches an almost Nathanael West–like postmodern sensitivity; editors and writers referred to themselves as "fiction factories," and artists usually painted over or discarded their cover painting, considering the canvas more valuable than the work covering it.[74] The pulps surpassed the nineteenth-century dime novels in variety, number, and audience appeal. They blazed the trail of market placement, the creation of audience and demand, and modern design techniques. Considering the accounts by pulp authors of their writing process, the term "fiction factory" is extremely apt. Frank Gruber writes of grueling days trying to break into the pulp racket, of pulp authors who could pump out upward of 200,000 words per month, of walking the circuit of magazine editors hoping for a last minute job writing filler stories at press time.[75] Norvell W. Page, creator of the pulp hero the Spider, stated that he wrote 100,000 to 120,000 words a month, but it was not uncommon for other pulp writers to turn out 200,000 words a month. Page also claimed that "the author of the Shadow series [Lester Dent], which runs around 50,000 words each, received an outline for a story on Tuesday and turned in the completed manuscript on Friday."[76] It is easy then to see why Hersey describes writing for the pulps as "the mill," and "the grind."

Between the wars, pulp authors earned anywhere from a quarter of a cent per word to four cents per word or more for the big name writers. Individuals might specialize in a particular genre (like Hammett or Chandler) or be equally skilled at pumping out a Western and romance simultaneously. Hard-boiled originator Carroll John Daly's writing diaries consisted of how many words he had written

---

[73] Adorno, 121.

[74] The term "fiction factory" was, and still is, often bandied about in regard to the pulp industry: Street and Smith, long-time producers of pulps and dime novels, chose it for the title of their history (1955), and, as Erin Smith has pointed out, pulp author Erle Stanley Gardner (like many other writers for the pulp) referred to himself as a fiction factory, Smith, 21. See Robert Lesser's *Pulp Art* (NY: Grammercy, 1997) for the history of pulp cover art.

[75] Gruber, 29.

[76] Norvell Page, "How I Write," in *James Van Hise Presents the Pulp Masters*, James Van Hise, ed. (Yucca Valley: Midnight Graffiti, [nd 1996?]), 72.

that day, how many stories he had out at one particular time, where he had sent them, when they were sent back—either rejected or accepted. If accepted, how much was paid, and if rejected, where they were sent to next. At any given time, a writer might have thirty stories circulating.

An example page from 1942 or 1943, when Daly's popularity and output were waning:[77]

"Dark Knights"	(4,500 [wds])	[rejected and received back]
11/20 [sent]	Sat. Eve. Post	Dec 1st
12/2	Cosmo	12/28
12/29	Ellery Queen Mag	1/26 (a nice letter)
1/27	Elks	2/6
2/10	Det. Story	3/15
3/[16?]	Det book mag	3/29
3/30	Black Mask	4/19th
7/19	Blue Book	8/13
8/14	Det. Fiction	8/26
Feb. 23	Detective tales	4/14

It is difficult to envision anything farther from the highbrow artist's agenda than the creative process of the pulp author: Hersey states "The professional [pulp writer] has attained an objective state of mind about his work, the amateur still talks about that inspiration and individuality in self-expression which are so precious to the serious writer and so utterly worthless to the quantity writer."[78] Contrast this with Joyce's years of poverty, laboriously working and reworking *Ulysses*. Pulp production is seemingly the epitome of that which modernism stood against.

Yet this epitome of capitalist literary production is exactly what ensured both originality and the eternal, mythic qualities of the pulps; just as the heightened production and mass circulation of the pulps make it anathema to the traditionally conceived idea of restrictive modernism, it is also this hyper-production of a literary form that embodies the marketplace and capitalist competition that ensured individualistic, nonclichéd, experimental, and, ultimately, *modernist* pulp fiction. Despite what cultural critics thought, the fiction factory produced writers whose characters, tone, themes, and style were entirely new: the stylistics of Bellem, Clark Ashton Smith, and Dashiell Hammett; the plotting of Harry Stephen Keeler; modern mythic characters like the Shadow, Flash Gordon, Tarzan who have passed into the cultural psyche. All these examples were groundbreaking because they reacted to, reinterpreted, and defied formula. Whereas the hero gets the girl in Hammett's *The Glass Key* and *Maltese Falcon*, the ends aren't uplifting— far from it: in both, the reader is ultimately left with a feeling of despondency exactly *because* the hero gets the girl: Ned Beaumont gets Janet but the reader is ultimately left with Paul Madvig's heartbreak; Sam Spade is stuck with Iva Archer and estranged from (his real interest) Effie. It would be impossible to consider

---

[77] UCLA Special Collections, Young Research Library. Carroll John Daly Correspondence and Clippings. Folder 2, 41.

[78] Hersey, 122.

Keeler's odd and montage inspired plots formulaic. And there were countless pulp characters and settings, which were set apart and flourished exactly due to the need to stand out among the thousands of other weekly, bi-weekly, and monthly stories that the pulps produced. Of course once one was successful it was copied enough to make them pulp conventions, but there was always an original, always a pulp avant-garde.

Whereas the pulp form seems to be the literary embodiment of Horkheimer and Adorno's fear of the rise of the culture industry and the death of critical thought, it is far from that simple. I would like to contend something different—that in the pulps exist the tensions and dynamics of modernism, albeit in a popular form. For Adorno, the aesthetics of modernism involve wholeness of diversity, a portrayal of modern dissonance and fracture with no reconciliation.[79] The pulps, through their very variety and kaleidoscopic portrayal of life approach this ideal when considered as a form *en total*. This is, admittedly, going out on a critical limb. But one of the points I hope to make is that Adorno and Horkheimer's position of intellectual and cultural elitism is itself totalizing, paralleling the traditional academic portrayal of modernism as elite, as the privileged space of the avant-garde that I described in the first section. Up to this point I have been establishing the relationship between the pulps and modernism as one of polarities; but in reality it is one of shared dynamics and themes, not so much a field of opposition as of fertile interchange.

Part 2

Dismantling the Binary: The Pulp/Modernist Nexus

Considering the great pace of production and sheer volume of the pulps—a literary production unequalled in history—it is possible to see the pulp magazine as a type of hyper-production. Both the speed with which they were written and the speed with which they tried to appeal to certain market niches guaranteed that they quickly reflected the tastes and composition of not only the mass market, but all aspects of society. Though much of pulp fiction certainly demanded a suspension of both disbelief and criticism on the part of the reader, it was far from apolitical, as Adorno and Horkheimer would contend. There were aspects of social and political criticism at work within the pulp formulas, as well as aspects of modernist aesthetics.

I would like to put this idea of the pulps as a literary catchall in another critical light than that of Adorno and Horkheimer: if we consider the academy, and more specifically English studies, with its qualitative and scientific process of canonization, as a manifestation of the power structure in the Foucauldian sense,

---

[79] See Peter Osbourne in "Adorno and the Metaphysics of Modernism: The Problem of a 'Postmodern' Art" in Andrew Benjamin, ed., *The Problems of Modernity* (NY: Routledge, 1989), 35–39.

then I am considering the pulp form as subjugated knowledge, a literature at the extremity where those dynamics of subjugation, as well as social dynamics in general, are made apparent. My contention in examining the pulps for aspects of modernism is not that the same depths and nuances of artistic, political, and psychological sophistication are common, but that those forces are present albeit in a popular or processed form, and that the pulp form as a historical gauge is overlooked. If it is possible to find commonalities with elite modernism, the pulp form's constructed opposite, then the historic artistic disavowal of the pulps must come under revision. The pulps offer a spectrum of literary and historic value. Due to their pure variety and volume, they are an extremely efficient meter of popular and social currents; they illustrate all manners of contradictions, levels of culture, and literary worth.

It is worth stating, again, that I am not contending that there is merit for a *"Norton Anthology of Pulp Fiction,"* or that the majority of pulp writing was more than turgid and formulaic, full of misogyny, racial and sexual stereotypes, and xenophobia so apparent on hundreds of pulp covers (especially those of the "shudder pulps"), but that literature of all types and quality were published in pulps, from the best to the worst—just as there were all types and quality of modernist literature including misogynistic and racist. It is its very extremity that makes pulp production valuable as a meter of modernist growth. Pulp magazines are so obviously on the opposite side of the literary scale from elite modernism that any dynamics contained in the pulps that embody or approach the dynamics of capital "L" Literature logically work against the mandarin nature of monolithic modernism as well as against the reductive definition of popular literature. There is little denying that some of the more purple passages of D.H. Lawrence, say, approach the excruciating prose of much pulp fiction, just as some passages of Hammett approach the terseness or experimentation of the modernists. What emerges then is a multileveled scale of interinfluences and similarities.

It is true that elite modernism defined itself against mass literature, but we should be circumspect about stopping there, about reaffirming the autonomy of high art. Horkheimer and Adorno state in "The Culture Industry" that "Light art has always been the shadow of autonomous art. It is the social bad conscience of serious art. The truth that the latter necessarily lacked because of its social premises gives the other the semblance of legitimacy. The division itself is the truth: it does at least express negativity of the culture, which the different spheres constitute. Least of all can the antithesis be reconciled by absorbing light into serious art or vice versa."[80] There is a disturbing underlying avowal of natural elitism and intellectualism in "*necessarily* lacked because of its *social premises*"; Horkheimer and Adorno would seem simultaneously to be allowing overlap between the poles, and disavowing any importance except the hierarchy itself. Their take on the culture industry here is seemingly black and white, odd for the inventors of negative dialectic. It is indeed possible, as I propose to illustrate, to reconcile these poles between high and low culture, for the pulps in actuality were

---

[80] Adorno, 135.

the *popularized* version of the dynamics and tensions of modernism in the public sphere; the pulp form was modernism consumable for the masses. It is possible to see many elements of avant-garde modernism in the pulp form, hence its efficacy as a foil for categorization and hierarchy.

Such a statement is difficult to defend, for much of the literature of the pulp genre is lacking (on the surface) many of the fundamental criteria of modernism, difficulty and experimentation of form being the most obvious. Indeed, one of the defining aspects of modernist art is its commitment to a worldly disillusionment, a refusal of standardized plots and utopian portrayals of the modern condition. The pulps, on the other hand, largely relied upon formula, cliché plots and characterizations, rudimentary prose, and happy endings. And, again, that is the foundation of my argument: if the pulps as a form of intrinsically oppositional literature can harbor integral aspects of modernism—including stylistic experimentation, then the simplistic hierarchies and definitions of modernism that have arisen from modern criticism begin to unravel. In pulp plots, the hero, against insurmountable odds, won the girl and vanquished the villain hordes. But before this happened, there were often glimpses of a purely modern world of technological dangers, of dark and mean streets, urban bleakness, the horrors of war, cruelty unimaginable. The images of the world that the pulps painted were often darker than any envisioned by Eliot; it was the portrait of a society unwinding.

Many of these writers experimented with, emulated, and graduated to not only the slick magazines, but high modernism as well. There are many examples of this overlap between the pulp form and modernism. Frank Gruber was one pulp author who was a frustrated aspiring literary author. Describing his descent into pulpdom, he wrote, "But by that time I had become a young intellectual and when I began writing again I was reading *Literature* with a capital L. I wrote stories and submitted them to magazines like the old *Smart Set*, *Atlantic Monthly*, and *Scribner's Magazine*. They were all rejected and I thought that I would lower my sights and try the more popular magazines, *The Saturday Evening Post*, *Collier's*, that type of trash. They wanted none of me and I found myself, at the age of twenty-two, with the ambition to write burning more brightly than ever, but nowhere to go [except the pulps]."[81] Frederick Schiller Faust is another such writer: he started as a poet, but adopted the pen name Max Brand and turned to writing popular fiction solely for income. Brand is the avowed king of the pulps, with 600 magazine publications and 900 copyrights, all of which earned him an Italian villa in which to pump out stories about the American West.[82] Yet he often referred to his pulp stories as pure trash. What he really cared about was his poetry, of which he published two books under his real name: *The Village Street and Other Poems* (Putnam 1922) and *Dionysus in Hades* (Blackwell 1931). In 1917, at the beginning of his career, Faust wrote, "At present I really care deeply for nothing but art. Don't laugh yourself to death. I mean what I say. *A-R-T!* In spite of the

---

[81] Gruber, 7–8.
[82] Tuska, xiii.

labors of Max Brand."[83] When William Rose Benét reviewed *The Village Street* in *Literary Review*, he wrote, "Here is a small book by a new poet. Delicate strength is in this book and vivid description. It is something to discover a modern writer so sensitive to the effectiveness of simplicity and clarity."[84] Whereas Brand was a pulp cash cow, Faust was a frequenter of Robert Campbell's bookshop and part of its literary circle, a fan of Joyce who drank and talked writing with Faulkner in Hollywood.[85]

Even more telling is the fact that many late modernist writers started in the pulps. For example, Tennessee Williams's first published short story was "The Vengeance of Nitocris," in a 1928 *Weird Tales* magazine.[86] Williams later said it was a "prelude to the violence which is considered my trademark."[87] Kenneth Fearing tried his hand at the hard-boiled thriller and initially published short stories in *Live Wire* in 1925. Robert Coates, future editor of *transition* (who I'll return to later), published in *Telling Tales*. As we have seen from Mencken and Nathan's pulp reliance described in the first chapter, there was an economic patronage. Besides Mencken and Nathan, other elite authors lived off the pulps as well: Sinclair Lewis was assistant editor of *Adventure*, just as Theodore Dreiser was earlier a staff writer for *Ainslee's* and editor of *Smith's Magazine,* two pulp prototypes.[88] The Jamaican author, W. Adolphe Roberts, a member of the Greenwhich Village set whose poems appeared alongside those of Djuna Barnes in 1920, was editor of both *Ainslee's* and, later, the pulp *Brief Stories* where he "discovered" and first published Edna St. Vincent Millay under the penname Nancy Boyd. As noted earlier, both Dawn Powell and Djuna Barnes published initially in the early all-fiction pulpwood magazines such as *All-Story* and *Snappy*.

The Pulps as Social and Political Conscience

One of the most uniform and damning criticisms against popular fiction is the seeming lack of social and political agenda in mass entertainment. The Frankfurt school considered mass entertainment as depoliticizing the working class, quelling abstract thought. The academy has disavowed the pulp genre as light, disposable. Many pulp editors and writers thought as much themselves, stating that their intention, if any, was purely to entertain. Yet many modernist authors, most notably Faulkner, made the same claim. The pulps held cultural and political criticism submerged, sometimes extremely subtly, within their pages.

---

[83] Tuska, 19.

[84] Quentin Reynolds, *The Fiction Factory* (NY: Random House, 1955), 180.

[85] On Brand and Joyce, see Reynolds, 183; on Brand and Faulkner, see Blotner, *Faulkner, A Biography* (NY: Vintage, 1984), 444.

[86] Tom Leverich, *Tom: The Unknown Tennessee Williams* (NY: Crown, 1995) 80–81; Williams's first publication was a fictional letter for a 1927 issue of *Smart Set.*

[87] Tony Goodstone, *The Pulps* (NY: Chelsea, 1970), 165.

[88] Goulart, 34; Reynolds, 150–151.

There is no better exploration of the political overtones in a pulp genre than Sean McCann's deftly written *Gumshoe America*, which concentrates on the emergence of the hard-boiled genre as a popular form of political and social criticism. In his first three chapters, McCann looks closely at the rise of the hard-boiled genre's populist voice and ethos as a critique of the Ku Klux Klan in the pages of *Black Mask* in 1923; at Dashiell Hammett's use of the popular detective genre as a venue for his own political "critique of liberalism"; and Raymond Chandler's aesthetic tensions between high and low art, which reflected a New Deal optimism/ pessimism. In general, the hard-boiled genre, Hammett, and Chandler have been exhaustively written about with much of the criticism exploring and building their relationships to literary modernism. In fact, of all the genres that grew out of pulps, it is the hard-boiled school that has garnered the most academic attention, exactly because it contains defined characteristics of monolithic modernism: it is cynical, urban, highly unsentimental, ardently masculine, and psychologically aware, it contains destabilized temporal and narrative structures, etc. Though still disregarding the larger pulp market, McCann's study works against the reductive modernist criticism of the pulps. Horkheimer and Adorno's claim was that cultural criticism didn't exist in the ineffectual and banal form of mass literature, a blanket disavowal of the culture industry— a stance that is underwritten by an intellectual effetism and a belief that true (high) culture offers a critique of capitalism. Adorno's statement that moments of slippage just prove the rule ("Least of all can the antithesis be reconciled by absorbing light into serious art or vice versa") falls short when standing outside such hierarchies, or when considering both the elitism of high culture and the shallowness of the popular form as constructions. Moments of political and cultural criticism as they existed in the pulps illustrate this.

Both McCann and Erin Smith describe how pulp magazines marketed themselves as based upon reader feedback in their letter columns—in this sense creating a symbiotic supply-and-demand relationship between reader and magazine. As I have formerly hinted, the relationship that the pulps had with their readers, whether a means of commercial pandering or not, had a dynamic like that of the public sphere, as illustrated in 1923 in the pages of *Black Mask* magazine.

Black Mask, the last of the "louse" pulps that Mencken started in order to subsidize the *Smart Set*, was initially, as its first issue claimed in 1920, "An Illustrated Magazine of Detective, Mystery, Adventure, Romance, and Spiritualism," but by 1923 this byline had been pared down to "Romantic Adventure, Mystery and Detective Stories."[89] And that was not all that was being pared down: the focus of the magazine was just beginning its move from parlor detective stories to the taut, colloquial, ultra-masculine and violent hard-boiled school of fiction.[90] It is

---

[89] William F. Nolan, *The Black Mask Boys* (NY: Mysterious, 1985), 20.

[90] Most critics cite the publication of Carroll John Daly's "The False Burton Combs," in the December issue of 1922, or his first Race Williams story, "Knight of the Open Palm," in June 1923, as the first hard-boiled story, but earlier, in the September 1922 issue, *Black Mask* was already streamlining its look and focus to darker, more psychological fiction. This issue marked many firsts: it was the first to carry editor blurbs before the stories, the first issue with George Sutton Jr. as editor, the first issue featuring Rose's art deco illustrations,

generally taken for granted that neither Mencken nor Nathan had anything to do with the magazine after they sold it to Warner and Crowe in 1921, but there is evidence that Mencken still had a hand in editing it through 1922—just as he had "advised" the editing of *Saucy Stories* and the *Parisienne* after selling those magazines. The fingerprints of Mencken can be found all over the early issues of *Black Mask* in ludicrous pen names and epigrams, and the fact remains that authors, most notably Hammett but also less known authors such as Carl Glick, appeared simultaneously in the *Smart Set, Saucy Stories,* and *Black Mask* well into the 20s.[91] There is also a more ineffable influence in how Mencken's stable of writers affected (even by second and third generations) the tone of the future publications. This interdependence is a fact that has long been studiously ignored by literary critics and historians devoted to either Mencken or detective studies alike, due again to that impassable border between highbrow and pulp.

Over the latter half of 1923, starting with the June 1 issue, *Black Mask* ran numerous stories and reader's letters devoted to the ongoing national debate over the Ku Klux Klan (see Figure 2.5).[92] As McCann points out, this was undeniably a marketing ploy used to cash in on one of the hot topics of the day, and ultimately, it worked—the response in the letter columns and the sporadic stories about the Klan continued for months. Whereas the "forum added little to this national debate over the Klan," it undeniably offered a venue to a public whose voice was not often heard. In this sense, the pulps were empowering to their readership.[93] The magazine itself took a stance of unbiased nonjudgment (a good policy with such a heated topic), and published stories both pro and con. The magazine's position, McCann hints, can be explained by *Black Mask*'s embattled stance as a pulp magazine: closer to the masses, a popular subculture fighting against corporate power, against the bourgeois magazines of popular opinion, the corruptions of "newspapers, ministers, and lawyers."[94] Whereas this rhetoric echoed that of the Klan, according to McCann, "The hard-boiled fiction created by Daly and

---

and, perhaps most importantly, the first story by Daly, entitled "Dolly"—a story that shows surprising psychological sophistication. According to the blurb that followed the story, "...with this number, Black Mask is beginning the publication of a new type of stories. It will continue to print fascinating, clever detective and mystery tales, which have proved so popular with readers. In addition, it will use other stories – like 'Dolly' and several others in this issue – that are founded on the deepest human emotion."

[91] Hammett's first published piece for the *Smart Set*, "The Parthian Shot," appeared in the October, 1922, his last, "The Green Elephant," in October of 1923; in between he published four times in *Black Mask*. He also published in *Saucy Stories* in October of 1923. His publications for both the *Smart Set* and *Saucy Stories* ended at the same time that Mencken severed his relationship with Warner, which leads me to believe that Mencken had more say in the content of *Black Mask,* hence in the formation of hard-boiled than hitherto thought. For information on Carl Glick's (who wrote mystery reviews for *Black Mask*) relationship with the *Smart Set* and the Mencken pulps, see the Glick collection, University of Iowa.

[92] *Black Mask*'s interest in the Klan can be seen as early as February of 1922, though no story inside seems to have the Klan as subject matter.

[93] Sean McCann, *Gumshoe America* (Durham: Duke U P, 2000), 44.

[94] Quoted in McCann, 56.

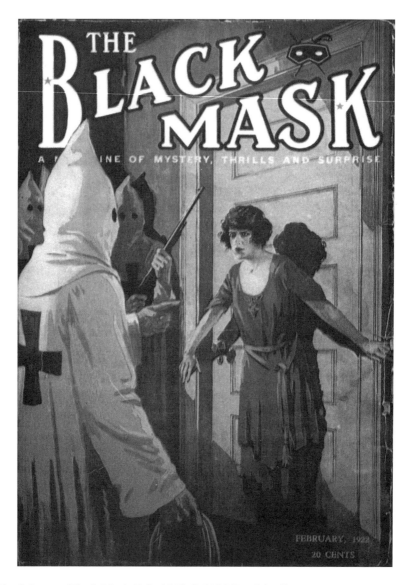

Fig. 2.5   *Black Mask*, Feb. 1922 © 1922 Pro-Distributers

Hammett suggested a deep skepticism about such a historical regression [to a pre-corporate economic order], though, and that skepticism can be traced in good part to the doubtfulness that these writers implied about the ideal of native community that supported the Klan's version of Republicanism" (and, I would add, Mencken's lingering influence).[95]

---

[95] Ibid.

Dashiell Hammett's writing especially resists claims of pulpish unsophistication. According to McCann, Hammett saw himself as something of an intellectual elitist who knew the necessity of instructing the masses through simplicity and clarity, of fighting the dangers of Klannish nativism and modern corruption, and he felt that the perfect means to do so was through a popular form—in fact by elevating that popular form—though I would argue that such an attitude developed later, after he learned the ropes by writing in the pulps. For Hammett, "The growing importance of the distinction between art and commercial entertainment thus became ... at once galling and enabling ...[His concerns] were Menckenian. He was consistently preoccupied with the distortions and dangers of what he later referred to as 'popular belief,' and he suggested that it was up to a vanguard of adventurous artists and intellectuals to overcome the baleful effects of 'common sense.'"[96] This bolsters the often-resisted idea that Mencken's iconoclastic stance greatly influenced the eventual socially conscious tone of the hard-boiled *Black Mask* via his stable of *Smart Set* writers who eloped to the pulps.[97] Hammett's fiction offers acute commentary on both popular politics and elite society. Writing about *The Dain Curse* (serialized in *Black Mask*, Nov. 1928—Feb. 1929), McCann points out that it is "as if the two sides of Hammett's authorial persona, the pulpster and the ironic modernist, were doing battle."[98]

Hammett's peripheral position with modernism has long been a standard for critics, just as, during his lifetime, he was the guilty pleasure for modernists—Gertrude Stein admitted to being a fan, as did Dorothy Parker, and Andre Gide called him, along with Faulkner, the greatest American writer of the time.[99] What has kept him out of the bastion of high modernists is only his (easy) accessibility, his chosen popular form. Hence Hammett is arguably a modernist in everything *but* reputation, a modernist outside the traditionally reductive definition, what Mark McGurl calls "the shadow modernist."[100] One element of Hammett's modernist aesthetics, explored in both McCann's book and McGurl's article, "Making 'Literature' of It: Hammett and High Culture," is the reflexive quality of his work, how Hammett's subjects and plots reflect the author's own art, the shortcomings of representation, and Hammett's own failure to bring to terms the polarities of his

---

[96] Ibid., 93–94.

[97] Case in point: in response to my request for access to some early *Black Mask*'s held by a Mencken collector, he wrote to me that these had nothing whatsoever to do with Mencken. Again, the unbroachable border between the pulps and highbrow literature.

[98] McCann, 113.

[99] When asked whom she would like to meet on a trip to New York City in 1934, Gertrude Stein singled out Hammett; see George Plimpton, *The Writer's Chapbook* (NY: Penguin, 1989), 349–350; Mark McGurl, "Making 'Literature' of It: Hammett and High Culture," *American Literary History*, Vol. 9, Issue 4 (Winter 1997), 706.

[100] McGurl, 714.

elite stance and populist agenda.¹⁰¹ The lead statue of the Maltese falcon represents *The Maltese Falcon*, ultimately an empty commodity: at the end of the book Spade is unable to communicate with Effie Perrin, and in life Hammett retreats from his art, frustrated.¹⁰² *The Maltese Falcon*, written for and conforming to the standards of the pulp magazine, should unquestionably be the insipid product of the culture industry in Horkheimer and Adorno's schema, yet in actuality it approaches their ideals of art. For Adorno, the work of art must portray stylistically the alienation of the subject in the modern world. Stylistics in Adorno's vision offers a critical distance from reality via dialectic—the gap or failure between reality and portrayal.¹⁰³ Considering Hammett's self-reflexive tension in *The Maltese Falcon* between resolution, subsequent failure, and conscious impossibility of portrayal, then does not the novel approach great art? Adorno and Horkheimer state, "The great artists were never those who embodied a wholly flawless and perfect style, but those who used style as a way of hardening themselves against the chaotic expression of suffering, as a negative truth."¹⁰⁴ This sounds to me like an excellent description of the hard-boiled style as Hammett saw and used it, despite what it later (d)evolved into with other writers such as Mickey Spillane.

Such dialectic tensions are likewise brought to bear in Raymond Chandler's fiction from *Black Mask*, but whereas Hammett took the high road, Chandler reveled in muddying his feet. For Chandler, the pulp form suited his pragmatic socialist leaning perfectly: he saw it as a wellspring for the poetry of the masses, rife with slang and creative exuberance. Chandler's fiction contains a reoccurring sense of loss for an idyllic working class brotherhood in opposition to the corrupt elite and powerful, such as degenerate old money families and crooked police or politicians, reflecting the author's search for balance between true representation and economic exploitation, as well as, according to McCann, the ideal of the New Deal Public Works and the corrupt monopolies that they might lead to. Chandler, McCann writes, "was a sentimental populist, and the core preoccupation of his work was the effort to hold onto an ever-fading democratic legitimacy." ¹⁰⁵

Referring to the self-reflexive style of Hammett and Chandler, McCann writes, "Driven by ambitions that they felt certain could not be realized, the major hard-boiled writers became, in effect, pulp avant-gardists – figures whose determination to overcome the limits of intractable cultural institutions could be measured by their willingness to embrace failure."¹⁰⁶ The political ethos and subagenda of either Hammett or Chandler should come as no surprise, though, to either readers

---

[101] James Naremore also identifies the self-reflexive vein in Hammett's writing. See Benstock, *Art in Crime Writing* (NY: St. Martin's, 1983), 54.

[102] See, for example, William Marling, *Roman Noir*, 39–92.

[103] See Haslett, *Marxist Literary and Cultural Theories* (NY: St. Martin's, 2000), 100–101.

[104] Adorno, 130.

[105] McCann, again, see 149.

[106] Ibid., 4.

or historians of American depression era literature. Due to the shared dynamics between the hard-boiled genre and modernism (urban growth, immigration, governmental and corporate distrust and corruption), finding such instances of depth and criticism in the hard-boiled genre is easy; hence the large amount of critical material devoted to it.[107]

Nor are Chandler and Hammett the only instances of political radicalism alive in the pulp form. Bruno Fischer, for example, turned to the pulps after writing for literary magazines and working as editor of *The Socialist Call*, the official publication of the Socialist Party, neither of which paid. He initially wrote for the bizarre shudder pulps, but eventually turned to detective stories. He took the proletariat hero to an extreme: he made a name for himself by creating detectives who were deformed or handicapped, such as Calvin Kane, called the 'Crab Detective" because of his useless and withered legs. Like Chandler, many of his detective stories feature corrupt politicians, district attorneys, or police, and support working class solidarity. For example, in "I'll Slay You in My Dreams" (*Dime Detective Magazine* 1944), a down-and-out ex-soldier is framed for the kidnapping and murder of a wealthy socialite. Though there are obvious holes in the case against him, neither the D.A. nor the chief of police care, intent only on closing the case to further their careers. Only a sergeant believes the narrator's innocence, saying, "Me, I've been on the force for nineteen years. I'll never be more than a sergeant. My eyes aren't clouded by ambition."[108] With the sergeant's help, the narrator proves that it is the socialite's powerful husband who committed the crime.

The connections between "tough guy" fiction and proletariat literature of the 1930s should be obvious. David Madden's companion volumes, *Tough Guy Writers of the Thirties* and *Proletarian Writers of the Thirties* (both 1968), intrinsically tie the two styles together, as well as go a long way toward saving the genres from disrepute—the hard-boiled style from its 1950s descent into Spillane-style, ultraviolent and misogynistic sensationalism, and the Proletarian novel from the blemish of its McCarthy-era disavowal. The novels of Farrell, West, Wright, Cain, McCoy, and even Hemingway and Dos Passos blur the lines between modernism, realism-naturalism, and pulpism. The long-standing debate within radicalism—whether populist, socialist, or Marxist—about the role/benefits of mass-culture, which stems from the years before World War I, ignores the pulp magazine as efficiently as does that debate between modernism and mass-culture. Yet the fact remains that the pulps were an outlet for numerous radical writers who were seeking a popular venue for their views. This is especially true with science fiction and socialism.

---

[107] See James Naremore's and Leon Arden's chapters on Hammett and Chandler respectively in Benstock.

[108] See Stefan R. Dziemianowicz, Martin H. Greenberg, and Robert Weinberg, eds. *Hard-Boiled Detectives* (NY: Gramercy, 1992), 317.

Science fiction, of course, has a long history of gestation and antecedents, but the rise of modern, pulp science fiction, which concerns us here, has been seen by some as a "previously unrecognized form of American modernism."[109] Eric Miles Drown, for one, finds many parallels in the formative science fiction of the Hugo Gernsback magazines with modernism, stating:

> Gernsback-era science fiction concerned itself with precisely the same problems as other modernisms. It conceived of the present as the very cusp of history, the moment when the past stopped being meaningful and the path of the future was determined. It granted fame and fortune, authority and prestige to culture makers, celebrating as heroes people who created new knowledge, and new ways of domesticating nature. It found meaning not in the divine but in the supreme fiction, that is, in the act of narration. It appropriated the symbolic material of the past, fragmented it, and reassembled it using the powerful formal features of the pulp narrative to give it coherence.[110]

Furthermore, these early magazines acted as an intellectual training ground or public sphere for preparing readers for modern technology and thought. Drown contends that, "To young, technically minded Americans busy finding their place in a highly ordered, but nevertheless confusing industrial economy, science fiction offered a powerful fantasy of individual agency just at the time wage earners were being denied precisely such agency."[111]

The suspension of belief that is innate to science fiction offered a venue to modernists for a stylistic freeing, an opportunity for dadaist binding of high- and lowbrow ephemera. Robert Coates's *Eater of Darkness,* for example, is rife with both pulp and modernist allusions even before the book itself starts—it is dedicated to, among others, the dime novel and pulp detective Nick Carter; "Sapper"—the pseudonym for H.C. McNeille, author of the highly successful Bulldog Drummond stories; Gertrude Stein; publisher Robert McAlmon; Harold Loeb; and Fantomas, the French fictional psychopath and arch villain. The novel itself waffles between pulpish mystery and *Ulysses*-inspired surrealism. It is about Charles Dograr, a modernist artist recently returned to New York City from Paris, who stumbles upon a scientist who has invented an x-ray gun that can look through objects thousands of yards away and send an invisible x-ray bullet. Together they start a killing spree—the "Radio Murders"—across the city. Victims even include (popular) literary critics Heywood Broun, Waldo Frank, Henry Seidl Canby, Asa Huddleberry, James Thurber, and George Jean Nathan. At one point, in a three-page tour de force, Coates lists the objects the x-ray machine looks through, such as:

---

[109] See Eric Mills Drown, *Usable Futures, Disposable Paper: Popular Science, Pulp Science Fiction and Modernization in America, 1908–1937* (Unpublished Dissertation, University of Minnesota, December 2001), 17.

[110] Ibid., 28.

[111] Ibid., 30.

a bottle of glue, [...] the mechanism of an alarm clock, [...] three pages of the Graphic, the hand of the readers, an orange, [...] two kissing lips, [...] a glass eye, two felt slippers, the C in a Chop Suey sign [...] Reginald Marsh [artist of NYC life], a bottle of gin, an art-bronze book-rack, Theodore Dreiser, a clogged drain pipe, a sheaf of Shulte Cigar Store coupons, H.L. Mencken, a stiletto, Kenneth Burke, a stethoscope, a Martini cocktail, [...] a copy of Ranch Romances, [...] the tassel on a lady's garter, Malcolm Cowley [...][112]

Besides the interplay and dichotomy between objects and persons (i.e., any subtle commentary between the pairings of Marsh and gin, Dreiser and a clogged pipe, or Mencken and stiletto), the seemingly randomness led Ford Madox Ford to call *The Eater of Darkness* "not the first but the best Dada novel."[113] And the novel's style follows a similar pattern of cultural contrast shifting between stylistic innovation (such as listing, conflation of news story and readers thoughts, reader disorientation) and pulp clichés. In the chapter "Tangled Trails," reminiscent of Joyce's "Nausicaa" episode, Coates writes in the purple style of a detective pulp story, replete with the single paragraph plot summary that always started serialized stories, Oriental villains, and poisonous snakes.

Though *The Eater of Darkness* is a "lost" modernist novel, a (very) few critics have looked at it in terms of its ties to Dadaism and to the fact that it was initially published in 1926 by McAlmon's Contact Press, or to that fact that Coates was a protégé of Stein and became the art critic for *The New Yorker*, but few have considered how he started as a pulp writer—his earliest publication in a 1924 issue of *Telling Tales*—and how this in turn influenced his more "modernist" novels.[114] He would soon write a highly successful book about the American West, *The Outlaw Years* (1930), something that is perhaps presaged by his inclusion of *Ranch Romances* in his list of x-rayed items. Regardless, his familiarity with the pulp form and reliance upon science fiction is central to his modernism.

Before the pulps, the utopian aspect of science fiction lent itself to the ideals of Bolshevism. In 1908, Alexander Bogdanov published *Red Star*, a novel that describes a socialist utopia on Mars. Later Granville Hicks, critic for the *New Masses*, published *The First to Awaken: A Novel of the Year 2040*, and V.F. Calverton, editor of the Marxist/Freudian critical journal, the *Modern Monthly*, wrote *The Man Inside: Being the Record of the Strange Adventures of Alien Steele among the Xulus* (1936). Of authors that published in the pulps, James

---

[112] Robert M. Coates, *The Eater of Darkness* (NY: Macauley, 1929) 29–32.

[113] Quoted in review in *Time Magazine*, Monday, August 5, 1929.

[114] I have only found two articles that mention *The Eater of Darkness*: Constance Peirce's "Gertrude Stein and her Thoroughly Modern Protege," *Modern Fiction Studies*, Vol. 42, No. 3 (1996) and "Language, Silence, Laughter: The Silent Film and the 'Eccentric' Modernist Writer," *Substance*, Vol. 16, No. 1, Issue 52 (1987). Coates is also one of the subjects of Robert Caserio's "Queer Passions, Queer Citizenship: Some Novels about the State of the American Nation 1946–1954," *Modern Fiction Studies*, Vol. 43, No.1 (Spring 1997).

Blish recounts: "in America in the 1930s quite a number of SF authors were sympathetic towards socialism, and one group in New York City, the Futurian Society, was formed exclusively for those who were either actual members of the communist party or espoused the Party's policies. Later the barriers were lowered a little to admit Trotskyites as well as Stalinists. The aim of the group, proclaimed publicly at a World-Con by John B. Michel [Michel published under the name Hugh Raymond] with a pamphlet to back him up, was to use SF to help bring about what they believed to be *the* future. They wrote and published SF stories with this intent."[115] This group included such prolific pulp authors (and members of the Young Communist League) as Donald Wollheim, Frederick Pohl, and Isaac Asimov. Many depression-era radical writers turned to the pulps as a vehicle once they found themselves alienated by the working class' craving for popular culture.[116] The Futurian Society wonderfully illustrates the type of grass roots communal fan-based pulp organization that considered itself a subculture, an alternative sphere, spawned by amateur fanzines as well as the pulps. They reflect perfectly the independent and alternative attitude held by the readers, writers, and editors of pulp magazines.

Even before the Futurian society was George Henry Rice, who wrote for the pulps under the name Francis Flagg. As Rice he wrote poetry for the *Daily Worker*, among other outlets, and was affiliated with the proletarian literature movement of the 1930s; as Flagg he published in *Amazing Stories* and *Weird Tales*. Less staunchly affiliated authors, such as the mechanical engineer Stanley Weinbaum, also took advantage of other worlds as case-scenarios of idealist politics. In "Valley of Dreams" (first published in *Wonder Stories* in 1934, and again in *Startling Stories* in 1940), Weinbaum describes Mars as a planet culturally advanced enough that their political system is utopian anarchism; Martians have "evolved, socially at least, to the point where they don't need government. They work together, that's all."[117] Jarvis, the narrator of the story, speaking to the space ship's crew that consists of members of autocratic, democratic, and communist societies on Earth, ruminates, "Queer isn't it – as if Mother Nature were carrying on two experiments, one at home and one on Mars. On Earth it's trial of an emotional, highly competitive race in a world of plenty; here it's the trial of a quiet, friendly race on a desert, unproductive, and inhospitable world. Everything here makes for cooperation." To which one of the crewmembers mutters, "'But Anarchy! ... It would show up on a dizzy, half dead pill like Mars.'" Weinbaum reflexively offers a juxtaposition to this utopian vision with one of Earthly excess embodied in a hallucination of moral anarchy inherent in the unchecked production of entertainment. The spacemen

---

[115] See R.D. Mullen and Darko Suvin, eds., *Science Fiction Studies* (Boston: Gregg Press, 1976), 51.

[116] There are plenty of histories of the futurians, but the most exhaustive is perhaps that of Damon Knight.

[117] Stanley G. Weinbaum, *A Martian Odyssey and Others* (Reading: Fantasy Press, 1949), 47.

stumble upon a valley of creatures that read others' deepest desires and use them to lure their victims to their death. The "dream-beasts," as they were called, show Jarvis all his desires: "'[the valley contained] Every good impulse, yes—but also every nasty little wish, every vicious thought, everything you'd ever desired, good or bad! The dream-beasts are marvelous salesmen, but they lack the moral sense! [We saw] even the forgotten [desires] that must have been drawn out of my subconscious. A Paradise – of sorts! ... I saw every beautiful woman I've ever known, and all of them pleading for my attention. I saw every lovely place I've wanted to be ... And I saw—other things.' He shook his head soberly. 'It wasn't all exactly pretty. Lord! How much of the beast is left in us! I suppose that if every man alive could have one look in that weird valley, and could see just once what nastiness is hidden in him—well, the world might gain by it.'"[118] In this story, and in its predecessor, "A Martian Odyssey," Weinbaum is said to offer the first sympathetic portrait of an alien, which reflects his own trailblazing against anti-Semitism in the pulp-publishing world of the 1930s.[119] Weinbaum published under his own name whereas most authors with Jewish-sounding names usually had to resort to pseudonyms to get published.

Pulp fiction and the ideals of a literature for the proletariat envisioned by socialist magazines such as *The Masses* seem a world apart. In histories of the little magazines *The Masses* is seen as the best balance of modernist avant-garde and political radicalism, even though it often came under fire as being too rarefied to truly appeal to the masses. Its initial byline stated: "A monthly magazine devoted to the interests of the working people," yet it was predominately written and published by middle-class socialists. As Genevieve Taggard puts it, "although [the magazine] did talk in a very specific and realistic tone of voice about the proletariat, it did not talk *to* the proletariat. Scoffers said, rightly enough: They draw nude women for *The Masses*, / Thick, fat, ungainly lasses— / How does that help the working classes?"[120] *The Masses* came under criticism by workers and other radicals alike for being elitist and bohemian, the writers and artists as just producing a magazine only for their own Greenwich Village coterie.[121]

The working class, on the other hand, undoubtedly read pulp magazines. As pulps grew into a type of proletariat subculture during the depression, certain magazines would approach socialist ideals closer than radical, avant-garde little magazines could, at least in praxis, if not by overt intention. Erin Smith points out, "A number of pulp magazines between the wars formalized their appeal to working men and women by sporting what amounted to union labels. Street and Smith's

---

[118] Ibid., 49–50.

[119] Sam Moskowitz, "The Marketing of Stanley G. Weinbaum," *Fantasy Commentator* (Fall, 1991), 107.

[120] Quoted in Fishebin, *Rebels in Bohemia: The Radicals of The Masses, 1911–1917* (Chapel Hill: U NC P, 1982), 184.

[121] See Morrisson, 188–195, and Zuhrier, *Art for The Masses* (Philadelphia: Temple U P, 1988), 65.

The Shadow: A Detective Magazine prominently featured the statement 'This magazine produced entirely by union labor' on its front cover in the early '30s, reassuring workers that their hard-earned cents would not be used to employ scabs. The title page of many Clayton publications, such as *Ranch Romances* and *Clues* went even further, pledging that its stories had been 'purchased under conditions approved by the Author's League of America,' that the magazines were 'manufactured in Union shops by American workmen,' and that 'each news dealer and agent is insured a fair profit.'"[122] It is doubtful that this mantle of popular front politics was just the absorption of the earlier radicalism espoused by *The Masses* into mainstream culture. I have already pointed out the feeling of fierce independence shared by pulps' creators and audience, of a reader's camaraderie based upon persecution by "established" literary tastes and forms, by the bourgeoisie: what McCann calls a "fraternal intimacy."[123] And stories such as "Legions of Starvation," from the December 1934 issue of *Operator #5* (see Figure 2.6), addressed proletariat concerns during the depression of corrupt government and food shortages, albeit in a manner more fitting to parable than pulp:

> Over the whole continent, little children clung whimpering to the skirts of distraught mothers, crying piteously for food. One of the most brilliant men in America, a national figure – backed by a powerful, efficient organization – drunk on ambition and the promise of supreme power, controlled all the reserve supplies of land. Hosts of voracious insects, bred at his command, were laying the plains waste, devouring all green things. Incendiarism and looting daily depleted the shrinking store of government-owned foodstuffs. The Four Horsemen of the Apocalypse laughed in their saddles as they thundered their mocking call of doom—forewarning the slavery of a once proud race of men. One man alone – Jimmy Christopher – can check their wild onslaught. Only he, Operator 5, can outwit the madman monarch.[124]

Other pulps, like *Popular Detective*, featured heroes displaced by the depression, such as Milton Lowe's Bagdad the hobo detective. In "Death Rides the Silver Streak" (August 1938), Bagdad must find out who murdered his fellow hobo; given the backdrop of postpanic America, it is no surprise that the culprit is a banker who was after $500,000 in securities. As pulp historians John Locke and John Wooley put it, such stories are "both romanticizing of and a show of empathy for all of those men thrown out of work by forces beyond their control and forced to ride boxcars, sleep in hobo jungles, and consist on the kindness of those better off. Not surprisingly, the fat cats – particularly bankers, tycoons and other members of the privileged classes – usually don't come off very sympathetic."[125]

---

[122] Smith, 23–24.

[123] McCann, 52.

[124] Quoted in Goodstone, lvii–liix, and also available as a Girasol pulp reprint (Mississauga, Ontario: Girasol, 2006).

[125] John Locke and John Wooley, *Thrilling Detective Stories* (Silver Spring, MD: Adventure House, 2007), 109.

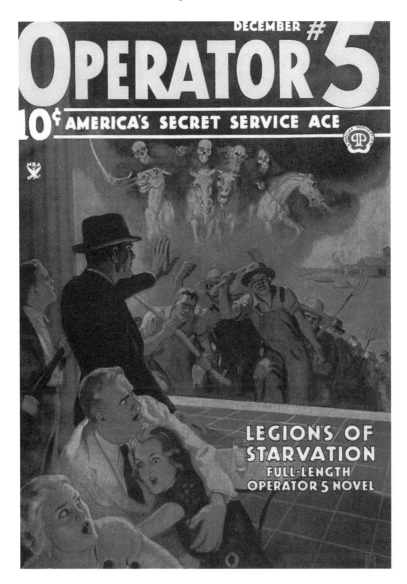

Fig. 2.6   *Operator #5*, Dec. 1934 © 1934 Popular Publications, image supplied by Girasol Collectibles

Mark Morrisson has commented upon *The Masses'* movement from leftist radicalism toward aesthetic modernism and modern marketing, as illustrated by its increasingly commercial cover art. A magazine's cover acts as its most important and rudimentary form of advertisement, and *The Masses'* use of stylized portraits of actresses and women on their covers, in other words, nonagendized illustrations, in order to attract an audience, parallels radical writers masking their agendas behind popular genre and pulp fiction. Indeed, there are some striking similarities between *The Masses* and the pulps: covers such as John Sloan's depiction of the Ludlow, Colorado riots has a certain pulpish feel, as do the expressionist covers of Ilanka Karasz or Frank Waltz, which parallel those by Rose for *Black Mask* in the early 1920s. Likewise, the proletariat boxing sketches of George Bellows foretells the covers of *Jack Dempsey's Fight Magazine* or *Knockout;* the January 1914 cover illustration of the Boer wars eerily parallels those from *Adventure* or *Blue Book*. Such comparisons may seem specious, until one realizes that *The Masses* was distributed alongside the early pulps: as the magazine itself pointed out, it was "on sale at news stands in 400 cities in the United States and Canada. In New York it is on sale throughout the Subway, at Brentano's and at [over a hundred] news stands" across the city.[126] And considered from a marketing viewpoint (and evident in these covers from *The Masses*), both the pulp and modernist little magazine pander to a certain sensationalism above and beyond any political or social ethos contained within the magazine. Yet even though *The Masses* aspired to "the language of the street," they alienated their working class audience as illustrated in the charges of elitism.

This use of mass-media marketing techniques for *The Masses* is somewhat ironic considering the schism in the magazine that occurred in 1916 when *The Masses'* artists demanded a movement toward editorial autonomy outside the overt political agenda of editor Max Eastman. The movement was voted down, resulting in the departure of the editorial board members who had started the "rebellion," namely John Sloan, Stuart Davis, Glenn Coleman, Maurice Becker, and, most importantly for us, Robert Carlton Brown.[127] This artists' rebellion underlines the tensions that exist between overt political radicalism and the understated politics of cultural/artistic avant-garde modernism, exacerbated in this case by the gulf between a magazine aimed at the working class yet implicated in modernist elitism. Bob Brown was one author who knew this gap well, for his career bridged it.

Brown is one of those liminal figures of modernism who seem always to be at the right place at the right time: in Greenwich Village for the Armory Show and *The Masses*; with Duchamp on the eve of the Independents' show; friend of Mencken; an expatriate in France who hobnobbed with Stein's circle and the writers around Jolas's *transition* including Harry Crosby, who published Brown's book *1450 –1950*. Brown himself established the Roving Eye Press in 1931. But before his involvement with elite modernism, Brown was a self-confessed pulp hack, who wrote for many of the early pulps, including *Argosy* and *Top-Notch*, as well as *The Smart Set*. According to Hugh Ford:

> [Brown had] a career that had made him a virtual writing machine. According to his own figures, he had, before his thirtieth birthday, written "1000 short and long fiction stories, one every three and 6/10th days, counting 100,000 word

---

[126] Morrisson, 248n 18.

[127] This rebellion, as it has become known, is infamous in the history of the *Masses*. Of the many accounts, see particularly Fishbein, 21–24, Zurier, 52–53.

typewriter busters and 3000 word playful finger-tip ticklers." Pulp magazines sometimes printed his stories in batches of five or six in a single issue, either under his own name or any of a dozen nom de plumes. In addition, he had produced a bestseller, *What Happened to Mary*, later a successful motion picture, and a popular book of detective stories, *The Remarkable Adventures of Christopher Poe*. Moreover, he had turned out "jokes, poems, epigrams, novelettes, anecdotes, articles, jingles, sketches, monologues, serials, digests, slogans, advertisements, *fueilletons*, reports, memoirs, confessions, tales, narratives, guides, monographs, descriptions, obituaries, wise-cracks, legends, journals, lives, plays, adventures, experiences, romances, fairy tales, parables, apologues, circulars, doggerel, sonnets, odes, episodes, lyrics, thrillers, dime novels, nickel novels, society verse, essays rondelets, biographies, codexes, broad-sheets, fly-leaves, pages, quires, and reams." After ten years of functioning as a "writing factory," disgorging in that time an astonishing ten million 'multi-colored words,' for fees ranging from one-tenth of a cent to ten cents a word – and earnings that occasionally reached fifteen thousand dollars a year – Brown understandably, concluded he had just about written himself out.[128]

Brown had a prolific career in all-fiction mags such as *All-Story*, *Cavalier*, *Top-Notch*, *Pearson's*, *Munsey's*, and *Everybody's*. Some (but not all) of his popular fiction contained an unstated socialist tendency, such as "The Making of an Anarchist," (*The Gray Goose*, Aug. 1908), or "The New Italy" (*Smart Set*, June 1914), which portrays the gritty reality of the American dream, full of hucksters, corruption and bureaucracy, as experienced by Italian immigrants. This agenda took a more aesthetic, less overt political turn with his modernist poetry, especially his invention of "The Readie," for which he is best known.

In the June 1930 issue of *transition*, Brown published a type of manifesto, stating the need for a modernist revolution in the way we read. Inspired by a tickertape machine, Brown envisioned a small, portable reading machine that projected a line of moving words onto a five-inch screen at high speed, in the manner of a movie (something like an early microfiche). The effect of this would be instantaneous absorption, a facilitated reception of the printed word by the reader. This facilitated absorption has a long series of modernist precursors, from Pater's idea that music is the ideal art because it works upon the emotions effortlessly, without need for interpretation, to Conrad's advocacy of the visuality of writing. Michael North considers "The Readies" as growing from the same modernist impulse to transform language, to break down lingual, cultural, and class barriers, evident in Pound's use of ideograms and Eugene Jolas's (along other members of the *transition* group) experimentation with multilingual poetry, and the use of film as a possible universal signifier that works outside of class and cultural hierarchies.[129] Indeed, Brown ends his *transition* essay by stating, "But the endless imaginative possibilities of the new medium [The Readies] shall not lead us astray. The low-brows are presently

---

[128] Hugh Ford, *Published in Paris* (NY: Macmillan, 1975), 303–304, source uncited.

[129] See North, *Camera Works* (Oxford: Oxford U P, 2005), esp. 72–76.

reveling in their Movies and their Talkies while the high-brow is content to sit at home sipping his thin alphabet soup out of archaic volumes of columns, mewling a little like a puling baby taking mush from the tip of an awkward spoon too gross for his musical rose-buddy temperamental mouth."[130] If one can get past Brown's verbosity, it is possible to see a hopeful vision for the transformation of reading from the marker of the intellectual elite (and I again remind you here of the numerous debates occurring at this time about the cultural position of the book) to an act visibly accessible to all classes. Inspired by Duchamp, Brown had formerly tried to capture the cubist's visuality in the printed word, and the readies were a logical extension of that. And it is obvious that Brown's idea caught on: two books of Readie poems were produced, Brown's own *The Readies* (1930) and *Readies For Bob Brown's Machine* (1931), which included contributions by Gertrude Stein, Hilaire Hilar, James T. Farrell, Ezra Pound, William Carlos Williams, Nancy Cunard, Robert McAlmon, and Eugene Jolas.[131]

Not only are Brown's socialist and proletarian tendencies obvious in the idea of the readies, but his early career as a pulp writer, because of its very extremity, is integral to its development as well. As a "writing machine," a pulp author is paid by the word; words therefore become objectified, commodified, and lose the aura (what Conrad calls the "light of magic suggestiveness"[132]) that modernism imposes upon them. The economics of writing not only gave Brown an appreciation of the physicality of words, but an ability to separate them from their aura, to see them as type and object. Hence he was enthralled with Duchamp's idea of capturing the "fourth Dimension," where the artist painted mundane objects imbued with a personal visuality of reception. It was this aspect that reenergized Brown, and reimbued words with a new dimension for him. According to Ford, Duchamp was amazed at how quickly Brown grasped and executed the cubist theory, and, in fact Duchamp published Brown's poem "Eyes" in *The Blindman*, the little magazine that was distributed for the Independents' Show.[133] Being a "writing machine" therefore inspired Brown's idea for a reading machine. North comments that "Brown has an astonishing faith in the effect of speed to overcome the conventional nature of alphabetic text."[134] This has to do, I believe, with Brown's earlier experience as a pulp writer, as much as any experience he might have had with the motion picture industry (which North hints at). Brown envisions being able to read "a hundred thousand words novel in ten minutes if I want to, and I want to," understandable for someone who had written (and gotten paid for) "100,000 word typewriter

---

[130] Quoted in *transition: a Paris Anthology,* Noel Riley Fitch, ed. (London: Secker and Warburg, 1990), 64.

[131] Brown's poetry, in general, attempted to capture an added visual element via placement on the page. It seems that the idea of the Readie poem was more of an abstraction in these books, since only one machine was built.

[132] Conrad's "preface" to *Nigger of the 'Narcissus'* (NY: Norton, 1979), 148.

[133] Hugh Ford, 303.

[134] North, *Camera*, 77.

busters." If the pulp writer is one who writes and produces fiction based upon speed, both as economically based process and as demand-based subject matter, the readies are the reception-based counterpoint—a reader who consumes at the modern speed. The readies therefore mark an endpoint in the popularization of literature, a pared down writing, fast and flowing, the speed of the pulps taken to the logical extreme—an effort to fuse pulp form and modernist agenda.[135]

Interestingly enough, as Michael North points out, Brown's own work in the readies relies upon stereotypical racial identifiers: "The close identification of ink with race in Brown's books suggests that without prejudice there would almost literally be nothing to see ... This is not simply a failure in Brown's ambitions, however, but a necessary effect of the whole utopian project to reduce specific verbal languages to a single utopian visual script."[136] I would likewise argue that Brown's use of the reductive, prejudiced markers in the readies, such as "flashing --- Afric-teeth" stem from his experience of quick and reductive characterization peculiar to fast-paced pulp writing.[137] Hence the undeniably modernist "readie," which Jerome McGann calls of overlooked but "single importance," is a direct result of the pulp form acting upon / influencing modernism."[138]

The Pulps as the Post-Harlem Form

Though Brown's effort to bridge a class-based gap in a manner that used racial stereotypes stems from the formulaic method of the pulps, this same form offered a means for African-Americans to break down these very stereotypes. This is often overlooked since the actual number of pulp writers of color is impossible to reconstruct. In *Dark Matter*, a book of African-American science fiction, Samual R. Delany recounts:

> I believe I first heard Harlan Ellison make the point that we know of dozens upon dozens of early pulp writers only as names: They conducted their careers entirely by mail – in a field and during an era when pen names were the rule rather than the exception. Among the 'Remington C. Scotts' and the 'Frank P. Joneses' who litter the contents pages of the early pulps, we have simply no way of knowing if one, three, or seven of them –or even many more—were blacks, Hispanics, women, Native Americans, Asians, or whatever. Writing is like that.[139]

---

[135] Needless to say, such an object parallels Chandler's and Hammett's politico-aesthetics.
[136] North, 81.
[137] Quoted in North, 80.
[138] McGann, *Black Riders: The Visible Language of Modernism* (Princeton, NJ: Princeton U P, 1993), 89.
[139] Delany, "Racism and Science Fiction," in R. Thomas Sheree, ed., *Dark Matter* (NY: Warner, 2000), 384.

We can identify at least one important member of the Harlem Renaissance who both wrote for and worked in the pulp industry: Wallace Thurman, who was the editor of *Fire!* and *Harlem* (New Negro little magazines) but also reader and ghostwriter for *True Story Magazine* and other McFadden pulps.

Thurman's most famous work, *Infants of Spring*, is one of the most caustic criticisms from within the Harlem Renaissance. In both its plot and in its own failure as a novel, it illustrates the movement's despairing search for an appropriate black voice. It can be read as the movement's soliloquy, criticizing through caricature figures such as Alain Locke, Zora Neale Hurston, and Aaron Douglas for either prostituting themselves and their race to the white fascination for black exoticism, or failing because of hyper race consciousness imbued with an instilled sense of inferiority.[140] Throughout, the artists of *Infants of Spring* waffle between adoration of white modernists and a seeming inability to produce any real African-American art that does not cater to or is colonized by the Anglo's taste for the exotic or primitive. The artists' inability is fueled by the hedonistic gin parties that gave rise to the white concept of Harlem primitivism. For Raymond Taylor, Thurman's semi-autobiographical main character, and his friends, Joyce and Hemingway made them "incontinently rhapsodic."[141] The only successful artist, Paul Arbian (based on Jean Toomer), kills himself in an effort to aspire to Huysmans and Wilde, inadvertently and ironically destroying his manuscript in the effort. Hence for Thurman the movement becomes marred between the autonomous space of elite, white modernism and the commodified and sensational image of Harlem.

The white cooption of the Harlem Renaissance resulted in not only the well-documented influx of white high society into the nightclubs and artist studios of Harlem, but a popular appropriation of Harlem even in the pulp sphere: Harold Hersey started the pulp magazine *Harlem Nights*, and Mencken and Nathan briefly considered starting an all-Negro pulp.[142] Thurman would have been well aware of such fascination, not only since he was a resident of Harlem, but also as an employee of the MacFadden pulp house. (The character of Jorgenson in *Infants of Spring* is most probably based upon Thurman's longtime friend, collaborator, and editor of *True Story*, William Jourdan Rapp.)

Thurman's criticism of the movement as a failed quest for form parallels the popular critical opinion that the movement failed by or about 1934. The movement's most eminent historians, David Levering Lewis and Nathan Huggins, would agree that by 1932 the Harlem Renaissance was quickly running out of steam, a victim of in-fighting, white cooption, and popular sensationalism.[143]

---

[140] Huggins, 191–195.

[141] *Infants of Spring* (NY: Macaulay Company, 1932 [AMS reprint, 1972]), 35–36.

[142] There is no record of a *Harlem Nights* magazine except in Hersey's memoir, but there is a record of a 1932 pulp titled *Harlem Stories* which lasted for two issues in 1932.

[143] See David Levering Lewis, *When Harlem Was In Vogue* (NY: Penguin, 1997), especially the last chapter, "It's dead now," and Huggins, 302–309. For more on Thurman, see Walden, "'The Canker Galls…,' or The Short Promising Life of Wallace Thurman," in Victor A. Kramer, ed., *The Harlem Renaissance Re-Examined* (NY: AMS Press, 1987). Such a statement is, of course, necessarily reductive.

Yet I would argue that rather than a failure, the New Negro movement led—at least for some writers—to a populist pulp form rather than a rarified modernist one. George Schuyler, whose "Negro Art Hokum" is if anything a more barbed attack of the inefficacy of the movement than Thurman's, is a key example.

Just as controversial as "Negro Art Hokum," Schuyler's *Black No More* (1931) has been called "The first full-length satire by a black American writer and *the* satire of the Harlem Renaissance."[144] Furthermore, it is the first genre novel of the Harlem Renaissance, if not the first genre novel by and about black Americans, predating Rudolph Fisher's *The Conjure Man Dies* by a matter of months. *Black No More* is a satirical tale about the invention of a process that turns black skin white. Along the way, he also sharply satirizes key figures of both the Harlem Renaissance, such as Du Bois (Dr. Shakespeare Agamemnon Beard), and white political leaders, such as Klan leaders, Senators, and Herbert Hoover (Harold Goosie). In the novel, the decolorization process becomes so popular that the blacks are a rarity in the North, and the South is crippled by the "ethnic migration"; color lines become nonexistent; the Knights of Nordica (the KKK), and the Anglo-Saxon association rely on compiling detailed genealogy of everyone in the states only to find out that the majority, if not all, of the Anglo leaders are actually of mixed blood. By the end, everyone relies on skin stains and suntan; mulatto is considered the norm. No one escapes Schuyler's pummeling. Schuyler therefore uses the possibilities offered to him via science fiction to undermine racial construction.

Ahead of its time and unflinching in its satire, *Black No More* was labeled "assimilationist," illustrating an "urge to whiteness" and "a plea for assimilation," and "the (white) American dream."[145] Hence Schuyler's criticism of the Harlem Renaissance was seen not as part of a blanket criticism of black and white alike, or of a treatise on racial construction (which it so obviously is when read through modern post-structuralism), but as self-reflexive racial hate. Schuyler's irony is lost in the translation.

A more blatant use of the pulp form by Schuyler are the dozens of sensational stories, serials, and novellas that Schuyler wrote throughout the 1930s for the *Pittsburgh Courier* under a variety of pennames. Serials like "Golden Gods: a Story of Love, Intrigue, and Adventure in African Jungles," or "The Beast of Bradhurst Avenue: A Gripping Tale of Adventure in the Heart of Harlem" were pure pulp sensationalism published in a newspaper since it was the only forum given the lack of African-American pulp magazines.[146] Of these, uncollected for almost 60 years, only two have been republished: *The Black Internationale: The Story of a Black Genius Against the World* and *Black Empire: An Imaginative Story of a Great New Modern Civilization in Modern Africa*. And even after its publication by Northeastern Press, it was widely ignored by critics as being apolitical, written

---

[144] Michael W. Peplow, *George S. Schuyler* (Boston: Twayne, 1980), 56.

[145] Quoted in Peplow, 82.

[146] For an enthralling list of these serials and stories, see the bibliography of Schuyler's *Courier* fiction in *Black Empire* (Boston: Northeastern U P, 1991), 337–344.

without "culturally specific ends."[147] Stephen Soitos cites it as being prejudiced, reductive, and "without a modicum of the satire, comic relief, of insight into black life that makes his novel *Black No More* so interesting."[148] This marks a prejudice of form, due to its obvious pulp milieu—the reason it was ignored for so long in the first place, and a resistance (or at least unfamiliarity) by critics to the methods of reading pulp fiction. Schuyler's stories offered both fantasy and cultural criticism largely unavailable to black audience in the accepted literary forms. Only Kali Tal has examined *Black Internationale* in the milieu of Black Militant Fiction and marked by a pessimism "impossible to deny"—a pessimism consistent, I would argue, with the cutting and uniform satire of *Black No More*.[149] After all, the headline for *The Black Internationale* was "Story of Black Genius Against the World."

Other African-American works that relied upon pulp genres were also overlooked due to either their popular form or deviance from the ethos of the Harlem Renaissance; for example, Rudolph Fisher's *The Conjure Man Dies*, which has been neglected except as one of the first black detective stories (it undoubtedly offers the first black urban detective). As a result, it has been written off by critics as *only* a detective story and beneath the considerable talents of Fisher, whom Langston Hughes called the "wittiest of the New Negroes."[150] But unlike Schuyler, Fisher's aim is more apparent: to write a popular and sensational genre novel that humanizes African-Americans, hence he uses the pulp form propagandistically. *The Conjure Man Dies* is therefore a more sophisticated work than Harlem Renaissance critics have allowed. Maria Balshaw recently wrote that *The Conjure Man Dies,* despite playing "fast and loose with tradition, urbanity, high and low culture, rationalism and primitivism," has been long overlooked "perhaps because there seems so little context for understanding an African American detective novel in this period; perhaps more because its 'inherent variety' of form makes it a difficult text to classify or respond to";[151] hopefully this project gives *The Conjure Man Dies* a suitable context.

The Conjure Man Dies uses a popular (trans-populace) genre as education and race relation through the conventions of the detective form, minstrelsy, and passing literature. In a radio interview, Fisher had earlier stated that he would be happy to be Harlem's interpreter—an attitude repeated in his 1927 *American Mercury* article "The Caucasian Storms Harlem" that optimistically concludes that through Harlem nightclub sensationalism "[m]aybe these Nordics at last have tuned in on

---

[147] Stephen F. Soitos, *The Blues Detective, A Study of African American Detective Fiction* (Amherst: U of Massachusetts P, 1996), 220.

[148] Ibid., 237.

[149] Kali Tal, "'That Just Kills Me' Black Militant Near-Future Fiction," *Social Text*, Vol. 20, No. 2 (2002), 79.

[150] *The Big Sea. The Collected Works of Langston Hughes*, Vol 13 (Columbia: U of Missouri P, 2002), 186.

[151] Balshaw, *Looking For Harlem: Urban Aesthetics in African American Literature* (London: Pluto Press, 2000), 38.

our wave-length. Maybe they are at last learning to speak our language"[152] Along these same lines, *Conjure Man* pairs stereotypical black characters with African-American Harvard graduates, doctors, and policemen. Fisher's double-voiced stylistics—the harmonization of the seemingly oppositional forms of modernist and pulp fiction—are apparent when Dr. Archer, the protagonist, tells Frimbo, an African King and the "conjure man" of the title, "You certainly have the gift of harmonizing apparently opposite concepts." Similarly, Fisher criticizes racial infighting: the murderer is criticized as one who puts his own needs in front of those of the black community, that is, he pursues "white" capitalist ideals. Racial solidarity is embodied by the book's two African-American detectives, a well-educated doctor and a working-class policeman.

Hence both Fisher's and Schuyler's books mark the quest for appropriate form that was supposedly the Harlem Renaissance's downfall. Their forms gave them a leeway and an audience that the forms of elite modernism criticized by Thurman did not. If we can consider Richard Wright, arguably the most important male African-American author directly following the Harlem Renaissance, in light of this history of the use of the pulp form, we see that what emerges from the Harlem Renaissance is a form that stands between the populist pulps and elite modernism, one that constitutes a powerful ideological weapon.

In *Black Boy* Wright confesses the importance of pulp magazines in both his education and as escapism: "[in school] I read tattered, second-hand copies of *Flynn's Detective Weekly* or the *Argosy All-Story Magazine*, or dreamed, weaving fantasies about cities I had never seen and about people I had never met," and he later counterpoints this by retelling what happens when he is discovered reading Mencken's *American Mercury*:

> One afternoon the boss lady entered the kitchen and found me sitting on a box reading a copy of the *American Mercury*.
> "What on earth are you reading?" she demanded.
> I was at once on guard, though I knew I did not have to be.
> "Oh, just a magazine," I said.
> "Where did you get it?" she asked.
> "Oh, I just found it," I lied; I had bought it.
> "Do you understand it?" she asked.
> "Yes, ma'am."
> "Well," she exclaimed, "the colored dishwasher reads the *American Mercury*!"
> She walked away, shaking her head. My feelings were mixed. I was glad that she had learned that I was not completely dumb, yet I felt a little angry because she seemed to think it odd for dishwashers to read magazines. Thereafter I kept my books and magazines wrapped in newspaper so that no one would see them, reading them at home and on the streetcar to and from work.[153]

---

[152] McClusky's introduction to Fisher's *The City of Refuge* (Columbia: U P of Missouri, 1987), xxxix; "The Caucasian Storms Harlem." *American Mercury*, Vol. 11 (August 1927), 398.

[153] Wright, *Black Boy* (NY: Perennial, 1998), 133, 273–274.

Ironically, Wright feels the need to hide the respectable magazines, while there is no mention of hiding his pulps in the earlier anecdote, inverting the usual guilt surrounding the pulps as described by white authors such as Fante, or even the Leo Dillon in Joyce's "An Encounter" who hides his dime novel inside a school book. And contrast this with Faulkner's Joe Christmas whose pulp reading marks his degeneration. This reversal is likewise acted out in *Native Son*, where Wright plays down the modernism of his text and heightens the pulp sensationalism.

The scene early in *Native Son* where Bigger and Jack openly masturbate in the theater contrasts with Fante's *Wait Until Spring, Bandini*, where the protagonist guiltily hides away, as if to masturbate, to read his dirty pulp magazine. Before this scene in *Native Son*, Bigger twice relates movies with pulps magazines: "He tried to decide if he wanted to buy a ten-cent magazine, or go to a movie," and "He wanted to run. Or listen to some swing music. Or laugh or joke. Or read a *Real Detective Story Magazine*. Or go to a movie."[154] For Bigger, the pulps and movies are a fantasy of fulfillment. What differentiates Wright's use of the pulps from the modernist trope of Bovarism—popular fiction's threat to morality—is that there is a sense that the violence and sensationalism of the pulp magazine is a real element in the life of African-Americans in the suppressed and urban environment of America. Whereas Madam Bovary's self-conception is built upon romantic novels, the fulfillment of Bigger's self-conception *surpasses* the fiction of the pulps: After murdering Mary and conceiving his plan of ransom, Bigger "felt that he had destiny in his grasp. He was more alive than he could ever remember having been; his mind and attention were pointed, focused toward a goal. For the first time in his life he moved consciously between two sharply defined poles: he was moving away from the threatening penalty of death, from the deathlike times that brought him that tightness and hotness in his chest; and he was moving towards that sense of fullness he had so often *but inadequately* felt in magazines and movies."[155]

The space that Bigger is caught in is the gap between reality and representation of life in America, between self-conception and self-realization, yet the fantasy or violence of the pulps inadequately portrays the violence of disparity, which Bigger enacts. If in earlier modernist texts, characters such as Bovary die because of the unbridgeable gap between reality and romantic representation, Bigger dies because he is able to bridge that gap, he lives the ideals represented to him on the screen, he finds himself within a pulp; hence the violent reality of the pulps is the reality of Bigger's life. He is not a product of the pulps as Bovary is, but a product of suppression that drives him to act. For Wright, the white "reality" of the American dream is the fiction, and the violence of the novel rises from the gap between Bigger acting out that fiction, and the reality of his situation. Hence, in *Black Boy*, Wright states, "But where had I got the notion of doing something in the future, of going away from home and accomplishing something that would be recognized by others?

---

[154] Wright, *Native Son* (NY: Perennial, 1998), 12–13, 28.
[155] Ibid., 149–150, italics mine.

I had, of course, read my Horatio Alger stories, my pulp stories, and I knew my Get-Rich-Quick Wallingford series from cover to cover."[156]

The sensationalism of the first half of *Native Son*, the brutal murders and the manhunt, are playing off (and using as a symbol) the standardized formula and atmosphere of just the type of pulp that Bigger enjoys; it works (and works well, considering the initial popularity of the book) like a pulp to capture a popular audience, drawing them into the coded core of the book. In *Black Boy*, Wright signifying to cover his high-cultural influences is a metaphor for his own art, which he covers under the sensationalism of the pulps, and later, under the detective form in *The Outsider*. As Paul Gilroy points out: Wright's "ambiguous relationship to literary modernism, namely the populist impulse inherent in his adaptation of the genre of detective fiction. The effect of this ploy is to demystify some of the preoccupations and themes of high modernism by transposing them into an accessible register, which confounds the European distinction between high and vernacular cultural forms and demonstrates yet again the correspondence between the everyday life-world of urban black Americans and the existential anxieties of the European Savant."[157] In other words, the liminal, overlooked, and repressed pulp form was appropriate for Wright's (and, later, others such as Chester Himes, Ishmael Reed, and Walter Mosely) depiction of the liminal and repressed position of African-Americans.[158]

Pulps, Formula, and the Speed of Writing

If the pulp form offered a promise of humanization to African-Americans and other ethnicities, of propaganda to socialists, of strong gender roles to women—it likewise resulted in stereotypical representations, vilification, and objectification. As we've seen with Brown's poetry and pulp stylistics in general, the speed of writing, reading, and identification caused innate reductivism in the pulps. And, as illustrated in criticism against this fast and formulaic aspect of the pulps, it was this very speedy formulism that delegated pulp literature to the cultural trash pile. Yet high modernism was just as enthralled, just as much enmeshed with speed and heightened technology as the pulps were. If one had to choose a single concept or sensation to describe modernity in the first few decades of the twentieth century, one could hardly do any better than "Speed." The concept of speed is an integral aspect of modernism: not only did elite modernism define itself against/apart

---

[156] Wright, *Black Boy*, 168–169.

[157] Paul Gilroy, *The Black Atlantic: Modernity and Double Consciousness* (Cambridge: Harvard U P, 1993), 171.

[158] It is possible to extend this to African-American women's writing and the romance or melodramatic pulp—Nella Larsen's *Passing*, for example, but it is also possible to argue that African-American Women's *even more* liminal position and stronger relationship to an oral folk literary tradition influenced their form more so than pulps, with Hurston (as anthropologist) being a conduit to modern authors such as Walker and Morrison.

from the technological speed of production and consumption—the years Joyce spent on *Ulysses* and the *Wake* again offer the best instance—but attempts to portray the modern condition tried, through various means, to capture the tempo of the modern world stylistically, as in Brown's Readies. Similarly, the trauma or clash innate in the general heightened speed of modern life, what Stephen Kern would consider the crisis of simultaneity, caused modernist movements such as vorticism and futurism to (often violently) portray the instability of time.[159] The reconsideration of temporal (in)stability was a predominant theme, whether as influenced by Einstein via Bertrand Russell or Vico via Yeats and Joyce or Bergson via Proust. Reality and temporal linearity breakdown, disorientation of the reader becomes the modernist norm: Woolf and Joyce attempt to capture simultaneity in *Mrs. Dalloway* and "Wandering Rocks" as do cubists such as Duchamp in *Nude Descending a Staircase*; Faulkner's narration of *The Sound and the Fury* jumps years via a single word or sense; in *The Secret Agent*, Conrad underscores man's attempt to control the arbitrary nature of time by making the Greenwich Observatory a symbolic target for anarchists. The temporal instability that so intrigues modernism likewise surfaces in the pulps, especially in science fiction and fantasy pulps, with time travel, or how the conflict between modern man and primitive world (or vice versa) becomes a standard plot device.[160] Much of the work of Edgar Rice Burroughs, *Tarzan* and *At the Earth's Core* for example, relies on these tensions, as does much of the fiction of Robert E. Howard, and innumerable science fiction pulps. Phillip Francis Nolan's "Armageddon 2419," which appeared in *Amazing Stories* in 1928, is one such short story, about Anthony Rogers, ex–World War I soldier, who is overcome by radioactive gas when a mineshaft collapses. He wakes up 492 years later in a war-torn and technologically advanced future. Rogers would also reemerge a year later in comic strip form as Buck Rogers. Many such stories offer allegories of modern life and man—modern heroes prove themselves as violent and brutal as the cavemen they are suddenly surrounded by, and the men of the utopian future prove themselves as corrupt, brutal, or foolish as those of the present day. Perhaps missing are the commentaries and stylistic complexities of elite modernism, yet what is obvious is that the pulps were working through, in an accessible way, the same tensions and dynamics that fed modernist works of the same period. And the unsubtle or popular form of these modernist aspects doesn't make them any less poignant or important. Patrick Brantlinger has pointed out, "the distinction

---

[159] See Stephen Kern, *The Culture of Time and Space* (Cambridge, MA: Harvard U P, 1993). Kern parallels the futurists with the advent of science fiction, but only tangentially examines the increased speed of production and distribution as it affects either the culture industry or modernism.

[160] Wells's *Time Machine* is of course the obvious correlation (perhaps too obvious) here. Stephen Kern examines the shift of Wells's view of the future from one of degeneration to one of possibilities. For Kern, science fiction writers "reached out to the future as if it were a piece of overripe fruit," 94.

between 'high' and 'mass' culture, dubious at best, breaks down when it comes to such widely shared phenomenon as the mythologization of history or apocalyptic doomsaying," and this is all the more obvious in "mass circulation science fiction stories and films."[161] Though Brantlinger is discussing more recent fictions, the pulps obviously illustrate this dynamic as well.

Since speed was perhaps the single most unifying and distinguishing element of the pulp genre (besides, possibly, its element of disposability, which, considering the heightened rate of production and consumption, could itself be an appropriate descriptor of the modern world), we should perhaps reconsider whether the modernist text is really the most appropriate written representation of modernity. Modernism's binary relationship to speed and technology, its attempts to portray the modern condition with both fascination and horror, mirrors tensions likewise available in the pulps, which, furthermore, were essentially more of a *physically modern* product, as illustrated by the resistance to them (and their ilk) during the "book wars" I've already described. Specialty pulp magazines, for example, developed around the new and enthralling technologies of speed, movement, and travel. The titles themselves point to this: *Speed, Exciting Stories, Action, Zeppelin Stories, Railroad Stories, Astounding Science, Wings!, Fighting Aces, Pep!, Scientific Detective Monthly; Miracle, Science and Fantasy Stories; Excitement!, Astounding Stories of Super Science*, etc. The magazines were quickly produced, containing fiction about quick and exciting living, quickly written in language meant to be quickly read. The topics themselves are completely involved with— spring from—the tensions of modernity, the problems of adaptation that arose from the new speed of modern life (just as Brown was trying to adapt reading to modern life). Contrast this with the rarefied book production of modernism—the use and fashion of handpresses, small publishers, autographed and illustrated editions—which was innately artesan-like, a return to medieval book production, as illustrated most blatantly in Pound's first three books of *The Cantos*, influenced by William Morris's Kelmscott Press;[162] hence the modernist book was innately unmodern. The pulp manner of production would be much more suitable.

An excellent example of how modern form and subject matter conflated in the pulps is the railroad genre of pulp, which approached a self-reflexive synaesthesia since subject matter, venue, and readership intersected: Railway stations were an important venue for the pulp magazine; the railroad pulps pandered to the commuting readership by taking as its subject the trains themselves and those who rode them, even publishing train schedules. Whereas modernism generally casts a suspicious glance at the railroad, what John Carey describes as a modernist criticism of the railroad as a symbol of the suburbs and the spread of the newly literate classes,[163] pulps like *Railroad Stories* concern themselves with speed and

---

[161] Brantlinger, *Bread and Circuses* (Ithaca, NY: Cornell, 1983), 39.

[162] See Jerome McGann's *Black Riders*, 79–81, for a discussion of the influence of medieval printing on the modernists via the Pre-Raphaelites.

[163] See Carey, 46.

the technological advancements both of rail and that rail made possible, but speed is often looked at as a danger, as well as something that, when controlled, deserved respect. "Mountain Job" by Ed Samples (October 1936 *Railroad Stories*), for example, depicts the danger of unchecked speed and technology as well as the necessity/power of it. Jimmie Dalton's father, a railroad engineer, elects to stay on a speeding train to ensure it will derail off the side of a cliff rather than crash into a slow-moving passenger train. Jimmie, who himself grows up to be an engineer, takes a slow-moving and safe job in respect for his mother's fear of danger for him, even though it costs him the respect of his co-workers. When the occasion arises to prove himself and his ability to maneuver down a mountainside at 70 miles per hour in order to divert disaster, he shows that "He's not afraid to ride the fast ones." Perry Miller has discussed how the railroad has traditionally been written about in American literature in terms of fecundity, as the mechanical mother that gave birth to the nation. Such a story as "Mountain Job" modernizes the traditional, naturalistic depiction of feminized technology, illustrating not only the need for masculine control of this femininity/fecundity, but how masculinity itself is gauged by it.[164] This portrayal within modernism became more complicated with the approach of World War I, when technology became destructive as well as generative.

Themes in the pulps constantly deal with the friction between old and new, urban and rural, action and complacency, technology and barbarism, west and east. *Wonder Stories*, an early science fiction pulp, grew from the popular fascination with new technology, specifically in *Electrical Invention, Science and Experimentation* magazine; the romance, true confession, and erotic pulps grew from the loosening morals of the 1920s, the clash between Edwardian propriety and flapperish freedom; the hero pulps and the detective pulps, especially hard-boiled, dealt with the tension of an urban population that had grown so fast as to threaten control; the Western pulps likewise played off the threat of the diminishing west and rural freedoms. Again, what we see in the pulps is often an extreme, popularized, and inflated aspect of modernism. The modernism of the avant-garde in the years before World War I was reflected in an ever-growing correlative popular manifestation, more and more obvious after the war. This gap of attrition or gestation between the modernist and popular can be accounted for by the war itself. Artists and intellectuals foresaw the advent and destruction of the war, realized or were fueled by the tensions of unchecked growth and technology. As Paul Fussell has so eloquently pointed out, World War I was the impetus for not only a popular cynicism and sense of irony, but an oppositional mindset as well. Hence it follows that the modernism that grew out of the postwar years was marked by preoccupation with its own cultural standing. The hierarchization of low-, middle-, and highbrow in both book and magazine publishing only cemented itself after the war: magazines such as *The Smart Set* or the early pulps were forced by the market to choose a cultural position or fail altogether.

---

[164] See Seltzer, *Bodies and Machines* (NY: Routledge, 1992), 27–29.

In the years following World War I, as the pulp magazine found and perfected its form, it also manifested, in a popular manner, the tensions of modernism. This is illustrated in the pulps' reconstruction of masculinity, their acting out via allegorical genre fictions of modernist technological tensions (science fiction), their fascination with war and threats against the West (i.e., Yellow Peril and the red scare personified by super villains in the hero pulps), and a wholesale pessimism (hard-boiled and war fiction). Writing of the postmodern fascination with and reconstruction of prewar futurism, Marjorie Perloff states, "For here, at the origins of a Modernism that was to turn increasingly elitist and formalist in its concern for self-sufficient structures and aesthetic distance, is the latent promise of an impure art world that might also be the place where we live"—and perhaps this impure art was already manifested in the popular form of the pulps.[165] Scott McCracken, for one, has pointed out similarities between science fiction and futurism: "It is possible to see some connections between modernism's experimental nature and early science fiction's enthusiasm for technical innovation as the path to the future. Modernist movements like futurism and constructivism were clearly motivated by similar concerns, while surrealism's interest in dreams and the unconscious has its counterpart in many science fiction stories."[166] I would go one step farther than either Perloff or McCracken, and state that the marketing techniques and tensions of modernism existed across the board, manifesting its nonelite side in the standardized and overtly commercial form of the pulp magazine. Elite modernism after the war found its most popular form for an elite audience (and aspiring elite audience) in *Vanity Fair* magazine, and for the proletariat in the pulps.

The varying relationships of the pulps and modernism to technology offer a powerful instance of such parallels. Modernist authors in turn feared unchecked technological growth and the loss of agrarian innocence or saw it as dehumanizing. Others, such as Bob Brown, saw technology as the means to bring about a cultural, modernist revolution. Futurists such as Marinetti promoted a vision of modern man amalgamated with machine as a means to bridge these tensions. As we shall see, all of these relationships inform modernism's elite status and its criticism of the bourgeoisie. There were equally complex negotiations between culture and technology in the pulp genres: the war pulps' fascination with science, technology, and the machinery of war (especially aviation); the Western pulps' wistful romance of an endangered wild West; hard-boiled fiction's urban corruption; science fiction's cautionary tales of technology run amuck. And the pulps were never forgetful of the fact that they were a product of technology.

Just as the pulps in general illustrate both the fascination of technology and trepidation at uncontrolled or misused technology, such is true of modernism, as earlier illustrated by Huxley. Morrisson has noted that the youthful need to destroy old idols and traditions that defined the futurists likewise accompanied

---

[165] Perloff, *The Futurist Moment* (Chicago: U of Chicago P, 1986), xviii.

[166] McCracken, *Pulp: Reading Popular Fiction* (Manchester: Manchester U P, 1998), 107.

the establishment of modernism as a youth movement.[167] The same type of youth-movement irrelevance is the popular, youth-aimed pulps like *Pep, Co-ed Campus Comedy,* and *College Stories.* Futurist catch phrases such as dynamism, futurism, and the violent titles of the different modernist European little magazines, such as *Blast, Die Aktion,* and *Der Sturm,* echo pulp titles such as *Action!, Dynamic Adventure, Shock,* and S*ure Fire.* Marinetti's fetishization of the automobile and airplane, and his commitment to the "beauty of speed," find their popular form in the material and composition of the pulp magazine: pulps devoted to the airplane and train were among the most popular directly after the war.

The futurists' onomatopoetic poetry can be seen, at least aesthetically, hand-in-hand with the manner in which pulp fiction attempted to capture the moment of action. Marinetti's description of/call for the futurist use of "[the] *Direct, imitative, elementary, realistic onomatopoeia,* which serves to enrich lyricism with brute reality, which keeps it from becoming too abstract or *artistic.* (e.g.: *ratta-tat-tat,* gunfire.)" resonates with the pulp genre's stereotypical use of the onomatopoeia sound effect: "He ducked, long after it had gone by, and he gunned the engine and yanked the trigger trips again. *Rat-tat-tat-tat!*"; or "The cannon yammered: '*Kachow! Chow!*' and vomited twin flame-streaks..."[168] But perhaps an even more apparent analogy can be found in the use of the body as a site of modernity's tensions by the modernists, especially Marinetti and Wyndham Lewis, and the pulps. As Tim Armstrong points out in his study of modernism and the body, "modernism brings both a fragmentation and an augmentation of the body in relation to technology; it offers the body as lack, at the same time as it offers technological compensation."[169] The dichotomy of simultaneous fascination and abhorrence marks both modernist and pulp war fiction alike. Hal Foster has called this modernist relationship between natural man and technological machine the "double logic of the prosthesis." Foster has examined the technological fascination of Marinetti and Lewis as an effort to control machinery, to re-create modern masculinity, to bind the mechanical and human, the masculine and feminine. The prescience of modernism, as a reaction to industrialization, made an effort to re-create the body, to re-create humanity, and specifically masculinity that had been destroyed/emasculated by first industrialization and then the wholesale slaughter of World War I. The prototypical futurist hybrid, reborn via the power of speed, has pulpish parallels in such heroes as Terence X. O'Leary or G-8 of the World War I aviation pulps, whose planes and bodies act as one, in heroes like Cannon Ball Toombs of the aforementioned "The High Jackers," who is admirable because of his ability to control his machinery at high speeds (throughout the story he is compared to World War I flying ace, Eddie Rickenbacker), or in the Shadow,

---

[167] Morrisson, 143.

[168] Marinetti, *Selected Writings* (NY: Farrar, Straus and Giroux, 1972), 101, italics Marinetti's; Allen R. Bosworth's "Windbag on the Loose," *War Birds* (1933), 79; Robert Leslie Bellem, "Death's Passport," reprinted in Goodstone, 118.

[169] Tim Armstrong, *Modernism, Technology and the Body* (NY: Cambridge, 1998), 3.

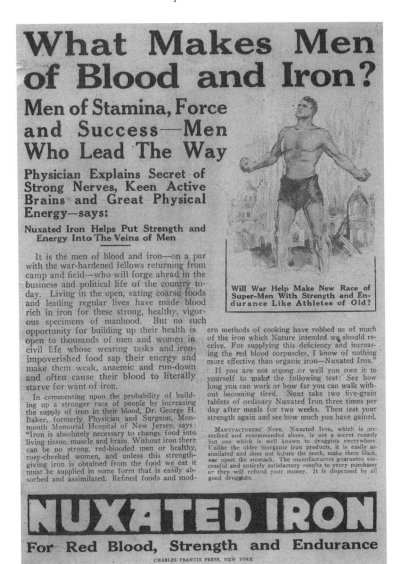

Fig. 2.7   Ad, Nuxated Iron from *Parisienne*, May 1919 inside back cover

whose twin 45s are extensions of his own hands. This binding is made even more explicit in the advertisements of the pulps: not only are ads for electrician, engineer, and radio operator training some of the most common, but other ads pair physical and mental improvement with being more machine-like, more prosthetic. A 1919 issue of *Parisienne* features an article-like ad for Nuxated Iron Supplement (see Figure 2.7), which starts: "It is the men of blood and iron—on par with the war-hardened fellows retuning from camp and field—who will forge ahead in the

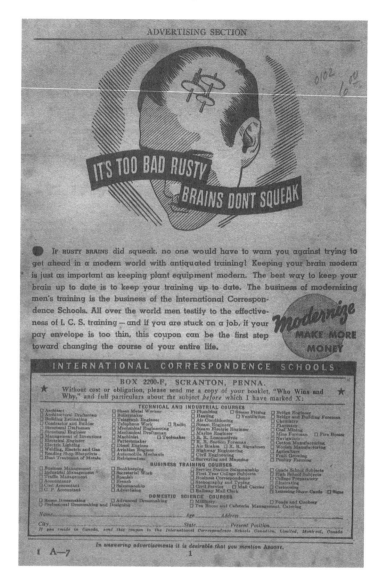

Fig. 2.8   Ad, International Correspondence School, *Argosy*, Aug. 7, 1937.

business and politics in the country today"; the picture's caption reads, "Will War Make New Race Of Super-Men With Strength And Endurance Like Athletes of Old?"[170] Similarly, an ad for correspondence school from a 1937 issue of *Argosy* reads: (see Figure 2.8) "It's Too Bad Rusty Brains Don't Squeak. If rusty brains did squeak, no one would have to warn you against trying to get ahead in a modern

---

[170] *Argosy* (Aug. 7, 1937), 1; *Parisienne* (May 1919), inside back cover.

world with antiquated training! Keeping your brain modern is just as important as keeping plant equipment modern ... Modernize[,] Make More Money."

Both Marinetti's and Lewis's utopian grasping of technology is an effort to bring into dialogue the polarities of the modern condition, an effort that leads them toward misogyny and fascism. Their efforts, though extreme, mirror the reaction to the cultural standardization of bourgeoisie art—Wyndham Lewis and *Blast*'s damning of "Dismal symbol, set round our bodies, of effeminate lout within" echoes Willard Huntington Wright's rallying in *The Smart Set* to fight "effeminacy and formalism."[171] Marinetti states, "I have had enough of the femininity of crowds and the weakness of their collective virginity."[172] Wright's and Lewis' comments should be considered in their surroundings, as statements made in pioneering avant-garde magazines that saw themselves as standing out above the tide of quality, bourgeoisie magazines that had been published for a female audience, whereas many pulp magazines (i.e., Western, adventure, many detective-themed pulps) saw themselves as an alternative to both mainstream, feminized literature and effeminate cultural highbrow literature—which again illuminates the reductive binary innate in Huyssman's general model of modernism, and specifically modernism's identification of "mass culture as woman."[173] Similarly, Bob Brown's efforts to bind elite modernism and popular audience via the speed and visual technology of the readie machine relied upon racially stereotypical imagery, just as the infamous racially stereotypical representations of the pulps grew out of the need for simple and speedy identifiers of otherness. The dualistic view of speed and technology in "Mountain Job" likewise relies upon a fear of femininity.

These acts of binding, whether man and machine, high and low culture, technocracy and technophobia, are ultimately violent acts in both modernism and the pulps alike. This is especially true of, and perhaps even emerges from, the dilemma of modernity as it affects the body: the representations of the body became a site of tension and recreation in modernism, with the neoclassical ideals at one extreme and the fractured or mechanical body at the other. Foster cites fascist art, and the work of Léger, Le Corbusier, and Lewis as points where the poles coexist. This was true before the war, but even more so afterward in reaction to the "mutilated bodies of World War I as well as the fragmented bodies

---

[171] Quoted in Foster, "Prosthetic Gods," *Modernism/Modernity*, Vol. 4, No. 2 (1997), 19; Dolmetsch, 34.

[172] Marinetti, *Selected Writings* (NY: Farrar, Straus and Giroux, 1972), 143.

[173] The idea that the pulps were purely masculine, as McCann and Smith portend, would likewise dismantle this model, but since the large body of pulps by and for women goes against this, it serves to illustrate the general trend of reduction in the academy. When Huyssen discusses "the exclusion of real women from the literary enterprise and with the misogyny of bourgeois patriarchy" (*After the Great Divide: Modernism, Mass Culture, Postmodernism* [Bloomington: Indiana U P, 1986], 45), he ignores recent revision that examines the role of women as editors, authors, and facilitators in modernism; it would be more appropriate if he examined the reductive tendencies of modernist criticism, rather than modernism itself.

of high modernism; and, on the other hand, various machinic modernisms, most of which were also concerned to make over this body-ego image that had been damaged in reality and representation alike."[174] Tim Armstrong likewise looks to the postwar male body as a dichotomous site of fracture and utopian prosthetics. Critics such as Paul Fussell, Elaine Showalter, and Joanna Bourke have written about the homo-eroticism and questioning of masculinity during World War I. The hyper-masculine fiction of Hemingway, Lewis, and Dos Passos can be seen as attempts to rewrite/reaffirm a postwar masculinity. The post–World War I pulp magazines evince a similar reconstruction of masculinity, not only in their literary mission—*Black Mask* was advertised as "The He-Man's Magazine," readers of *Action Stories Magazine* were "entitled to enroll in the Brotherhood of He-Men"—but in their advertisements as well, in the many Charles Atlas–type ads for physical improvement and standardization, and in the many ads for learning the electrical trade in order to become wealthy, self-sufficient, and more modern.[175] Whereas modernism looked upon the melodrama of bourgeois fiction that appeared in the quality magazines as feminine, concerned overtly with advertising and sales (women were of course seen as the majority of magazine buyers), the pulp magazines saw both middle-class *and* highbrow fiction as effeminate, the latter being nonutilitarian, too artsy and concerned with aesthetics. And this pulp view of highbrow literature echoes Marinetti's (reflexive) damnation of art as a city of "Paralysis with its henhouse cackle."[176] These tensions that grew out of the war reached their pinnacle in the trope of the robot in both modernist and pulp literature, as we shall see.

The role that dime novels and popular fiction played in constructing the ideals of Victorian masculinity—honorable, nationalistic, courageous—before the war (G.A. Henty, Alger, Hughes's *Tom Browne's School Days*), had a parallel role in reconstructing those ideals after they had been destroyed by the reality and horrors of war.[177] It is telling that the contradiction that existed in modernism behind the simultaneous fascination with war, from the futurists to Hemingway, and the abhorrence of war, from Hemingway to Sassoon, likewise existed in the pulps. Consider these excerpts from two stories from World War I aviation pulps: "Dorme, The Impenetrable," a "True Feature" from a 1933 *War Birds*, "The Oldest Air War Magazine," and "The Flaming Arrow," an Ace Avery story by George Bruce from a 1934 *The Lone Eagle* magazine.

> The French Army, which selects with care its nicknames called him "Father" Dorme and "Dorme the Beloved." This for obvious reasons—superlative comradeship and devotion. But it had another name for Rene Dorme; and earning

---

[174] Foster, 6–7.

[175] Goulart, 30.

[176] Marinetti, 47.

[177] On the role of dime novels and popular fiction on the "great adventure" mentality, see Fussell, *The Great War and Modern Memory* (NY: Oxford U P, 2000), 21, as well as Michael Adams, *The Great Adventure* (Bloomington: Indiana U P, 1990).

it made him one of the greatest of all fighters. "Dorme, the Impenetrable." Side by side, that title stands with Eric the Red, Richard the Lionhearted. An airman almost too tough to kill! Less than a year at the Front, and twenty-four air victories. No wonder dorme [sic] wore every medal France had, Legion of Honor, Military Medal, Croix de Guerre with nine palms. He didn't wear them on his chest, but in a tangled wad in his pocket!

Such stories of the "Knights of the Air" hearken back to a Tennyson-like romanticism of war. How much different from Bruce's story:

> Kill! The word stalked through Avery's brain. Kill! Smash, crush, destroy! Burn, rend, murder. Kill! Every beautiful thing. Months now, since he had come to the front, that was the one word that haunted him. It lived with him, walked with him, slept with him. Kill! Even in his dreams, he was busy with the business of killing. The faces of the men he had killed, imaginary faces, peered horrifyingly out of the depths of these dreams. He was "Ace" Avery! No identity of his own. Nothing left of the kid who had crossed an ocean from the States to follow the Path of Glory, whose nose was eager to sniff the tang of battle, and whose soul strummed to the thrill of flying. None of that boy left.[178]

Such a portrait is replete with the disillusionment and emptiness of humanity that marks Hemingway's, Cumming's, Remarque's wartime fiction. Furthermore, it illustrates the important fear of the loss of humanity—not just in numbers of human life, but in individualism as well—that unavoidably happens in the world of technology and modern production. Yet pulp aviation magazines such as *Flying Aces* and *Bill Barnes Air Trails* sensationally marketed themselves to technophiles; articles about and model diagrams for warplanes accompanied war fiction. Marinetti would have approved, as would Faulkner on this side of the Atlantic.[179]

This duality of violence/mechanics was, of course, not peculiar to modernism or the pulp genre, but common in all aspects of society as an aspect of the modern condition. A telling example of the widespread fascination with the popular mechanics of war can be seen in magazines such as *Illustrated World*—not a pulp magazine but a monthly news magazine dealing with science and mechanics—which, during World War I, filled its pages with stories and essays about tanks, submarines, trench life, and, overall, the technological side of warfare. We can look to the December 1916 issue to get a good idea of its contents (note the reliance upon dichotomies): "The Etiquette of Submarining—The formula to be followed in destroying an enemy's shipping"; "Destroying the Frigate Franklin"; "Catching Torpedoes"; "Baseballs of Death," a story about hand grenades; "War's Maelstrom—The humor and horror of war abroad [!!!]"; and "For the Nursery Battalion," a story about war-themed children's toys. There are also stories about the Gyroscopic Unicycle, "What a Glass of Whiskey Does to You," "New Uses for the Electric Giant" (electricity), and "Motion Pictures That Really Talk."

---

[178] Goodstone, 46–47.

[179] See the next chapter for more on Faulkner's aviation fetish.

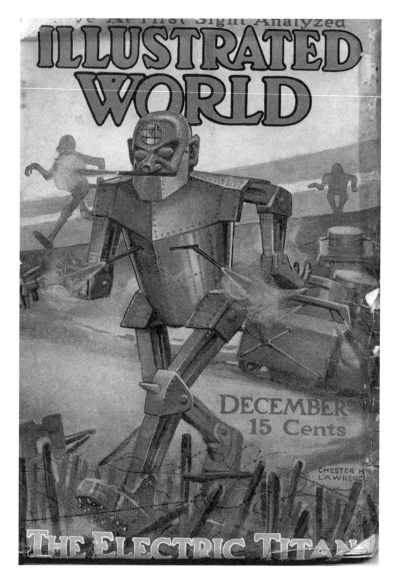

Fig. 2.9   *Illustrated World*, Dec. 1916 © 1916 Illustrated World

But most striking of all is the cover story (see Figure 2.9), "The Electric Titan," about a "mechanical marvel [that] may furnish the warring armies of Europe with a new engine of destruction." The electric titan, is in fact, a robot—a machine that mimics the walking motor skills (and shape) of a human. The cover, with what must be one of the earliest depictions of a robot, depicts a metal giant with blazing machine guns emerging from its chest and (cigar-like) from its mouth, and pulling a tank across a battlefield. The photos of the real machine inside the magazine show something quite different, something more like a box of gears on top of two buxom metal legs, but what captures the writer's imagination is the mimicry of man who would enable it to leap trenches and stomp troops: "there is a possibility that before the close of the present conflict we will see his fearsome bulk adapted to the grim business of war. We may soon receive reports of him, wearing a German helmet or a French shako, and creating devastation in the ranks of the enemy." The article goes on to cite the major inventions of the war—the tank, the submarine, "machine guns that mow down winnows of men as fast as the harvest machine mows grain in the field. [...] Why may not such an Electric Titan be part of the mechanical equipment of the armies of the future?"

The article predates, by four years, Karel Čapek's invention of the word "robot," in his play *R.U.R.* (Rossum's Universal Robots), yet it underlines certain tensions that inspired Čapek, as well as moderns such as Huxley and Orwell and hundreds of pulp authors. Čapek's play, written in Czechoslovakia in 1920, was performed there in 1921 and in New York in 1922, and published in English in 1923. The play met with worldwide critical success: George Bernard Shaw, for example, was one of Čapek's fans. The play, which describes the invention and evolution of mechanical workers that eventually kill off the human race, is an anti-utopian commentary on the dangers of over-mechanization, over-production, over-industrialization. Čapek does end *R.U.R.* on a positive note though: after the extinction of the human race by the robots, two Adam and Eve–like robots evolve, fall in love, and go forth to repopulate the earth. Less optimistic portrayals of the mechanization of man were made in much expressionist art, as Harold Segel has noted, notably in the drama of Iwan Goll (the German translator of *Ulysses* and prominent figure in both Bauhaus and Surrealism), which criticized how bourgeoisie society de-individualizes man, makes him into a capitalist automaton. Such works again bring us back to modernism's criticism of Fordism. Ironically, the robot as a symbol of bound worker and machine, armored and aggressive, mirrors the proto-fascist formula of Marinetti and Lewis, as well as their critique of the conditions of bourgeois society. Marinetti's instructions for the futurist to "metallize" his voice, dehumanize his face, and "gesticulate geometrically" and Lewis's call for the modernist artist to, in Foster's words, "mold this flaccid feminine modernity into an armored masculine modernism," though different in many aspects, agree in that they rely upon using the mechanical alienation of modernity as a means to re-create and strengthen a utopian masculinity.[180] Conrad offers another, more humanist angle in *Heart of Darkness*, when he depicts the dying natives in the grove as "mere shapes" and "Bundles of acute angles." Imperialism, as well as mechanization, dehumanizes.

Such themes as the mechanization of the proletariat in pulp magazines were all the more poignant, for they were the reading matter of the working class, hence all the more close to home just as the depiction of the workers in, say, *Metropolis* or *Modern Times*, would evoke entirely different connotations and emotions to a

---

[180] Foster, 18.

factory worker than to an industrialist. The conflict between man and machine, or, to put it another way, the mechanization of man, as embodied by the trope of the robot, in a world where men were becoming statistics, cogs in factories, and the industrial machine is another manifestation/byproduct of modern standardization. For Conrad, the modern condition in general is one of cold mechanization, as illustrated by his famous existential analogy of the universe as a "knitting machine." Only art offers any possible relief from the cold, ineluctable threat of entropy, of, in Frederick Karl's words, "holding off the onslaughts of scientific ideology."[181]

The promise that art holds against the technocracy of modern life is likewise evident in the pulp genre. A. Merritt's short story, "The Last Poet and the Robots," (1934, *Fantasy Magazine*) offers another example of the modern/pulp nexus. In it, Narodny, the world's last poet and greatest scientist, has evolved into an ageless, god-like being and has ensconced himself far underground in a series of vast caves where he spends his time re-creating famous historical events, discoursing with history's greatest minds, and playing planetary vibrations like vast musical scores. In the outside world, robots have evolved from men's servants into sentient beings who are threatening to take over the Earth. Nardony, comes to the humans' aid, stating that, "I care nothing for mankind—yet I would not harm them, willingly. And it has occurred to me that I owe them, after all, a great debt. Except for them – I would not be. Also, it occurs to me that the robots have never produced a poet, a musician, an artist."[182] The robots are portrayed as a single militant entity, with no individualism. Narodny understands that they have formed a group identity in fear of extinction, which denotes a degree of emotion. He uses music, rhythm, and vibration in mathematical sequences to take advantage of the robots' emotion by causing them to dance until their metal bodies crack, to, more or less, dance to their deaths "in grotesque rigadoons, in bizarre sarabands, with shuffle and hop, and jig the robots danced while the people fled in panic (…) everywhere the sound was heard – and it was heard everywhere – the robots danced … to the piping of Narodny, the last great poet … the last great musician."[183] After the war with the robots, and much collateral damage ("many men died, but many are left. They may not understand –but to them it was worth it"), Narodny states, "It drives home a lesson, what man does not pay for, he values little."[184] Besides offering a critique of fascism, Merritt offers hope for mankind in the melding of art and science. Despite the pulps' self-effacing tendencies (that mirror the elitist mantle of modernism), which are apparent here in Narodny's elite cultural/artistic/evolutionary status, this marriage of science and art can itself be seen as an analogy for the pulp magazine: the product of both technology and hyper-production, seen as destroying and creating individualism via its creation of/pandering to a proletariat readership.

---

[181] Karl, *Modern and Modernism, The Sovereignty of the Artist 1885–1925* (NY: Atheneum, 1988), 201.

[182] Merritt, *The Fox Woman and Other Stories* (NY: Avon, 1977), 118.

[183] Ibid., 124.

[184] Ibid., 126.

The modern condition of production—whether embodied by Adorno and Horkheimer's culture industry or Conrad's European imperialism—deprives the masses of individualism: as Marshall Berman puts it, "Individuality itself may be melting into the modern air."[185] Similarly, for the modernist intellectual, the pulps were regarded as not only an instrument of cultural standardization, but a threat of overpowering mass(es') production. The irony is that as the culturally elite came to identify the pulps as a symbol of the mechanization of literature, as well as culture as a whole, the pulps were themselves criticizing and navigating the modernist ground, albeit via formulas that were digestible yet not condescending to the masses. The pulps became something of a mass subculture (if such a thing is possible), either carefully ignored or bashed by the purveyors of culture. The pulps became a popular modernist nexus.

But the most glaring omission in this pulp/modernist nexus is that of modernist stylistics—those of experimentation, inscrutability, and carefully constructed difficulty. Sure, futurist poetry and pulp sound effects are a commonality, more important are the urban patois of hard-boiled and the symbolism of Chandler and Hammett, but none of these come close to the fiction and plotting of the great Harry Stephen Keeler, a true pulp modernist.

The Strange Case of Harry Stephen Keeler

Harry Stephen Keeler was the author of more than 75 books, many of which were expansions of serials initially published in the pulps. He was also editor of the girlie pulp *10 Story Book Magazine*, the originator of the Webwork Plot Design formula, and is perhaps the most intriguing yet forgotten pulp craftsman in a pantheon of admittedly intriguing authors. At the height of his success, his books went through numerous editions, were printed on both sides of the Atlantic by established publishers and reprint houses alike; he was said to have the lengthiest mystery story ever written (*The Box From Japan*, 1932, 765 pages); and in the late 1920s he influenced many mystery writers with his idiosyncratic plotting device. By the end of his life he was forgotten, published only in Spain and Portugal after being dropped from the lists of increasingly disreputable American or English publishers. Today, though still largely forgotten, he is a cult figure: his books are highly collectible, there is a Harry Stephen Keeler Society, and his novels are finally available through the print-on-demand publisher Ramble House. Yet even in his current small but avid fan base he is lauded as an oddball, known for his insane plots and characters, and often thought of as "unreadable": Francis Nevins, who was responsible for rediscovering Keeler through a series of articles in *The Journal of Popular Culture*, labeled him the "great wack of American letters"; in a recent *Wall Street Journal Article* about the small internet inspired Keeler resurgence, Carlos Tejada called Keeler "so bad [he's] good as gold." Webpages, jacket blurbs, and book reviews often wonder whether Keeler was a genius or insane.

---

[185] Berman, *All That is Solid Melts into Air* (NY: Penguin, 1988), 110.

The question is understandable for not only is insanity a reoccurring theme in Keeler's novels (as are skulls, trepanning, and sideshow freak whorehouses), but to read a Keeler mystery is to be immersed in a plot structure so intricate and vast that the overall feeling is of vertigo, of surreal yet seductive disbelief. A reader doesn't so much read a Keeler book as jumps on for a ride full of impossible coincidences, whimsical names, and such a convoluted plot that there is no possibility for a "whodunit" ending. According to traditional mystery conventions (i.e., for a mystery to "work") characters and plots must be founded in reality; this is exactly the convention that Paul Auster's New York Trilogy works off of and against, and it is exactly what Keeler suspends.

It would be almost impossible to synopsize the plot of a Keeler book, but it is necessary to try so as to convey their complexity. *The Green Jade Hand* (1930), for example, involves the murder of Casimer Jech, a curio dealer whose safe contains both a stolen priceless book and a small green jade hand, which holds the clue to where thousands in embezzled bank bills are hidden. Before his death, Jech buys the jade hand from a hobo who found it in a bowl of chop suey where it was thrown by a Chinese cook who stole it from the now deceased Wong Kwei, the cook's former roommate in a boarding house in Cleveland who embezzled $200,000. The hand is being sought after by Sadie Hippolyte, the boarding house owner, who is in reality the ex-wife of Luke McCracken, ex-convict and safe cracker, who was set up and jailed by Sadie and her lover. McCracken is childhood friends with Dirk Mattox, who is engaged to Iolanthe Silverthorne whose father, an avid book collector, is opposed to the marriage unless Mattox can retrieve the priceless book from Jech. This all, of course, is slowly divulged over hundreds of pages. Before the end, it turns out that the hobo, who gets back on his feet with the money from Jech and is hired by Mattox, is actually the estranged brother of Iolanthe Silverthorne. The family's reunion allows Dirk and Iolanthe's marriage, and the murder, which ends up being an accidental shooting, is solved by the detective, Simon Grundt, who is the retarded janitor at the police station and "formerly of the Lincoln School for the Feeble Minded."

While this in no way does justice to the book, leaving out dozens of important characters and plot twists, it conveys the complexity and absurdity of a Keeler novel. Some contemporary reviewers, who were obviously just not open to the Keeler experience, felt that "one gets the impression that [Keeler] starts without knowing where he is going, bringing in all the complications he can think of and winds the story up as best he can"; but in actuality, Keeler, who was initially trained as an engineer, devised a plot construction formula itself so complex that it is resembles electrical system schematics rather than Freytag's pyramid (see Figure 2.10).[186] Such plot designs were likewise similar to Faulkner's famous Yoknapahtowpha timeline written across the wall of his study. Keeler outlined his methodology in a series of seven articles published in *Author and Journalist* from April to November of 1928 (see Figure 2.11), entitled "The Mechanics

---

[186] *New York Times* (Sept. 8, 1935), BR16.

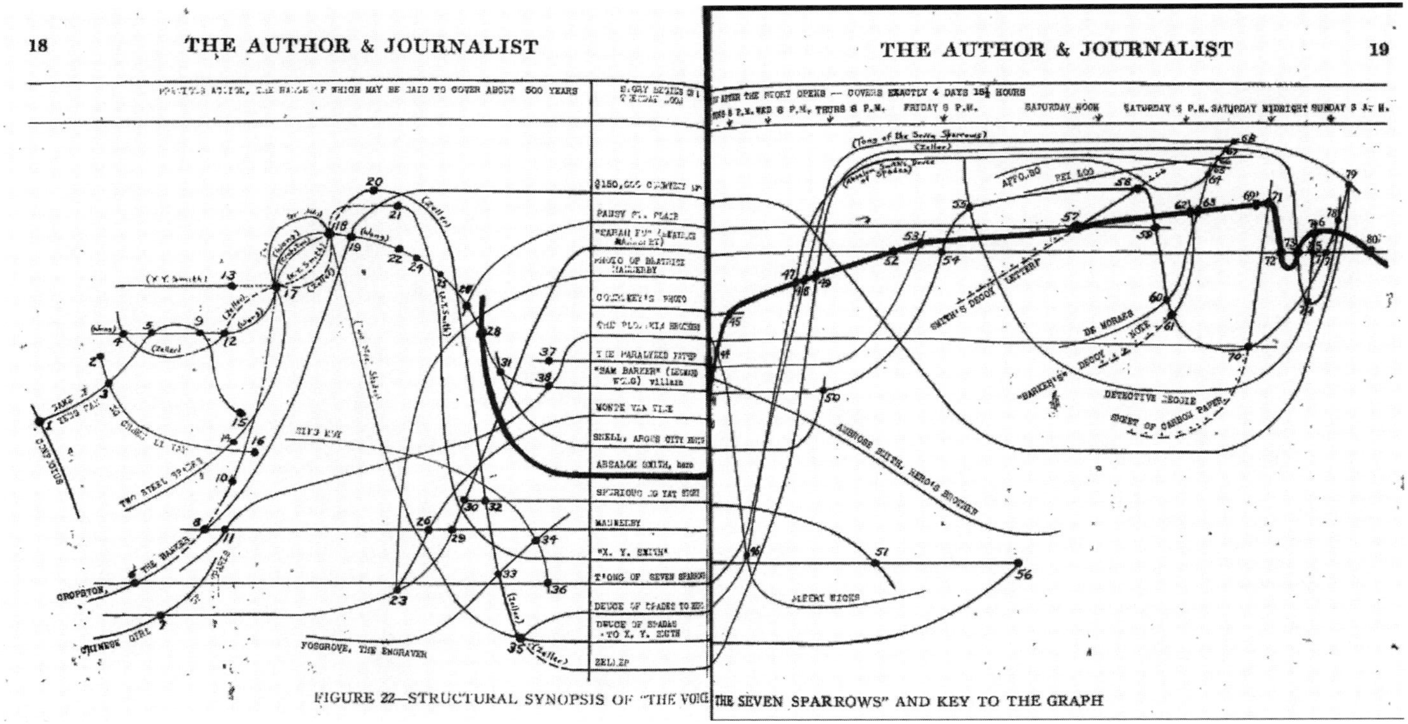

Fig. 2.10   Keeler Graph, *The Author and Journalist*, April 1928. Copyright never renewed

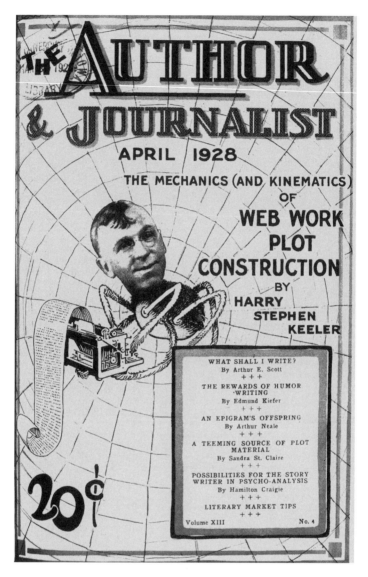

Fig. 2.11   *The Author and Journalist*, April 1928 © 1925 The Author and Journalist

(and Kinematics) of Webwork Plot Construction." As a way of illustrating his technique, he published the schematics for his *Voice of the Seven Sparrows* [See Illustrations], which, if nothing else, illustrates the complexity of his formula. The formulaic aspect of his design is even more blatant in its initial presentation in three issues of *The Student Writer* (the forerunner of *Author and Journalist*) in 1917, an excerpt of which runs:

Combining this with the interrelation that must exist between all the incidents of a story we have what may be termed a mathematical rule which may be expressed: if the thread A, or viewpoint character, should figure with the thread B in an opening incident of numerical order "n" (with respect to the incident in the conditions precedent) there must be invented a following incident "n + 1" involving threads A and C; and incident "n + 2" involving threads A and D; an incident "n + 3" involving threads A and E; and so on up to perhaps at least "n + 4" or "n + 5"; and furthermore "n" must cause "n + 1"; "n + 1" must cause "n + 2"; "n + 2" must cause "n + 3" and so on.[187]

Next to this, the *Plot Genie* looks like a child's game. Keeler takes formulaic and pulp conventions and multiplies/compounds them to such an extent that they become absurd. Coincidences don't offer easy closure, but are so ubiquitous that they are the engine that moves his books forward, involving not one mystery, but dozens. Many of his books adopt an *A Thousand and One Arabian Nights* like structure wherein stories are often layered upon other stories and seemingly unrelated fictional tales appear within larger works in a Russian-box narrative. This allowed Keeler to reuse short stories that appeared earlier in pulp magazines, but these often affect the outer narrative framework, with fictional characters or even references to Keeler himself suddenly appearing in the framing narrative. Aspects like character and characterization become just something used to confuse the plot or add another layer. Racist pulp conventions are brought to the extreme in Keeler's books in that everyone seems a bigot, though there are many places where Keeler destroys racial stereotypes—a stereotyped, pidgin-English-speaking American Indian actually has a PhD; a white racist is suddenly turned into an African-American. Seemingly, Keeler himself was relatively liberal, both culturally and politically. In general, Keeler is the pulp author in extremis; as Jay Lewis of the Norfolk, Virginia *Ledger-Dispatch* wrote, "Harry Stephen Keeler is a one man fiction factory, who turns out mystery thrillers with the ease, speed and skill of a Ford plant producing cars."[188]

Yet Keeler, despite or even because of his hyper-pulpism, arrived at the same modernist sensibilities as James Joyce and William Faulkner. His books have philosophical resonance, stylistic inscrutability, and a sophistication of plot structure that rivals *Ulysses*. His "Chameleon" books, *The Chameleon* and *The Mysterious Mr. I*, which were originally written as a single novel but published by Dutton in two volumes in 1938, feature the apex of the unreliable narrator who changes personas more than 50 times. The book (for so am I calling it according to its original construction) is arguably Keeler's masterpiece and, like *Ulysses*, follows the narrator for twenty consecutive hours but through the streets of Chicago rather than Dublin. The narrator, whose true name the reader doesn't discover until the last page, constantly shifts identities from an escaped con man to an optometrist

---

[187] *The Student Writer*, Vol. 11, No. 7, 1.
[188] N.d. quoted in *Keeler News: the Bulletin of the Harry Stephen Keeler Society*, No. 27 (June 2000), 10.

to a safecracker to a character impersonator to a sneak thief to a numismatist, etc. Like Ford's *The Good Soldier*, the plot is layered, with the narrator constantly playing with the reader's expectations. The plot and manipulations are so intricate that it is easy to lose track of all the subplots, many of which—again, like in *Ulysses*—are not tied together for hundreds of pages.

Other works, such as *The Portrait of Jirjohn Cobb* about four men stranded on a small island during a flood, are decidedly Faulknerian with similar settings, dialect, and even sentence structure: "Though no mere 'conference' was this, being held between the Sheriff and the 3 men, all equidistant about the flat stone government marker, and with feet of all practically touching this improvised table; rather was it, instead, a poker party – a poker party being held not, as customarily, in a comfortable gambling room, but on a lonely, fog-ridden, and now boatless island: a poker party minus cards – minus chips – minus money!"[189] As in Faulkner, the mentally handicapped are integral to the overall grotesque atmosphere of the author's constructed world: the detective of *The Green Jade Hand*, which was published in 1936 but based on pulp short stories published as early as 1922, is reminiscent of *The Sound and the Fury* and *The Hamlet*. Many of Keeler's later novels feature "Idiot's Valley," a Yoknapawtopha like county where all the residents are "a slew of gun-toting mental defectives."[190] Other books, such as *The Marceau Case* are reminiscent of John Dos Passos's newsreel style in that they are told entirely through telegrams, news clippings, excerpts, and epigrams.

Oddly enough, despairing reviews of Keeler often make parallels between him and modernism: the reviewer for the *Baltimore Evening Sun* stated that "Harry Stephen Keeler has a large following which would seem immense were he content to write his stories once in English, instead of three or four times in a strange jargon which eschews distinction between the parts of speech, and employs such a system of punctuation as no other writer, save, perhaps, Gertrude Stein ever dared."[191] The humorous contention that Keeler's writing is in other than English reoccurs often in reviews. One reviewer contended that Keeler's books were written in Choctaw; *The Translation Index* pointed out that "Of Keeler's half a hundred or more books published up to the end of 1953 in Great Britain and America, 77 translations have been made in Spain, Germany, Italy, Portugal, Czechoslovakia, Finland, Holland, France (in Russian for Russian readers; in French for French readers), and Sweden. It would be fascinating to read one of his yarns that had been translated into English."[192] This was very similar to the popular reaction that *Finnegans Wake* received: Arnold Bennet's claim that *Anna Livia Plurabelle* be published with a "Joyce Dictionary," or that *The Wake* was an onslaught on the English language.

---

[189] *The Portrait of Jirjohn Cobb* (NY: Dutton, 1940), 10.

[190] Francis Nivens, "The Wild and Woolly World of Harry Stephen Keeler, part 4" *Journal of Popular Culture*, Vol. 7, No. 1, 160.

[191] N.d. quoted in *Keeler News: the Bulletin of the Harry Stephen Keeler Society*, No. 27 (June 2000), 10.

[192] Ibid.

More recently, in response to the republication of Keeler's *The Riddle of the Traveling Skull*, Otto Penzler of the *New York Sun* wrote in an article titled "The Worst Writer in the World," "To be fair, there are several scholars of the mystery genre who believe reading Keeler is fun. I expect they take home the Christmas tree that is lopsided and the ugliest dog in the pound because it's so achingly homely that it's cute. They go to Ed Wood movies and listen to the music of John Cage because they feel they're the only ones who can appreciate the truly dreadful." It is telling that Penzler relates Keeler to the music of John Cage, especially since Cage was infamous for compositions based upon and inspired by *Finnegans Wake*. Compositions such as his "Roaratorio: an Irish Circus on *Finnegans Wake*" (1979) used his methodology of "chance" wherein arbitrariness dictates results.[193] This parallels not only the composition method of Joyce, but Keeler's as well.

Perhaps the most telling link though between Keeler's extreme form of pulp story construction and high-modernism is the similarity between his methodology and Joyce's composition of *Finnegans Wake*. The *Wake* is a web of allusions culled from whatever interested Joyce in his wide-ranging reading, recorded in stacks of notebooks, written into an ever-enlarging structure and linked via word play and themes of anti-structuralism. Similarly, Keeler kept files of random newspaper clippings that he then wrote into his stories, linking them together via an intricate webwork of plot and coincidence, but rather than a form based upon anti-structuralism, Keeler's is formula and structure consciously taken to the point of absurdity. The similarities of these two authors are a melding of extremes where randomness, complexity, and playfulness are integral.

But Keeler's plot construction is more than just an exercise in form, for it offers a portrait of the world where, since coincidence is paramount, personal choice is ultimately absurd. Webwork-designed novels allowed for randomness and coincidence, but not deus ex machina coincidences that were a pulp convention, but such a web of random coincidences, beautifully constructed, that they hint at an existential message. It, like many modernist philosophies, is influenced by the ideas of entropy and the instability of time. In the section of *The Chameleon* where the narrator impersonates the philosophy professor Scopester Glendenning, Keeler not only offers a rationale for such plot technique where the professor proves how effect results in cause, but also reflexively equates Glendinning with the author himself by referencing the implausibility of the plot for Keeler's earlier book, *The Marceau Case*.

In his lecture, Glendinning proves that "effect" actually produces "cause," that what is deduced by man as randomness can in actuality be a pattern but one that man doesn't have the critical distance (or scope of time) to recognize. The description, which sounds suspiciously like chaos theory, segues to a Duchampesque one about how the passage of time is just the third dimension trying to impose structure on the fourth; by way of example, he shows how this undermines

---

[193] See Marjorie Perloff's essay on *Roaratorio* in her *Postmodern Genres* (Norman: U of Oklahoma P, 1995), 211–227.

the plausibility of "locked-room" mystery stories: "'And so, answering this last question succinctly, Time is, in essence, only Space! And were the fact of the 4-dimensionality of the Universe full understood--" I added, "—grasped completely, that is, by magazine and mystery novel readers, fiction writers could no longer write mystery stories known as 'locked-room murders[.]'" A student then asks the professor how he would solve the Marceau Murder Mystery "if, as an author, you'd invented the mystery?", blatantly referencing Keeler's own novel of the year before.

Such self-references are common to Keeler (there are Keeleresque characters who are editors of the magazines—*10-Story Book* and *America's Humor*—that Keeler edited), but this instance is especially telling in that it is linked to not only a philosophical (and mathematical) treatise that rationalizes Keeler's use of coincidence and randomness, but also one that is applied to mystery stories. Unquestionably, Keeler is explaining his destruction of the formulaic and traditional mystery while reflexively adhering to the form. In a Keeler webwork plot, randomness—or chaos—becomes the form or structure itself, form in chaos.

Numerous scholars —Thomas Rice, Michael Gillespie, Peter Francis Mackey, to name the major proponents—have written persuasively about chaos theory as integral elements in Joyce's structure for both *Ulysses* and the *Wake*.[194] It is evident in the "Wandering Rocks" episode of *Ulysses* and in Bloom's general wandering around Dublin. For Mackey, whose *Chaos Theory and James Joyce's Everyman* looks exclusively at *Ulysses*, chaos theory as a useful tool for entering into a Joycean philosophy of freewill. For Rice, science from Euclidian geometry, relativity, and chaos theory imbue all of Joyce's work, from *Dubliners* to the *Wake*—Euclidean science concretely influences his earlier work and the new sciences are analogous in the construction of *Ulysses* and the *Wake*. For Gillespie, the use of a nonlinear narrative of complexity, which rises from modern scientific theory, is a valuable tool for the reader to enter into the *Wake*. Regardless, Joyce's construction of the *Wake* was mathematical, as was both Keeler's webwork construction and his philosophy of structure in randomness.[195]

There is no evidence that Keeler was familiar with any of the modernists, or that he ever read them; according to Richard Polt, a philosophy professor at Xavier University and the head of the Harry Stephen Keeler Society, Keeler's later reading consisted mostly of fellow pulp writers and books on science, history, religion, and philosophy.[196] And since Keeler's theories of plot construction were firmly in place

---

[194] Thomas Rice, *Joyce, Chaos, and Complexity* (Urbana: U of Illinois P, 1997); Michael Patrick Gillespie, "Reading on the Edge of Chaos: *Finnegans Wake* and the Burden of Linearity," *Journal of Modern Literature*, Vol. 22, No. 2 (1999), 359–371; Peter Francis Mackey, *Chaos Theory and James Joyce's Everyman* (Gainesville: U P Florida, 1999).

[195] According to Caresse Crosby in a letter to Richard Ellman, Joyce's biographer, Joyce claimed that the structure behind *Finnegans Wake* was mathematical; see Ellman, 614.

[196] E-mail to the author, Sept. 9, 2007.

as early as 1917, it is safe to say that he arrived at what is traditionally lauded as the sensibilities of modernism from an entirely pulp milieu.

The detective story is innately modernist since it challenges and involves the reader, an ethos that drove the modernist tendency for difficulty and one that is perhaps most famously apparent in Conrad's stated goal to awake the reader and language alike from complacency.[197] The type of complexity that both modernists and Harry Stephen Keeler practiced unquestionably did this, but so did the less complex but linguistically rich stylistics of pulp authors such as Robert Leslie Bellem, with whom I started this chapter. Ludwig Wittgenstein agreed, for during the late 1930s and early 1940s, as he was championing the direct action and utility of language (in contrast to the disingenuous ways of philosophical debate), he was an ardent fan of Street and Smith's detective magazines, having them sent overseas by his friend Norman Malcolm, a philosophy professor at Cornell. Numerous times, Wittgenstein's letters prompt Malcolm for a fresh supply, stating "my mind feels underfed," and "Thanks for the detective mags! They are rich in mental vitamins and calories." In 1948, after reading a detective story by the (very un-pulpish) Dorothy Sayers that was so "bloody foul that it depressed me," Wittgenstein stated that opening a pulp magazine was "like getting out of a stuffy room and into the fresh air."[198]

For Wittgenstein, the pulps held a directness and vigor that academic debate didn't. In a letter of March, 1948, he wrote to Malcolm that "Your mags are wonderful. How can people read *Mind* [the philosophical journal] if they could read Street and Smith beats me. If philosophy has anything to do with wisdom there's certainly not a grain of that in *Mind*, & quite often a grain in the detective stories."[199]

For the history of literary modernism, the pulps hold that same promise of vigor and wisdom.

---

[197] Just as science fiction is innately postmodern. Brian McHale points to this about detective fiction (though for differing reasons). See *Postmodernist Fictions* (NY: Routledge, 1987), 16.

[198] See Alfred Jan, "Doan, Carstairs, and Ludwig" in *Blood 'n' Thunder* (Fall, 2006), 16–19. Wittgenstein quoted from Norman Malcolm's *Ludwig Wittgenstein: A Memoir* (Oxford: Oxford U P, 2001).

[199] Quoted in Jan, 17.

Chapter 3
Lurid Paperbacks and the Re-Covering of Modernism

It used to be thought that 'serious writing' and 'best sellers' were mutually exclusive categories: the popular book never had literary merit, and the work of distinction would never be popular. The paperback experiment has destroyed that superstition and has proved that literary merit doesn't interfere with the broadest sort of popular success – unless the merit depends upon subtlety, allusion, or the defiance of popular notions. If the merit has come to be widely recognized and the book is regarded as something of a classic, the public will buy it in quantities simply for that reason, as happened with the paperback editions of *A Farewell to Arms* and *The Great Gatsby* – though I doubt that it could happen with Kafka's *The Castle*.

—Malcolm Cowley, *The Literary Situation* (1954)[1]

As I read more and more original novels in paperback, it strikes me that this method of publishing has replaced some of the older media of training, experimentation and exploration in fiction.

Years ago the pulp magazines and the avant-garde magazines provided two areas in which writers could prepare. Now the pulps are gone and the avant-garde is for the most part languishing. Paperback originals, with their demand for action and movement, their need to satisfy and compel the reader, their freedom of subject matter, have moved in to fulfill this need …

—Robert Kirsch, March 11, 1960[2]

Part 1

Modernism on the Wrong Side of the Tracks

Naked Bodies For Sale. Night after night the girl sold her body in the dark streets of Paris. In the rented room she would slowly strip herself naked before the men who paid for love …

Toward morning she would return to the arms of the man who took her earnings—the same man who beat her until she cried out aloud for the sensual release of his savage love making …

---

[1] Cowley, *The Literary Situation*, 106.
[2] Robert Kirsch, *Lives, Works & Transformations: A Quarter Century of Book Reviews and Essays* (Santa Barbara: Capra Press, 1978), 133.

Fig. 3.1   *Bubu of Montparnasse.* Berkley Publishing Corporation, 1957

So reads the back cover of the 1957 Berkley Press edition of Charles-Luis Philippe's *Bubu of Montparnasse.* This, like many mid-1950s paperbacks, promises some pretty tawdry stuff. Turn the book over and its front cover continues the tone of racy Parisienne lasciviousness (see Figure 3.1): glaringly red, it depicts an attractive, dark-haired woman dressed revealingly in a low-cut blouse that accentuates her figure. She is leaning back suggestively on a bar stool, her garter belt and fishnet stockings visible through the slit in her short skirt. She stares brazenly at the viewer and smokes a cigarette. Next to her is the title in lurid yellow block letters. And the publishers let us know that the work isn't censored: on the bottom of the cover, right underneath T.S. Eliot's name, is the phrase "complete and unabridged." Wait. T.S. Eliot? Yes, in big bold yellow letters: "Preface By T.S. Eliot."

Why does the idea of Eliot being associated with such a gaudily marketed book seem incongruous to us (which it invariably does, especially if one is unaware of Philippe's little known naturalistic work)?[3] In reality, the edition promises more than it delivers, for Eliot's introduction is mostly nostalgic for the time when he was first introduced to Paris, which *Bubu* recalls. He praises Philippe for his impartiality and dispassionate depiction of street life, and, ultimately, for his realism, stating in the last line of the intro that "… even the most virtuous, in reading it [*Bubu*], may feel: I have sinned exceedingly in thought, word and deed."[4] It is the marketing of the edition that warrants our reaction though, for the pairing of it and Eliot's reputation is so incongruous. Critics have involved Eliot's name for decades as being instrumental in the New Critical establishment of modernism as a cohesive, autonomous movement directly opposed to such crass, popular works and forms as the paperback. This was especially true in the 1950s when modernism had been established as a literary institution by the academy and general reading public at large. The fact that this bifurcation between high and low is still to be found in our literary tradition is proven by the current scholarly battle being waged against it in recent critical publications.[5] The post–World War II years that deepened this schism also saw numerous manifestations of avant-garde modernism in popular culture, especially masculine writers like Hemingway and Fitzgerald, or Faulkner, whose many long out-of-print titles were republished between 1947 and 1957 in popular paperback versions.[6]

What, therefore, can we make out of such seemingly unmodernist books as this *Bubu*, which, considering the hundreds of thousands of copies published, was invariably many readers' first introduction to Eliot? Or, for that matter, what happens to the idea of a writer's presumed audience when we consider the Armed Services Edition of Virginia Woolf's *The Years*, which had a circulation of 155,000. It is hard to conceive of Woolf imagining a book of hers being passed around a foxhole in the South Pacific. In such instances, the author is not introduced into a modernist sphere of consumption, for the milieu is not even literary,

---

[3] The reaction to this volume, when I used it as an illustration for a talk on pulp modernism given at the "Material Modernism" conference in Vancouver, was uniform: a guffaw at the pure disparity that exists between Eliot and, well, everything else corporal, material, or otherwise symbolized by the pinup on the front cover.

[4] *Bubu*, 9.

[5] The last few years have seen a glut of critical books exploring the relationship between highbrow and popular; a sampling would include Latham's *Am I a Snob?*, David Chinitz's *T.S. Eliot and the Cultural Divide*, Morrisson's *The Public Face of Modernism*, Bornstein's *Material Modernism*, Pease's *Modernism, Mass Culture and the Aesthetics of Obscenity*.

[6] For more on Faulkner's paperback career, see part two, section one of this chapter.

as in a book store, but a proletariat sphere—a Woolworth's, Kresge's, or army hospital. In this realm, Woolf's and Eliot's peers are not Joyce, Pound, and Stein, but Edgar Rice Burroughs, H.P. Lovecraft, and Mickey Spillane.

Despite any surprise on the part of academics at these seemingly inappropriate pairings, the rise of the paperback retroactively illustrates how nonelitist, popular aspects of modernism existed at the movement's inception, and the paperback phenomenon does so despite the years of hierarchization on the part of the academy. Considering this, the modernist reputation of autonomous art can be seen as a marketing ploy, which again becomes evident in the mass distribution and reception of popular and sensational forms of the material book.

The initial idea, which I am evoking with *Bubu*, that these paperbacks pose a threat to monolithic modernism isn't new: Malcolm Cowley, whose role is undeniable in the academic definition of modernism, dedicates two chapters to the popular paperback phenomenon in his 1954 book *The Literary Situation*. He begins by describing his rambles through Chicago on either side of the "jagged, gradually changing, and indefinite line that separates the Gold Coast from the rest of the Near North Side."[7] On the East side of this line are the Newberry Library, art galleries, big apartment buildings: in a word, culture. West of the line are the "shabbier houses," "honkytonks," Negro and Polish neighborhoods. Tellingly, it is on this side of the line that the drugstores, newsstands, and department stores that sell paperbacks can be found, as opposed to the bookstores of the east side, which he describes as hallowed depositories of culture. Cowley recounts his paperback slumming, as it were, in the many Walgreen stores, newsstands, and drugstores in the poorer sections of town. He recounts the wide variety of paperback books published, from art, history, and psychology books to the more common westerns, detective, and sex thrillers; he wonders over a sensationally marketed collection of Sartre short stories, *Intimacy*; he appreciates the variety of books offered, but marvels at the lack of distinction between the "mud" and "sapphires." Yet there is something slightly noxious about his descriptions: in a Walgreen's he notes that a rack of books has been removed for an expansion of the "bottled goods" (read "booze") department; he notes that people can buy these books along with "rubber goods" and "bottled goods," and people can buy these books while "drinking the liquor," and "curing one's hangovers at the drug counter"; he watches the typical paperback purchaser: for example there's an old man in a shabby overcoat who looks but does not buy, and a "broad-beamed housewife, her head wrapped in a soiled babushka," who buys Mickey Spillane's *The Big Kill* in lieu of the Sartre. Cowley himself is "tempted to answer their [the books'] plea, fill my overcoat pocket with books, buy a pint of whiskey at the liquor counter," but instead he heads over to the other side of the tracks to cleanse himself in the healthier cultural atmosphere of real bookstores.[8]

The point of Cowley's odyssey is to illustrate not only the need of cultural leadership that exists in bookstores, cultural magazines, and book reviews, but

---

[7] Malcolm Cowley, *The Literary Situation* (NY: Viking, 1954), 96.
[8] Cowley, *Situation*, 99.

also the threat that mass paperbacks with their uniformly sensational and saturation marketing pose to American culture. For paperbacks, due to their very availability, their sheer mass of titles, and their lack of cultural distinction, threaten to overrun the governing cultural pressure that exists in intellectual spheres of the bookstores, book review sections, and literary magazines. The picture that Cowley paints of the lower masses that feed upon the paperback is one of slovenly, alcoholic, fecund illiterates who cannot tell the difference between Sartre and Spillane, and the evil of paperbacks is that they don't draw such defining lines themselves. What Cowley is doing in these pages is policing the cultural borders between elite literature and popular literature. He is, as it were, protecting his own intellectual and professional stake in American culture and letters.

This paperback debate is yet another episode in the long feud that the cultural elite has with the masses, similar to the debates about book clubs and pulp magazines discussed earlier. Yet the paperback debate still has resonance; the rise of the paperback changed modern publishing in ways that are with us today. And the prejudices of Cowley's time still exist in the academy. For example, Thomas Roberts's *An Aesthetics of Junk Fiction* (1990) uses the moniker "paperback fiction" to stand for the lowest category on the literary scale of sophistication, and "paperback reader" as the least sophisticated or dedicated type of reader. We shall avoid discussing the limitations and dangers (as well as the innate cultural and economic prejudice) of Roberts's categorizations. Let it suffice to note the use of a physical form to identify a type or quality of literature—Roberts does not identify the "serious reader," the most sophisticated type who "include the reading of certain novels among the most important experiences in their lives," as the "hardback reader," or as the "limited edition," or "first edition" reader.[9] There is a prejudice of form that can be traced back to the pulp beginnings of the paperback, despite the fact that many of the modern classics appeared in mass paperback.[10] And despite the fact that, for example, the early 1950s saw mass-paperback houses publishing collections of avant-garde writing and cultural criticism (including that of Cowley himself)—such as NAL's *New World Writing*, Avon's *Modern Writing*, Pocket's collection of *The Pocket Atlantic*, Bantam's *Saturday Review Readers*—all of which reached a mass audience with a circulation that little magazines such as the *New Masses* or *Poetry* could never approach.

Even earlier paperback ventures defy the concept of modernism's form as purely elite; I have already mentioned Haldeman-Julius' Little Blue Books with their socialist-leaning modernist authors and strictly utilitarian form. If the Little Blue Books were *The Masses* of paperbacks, then Charles Boni's Paper Books were the *Vanity Fair*.

---

[9] Roberts, *An Aesthetic of Junk Fiction* (Athens: U of Georgia P, 1990), 31.

[10] In Europe, the publishing of books in unbound boards—precursors of the paperback—has been standard for centuries, and this held true for modern publications. For example, the Odyssey Press's edition of *Ulysses* (1933, printed in Hamburg) was paperbound. The success of the first two European popular paperback houses, Albatross and Tauchnitz, sparked the mass-paperback phenomenon in England and America.

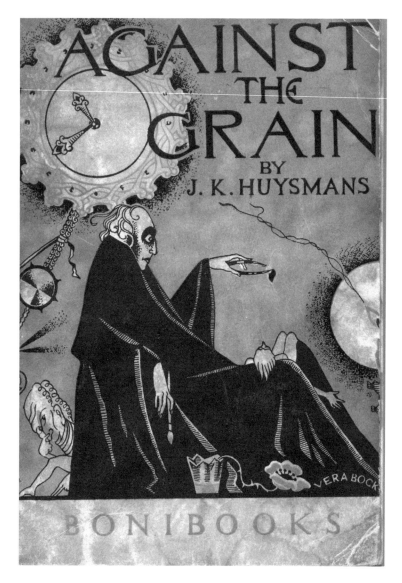

Fig. 3.2   *Against the Grain.* Albert and Charles Boni, 1930

In 1929, Boni, the creator of the Modern Library, developed a modern, highly stylized paperback form that featured highbrow, mainly modernist authors. The Boni Paper Books series published works by Wilder, Lawrence, Anderson, and Gorky with cover illustrations by Rockwell Kent and Vera Bock (see Figure 3.2). They were made out of high-quality paper, and could even be, for the price of a dollar, sent back to the publisher and rebound in a Kent-designed cloth binding. According to a press release, Boni promised, "Only quality production will make it possible to publish good books, better printed than those now offered in cloth bindings, on equally good paper, at one-seventh of the current book price."[11] Unfortunately, Boni's attempt was short-lived due to the depression and his marketing the books via a subscription method rather than through popular marketing. Despite its short life, Boni's paperback series is an example of coalesced mass and modernist form. Others existed: Albatross Press, for example, started their paperback publishing in 1932 with *Dubliners*.[12]

Although these imprints might seem singular exceptions to a general rule, I still contend that the very physicality of the paperback has a critical resonance and aptness for modernism due not so much to the fact that both sides of the cultural debate—the trade press and the mass paperback press—have seemingly merged in modern publishing, but because the paperback is a peculiarly modernist form.[13]

This last claim is perhaps as shocking as finding Eliot's name on the cover of a tawdry and sensational paperback, for the idea of a modernist work being presented in a popular, disposable form goes against not only the idea of modernism's culturally elite position, but against modernism's aspirations—even self-definition—of permanence. It begs the question whether or not modernist art necessarily needs to be in a form designed for posterity. The physical form of literary modernism, as a reaction to the dilution of a privileged readership, became rarefied: specialized publishers, limited editions, collectible manuscripts and galleys. What is it that rubs us wrong, as inheritors of modernism's mantle of cultural nobility, about a book marketed for its sexual explicitness rather than exclusivity or obscurity if the work contains both elements? If modernist elitism is a construction, as I have previously argued, then the idea of Eliot, Lawrence, or Joyce being sold sensationally to a mass audience doesn't seem so very ludicrous. The very fact that modernism appeared in the marketplace works against the constructions of elitism—no matter if the basis of such constructions lay with the author or with the subsequent criticism. Even recent revisionist criticism that places modernism in the marketplace, such as Lawrence Rainey's *Institutions of Modernism*, which looks at *Ulysses* in the rare-book trade, still ignores much more explicit examples of commercial modernism like paperbacks. Indeed, modernism's claim to timeliness, to capturing the existing, contemporary, modern moment is itself an ephemeral act: not only

---

[11] Thomas L. Bonn, *Undercover: an Illustrated History of American Mass Market Paperbacks* (NY: Penguin, 1982), 33.

[12] According to Slocum and Cahoon, "In 1932 *Dubliners* was published in a copyright edition by the Albatross Verlog, Hamburg, Paris, Milan, as Vol. I of the Albatross Modern Continental Library. ...There was also a special edition of ten copies *hors commerce* printed on Japanese vellum and bound in green half-leather," *A Bibliography of James Joyce* (New Haven: Yale U P, 1953), 18–19.

[13] There are remnants of the prejudices of form against the modern paperback in that a respectable author must be published initially in hardcover—hence those affluent enough to buy a hardcover are that much closer to the author's aura, more in the know—before the book is released in a mass edition. But, granted, such prejudices are much less than during the time of modernism.

dedicated to capturing a fleeting impression of time and place, but enmeshed in a depiction that is, by modernity's very pace and nature, doomed to be outmoded.

In earlier chapters, I discussed ways in which popular and modernist dynamics coexisted at the advent of modernism before the schism between high and low or varied genre literature; this chapter considers how different manners of marketing modernism—whether elite or sensational—can be used to exhume such interrelationships. In other words, how the physical products of modernist or popular literary output—the books, advertisements, dustwrappers—can be used archaeologically (in the Foucauldian sense) to re-create aspects of modernism lost due to the accumulation of critical or cultural capital.

Comparing, say, a first edition of *The Sun Also Rises* with a popular 1940s paperback edition may initially seem frivolous, but whereas they are very different publications, they are undeniably the same "book." And any reaction against such a comparison stems from the fetishization or fallacy of the first appearance, that privileging of early and first editions (ironic because this itself emanates from the marketplace of the book collector). No work of literature can exist in a vacuum; the physicality of a book—the dustwrapper, illustrations, typeface, quality of paper, where it is bought, the price paid, etc.—all play a part in the initial interpretation of a book, all are integrally linked to the author and publisher's intended, even constructed audience, how it is read by the individual as well as the public en masse. Hence the marketing provenance of a book, its very materiality, constitutes a literature of its own, a constructed aura or psychology of the physical book that is symbiotic to the fiction as well as our understanding of it. In the marketplace, the basic look of a book at the moment of decision to buy or not transforms all buyers into primal literary critics.[14] The book, whether ephemeral or fine edition, is indeed the most primary or rudimentary form of advertising (and in many instances holds both overt and complex clues to the text and its production). Given this, the dust covers of a Scribners first edition or a later Bantam paperback are each texts in themselves that tell very different stories. As Jerome McGann asserts in *The Textual Condition*, "To read, for example, a translation of Homer's *Iliad* in the Signet paperback, in the edition published by the University of Chicago Press, in the Norton Critical Edition, or in the limited edition put out by the Folio Society (with illustrations), is to read Homer's *Iliad* in four very different ways. Each of these texts is visually and materially coded for different audiences and different purposes."[15] I propose to look at one type of coding and the ramifications that this has on the long-term reception of modernism.

---

[14] For a similar textual reading, see Ted Bishop, "Re: Covering Modernism – Format and Function in the Little Magazines," in *Marketing Modernism*, 287–288. Bishop relies on the terms of Jerome McGann's Bibliographic Environment, in considering the physical material of the book in an attempt to return aesthetic modernism to the dynamics of the marketplace. Also useful is the first chapter of George Bornstein's *Material Modernism* (Cambridge U P, 2001).

[15] Jerome McGann, *Textual Condition* (Princeton, NJ: Princeton U P, 1991), 115.

Cultural Prejudice and the Visuality of the Book

The visual coding of the popular paperback, seemingly oppositional to modernism, is unavoidable because of its extremity and sensationalism—even if the paperback form itself has been efficiently avoided in literary criticism exactly because of this visual coding. This prejudice against the blatant visuality of the form is even more pronounced when considering the emergent influence of visual studies upon literary criticism—though perhaps too established now to be considered emergent. Informed generally by visual arts and film studies, and specifically by Guy DeBord's ideas of modern society as one of spectacle, by Benjamin's flanneur, Foucault's panopticon, Lacan's gaze and Mulvey's male gaze, the study of modernism has been invigorated by visual culture.[16] Comparisons between literature and spectacle are not new, at least when it comes to the visual arts, but these traditionally were constrained to fine arts: modernism and cubism; Conrad and impressionism; Stein, Picasso, and African folk art. Studies such as Deborah Schnitzer's *The Pictorial in Modernist Fiction from Stephen Crane to Ernest Hemingway* (1988), which examines high modernists in regard to impressionism, cubism, and postimpressionism, are ultimately a reciprocal substantiation of the interdisciplinary influences among privileged audiences and coterie producers. Schnitzer's work, for example, entirely ignores the presence of mass audiences and the milieu of mass culture. Worse, such studies propagate class-based prejudices that arose with the establishment of modern aesthetic judgment in the eighteenth century.

In "Who's Afraid of Visual Culture?," art critic Johanna Drucker states the need for a reassessment of the oppositional relationship between fine and popular arts: "There has to be a way to take seriously early twentieth-century visual forms of response to modern life that were not exclusively concerned with either transcending it in favor of a universal language of abstraction or with radical political negation."[17] She cites groundbreaking art retrospectives, such as *Graphic Design in the Mechanical Age* (1999, Cooper-Hewitt Museum), as offering an alternative. If looking to commercial art (especially graphic art) is a productive solution, can it also solve a similar problem in literary studies? Obviously so. The many recent works that examine modernist literature in relation to popular culture point to this trend. Karen Jacobs's *The Eye's Mind* looks at authors from Henry James to Zora Neale Hurston in order to "reconceiv[e] modernist fiction as an intimate participant in the period's broad and ambivalent preoccupation with visual perception," and Jacobs does so by establishing how modernist authors are informed by popular spectacle (Woolf by the village pageant, Nathanael West by

---

[16] In universities, freshmen composition has been moving in that direction for years, with texts such as *Ways of Seeing* replacing *Ways of Reading*.

[17] Johanna Drucker, "Who's Afraid of Visual Culture," *Art Journal*, Vol. 58, No. 4 (Winter, 1999), 36.

popular film).[18] Other studies, such as Maggie Humm's *Modernist Women and Visual Culture: Virginia Woolf, Vanessa Bell, Photography and Cinema,* consider the interchange of literature and photography. There are likewise many recent books that consider how visuality surfaces in the texts of single authors, such as Peter Luries' *Vision's Immanence: Faulkner, Film, and the Popular Imagination,* Roy Gottfried's *Joyce's Iritis and the Irritated Text* (1995), Joseph Valente and James Hansen's forthcoming *Joyce and Visual Culture.*

Joyce, half-blind, lends himself particularly well to studies of visual spectacle. The term visuality seems to reify an agenda that already existed in modernism; consider the history of such publications in Joyce studies: Cheryl Herr's work on music halls, Jennifer Wicke's work on advertisements, Brandy Kershner's work on photography. I'd even argue that Jackson and McGinley's illustrated and annotated *Dubliners* relies upon exploring the visual aspects of Joyce's time, and his works' milieu; they explore the shift from a literate to visual culture.

The majority of literary visual criticism is comparative: Faulkner and film, Joyce and photography, Modernism and sculpture, etc., rather than about the visuality of the text (typography, etc.) or the book itself (dustwrapper, marketing, etc.). This is due to the conceived modernist prejudice against the material aspect of literature, in other words, that modernism isn't concerned with the material issues or the marketplace—and if not a conceived modernist prejudice, then an actual academic one. Hence, it is safe to consider literature in relation to accepted forms of high plastic arts, or forms as obviously different as film, but we dare not consider the work itself within the dynamics of a market driven society, or on the same continuum as such obvious products as popular literature, pulp magazines, etc. There is no escaping the basic materiality of the text, just as there is no escaping the visuality of the written word.

What these studies that compare visual media to literature do is facilitate our understanding of the text. And this brings us to the reason why Joyce (and modernism) is so appropriate for visual studies, a reason that has been traditionally overlooked. The idea of visuality is one of accessibility; the visual is contrapuntal to the idea of a restricted or elite text. In order to clarify this, let me dwell for a moment upon a goal of modernist stylistics: perhaps Conrad wrote it best when he stated that the goal of the artist was "above all, to make [the reader] see!" Conrad, Joyce, and other modernists used their stylistics to give the reader a sense of hyper-reality, a physical dimension. Their goal was to teach, not to ostracize. Joyce's ephemera, and Leopold Bloom's flanneuristic gaze is the personification of Stephen's ruminations on Sandymount Strand about the transformation of immediate (popular, mundane) experience into art (though this, like so much high-modernism, depends upon the male gaze and the objectification of the female body. Remember that Stephen's stroll and aesthetic diatribe in "Eumaeus" returns him to the place of his initial epiphany in *Portrait,* inspired by his voyeuristic stare at the "bird girl's" naked legs).

---

[18] Karen Jacobs, *The Eye's Mind* (Ithaca: Cornell U P, 2001).

The conception of the popular audience in traditional literary and film studies is one of passivity, as illustrated by Frederic Jameson's statement that "the visual is *essentially* pornographic, which is to say that it has its end in rapt, mindless fascination."[19] Yet this concept of audience, like Adorno's, is reductive, especially when considering the act of reading, which, as recent cognitive theory has shown, is dialectic rather than passive.[20] This restrictive idea of audience is one of a mass or populist entity being acted upon; what visual criticism should aspire to and reconstruct is an audience more like the active reader. The term "reader" denotes a dialectic of interpretation, of interaction rather than passivity. The reason there are visual aspects in, say, Joyce's work are to instruct the reader into how to read and interpret, to destroy passivity. Therefore, visual aspects of the written word blurs considerations of highbrow or lowbrow, or perhaps exists simultaneously within such designations.

Perhaps an example: the Sigla of *Finnegans Wake* grew out of Joyce's own shorthand, but they offer a shorthand note to the reader, a solid, nonalphabetical (hence uncorruptible, untranslatable or trans-translatable) signifier of an anomalous concept. Hence with "E" or "Ш" Joyce conflates "character," as in a typographical pheme, and "character," as in HCE. The *Wake* levels the playing field for all readers, beyond culture and class, and the sigla becomes a symbol for this, literally.

I've used this typographical example consciously, because it is very nontraditional to consider textual or typographical matters in visual criticism. Whereas such studies as those mentioned above are (for the most part) correct to try and find visuality within the text, notice how none are dedicated to the visuality *of* the text, of the book as object. This is due in part to the last 50 years' devaluation of bibliographic scholarship in favor of criticism, but it is also due to the prejudice against seeing literature as visual, hence material, hence a commodity. Bringing visuality back to the book is long overdue. Two studies that do consider the book and literature as object are Drucker's *The Visible Word: Experimental Typography and Modern Art, 1909–1923* (1994), which is as much concerned with visual art as literature, and Jerome McGann's now standard *Black Riders: The Visible Language of Modernism* (1993). Likewise, *Re-Covering Modernism* refocuses visuality (pun intended) back to the material cohesiveness and unity of printed material.[21]

This argument is alike in spirit to McGann's, which stresses the visuality of the text and the necessity for critics to pay attention to the integrity of such, to research the flaws or degeneration of translation from edition to edition (the loss of original type face, line breaks; the milieu of the printed book); yet unlike

---

[19] Fredric Jameson, *Signatures of the Visible* (NY: Routledge, 1990), 1.

[20] See, for example, Linda Flower and Christina Haas, "Rhetorical Reading Strategies and the Construction of Reading," *College Composition and Communication*, Vol. 39, No. 2 (May 1988), 167–183.

[21] This is not to say that the works of modernism are cohesive (as new Criticism would have it). In fact, this chapter forwards the idea of the instability of both modernism and its reception.

McGann (though toward a similar purpose) and Drucker, who more or less limit their studies to typography, hence semiotics and experimentation—I would extend the focus rather to both the reception of the different manifestations of text and on the book as a whole: how a book under different auspices or wrappers, sold as a reprint in a different market evinces different textual and hermeneutical dynamics, hence underlining—and this is where McGann and I again intersect—how the marketplace affects reception and even constitutes a poetry or literature of its own, inextricably grounded in the material.[22] Yet, just as Bob Brown's visual literary modernism relied upon racial signifiers (as pointed out by Michael North and discussed in the last chapter), the visuality and materiality of modernism as divulged by the paperback evinces or builds off of a strain of misogynistic visual signifiers that deconstruct elite and popular categories.

Let us momentarily return to Joyce for an example, specifically the 1947 Signet paperback of *Portrait* (see Figure 3.3). Of all of Joyce's covers, it is illustrative, attempting to capture more fully the themes and dynamics of the text; it works toward narration and exegesis. Modern readers must get over the surprise—perhaps even prejudice—of the popular paperback form of the '48 Signet to see that the artist Robert Jonas, who Signet reserved for the covers of their more "literary" works, has managed to capture a surprising amount of nuance: Stephen's stance displays both his cultivated artistic distance and awakening sensuality, the opposing tensions of church and exile are neatly illustrated in the unequal balance between steeples and masts. Importantly, the cover is not as naturalistically rendered as most of the era's paperback covers, but drawn with an element of abstraction. Therefore, the cover attempts to not only attract the reader, but explicate as well.

This parallels Joyce's own concerns about the Shakespeare and Company edition. He painstakingly searched and demanded just the right color blue for the cover—that of the Greek flag, and white islands of letters rising from the blue Aegean in order, along with the title, to clue the early reader into the classical parallel. The cover is more than just decorative, but instructive in a way that later covers weren't. Ted Bishop has pointed out that later covers like the Random house just reified the modernist, elite position.[23] They are decorative, not narrative.

But more than this, the Signet also captures—if not misogyny, then a reliance or element of objectification of the female body innate to androcentric modernism. I once had a colleague misconstrue this cover as an illustration of one of Stephen's dalliances with a prostitute, rather than his moment of epiphany. This mistake is telling, for the climax of *Portrait* is Stephen's learning to channel the mundane or physical into elevated art, yet rather than pure aesthetics, it is yet still embroiled, dependant upon, and incorporating the physical, sexual, or ephemeral. The same with modernism, which portends to separate itself from the mundane marketplace,

---

[22] McGann looks to the postmodern poets Jack Spicer and Ron Silliman who utilize/pay attention to the extraneous or metatext of book covers, ISBN numbers, etc., as extension of their poetics, *Black Riders* (Princeton, NJ: Princeton U P, 1993), 107.

[23] See Bishop, "Re: Covering Ulysses," *Joyce Studies Annual*, Vol. 5 (1994), 22–55.

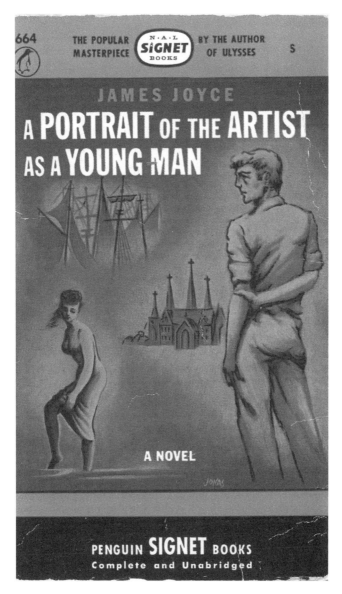

Fig. 3.3   *Portrait of the Artist as a Young Man.* Penguin Signet, 1948

still exists as physical material in the marketplace. Joyce incorporated this in *Ulysses* when he continually brings Stephen Dedalus's attempts to escape to the ethereal aesthetic plane crashing down to earth: his physical needs end "Proteus" just as Bloom's begin "Calypso"; his absinthe-fueled bohemian performance in Nighttown ends with his literally falling to the ground, a deflation of his pretensions.

What this popular text illustrates is a type of accessibility of Joyce, though the sanctioned reception would have us consider such marketing "misreadings." The multivalency of Joyce should negate the idea of a misreading. Applying the idea of a misreading to *The Wake*, for example, is, well, difficult to say the least. What I would like to propose is that such editions are on a continuum with the packaging of the first edition of *Ulysses* and that they inform or explicate or offer a way to read the text, and that these are likewise on the same material continuum as Joyce's typographical play, and the larger overarching modernist goal to bring a dimension of visuality to the written. Paperback marketing offers a way to rediscover this popular aspect.

The paperback is a form that marks the obvious (visual, corporal) end to modernist elitism at a time when modernism's avant-garde status is in tension with its popular manifestations in mainstream culture. Ultimately, though, this mantle of elitism was not dropped or reassessed or eyed critically, but, if anything, propagated with renewed vigor, its borders policed all the more stringently due, in part, to its manifestation (and cooption) by the popular, paperback form. Since I shall be returning to and framing arguments, authors, and books by the paperback form, it is necessary to give a brief account of its history and major publishers.

The Paperback

The paperback has a long and successful tradition in Europe, ranging from the classic publications of Venetian Aldus Manutius in the sixteenth century to the German Tauchnitz books of the nineteenth.[24] What is common to these editions is that they were intended to bring inexpensive quality books, in both form and content, to a large audience.

Such an ethos is similar to that of Arnold Bennett, who, in *Literary Taste, and How to Get It* (1909) proposed not only a list of important authors necessary to the cultivation of literary taste, but the price one should pay for inexpensive editions. Both John Carey and Sean Latham have examined Bennett: Carey sees him as an author and critic whose "writings represent a systematic dismemberment of the intellectual's case against the masses"; Latham sees him as a figure that straddles the line between low- and highbrow, who (like Joyce) was a fan of both Pound and Corelli.[25] Bennett becomes therefore, a prototypical embodiment of the English

---

[24] I have used numerous sources for the history of the paperback, most importantly Frank L. Schick's 1958 *The Paperbound Book in America*, Thomas L. Bon's *Undercover: An Illustrated History of American Mass Market Paperbacks*. For the history of the New American Library *Heavy Traffic and High Culture* (Carbondale, IL: Southern Illinois U P, 1989), also by Bonn, is integral. Also important are: Allen Billy Crider, ed., *Mass Market Publishing in America* (Boston: G.K. Hall, 1982); William H. Lyles, *Putting Dell on the Map* (Westport: Greenwood P, 1983); Piet Schreuders, *Paperbacks, U.S.A.* (San Diego: Blue Dolphin, 1981).

[25] Carey, 152; Latham, *Snob*, 72–73.

middlebrow intellectual, one who was raised on *Tit-Bits*, the English parallel to an early pulp literary magazine such as the *Ainslee's* or *The Popular Magazine*.[26]

Rather than examine Bennett's blatantly economic-based approach to reading and writing, which both Latham and Carey have already done, it is sufficient to league Bennett's aim to bring culture to the middle class (which invariable brought the wrath of Pound, Eliot, Woolf, Lewis, and most of the other prominent modernists) with the motivation behind the rise of English paperback publishers such as Albatross Press (actually an international effort) in 1931, and Penguin Books in 1935. There were numerous experiments and attempts to create a demand for mass-market paperbacks in America during the early part of the twentieth century, most notably the pulp house Street and Smith, and the Arthur Westbrook Co. of Cleveland. Yet none lasted long, and all, with one or two noteworthy exceptions, were popular and genre fiction, competing with (and growing out of) the yellow backs, dime novels, and pulp magazines. This all changed when Robert de Graff started Pocket Books, which was based, more or less, on the success of Penguin in England. De Graff, like Penguin's Sir Allen Lane before him, figured that inexpensive quality books, distributed like magazines in newsstands, drugstores, and department stores, would appeal to the American public. De Graff, unlike Lane, relied upon pulp magazine-like covers to catch the eye. Whereas Penguin books were stolidly marketed via uniform, nonillustrated covers, Pocket Books used full color, glossy covers. It is worth quoting De Graff's initial full-page ad for the *New York Times* at length:

> Today is the most important literary coming-out party in the memory of New York's oldest book lover. Today your .25¢ piece leaps to a par with dollar bills. Now for less than the few cents you spend each week for your morning newspaper you can own one of the great books for which thousands of people have paid $2 to $4.
> These new Pocket Books are designed to fit both the tempo of our times and the needs of New Yorkers. They're as handy as a pencil, as modern and convenient as a portable radio – and as good looking. They were designed specially for busy people – people who are continually on the go, yet who want to make the most of every minute.
> Never again need you say "I wish I had time to read" because Pocket Books gives you the time. Never again need you dawdle idly in reception rooms, fret on train or bus rides, sit vacantly staring at a restaurant table. The books you have always meant to read "when you had time" will fill the waits with enjoyment.[27]

Against the expectations of the publishing industry, Pocket Books was an instant success, sparking a glut of new paperback publishers, the first being an American division of Penguin. Other houses included Red Arrow, Avon, Popular Library,

---

[26] Interestingly enough, Conrad, Joyce, and Woolf all attempted, at one time or another, to publish in *Tit-Bits*, and failed, while Bennett succeeded.

[27] Quoted in *Under Cover*, 35–36.

and American Library. The war and paper shortages put a hold on new ventures, but by 1949 Dell, Fawcett, Lion, Bantam, Ballantine, the New American Library (NAL), Graphic, Pyramid, and Checker books had all started paperback lines. The majority of these were formerly (or concurrently) pulp houses that already had the distribution and resources to start paperback branches of their own.[28] Since the majority of paperbacks were reprints of trade publisher hardbacks, the paperback marked the demise of the pulp form, or—in the case of the paperback originals (PBOs) that Fawcett pioneered in 1950 and that eventually took over the market— its evolution.[29]

The books published by these early paperback companies ran the gamut of fiction to nonfiction, "serious literature," movie tie-ins, and how-to manuals. As Geoffrey O'Brien puts it:

> The paperbacks provide just such a stew of high and low, of vigorous and decayed; they are the common ground of Shakespeare and Irving Shulman and Bishop Fulton J. Sheen, of *Light in August* and *Lust Party*, indiscriminately mingled and mating. In short, they partake of the characteristic American atmosphere. It is useless to distinguish between "high art," "personal art," "folk art," "commercial art," or "Exploitation"; in the living situation, they all float about in the same pond.[30]

Malcolm Cowley's nervousness about the cultural scene at the dawn of the paperback revolution is understandable, then, seeing as his career was one of designating good literature from bad, and the paperback, as a form, ignored such designations. In 1947, there were 297 new titles and approximately 95 million paperbacks sold.[31] Cowley's criticism and fear of literary fecundity parallel that generated by the pulps decades earlier.

The choice of works for paperback publishers depended upon many factors, not the least of which was availability. For the most part, "pb" publishers were at the mercy of the trade hardback publishers, who must first be willing to sell the rights for reprint of a title. And even then, the first option to buy/print would go to the established hardback reprint houses, such as Grosset and Dunlap; if they turned down the option, or two years had passed since the initial hardback republication, then the paperback publisher could buy the rights to republish a title. It took some time for new publishing houses to "find" their audience. In his history of the NAL, Charles Bonn describes the gambles taken by the publishers Victor Weybright and Kurt Enoch in obtaining authors they thought would sell, such as Faulkner (who did) or Edna Ferber (who didn't).

---

[28] See Bonn, *Heavy Traffic*, 8; *Under Cover*, 46–51; Schick, 155–176.

[29] At least one prominent literary critic saw the paperback originals as having the same avant-garde dynamic of the little mags; see Robert Kirsch's epigram for the chapter.

[30] O'Brien, *Hardboiled America, Lurid Paperbacks and the Masters of Noir* (NY: DeCapo, 1997), 13.

[31] Schick, 81.

The line between capturing an audience and constructing an audience was often blurred. The paperback technique of distributing books via saturation in every possible venue parallels the method of publishing books that would appeal to any type of possible interest. Besides the obvious physical similarities of cover design, this type of marketing is the most evident illustration that the paperback grew out of the pulp magazine. Each publishing house had divisions for nonfiction and even specific types within those divisions (such as the Pocket Library of Great Art or Signet's scholarly Mentor Series of nonfiction and Key series of popular nonfiction); and each had different imprints for fiction and, within them, genres of fiction (such as Dell First Editions series of PBOs, Penguin Classics of world masterpieces, etc.). Already by the late-1940s/early-1950s, the wide-ranging breadth of titles and genres is striking; a single publisher like Signet (NAL formerly a division of Penguin) featured not only classics, but sensational literature as well. Signet broke away from Penguin in 1948 and was soon one of the most distinguished paperback publishers, known for the quality of their titles and their outstanding cover illustrations. In that year they published 26 titles, including: *100 American Poems*, edited by Selden Rodman; Erskine Caldwell's *Tragic Ground;* Thomas B. Dewey's *As Good As Dead*; Joyce's *A Portrait of the Artist as a Young Man*; Basil Heatter's *The Dim View*; Horace McCoy's *They Shoot Horses, Don't They?* and *No Pockets in a Shroud*; Arthur Koestler's *Darkness at Noon*; William MacLeod Raine's *Sons of the Saddle*; Enid Currie and Donald Geddes's *About the Kinsey Report*; James M. Cain's *Past All Dishonor*; Charles Jackson's *The Lost Weekend*; Hugh Holman's *Slay the Murderer*; William Faulkner's *The Old Man*; Thomas Wolfe's *Look Homeward, Angel*; and Mickey Spillane's *I, the Jury*.

Over the next few years, Signet would publish more paperback originals such as *I, the Jury*, as well as reprint such modern classics as Lawrence's *Lady Chatterley's Lover* and *Sons and Lovers*, James T. Farrell's *Young Lonigan*, Conrad's *Heart of Darkness*, numerous more Faulkner titles, Flannery O'Conner's *Wise Blood*, Ralph Ellison's *Invisible Man*, Erich Maria Remarque's *Arch of Triumph* and *Spark Of Life*, Salinger's *Catcher in the Rye*, Christopher Isherwood's *Goodbye to Berlin*, Tennessee Williams' *A Streetcar Named Desire* and *Glass Harp*, George Orwell's *1984*, Chester Himes' *If He Hollers Let Him Go*, Dreiser's *An American Tragedy*, etc.

What is important to consider about these titles is that no matter the relative success in terms of paperback sales, they sold in this popular form almost without exception many, many more times than any earlier publication. This was true of even a formerly popular title such as Caldwell's *God's Little Acre*.

Originally published by Viking in 1933, *God's Little Acre* had sold 8,300 copies—a relatively large run. As a Modern Library book, it had sold more than 66,000 copies, and as a Grosset and Dunlap hardback reprint, it had sold 150,000 copies—a total of roughly 225,000 copies. As a Signet paperback, *God's Little Acre* sold *3.5 million in only a year and a half*![32] The usual initial Signet run of a new

---

[32] Schick, 142.

title was 200,000 copies, for Fawcett 300,000. To put this into perspective, most first edition runs by modernist authors ran from around 5,000 (the first edition of *The Sun Also Rises* was 5,090 copies) to 30,000 for the more popular or fashionable authors (*A Farewell to Arms* was 31,050 copies following the success of the earlier novel, and *The Great Gatsby* was 20,870). Other modernist classics sold far, far less than their initial run; *The Sound and the Fury* only sold 500 copies.[33]

Similarly, between 1943 and 1946, the Armed Services Editions published nearly 120 million volumes of books, including popular and highbrow alike. John Cole states in *Books In Action, The Armed Services Editions*:

> The Armed Services introduced thousands of Americans soldiers and sailors to the pleasure of reading. Between 1943 and 1947, nearly 123 million copies of 1,322 titles of these flat, wide and very pocketable paperbacks were distributed to U.S. Armed Forces around the world. Best-sellers, classics, mysteries, history, westerns, and poetry were part of each shipment. For most of the U.S. troops overseas, Armed Services Editions were the only books easily available. And never had so many books found so many enthusiastic readers.[34]

Authors included Sherwood Anderson, Robert Benchley, Kay Boyle, Rupert Brooke, Joseph Conrad, William Faulkner, F. Scott Fitzgerald, Ernest Hemingway, A.E. Housman, Aldous Huxley, Thomas Mann, Katherine Mansfield, H.L. Mencken, George Bernard Shaw, and, of course, Virginia Woolf. The Armed Services editions are all uniformly marketed and include any and every type of literature. Due to their essential utilitarianism, they are probably the one physical book form published in the twentieth century that is devoid of any marketing or cultural signifier. While (as we shall see) the trade paperbacks became a common denominator of literature by their very sensationalism and extremity of advertising, the Armed Services Editions became a nonhierarchical literary product due to their lack of advertising and, needless to say, their somewhat captive audience.

Hence, the paperback form undeniably introduced more modernist authors to a much larger audience than ever before. It is possible that the 1950s accelerated canonization of modernism owes a debt to the pulp paperback form in two ways: 1) by pure numbers, these authors were finding their largest audience ever, and 2) because the academy was redoubling its efforts to hold onto the modernist pretense of elitism as a reaction against the popularizing of the avant-garde form. Hence we see reactions such as Cowley's, who was likewise at this time rewriting and republishing his influential *Exile's Return*. Yet the sense of the contamination of modernism by this new, seemingly fecund and uneducated reading public that pervades Cowley's account of his adventures in the mass marketplace(s) was usually subsumed in the more popular and pervasive criticism of the paperback form—that of their sensational cover art.

---

[33] See Hanneman; Schwartz, 11.

[34] Cole, *Books In Action, the Armed Services Editions* (Washington, DC: Library of Congress, 1984), 3.

Re-Covering Modernism

Early paperbacks of the late 1930s and early 1940s were quite staid compared to a decade later. Many, such as the early Penguin, Pelican, and Albatross books, stuck with wholly (and wholesome) typographic covers. Early pictorial covers were likewise muted, with exceptions being Pocket's 1941 edition of Zola's *Nana* (whose nipples are visible through her blouse), which, according to Bonn, became one of the most popular titles with the armed services throughout the decade, despite the outcry against the cover (see Figure 3.4).[35] By the late-1940s though, book designers turned to the pulp magazines for inspiration due to heightened competition. Paperback covers relied upon what Schick calls the "Three S's" of Sadism, Sex, and Smoking Gun.[36] As Cowley points out, paperbacks, regardless of their content, were marketed by homogenizing sensationalism. This was likewise noted in 1952 by the Congressional Gathering Committee on Current Pornographic Material, which stated that "the covers of many of these [paperback] volumes are extreme and in bad taste [but] in many cases the covers do not reflect the content of the book and are designed to promote sales by catering to the sensational."[37] Yet often these covers depicted aspects that were in the text, albeit heightened or out of context. How dishonest or misleading is depicting Stephen Dedalus staring at a woman who is lifting her dress and exposing her thighs, or illustrating Faulkner's *Sanctuary* with a scene of violence or *Pylon* with a thinly veiled ménage à trois, or showing an embracing couple on the cover of Lawrence's *Women In Love*? Those elements are undeniably in the texts.

Granted, the idea of D.H. Lawrence, or many of these other modernist authors, being marketed through their reputations for risqué literature seems less inappropriate than Eliot's name appearing on the cover of *Bubu of Montparnasse*. What might bother an academic like Cowley about these specific volumes is not so much the sensational marketing as the fact that they are offered in these editions at all, which seems to disprove the aura of modernism. Published in the hundreds of thousands, marketed sensationally via saturation, the pulp paperback as a form seems anathema to the origin and aura of the author/artist; it worries Benjamin's idea of "form-value" of the work of art in the modern age of mechanical reproduction by replacing it with sales value. Yet these sensational covers illustrate elements that are indeed apparent in the texts. In fact, they sometimes offer clues to elements that academic critics have historically ignored due to the fact that it would be unthinkable to consider canonized (and idealized) works of modernism in this context.

One such example is Bantam's 1949 edition of *The Great Gatsby* (see Figure 3.5). Originally published in 1946 with a cover illustration depicting a jazz-age party scene, the 1949 edition was released with a much racier dustwrapper to

---

[35] Bonn, *Undercover*, 100.
[36] Schick, 85.
[37] Quoted in Schick, 113.

Fig. 3.4   *Nana*. Pocket Books, 1945

be placed over the already existing 1946 cover art in order to pick up lagging sales and tie into the Paramount film starring Alan Ladd as Gatsby.[38] The new dustwrapper depicts a shirtless, muscular Jay Gatsby, hands on belt as if about to take his pants off. Behind him is a man, hand at waist, pointing a large revolver at

---

[38] Many paperback companies also used dustwrappers to cover other publisher's returns and back stock after a merger or buyout.

Lurid Paperbacks and the Re-Covering of Modernism 171

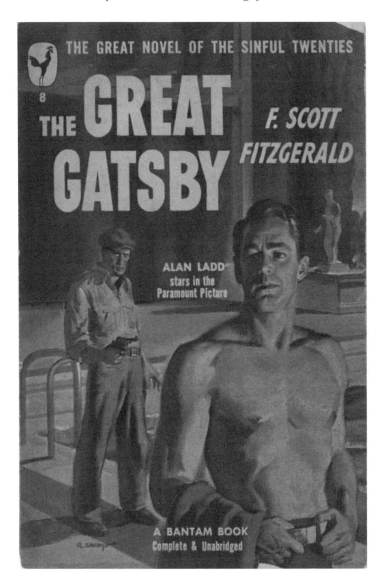

Fig. 3.5   *The Great Gatsby.* Bantam Books, 1946

Gatsby's back. The latent homo-eroticism in the image is undeniable, and, though constructed entirely for reasons of sensationalism, suggests a submerged element of the book. Likewise, the heading, "The Great Novel of the Sinful Twenties," missing from the earlier cover, leads a reader to expect more sex rather than parties. It is telling, especially considering the primacy of *Gatsby* as a canonical text, that critics did not notice the submerged themes of homosexuality until the late 1970s. Social passing is a theme in the novel, but so is sexual passing evident in unspoken tensions, such as that between Jordon and Nick, or troublesome gaps in discursive action, innuendos, and a "cultivated ambiguity."[39] The adumbrated scene and interaction between Mr. McKee, "a pale, feminine man" and Nick is the most obvious example. Nick tenderly wipes a spot of shaving cream off McKee's cheek; Nick and McKee "groan" down in the elevator, where the elevator boy snaps at McKee for holding the elevator lever; and most telling is the gap in action between the elevator ride and "…I was standing beside his bed and he was sitting up between the sheets, clad in his underwear, with a great portfolio in his hands."[40] Such ellipses, like those on the back cover of *Bubu* are a staple omission for the sexual act in risqué pulp fiction, and point toward Nick's sexual passing, hence his identification with Gatsby's passing.

That paperback publishers utilized such dustwrappers, cover illustrations, blurbs, and out-of-context quotations in order to sensationalize aspects of the text, and even went so far as to change titles of lesser-known books to more sensational ones—for example, the Bantam edition of Somerset Maugham's *Christmas Holiday* was retitled *Stranger in Paris*—raises the question of the sanctity of an author's work. Modernist criticism has repeatedly debated the sanctity of the text, especially in matters of editorship, and most infamously in the debate about the revised Gabler edition or Danis Rose's recent Reader's Edition of *Ulysses*. The text becomes unstable once it has been released into the world due to the ensuing involvement of publisher, editor, book designer, even bookseller: all play a role in the construction and reception of a text, and all deflate or dilute the author's intention. Jerome McGann contends, "literary works are coded bibliographically as well as linguistically. In the case of the bibliographic codes, 'author's intentions' rarely control the state or transmission of the text."[41] The modernist trend of specialty, do-it-yourself, or little press publishing was one way to circumnavigate this (I shall later examine this phenomenon with *Lady Chatterley's Lover*), but despite the original textual production, consequent publications likewise bring a work further away from the author's original construction, or "aura," to use Benjamin's term. This gap between writerly intent and audience reception is best illustrated in the pulp paperback. Yet it is important to note that many publishers, as well as authors, looked for and actively sought paperback reprinting. Such editions often brought more income to the author than the earlier editions, and, along with Hollywood film rights, were necessary support for many modernist authors.

---

[39] See Keath Fraser's 1979 article "Another Reading of *Great Gatsby*" in *F. Scott Fitzgerald's The Great Gatsby* (Harold Bloom, ed. [NY: Chelsea House, 1986]), which is the earliest mention I can find of the text's submerged homosexuality. Another example of such a paperback cover capturing submerged text would be Jonas's abstract cover for Penguins' *Sanctuary,* see article by Madden in Abadie and Fowler's *Faulkner and Popular Culture* (Jackson: U P of Mississippi, 1990).

[40] *The Great Gatsby* (NY: Scribners, 1953), 38. Fitzgerald's ellipses.

[41] McGann, *Textual*, 60.

This was certainly true for Faulkner, whose long out-of-print titles, never too successful in the first place, found new life in the popular paperback market.

The fact that modernist authors were often deeply concerned with the look of first or early editions of their works, but paid scant if any attention to the paperback editions doesn't so much reflect the authors' lack of control over reprints as much as the ephemeral quality of the paperback and the elitist stance of many authors. I shall return to some of these themes later in the chapter, but what is important to stress is that the paperback form is critically valuable because it is seemingly opposed to the traditional modernist form, yet it is undeniably modern. The form's absorption into the dynamics of publishing coincided with the end of literary modernism as a practice, as its reification in the academic canon. With each new generation of reader, the literary culture beforehand is rediscovered, reexamined, and reconstructed. As literary critics we know this better than anyone; each new generation of literary criticism reassesses and resituates the canon according to its generational ethos. Just as the literary academy returned to the scene and form of modernism (re-creating the little press and little magazines, reconfirming the canon and form of modernism, etc.), I would like to use the paperback form, as well as the pulp genre in general, to return to the pre-elitist dynamics of modernism and assert that the very ephemeral nature of the pulps and paperbacks alike is, as I have stated earlier, peculiarly appropriate for modernism, for these genres physically strip the text of academic preconceptions. Granted, they often replace them with sensational connotations, but it is this very disjunction or incongruity that begs examination.[42]

George Bornstein, in discussing the validity and simultaneous difficulty of Gabler's synoptic edition of *Ulysses*, states "that very difficulty also confers an advantage – it fractures the deceptive unity of any single 'clear text' edition, which always encourages the notion that it offers us 'the' novel."[43] Though Bornstein is discussing the dual presence of multiple textual representations in the synoptic edition of *Ulysses*, the overall and well-publicized instability of the book, its "hybrid material textuality [that] both reveals and reflects its hybrid thematic," can be used as a parallel to modernism itself; in other words, the instability of *Ulysses* as a text, indeed as *the* text of modernism, illustrates the instability of modernism.[44] Similarly, the differing texts of the synoptic edition parallel in general the gap between multiple editions of the same book, including a modernist first and a later sensational paperback. I would like to consider modernism *en toto* as a text and argue that its pulp and paperback forms (either alongside or independent from its accepted textual forms) both reveal and reflect its hybrid nature: they defy the traditional view that there is a "proper" or normative form for modernism, and reveal and reflect its high/low nature.

---

[42] My efforts here are similar to those of George Bornstein, Wim Van Mierlo, Edward Bishop, and others of the "material modernist" school, which attempt to broaden or debunk what narrowly constitutes a proper or definitive or complete text.

[43] Bornstein, *Material Modernism* (NY: Cambridge, 2001), 138.

[44] Ibid., 139.

Paperback Modernism and the Great Divide

In making the above claim about the fitting nature of the ephemeral paperback in regard to modernism, I have in mind Baudelaire's 1863 statement that "Modernity is the transitory, the ephemeral, the contingent, one half of art, the other half being the eternal and immutable."[45] These tensions identified by Baudelaire remain vibrant throughout the age of modernism, with authors such as Woolf and Joyce attempting to capture and transform ephemeral material such as advertisements, or ephemeral moments such as epiphanies, into permanent high art. Yet the material aspect of modernism disavows/avoids its own ephemeral or material nature, and the traditional academic definition of modernism (until recent revisionist practices) would ignore modernism's subjective reliance upon the mundane or popular. Hence, this is a definition that would seemingly work against the exclusive modernism that the academy has long attributed to Ezra Pound, T.S. Eliot, and Virginia Woolf. For Baudelaire, modernism was a product of tensions of the ephemeral *and* eternal, of the mundane *and* the artistic (or, in similar terms, the popular and the elite). Manet, as an example of an artist influenced firsthand by Baudelaire's ideas, filled his pictures with graphic and—for the time—shocking realism of Parisian street life, transforming the transitory into a poetry of beggars and prostitutes: Pierre Bourdieu names Manet's *Absinthe Drinker* (1859) as marking the seminal break with the academy and the beginning of an autonomous network of modernist symbols. Indeed, the primary venue of impressionism was not the elite museum or gallery, but the Parisian street café. Somewhere between Baudelaire and, say, Woolf the conscious (or admitted) knowledge of this interdependence between the mundane and the ethereal—and, more importantly in regard to form, the elite and popular—became if not overlooked, certainly unstressed. In light of Baudelaire's quote, the ephemeral and sensational form—both literary and actual—of the pulp magazine and/or paperback makes them appropriate to modernism and not solely as the stimulus for reaction, as something for modernism to define itself against.[46]

In apparent contrast to Baudelaire's claim, and less than a decade earlier, is Flaubert's *Madame Bovary*, an ur-text for the modernist novel, which utilizes the binary between the elite and the popular, reality and romance as a contrapuntal source of irony and disillusionment. For Flaubert, Emma Bovary's adolescent devouring of romance novels, how she "tried to find out what one meant exactly in life by the words *bliss, passion, ecstasy,* that had seemed to her so beautiful in

---

[45] Duchting, *Edouard Manet: Images of Parisian Life* (NY: Prestel, 1995), 25.

[46] The pulp magazine is even more ephemeral (read disposable, transitory) than advertisements, for the ad slogan, logo, or jingle is designed to be memorable again and again, creating a repetitive need for a product. The pulp, on the other hand, was designed for instant appeal and disposal, the cover art usually misrepresenting or further sensationalizing the magazine's contents; each month's design again trying to capture the reader's attention anew. Magazines often built their reputations on their specific styles of fiction as much as on their quality of fiction.

books" leads to her end.⁴⁷ The poison she swallows isn't arsenic, but romance. Despite these elements of criticism innate to Flaubert's use of the popular romance, it becomes integral in the construction/projection of self-hood (or *bovarism*, as it has come to be known, thanks to Gaultier), as it does to the ironic (modernist) voice of the novel.

Before proceeding to Flaubert's own relationship to writing and popular culture, it is necessary to divert attention a moment to the idea of popular culture—specifically popular literature as feminine. Andreas Huyssen, as a means to define the postmodern against modernism, labeled mass-culture feminine and "Modernism's Other." This brought an irate reaction from cultural critics and modernist revisionists who soon showed the "great divide" as not so very great. Of course, there was a certain element of high-modernism, the patriarchal element, who defined themselves as reacting against what they saw as a feminine popular literature and whom were canonized exactly because of their patriarchy. But this was only one segment of modernism reacting against one segment of popular literature. As earlier chapters of this study have shown, there was both a vibrant masculine and feminine mass-culture, there was both romance and domestic fiction just as there were dime novel Westerns and masculine detective yarns. Huyssen's definition was based upon the monolithic canonized idea of modernism, and was really more concerned with the postmodern than the modern, as he himself has pointed out more recently.⁴⁸ The Bovarism of characters such as Conrad's Lord Jim, the narrator from Joyce's "Araby," the tall convict in Faulkner's "The Old Man," and Richard Wright's Bigger Thomas is a reaction to and constructed by male-oriented mass-fiction, which goes to show how slanted or specific Huyssen's initial definition is.

It is important to note again that working class pulp magazines considered both mass-market slicks and highbrow little magazines as effeminate. More than this, though, the idea of an androcentric modernism remasculating fiction has as much to do with economic consumption of mass-circulated magazines that constructed the female consumer—but the overall scene of magazine production was much more varied than just little magazines and those types of slicks. The modernist reaction to both the feminine and the popular is more complex than a certain avant-garde art-for-money's-sake emasculation left over from the decadents; if modernists like Ernest Hemingway and Ezra Pound defined their movement against both mass-consumption and mass-literature, they still sought out popular venues, played with mass-cultural genres, and often relied upon mass-circulated venues. Furthermore, their works, names, and reputations became mass-circulated themselves, for ultimately it is impossible to guarantee the evolution or reception of a work once it has left the hands of the author, as Flaubert found out.

---

⁴⁷ Flaubert, *Madame Bovary* (NY: Norton, 1965), 24.
⁴⁸ Andreas Huyssen, "High/Low in an Expanded Field," *Modernism/Modernity*, Vol. 9, No. 3, 373n7.

As early as 1839, in an essay entitled "Les Arts et le commerce," Flaubert attempts to establish, rather idealistically, the transcendence of the artist above the material and physical world of the marketplace, but, as Mark Conroy points out, Flaubert's polarities of spiritual art and materialist commerce are actually inextricably entangled.[49] Writing about *L'Education Sentimentale*, Conroy asserts that Flaubert's criticism of the spread and taint ("the corruptibility") of the marketplace in modern life cannot be disassociated from the very means by which he presents that criticism since the book is ultimately a commodity. Therefore, "Throughout his career, then, Flaubert seems to have fluctuated between the desire not to be a commodity at all, and the desire to be merely a very high-toned one."[50] This discomfort/resistance to his audience led Flaubert to avoid clichéd, bourgeois language, to depersonalize the narrator and audience alike in an effort to refute a public that, ultimately, he needed. Sartre, as well, points out that Flaubert, through his very disdain toward popular acclaim, won it.[51] Hence with Flaubert, the future oppositional relationship between high and mass literature is far from a simple binary. If Flaubert marks the earliest conflation of the literary modernist ethos and popular acceptance, the paperbacks of the mid-1940s and early 1950s mark its finale.

We can look to Joseph Conrad's use of the imperial adventure form as an overture or introduction to the modernist use of the pulp genre. According to Ford, Conrad is *the* proponent of Flaubert's idea of *le mot juste*, the inheritor and disseminator of the Flaubertian form in English letters, which is reflected in his aim to make every line of the text carry its justification. Numerous critics have established the debt Conrad owed to Flaubert; it is commonplace to treat *Almayer's Folly* as Conrad's *Bovary*, and Ian Watt has noted that Conrad himself admitted to the overall influence of *L'Education sentimentale*.[52] Conroy examines both Flaubert and Conrad together in terms of the gap between an author's constructed/imagined audience and actual readership "because of the specific pressures, the particular strictures applied to narratives of the recent past, and the unique ideological web in which each is implicated. [Furthermore...], because they are acutely aware of their delicate positions in the culture of their time, and [...] because—above all in their works that are discussed here—they help make connections between their own micropolitical position as authors with readers and the macropolitical social element they portray in their narratives."[53] Conroy, influenced by Jameson's *The Political Unconscious*, is working within the recent trend to rehistoricize Conrad. This trend can likewise be seen in books such as Andrea White's *Joseph Conrad and the Adventure Tradition* and

---

[49] See the fourth and fifth chapter of Conroy's *Modernism and Authority: Strategies of Legitimization in Flaubert and Conrad* (Baltimore: John Hopkins U P, 1985).

[50] Ibid., 77.

[51] Ibid., 75–77.

[52] Ibid., 61; 51.

[53] Ibid., 39.

Linda Dryden's *Joseph Conrad and the Imperial Romance*, both of which return Conrad's early stories and novels to the popular milieu of their initial appearance. White's contextualization of Conrad is, for the most part, a postcolonial attempt to come to terms with the writer's often-ambiguous stance toward Imperialism, rather than an effort to come to terms with Conrad's ambiguous stance between high modernism and popular genre. Dryden's study, on the other hand, utilizes the initial critical reaction, which treated Conrad's work within the popular adventure story genre, in order to trace Conrad's critique of imperialism via the form and dynamics of the Imperial romance—subversively at first, but explicitly by the time of *Lord Jim*. Over the course of Conrad's sea stories, therefore, he "colonizes" a popular form, not only to challenge "the assumptions of romance rather than perpetuating them," but also in order to garner publication interest. Thus, with *Almayer's Folly*, he relies upon the "romantic appeal" of the Malay Archipelago, and the pseudonym "Kamudi," to secure publication.[54] Other critics have looked to Conrad's ambiguous (or multivalent) stance between poles in an effort to break down modernist elitism: Cedric Watts, for example, has written about the overt American marketing of *Chance* to a female audience and its ensuing commercial success.[55] Jameson looks to Conrad's fiction as proof that the forces that led to modernism likewise led to forms of popular literature; he sees *Lord Jim* as "a virtual paradigm of romance […which] comes before us as the prototype of the various 'degraded' subgenres into which mass culture will be articulated (adventure story, gothic, science fiction, bestseller, detective story and the like)."[56] The gap, or discontinuity between the two halves of the novel, the infamous schism, therefore marks the divergence of high and low forms.

The reflexive nature of *Lord Jim* makes such postmodern readings apt, for popular fiction supplies the integral impetus for both Lord Jim's self-disillusionment and the novel's action. The traditional academic view on Conrad since his "rediscovery" and canonization in the late 1950s has been that of an early albeit uneven modernist whose first great novel, like his oeuvre, falls into clichéd banality; what Daphna Erdinast-Vulcan calls the "almost unanimous, if qualified to various degrees, critical dismissal of the second part as a regrettable artistic lapse."[57] (This gap in *Lord Jim* parallels the gap between Conrad's early and late fiction, not only are many of the later novels such as *Chance* neglected by academia, but they are usually written off as commercial pandering.) These modernist critics were writing and judging from their privileged position after the

---

[54] Linda Dryden, *Joseph Conrad and the Imperial Romance* (NY: St. Martins, 2000), 51–54.

[55] See "Marketing Modernism: How Conrad Prospered," in Cherniak, Gould, and Willison, 81–88.

[56] Jameson, *The Political Unconscious* (Ithaca: Cornell, 1981), 207.

[57] Erdnast-Vulcan, *Joseph Conrad and the Modern Temper* (Oxford: Clarendon, 1991), 32; see Daniel Schwarz's *Conrad: The Later Fiction* (London: Macmillan, 1982) for more on the critical history of these works.

establishment of modernism as a cohesive, canonized movement, looking back at a work that was written before such classifications were conscious, when the space between genres was fuzzy. Zdzislaw Najder has written "Conrad was never a writer of and for an elite. At the time when withdrawing into high art's ivory tower was becoming increasingly common among the more ambitious writers, he, not lowering his exacting standards, wrote for all"—yet it is undeniable that Conrad craved literary respectability just as he craved (obsessed about) salability.[58] Scholars of modernism have therefore approached Conrad wearing the blinders of their own inflated cultural position—the elite vantage point that was yet to be constructed at the time of the novel's composition. Such critics not only overlook Conrad's shaping his fiction towards popular reception, but they ignore the amorphous aspect of early modernism/late Victorian fiction, a literary scene less concerned with classifications. Ultimately, the slanted modernist adoption of Conrad, replete with castigations of the popular aspects of his writing, proves the emptiness of the mantle of autonomy.

More recent critics, such as White, have seen the first half of *Lord Jim* subverting the popular form of the second half, the entire novel a criticism of the popular form: Jim decides upon his vocation after a "course of light holiday literature." And, in the section directly preceding Jim's first lost opportunity to prove himself:

> On the lower deck in the babel of 200 voices he would forget himself, and *beforehand* live in his mind the sea-life of light literature. He saw himself saving people from sinking ships, cutting away masts in a hurricane, swimming through surf with a line; or as a lonely castaway, barefooted and half naked, walking on uncovered reefs in search of shellfish to stave off starvation. He confronted savages on tropical shores, quelled mutinies in the high seas, and in a small boat upon the ocean kept up the hearts of despairing men – always an example of devotion to duty, and as unflinching as a hero in a book.[59]

Jim's persona (bovarism) was constructed by the unrealistic adventure stories he read either below deck (the deck demarcates both the physical space of reading and the psychological place of absorption/affect) or before boarding ship, his impetus to sea. Notice Conrad's use of the word "beforehand." Jim, like Emma Bovary is a product of his reading, which immediately results in a gap between reality and construction, between interior and exterior, between—and I am using the analogy in every sense—the book and its cover. The fascination that Jim holds for Marlow is that he *appears* in every sense "one of us." Jim's self-destruction reflects the impossibility of living up to the popular and imperial ethos, but his saga also reflects a book trying to live up to its cover, as it were. *Lord Jim*'s gap has therefore become the *locus* of modernist preoccupation with cultural positioning. Is it Conrad

---

[58] Najder, *Conrad in Perspective* (Cambridge: Cambridge U P, 1997), 177; see Dryden, 110–111 about Conrad's making stories "'Magazine'ish."

[59] *Lord Jim* (NY: Norton, 1996), 47, italics mine.

losing control of his original story or pandering to a magazine crowd, as early critics originally thought? Is it the break between high and low, or Jameson's gap? Or is it an amalgamation between high and low? Is it an antagonistic relationship, wherein the author uses the form to critique the form? I do not believe that there is any easy or clear-cut answer. Such questions, in fact, evoke yet another: why does it have to be one or the other? Conrad's form, which was examined for so long through the lens of either modernism or genre fiction, is multivalent. Conrad's own artistic philosophy was based upon the necessary aesthetic endeavor to capture reality despite the conscious impossibility of success; it is the artistic endeavor that holds potency. Conrad's ethos is innately nonreductive and dialogic in the Bakhtinian sense for it accepts the irony, ambiguity, cynicism, and polyphony of modern life.

Consider, for example, the idea that Conrad uses the form of the adventure story in order to critique it as well as the ethos it informs. This type of literary colonization, or covert act, is dialectical, mediating and existing between the extremes. Toward whatever end, the form still has simultaneous aspects of elite *and* popular, and works (consciously, I would argue) as both. This essential resistance to reduction offers an entry point into the question of audience and form as linked to reception. If Conrad's intent, or Lawrence's, or Flaubert's for that matter, is to criticize a popular form, such as adventure or romance, by adopting and parodying that same popular form/vernacular, what happens if the book is itself marketed to the same audience that it is criticizing?

Similarly, we can look at the emulation and adoption of Conrad by pulp writers of the 1920s and 1930s in magazines such as *Adventure*, *Short Story*, and *Blue Book* (as well as early *Black Mask*, as Sean McCann has pointed out). The iconization of Conrad in lowbrow fiction parallels the later adoption of Hemingway in masculine and hard-boiled pulp writing of the 1950s and 1960s. But Conrad's standing in academia sits upon the shoulders of modernists such as Eliot, who uses a passage from *Heart of Darkness* as an epigraph to "The Hollow Men" and in earlier drafts of *The Waste Land*, and such as Virginia Woolf, who lauded "Youth" as superior to *Ulysses*. Hemingway, Ford, and Fitzgerald all cited Conrad as an influence, which ignores any popular, hence shunned, cooption of him.[60]

The stylistic or subjective gap in *Lord Jim* uncovers the static nature of reception and the unstable nature of form; by extension, it is the same gap that exists between "modernist" and popular editions of a work, such as 1940s and 1950s paperbacks, and parallels any existing gap between marketing and content—a gap that certain modernist authors tried to literally navigate within their fiction (as I shall expand upon later when discussing the paperback career of William Faulkner), but other authors attempted unsuccessfully to guide the reception of their work by controlling the material nature of production. This attempt was especially unsuccessful and ironic in the case of D.H. Lawrence, as explicitly illustrated by the sexually charged covers of his American paperback editions. These covers retroactively undermine

---

[60] See Cedric Watts, *A preface to Conrad* (NY: Longman, 1993), 184–190.

Lawrence's modernist self-marketing and substantiate readings of his work that the author tried to counteract. This in itself reflects the attempt in Lawrence's fiction, seldom successful, to balance aesthetics and sexuality, to control his material prose while writing about exuberant sensuality.

D.H. Lawrence and the Book as Body

There has been a recent movement to treat the more purple moments of Lawrence's prose as a parodic use of the language of the popular romance or love story. Indeed, today the clumsily veiled symbolism of Lawrence's phallic prose can be read like the most torrid of pulp romances. David Lodge believes that Lawrence's use of such rapturous prose of popular fiction in *Women in Love* is a means to put "the reader on his guard against identifying to[o] readily and deeply with the emotion of the character that is being described, against confusing sincerity with truth."[61] Lodge, Avrom Fleishman, and David Trotter have all examined Lawrence through Bakhtin's idea of double-voiced stylization, specifically in the novel's use of parody. Fleishman, for example, states that with the opening of *Women in Love*, Lawrence "explodes a mine under the whole shebang, the [romantic] subject of English novels from Jane Austen down to romantic pulp."[62] Such use of parody, and Joyce's "Nausicaa" is another often-cited example (though likewise troublesome), seems to confirm the superior stance of modernism, yet this use also entails a necessary dependence. This irony is compounded when we consider that Lawrence's use of a popular literary form, used initially for ironic ends, was then taken at face value and used by later paperback publishers.

We can look, for example, at two Lawrence titles from Avon's "Red and Gold" editions: *Women in Love* (1951) and *Aaron's Rod* (1956, Figures 3.6 and 3.7). The cover of *Women in Love* depicts a woman undressing, her gown falling off her shoulders. We can see, by the mirror behind her, that there is a man watching her undress. The red banner at the top of the book lets us know "BY THE AUTHOR OF 'LADY CHATTERLEY'S LOVER.'" The viewer/reader seems to be personified by the presence of the man's image, leading us to believe that the story shall be told from his point of view, and suggesting that the story should be read lasciviously. Whereas this edition plays upon both *Chatterley's* and Lawrence's infamy, *Aaron's Rod*, which does not mention *Chatterley*, stands upon its own. The illustration depicts a man and women embracing, her cleavage quite apparent; next to the illustration it states "A book for men and women who are mentally as well as physically grown up. ... Extraordinary," and on the back cover, it claims that Lawrence is a "poet of the spirit and the flesh of a woman...." Judging purely by these covers, the books are exactly that which Lawrence is criticizing: his ironic dialogic elements are lost in the popular form of the book, adding an additional element of irony by deflating the original cultural stance/milieu of the

---

[61] David Lodge, "Lawrence, Dostoevzky, Bakhtin: Lawrence and Dialogic Fiction," in Keith Brown, ed., *Rethinking Lawrence* (Philadelphia: Open University Press, 1990), 101.

[62] Fleishman in Brown, 113.

Fig. 3.6   *Women in Love*. Avon, 1951

book. The original elitist criticism of the popular form is at once deflated and ironically proven. The popular form, at a later time of modernist canonization, retroactively reveals elements of polyphony via the tensions between the reader's expectations built upon the "anti-modernist" sensational packaging (itself misconstrued from the deflated parody) and the book's other modernist elements.

This dichotomy of form and content heightens the tensions between art and commerce that so plagued Lawrence. Joyce Wexler, for example, has written about

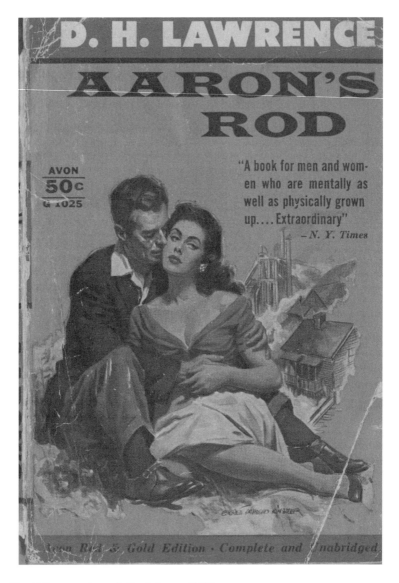

Fig. 3.7   *Aaron's Rod.* Avon, 1956

Lawrence's constant battle, pandering to and searching for an audience while still attempting to maintain his modernist ethos. It is telling that "The Sisters," the prototype for *The Rainbow,* was originally written as a "pot-boiler," to use Lawrence's term.[63] Wexler states that for Lawrence, "'Hack work,' trying to please an audience, was pandering, but changing it [the audience] was a writer's duty.

---

[63] Wexler, *Who Paid for Modernism?* (Fayetteville: U of Arkansas P, 1997), 88.

Lawrence's justification for seeking a publisher was that he had to transform his readers' lives."[64] Yet it is undeniable that Lawrence often subdued his writing and shaped it toward his readers.

Lawrence's own stance toward the masses is equally tortured. He emulated an idealized peasantry and natural aristocracy, such as Mellors in *Lady Chatterley's Lover*, yet his antipathy toward the "idiotic people who read" is well noted.[65] Allison Pease sees that with *Lady Chatterley*, Lawrence "distinguish[es] between two kinds of social leveling; a positive leveling, or breaking of barriers, that is achieved on an individual basis through human contact, and a negative leveling that is achieved through abstracting the humanity of individuals and diffusing them through mass-cultural media. Real equalizing cannot occur at a disembodied level."[66] Throughout Lawrence's oeuvre, he attempted to "reinscribe" the body as the "disinterested" locus of purity and truth, outside the discourses of materiality; "The sexual body, in its profound disinterest, erases class difference, indeed erases individual difference."[67] Pease believes that Lawrence ultimately failed, not simply because he fell into the prose of popular and sensational pornography, but because his very form was intrinsically material. This is perhaps best illustrated by the many pirated editions of *Chatterley* that overtly played up the pornographic elements in the text.

I would take Pease's argument one step further into the material aspect and state that Lawrence's efforts to write the disinterested body found their actual *physical* manifestation in his privately printed, limited, and signed first Florence edition of *Lady Chatterley's Lover*—a book that he rewrote specifically because he knew that he had carte blanche as publisher and writer. As an artistically crafted volume marketed to the literary elite, it represents/personifies the "disinterested" erotic body—form and subject merge—but it also seems to undermine Lawrence's earlier need to "write because I want folk – English folk – to alter, and have more sense."[68] The fact that Lawrence was soon to put out a popular, inexpensive edition has more to do with undercutting the many pirated editions of *Chatterley*, as John Worthen has established, than any sense of public uplift.[69] The unauthorized pirated editions, and more so the *authorized* later pulp paperback editions of Lawrence's work, which cater to the lusty sensation that Lawrence was attempting to avoid (according to Pease, *needed* to avoid for his modernist agenda), illustrate the constructed line between modernist ethos and popular form. If Lawrence's purple prose is indeed suffused with irony (which I see little evidence for one way or another) it comes to naught when we consider his popular audience and

---

[64] Ibid., 90.

[65] Quoted in Wexler 94; see Carey, passim, as well as Wexler, 94–95, Pease, 136–165.

[66] Pease, *Modernism, Mass Culture and the Aesthetics of Obscenity* (NY: Cambridge U P, 2000), 152.

[67] Pease, 143–144.

[68] Quoted in Wexler, 88.

[69] See Wothen, "Lawrence and the 'Expensive Edition Business,'" in Cherniak et al., *Modernist Writers in the Marketplace*, 105–123.

books such as these paperbacks or earlier pirated editions of *Lady Chatterley's Lover* like that in William Faro Incorporated's "Modern Amatory Classic Series" (1930), which was soon followed by the anonymously written *Lady Chatterley's Husbands* (1931) and *Lady Chatterley's Friends* (1932). Poor Lady Chatterley! When will she get some rest?

Decadence, Pornography, Joyce, and the Instability of the Text

It is perhaps Joyce who most complicates the modernists' use/adaptation of the popular form. Many critics have noted that Joyce's work, from *Dubliners* through *Finnegans Wake*, relies upon popular ephemera—whether that of a commodity (a bar of soap, a can of sardines), a common advertisement (a flyer for Agendath Netaim), a newspaper, or a popular literary form. Garry Leonard, for example, has noted that the essence of the epiphany, for Stephen, is the transformation of the "commonest object" into a "radiant" object—I would add that this is similar to Baudelaire's "eternal and immutable" work of art.[70] Despite the fact that Leonard also compares the epiphany to an advertisement, Derek Attridge points out that such explorations sometimes propagate an elitist discourse: "since what they often document is the process whereby a highly refined author catering for a minority audience transmutes the dross second-rate material into the gold of high art."[71] If Joyce takes the "throwaway" debris of culture and transforms it into immutable art, his dependence is never purely ironic and/or critical. As Brandon Kershner states in his introduction to *Joyce and Popular Culture*, "Joyce's invocation of a work of popular fiction is virtually never simple citation or quotation, and the relationship between the two is seldom simply ironic."[72] Joyce's appreciation of the popular form always seems much more gleeful than damning.

A large body of criticism examining Joyce's use of popular culture and literature now exists: explorations of masculinity in references to Eugene Sandow, of the music hall and popular song, of femininity and Victorian advertising, of references to tattoos and absinthe, of boy's magazines, dime westerns, abstinence tracts and white slavery, of postcards and pornography.[73] Rather than rehash this

---

[70] Garry Leonard, *Advertising and Commodity Culture in Joyce* (Gainesville: U P of Florida, 1998), 2.

[71] Kershner, *Joyce and Popular Culture* (Gainesville: U P of Florida, 1996), 23.

[72] Ibid., 11.

[73] For obvious reasons, Joyce has been exceptionally fertile for cultural studies, see especially Garry Leonard's *Advertising and Commodity Culture in Joyce* examines advertising, kitsch, pornographic postcards in Joyce; Cheryl Herr's *Joyce's Anatomy of Culture* on religious tracts, newspapers, and the music hall in Joyce; Brandon Kershner's *James Joyce and Popular Culture*, as well as "Framing Rudy and Photography" in Levitt's *Joyce and the Joyceans* (Syracuse: Syracuse U P, 2002), and "The Strongest Man in the World: Joyce or Sandow?" in Leonard and Wicke's edited *James Joyce Quarterly* (1998), 35; Jennifer Levine's "James Joyce, Tattoo Artist" in Valente's *Quare Joyce* (Ann Arbor: U of Michigan P, 2000).

existing criticism, I would like to examine the reception of Joyce's work and its reputation of being erotic, sensational, or pornographic—a reputation that exists even today. The role that *Ulysses* played in the history of censorship and modernism alike ensures its constant reappraisal in critical works. Katherine Mullin's *James Joyce, Sexuality and Social Purity* (2003) is just the latest volume that considers the "scandal of *Ulysses*" in terms of its initial reception. The fact that the Woolsey decision aided in furthering the autonomy of the modernist work is not so readily apparent today, nor is the oft times ambiguous line between art and obscenity as it existed before the decision.

The relationship between pornography and mass literature, which I am invoking here, relies upon the cultural fear of a large fecund reading public, unable to both control bodily urges and differentiate between good and bad, moral and immoral literature—hence it is a relationship on the same continuum as Cowley's criticism of the paperback and Jameson's definition of the visual. Pornography embodied the worst fears of the elite reading public in the nineteenth century. Furthermore, pornography seeks to directly affect the body, in opposition to the goals of high art, which deal instead with intellectual distance. Pease states that "Sexual literature written for profit with the specific purpose of identifying with and / or creating a physical subjectivity and a bodily reading / consumption, is the antithesis of the art of the aura, for distance is antithesis to bodily reading. Reaching its zenith in an age of mass reproduction, pornography, especially in its visual forms, represents mass-culture and its physical repudiation of distance."[74] Yet pornography has a convoluted relationship with modernism and decadence before it: like both, it often looked to classicism as a means of reinvigoration and respectability.

Numerous critics have argued that decadence played a much larger role in inspiring or sparking modernism than heretofore noticed. David Weir in *Decadence and the Making of Modernism* establishes how important the decadent movement was as a buffer between romanticism and modernism; Cassandra Laity has written about Swinburne's influence (however problematic or "un-modernist") upon H.D; the influences of Wilde and Baudelaire upon Joyce are well documented and surface in numerous ways throughout *Ulysses;* Stephen Dedalus's aestheticism and pretentious bohemianism is the obvious example. Yeats and Pound, as well as numerous modernist publishers—most obviously Black Sun Press' Harry Crosby— were inheritors of the decadent stylistics of fine art publishing.[75] Yeats's own publishing ventures with the Cuala Press and Pound's with his various publishers were inspired by Leonard Smithers and the Bodley Head Press. Just as *The Smart Set* was financed by the popular form of the pulp magazine, pornography played a large role behind the scene of decadent publishing. And this carried through to modernism as well; *Fin de Siecle* purveyors of smut were often the publishers of important or challenging literature, most obviously Smithers, publisher of

---

[74] Pease, 79.
[75] McGann, *Black Riders*, particularly 3–23.

The Savoy, Beardsley, and Wilde.[76] Decadents and early modernists such as Ernest Dowson, Wilde, Arthur Machen, and Arthur Symons were hired as translators and editors of erotica. Swinburne had to turn to a questionable publisher to get his poems published at all. This trend continued into modernism, most obviously with Jack Kahane's Obelisk press, which published *The Rock Pool,* Cyril Connolly's book about debauched expats in France; Joyce's *Pomes Penyeach;* and Henry Miller's *Tropic of Cancer;* all financed by suggestive erotica for English tourists or banned books about homosexuality. It was the predecessor to the more famous Olympia press.[77]

As the Victorian age waned, naturalism and realism pushed the boundaries of acceptable representation. In the twentieth century, both modernist art and pornography looked to classical form and stylistics, or to exoticism and primitivism: modernism in order to play off of or reinvigorate archetypes, to look to earlier, pre-Christian representations. For pornography, classicism both offered a mantle of respectability, historicity, or culture, and its historical-based sexual freedom or openness offered an excellent rationale against repressive morality. One of hundreds of examples of the convergence of erotica and modernism is the privately printed paperback of *The Pleasures of Being Beaten and Other Fleshly Delights and other Fleshly Delights* (c. 1935), which was in actuality pirated from earlier volumes, retitled, recovered with an incredibly quirky, nonsexy "erotic" photo of a nude woman surrounded by shop mannequins holding whips, and sold from under the counter and advertised in the back of pulp magazines. The earlier editions were Pierre Louys's *Cyprian Masques*, originally published by London's Fortune Press, circa 1929, and Charles Cullen's illustrations from the Press of Classic Lore's 1928 edition of Lucian's *The Mimes of the Courtesans,* translated by A.L. Hillman, which was republished in a more popular/readily available edition by Rarity Press in 1931 (Rarity also republished, as part of the same erotica series, a 1931 edition of *The Natural Philosophy of Love* with a postscript and translation by Ezra Pound).[78] This "pornographic" edition retained some of Fortune Press's decadent illustrations by Beresford Egan and all of Rarity Press's wispy deco illustrations by Charles Cullen who also illustrated Countee Cullen's *Copper Sun* and *The Black Christ and Other Poems*. Egan is famous for having illustrated Baudelaire *Les Fleurs du Mal*, Radclyffe Hall's *Well of Loneliness*, Aleistar Crowley's *Moonchild*, and works for Mandrake Press in London. His illustrations

---

[76] See James Nelson, *Publisher to the Decadents: Leonard Smithers in the Careers of Beardsley, Wilde, Dowson* (University Park, PA: Penn State U P, 2000), especially appendix A, an overview of Smithers' career as publisher of pornographic material by Peter Mendes, 287–294.

[77] See the first few chapters of John De St Jorre's history of the Olympia Press, *Venus Bound*, for an overview of the Obelisk (NY: Random House, 1995).

[78] For a History of the 1928 edition, see Thomas Jenkin's "An American 'Classic': Hillman and Cullin's *Mimes of the Courtesians*," *Arethusa*, Vol. 38 (2005), 387–414. Pound's 1922 introduction, and the Rarity Press erotica edition confirm the blurring of popular erotica and modernism.

are an excellent conflation of decadence and modernist art deco. The unmistakable influence of Aubrey Beardsley points to a larger conflation of art styles utilized by a *symboliste*/decadence-influenced modernism, a debauched deco.

Likewise, the dynamics of erotica publishing mirror those of modernist publishing in that there was a definite hierarchy to form: *The Pleasures of Being Beaten* was also published in hardcover, with one of Cullen's illustration on the cover rather than the surreally bad photo—erotica emulated modernist production, yet relied upon paperback sensationalism. The visual stylistics of decadence moved fluidly between British and European modernism and American popular culture and erotica. This is also evident in the cover of Boni Paper Books' *Against the Grain*, in the first issue of Harold Hersey's pulp *Courtroom Stories*, which featured a cover story on "The Trial of Oscar Wilde" (see Figure 2.1), in dozens of 1940s and 1950s paperback covers such as Pierre Louys's *Aphrodite* and Zola's *Nana*, which marketed the books' sensationalism, and in the overall feel and design of dozens of spicy pulp magazines, some of which advertised *The Pleasure of Being Beaten.*

Despite this popular marketing, these books still contained their elements of decadence, realism, and modernism, such as innate cultural criticism and challenging of a morally repressive society. According to Thomas Jenkins, Hillman's translation of Lucien both heightened the racy aspect of the novel and was used to challenge modern prudery; there is a similar argument in Pierre Louys's forward, which urges modern novelists to turn to Lucien for inspiration in capturing a timeless reality and "a really French character." Jenkins considers that Cullen's illustrations hold an advocacy of homosexuality, a blurring of gender roles, in order to show how classic texts are adopted—and adapted by contemporary times. There is, I think, a tendency for Jenkins to over-read these illustrations but, regardless, this tawdry paperback edition, with its new title, cover, and conflation of Egan's grotesque illustrations with Cullen's, is somehow in keeping with both a modernist and decadent tradition in being both androgynous and patriarchal.

The title itself is something of a misnomer—especially as paired with the cover photo of a store manikin "whipping" a nude woman. There is in fact no sadomasochism in the book; whoever put out this pirated edition latched onto one of Hillman's chapter subtitles—controversial in a book that features the humiliation, beating, and rape of a prostitute by three soldiers: something distinctly not a "pleasure." Cullen's illustration seemingly turns this scene into a joyous expression of deco style, the woman seems not to resist but throws her arms out and head back, almost as if to receive the soldier in front of her, his phallic sword pommel at crotch level, a vortex of art deco line design swirling from it. My reading of this picture deviates greatly from Jenkin's who sees it as a violent struggle; he also sees the ram's head loincloth on one soldier as symbolizing a vagina, despite the obvious male and phallic connotations.

But *The Pleasure of being Beaten*, made up as it were from French and American translations of a classic Greek text, with illustrations that combined American art deco and British decadence, and sold as an erotic pulp paperback, also illustrates the blurring of boundaries and hierarchies that is often the result of the transatlantic (and transgenerational) journey of decadent modernism into the American marketplace. David Weir describes this as the American "decline" of decadence, initially diluted by Huneker who refocused it to the bourgeoisie, then by Ben Hecht who used it to challenge American moral hypocrisy and spread this diluted version of decadence through his writing for popular cinema.[79] Whether or not this loss of specificity of agenda is a decline or not (I daresay that Weir's consideration of the class shift involved with decadence as a dilution may just be an extension of the modernist class-based prejudice of form), what does translate into popular American modernist decadence is the patriarchy innate to European decadence, evident in both Huneker's and Hecht's novels as well as in popular modernism/erotica such as *The Pleasure of Being Beaten*.

Weir, Cassandra Laity, and Elaine Showalter have discussed how decadence was able to participate "in patriarchy even as it rejected masculinity," hence facilitating its appeal to an androcentric modernism possible. We can see this carried over to Cullen's smooth, effeminate male figures, equally indicative in the phallic modernity of art deco (as compared to the fluid feminine lines of romantic art nouveau). Even if Jenkins's argument that Cullen is blurring gender lines through his illustrations is true, it still propagates a male-centered fantasy driven caricature, albeit homosexual, in that only the male figures are androgynous; all the females are voluptuously drawn. This parallels the fact that numerous female critics have seen that the lesbian images of decadence (in particular Swinburne's) "are perceived as pornographic male fantasies shaped by the 'male gaze.'"[80]

"At worst," writes Laity when discussing H.D.'s reimagining of Swinburne's *Lesbia Brandon*, "decadent influence clearly marked the ways in which the feminist revisionist text falls prey to its submerged male discourse"—a phenomenon that can be seen not only in the retitling of Lucien's *Courtesans*, but also in numerous pulp paperbacks.[81] Laity also identifies the paradox of a decadent influenced modernism: if the decadents were fascinated with gender borders and androgyny, patriarchal modernism was interested in the remasculation of literature. This was the stated goal of Pound, Lewis, and Marinetti. We could also add Willard Huntington Wright—at least in avowed purpose of making *The Smart Set* a journal dedicated to countering effeminate literature and society.

With modernism, since cultural hierarchies did not translate so readily across the Atlantic due to the lack of an American aristocracy (resulting in a more visual popular modernism), what did translate were the gendered tensions seen overtly in the sexual marketing of paperbacks. *The Pleasure of Being Beaten* is an extreme example of how the masculine canonization innate to the reification of modernism was echoed at an extreme in the paperback form; the process of what authors were

---

[79] Weir, *Decadence and the Making of Modernism* (Amhurst: U Massachusetts P, 1995), 170–180.

[80] See Laity, "H.D. and A.C. Swinburne: Decadence and Women's Poetic Modernism," in Hoffman and Murphy, eds., *Critical Essays on American Modernism* (NY: Hall, 1992), 222n8.

[81] Laity argues that H.D.'s response to Swinburne distinguishes "at least one strain of female modernism from the prevailing male modernism," 212.

chosen for paperbacks, and what sensational aspects of modernism were used as marketing techniques for paperback companies (from shadow erotica to popular mass-distributed editions) is a "corrupted" or hyper-commercial manifestation of masculine modernism made obvious via the negation of the mantle of nonphysicality or sensuality innate to modernist stylistics and marketing. In other words: decadent eroticism illuminates a cross relationship, a sameness, between popular literature and the male centered high modernism of Lawrence, Pound, and the boys. One of the reasons that I have paid so much attention to decadence as a precursor to modernism is to show how the sameness of highbrow literature and popular erotic existed at the dawn of modernism and was carried on through the censorship trials of Joyce's *Ulysses*—a book that has obvious decadent resonance, especially in the pairing contrast between Bloom as sensualist and Dedalus as Aesthete. The conflation of modern stylistics illustrates three things: first, that such erotica illuminates another aspect of popular modernism; second, that this wasn't a case of usury or simple adoption by smuthounds, of the avant-garde being absorbed by popular culture, but that they arose simultaneously, were different sides of the same coin; and finally, it points to the evolution of patriarchal modernism. Just as male-centered eroticism, regardless of whether it was hetero or homosexual, coexisted with decadence, a male centered eroticism shored up the patriarchal elements of high-modernism, surfacing in the hyper-masculinity of the futurists, of Lewis and Pound, and, by proxy, Hemingway—though, to be fair, Hemingway would work through these issues in his themes of writerly centered androgyny in *Garden of Eden* and other such male/female twinning, much like Faulkner's trying to navigate, however unsuccessfully, the issues of race.

This lack of hierarchy is explicit in the watch and ward societies' lack of differentiation between high and low, art and pornography. It is undeniable that the places where finely bound books of literature, little magazines, *Ulysses*, *Lady Chatterley's Lover*, pornography, and the seedy pulp magazine commingled freely were on the lists of banned books and, ultimately and for however short a time, in the furnaces of the New York Society for the Suppression of Vice. Book hounds disregarded a work's stylistics and aesthetic aspirations much more easily than any postmodern critic.[82]

Pease has established that Joyce's "mastery of form," like that of Aubrey Beardsley, "de-emphasizes the body," by placing emphasis on the representation rather than the represented.[83] Yet what happens when the consumer is not familiar with that language of mastery? The "scandal" of *Ulysses,* particularly the original obscenity trial, usually concerned itself with what would happen (indeed, happened) if the book fell into the hands of those who were not versed in highbrow aesthetics. This again stresses the fact that the physical composition of the published work (cover, price, availability, venue, etc.) constitutes an effort on the part of writer and publisher to control his or her expected audience once the work has been released

---

[82] See Gertzman, *Bookleggers and Smuthounds* (Philadelphia: U of Pennsylvania P, 1999), Chapter 4.

[83] Pease, 134.

to the world, even though, ultimately, there is no assurance of reception (this is all the more obvious in early popular paperbacks). Furthermore, differentiations between art and erotic became fuzzy.

Even the racier pulp magazines such as the overtly risqué *Snappy* (different from the magazine of the same name featured in Chapter 1) paid close attention to the avant-garde literary world (see Figure 3.8).[84] Every month, *Snappy* featured "Torrid Tomes," a book section that not only reviewed current books for their titillation factor, but highlighted modernist books for their racier sections, such as "The description of Spanish 'ladies of the evening' in Ernest Hemingway's *Death In The Afternoon*...The last chapter (and most of the others) in Henry Roth's *Call It Sleep*..." Worth quoting at length is the blurb about the little magazine, *Story*:

>Story Goes Snappy!
>Probably the artiest literary magazine coming off the printing presses today is Whit Burnett's and Martha Foley's *Story*, a little fattish publication serving as a catalytic agent for up-and-coming writers of this day and age. If you write with pebbles in your mouth, holding a pencil in your left foot and can get a little of Gertrude Stein and a lot of William Saroyan into your manuscript, you're a *Story* prospect. Imagine our surprise, therefore, when the June issue of this *ne plus ultra* of mags reached this desk to find a yarn in it titled "*Bare Legs*," penned by Edward Anderson, and to further discover that "*Bare Legs*" means just what it says, having to do with a man hobo who meets a lady hobo and is attracted first to her bare legs, then to her bare thighs, then to her bare hips, then—! Well, you get the idea. Anyway, on page 72! "the breasts moved and swelled under the green jersey." Tsk! Tsk! Tsk! What *is* the world coming to?[85]

Such meta-underlining of the dirty passages of modernist texts illustrates an aspect of modernism that lives outside of the halls of academia: it is an extreme example of the gap between the scholarly marketing of a text and a certain kind of common reader outside the text.

The stylistic inscrutability of *Ulysses* could not save it from such pornographic colonization as illustrated by Samuel Roth's pirating of *Ulysses*, and even more explicitly in the Marvin Miller's Collector's Publications' pirated edition of *Ulysses* of the late 1960s, "Complete and Unexpurgated," replete with 43 pages of advertisements for other adult publications and sex toys (see Figure 3.9). Such examples are extreme illustrations of the gap between content and representation, much further down the continuum from Signet's edition of *A Portrait of the Artist as a Young Man*.

With the inclusion of Judge Woolsey's decision into the Random House edition of *Ulysses*, the publisher effectively attempted to raise the appeal of *Ulysses* by widening the distance between sensational literature and important literature.

---

[84] Though nominally the same, this *Snappy* is not to be confused with the *Snappy* discussed in Chapter 1. This one was published by Merwil/D.M. Publishing starting in 1932.

[85] *Snappy* (Sept. 1935), 61, 15.

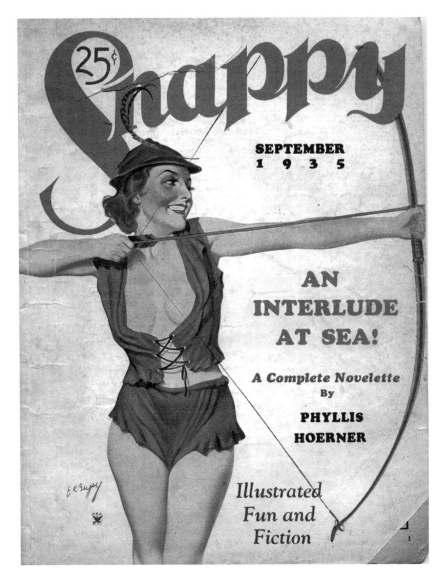

Fig. 3.8 *Snappy Magazine*, Sept. 1935 © 1935 D.M. Publishing Company

The inclusion of the transcripts: a) placed *Ulysses* in a pivotal social rather than a difficult literary context and b) defended it against further claims of pornography, yet c) simultaneously advertised its former morally nebulous state and risqué nature. The importance of *Ulysses,* therefore, went beyond any cultural or stylistic experimentation or difficulty and became a socially/politically important text.

There is some question as to what Joyce's own stance and motivation was. Critics such as Richard Brown believe that Joyce played down the role of radical

Fig. 3.9 Ad, Uthaid from *Ulysses*, A Collectors Publication (pirated) n.d.

sexual portrayal in his texts, while Katherine Mullin believes that "Joyce's fiction daringly incited the cultural conflict which would make him notorious" by reworking his text to be purposefully critical of and enticing to moral critics and watch and ward societies.[86] Mullin discusses, for example, how Joyce deflates the idea of the pure and isolated innocence of childhood via the character of Gerty.

---

[86] Mullin, *James Joyce, Sexuality and Social Purity* (NY: Cambridge U P, 2003), 3.

While it is unlikely that Joyce would have consciously sought the publishing troubles that he met, it is also undeniable that he foresaw the moral indignation that would rise up against *Ulysses* and wrote it into his text, most conspicuously in Bloom's persecution in "Circe." In Bloom's dream sequence Philip Beaufoy accuses Bloom not only of plagiarism, which hearkens to Joyce's own pillaging of popular texts, but also of "moral rottenness."[87]

The well-known picture of Joyce and Sylvia Beach sitting under an enlargement of *The Sporting Times'* headline "The Scandal of Ulysses" illustrates a certain hubris at the flaunting of moral convention. And indeed, Shakespeare and Company utilized *Ulysses'* suppression as an advertising ploy. The idea that Joyce marketed *Ulysses* sensationally, or at least took advantage of an outside sensationalism to sell the book, is somewhat moot, for what is important is that a certain portion of the audience, for whatever reason, moral or otherwise, did in fact read a different book (i.e., see a different aspect of it) than modern (or modernist) academics have been trained to see. To a certain point, we are products of the *form* of *Ulysses*. Sebastian Knowles, in his delightful *The Dublin Helix*, discusses why he loves the 1934 Random House edition of *Ulysses*, stating that "we all love the edition we grew up with." While many experts prefer the corrected Gabler edition, Knowles attests, "The Gabler edition may be the text for the new millennium, but it resembles Joyce as a dead nettle resembles life."[88] But imagine if you had first approached *Ulysses* with no preconceived notions, and read the 1960s erotic edition, or a sensationally covered early 1950s paperback.

Malcolm Cowley, in *The Literary Situation*, relates how a "newcomer in the field [of paperback publishing], who was fresh from directing pulp-paper magazines," stated "'Give me the right cover ...and I could sell two hundred blank pages. I could sell *Finnegans Wake* on Skid Road as a book of Irish jokes.'" Cowley warns that "It is possible that he could sell a first soft-cover printing of *Finnegans Wake* in the shabbiest neighborhoods, but he couldn't sell a second";[89] but what about those hundred or so thousand who were introduced to Joyce via that sensational edition? Or what about *A Portrait* or *Ulysses*? Stripped of their elite mantle and marketed for a popular audience, would it be a practical joke as Cowley would have us believe or just a fitting, popular edition?

Ultimately, there is a gap between the academic and the "common reader," a gap that is illustrated inversely by the gap between paperback marketing and textual content. And it is this space in between where the dynamics of cultural exclusion, academic construction, modernist marketing are most visible. The portrait of modernism established by those impresarios like Eliot, Pound, even Woolf, and critics like Cowley and Hugh Kenner would not only have a wall up between popular and elite literature, but it would also have us overlook modernist writers' concerns with popular forms and monetary gain. Paperbacks force those issues

---

[87] Joyce, *Ulysses* (NY: Vintage, 1986), 15.843.
[88] Knowles, *The Dublin Helix* (Gainesville: U P of Florida, 2001), 1, 4.
[89] Cowley, *Situation*, 120.

and also illustrate the importance of extending genetic criticism (which traces a work's lineage of publication back to the manuscripts) forward to publications subsequent to the first edition.

Part 2

Reading Pulp Modernism: Two Case Studies

The last three chapters have established the rich history of a popular modernism. I would like to finish with two examples of reading "pulp modernism" into a few classic, though rarely explored modernist texts: William Faulkner's *Pylon* and *Wild Palms*, and Ernest Hemingway's *To Have and Have Not*. These texts and authors lend themselves to such a reading, and through them they offer a culmination of many of the dynamics explored in this study: they are undeniably modernist products, "steeped" in allusions to seminal modernist texts such as *Ulysses* and *The Waste Land*, yet also allude to pulp magazines and popular fiction; they evince a seemingly oxymoronic reliance upon pulp forms and genres while simultaneously damning them; they have the economics of writing as a subtext; they have innate sensationalism; they were printed, marketed, and most widely read as popular paperbacks; and they have been pretty well neglected by academia. More so, it is possible to extrapolate from these works about the more general relationships the authors had with their artistic reputations and their popular audience. The conflict of popular acceptance (as most clearly illustrated in mass-market paperback editions) and avant-garde identity is especially poignant in the cases of Faulkner and Hemingway, affecting directly the construction (or attempted deconstruction) of their public personas. This section works off of many of the marketing issues explored in the first half of this section, most obviously the appropriation of the pulp form within modernist literature for economic, symbolic, or formulaic ends, but also the conflation of modernism and pulpism upon the plain of sensational marketing, whether as the actual means of selling the physical book in the market place, or in the extremities of sensation—violent or, more commonly, sexual—included in the fiction itself, which determines indirectly the reputation and reception of a single work or an author in general.

My choice in these readings is admittedly canonical and masculine, and purposefully so since these works and authors—or at least the marketing of them, illustrate how the insidious misogyny of the canonical modernist—reified through new criticism—existed in both the elite and popular spheres. It is important to point out that pulp modernism doesn't exclude female authors, as the presence in the first two chapters of flappers, gun molls, and working girls proves. There was a presence in paperbacks of Edna Ferber, Ann Petry, and other best-selling authors, but of female modernists, there were only a few: Woolf's *Orlando*, poems by Millay, Radclyffe Hall's *Well of Loneliness*. Lesbian authors such as Ann Bannon found a large audience for her paperback originals, which has resulted in recent critical attention, but for the most part the patriarchical dynamics of canon formation were already well in place by the time the paperback phenomenon was under way, and the wave of feminist canon revision was 20 years off. Dawn Powell, for example, would have made an obvious choice for republishing in softcover. Plus, I think that it was more difficult to subsume the novels of authors like Gertrude Stein and Mary Butts into sensational marketing. My argument has been that despite the seeming incongruity of these paperback covers, they portray aspects of the texts, and any sense of incongruity comes from the tension between sensational marketing and the constructed marketing of elite modernism. Hence my focus on Faulkner and Hemingway, whose reputations as elite modernists are particularly at odds with their popular appeal, divulges the eminence of popular forms to and within the movement.

William Faulkner in the Pulp Milieu: Paperback Money

Judging by the history of Faulkner criticism, he is a mythic writer; he is a modernist writer. He is not a popular writer. In "'When I showed Him the Check, He Asked If It Was Legal': What William Faulkner Got and Gave Us From Pop Culture," an essay that more or less reaffirms the autonomous separateness of Faulkner's work from modern popular culture, George Garrett ruminates upon the fact that magazines, the like of which Faulkner depended upon as an outlet for his stories, generally fail to turn up in Faulkner's work, the major exception being the slick magazine in *The Sound and The Fury* that carries Caddy's photo.[90] But Garrett tellingly overlooks the presence of the pulp magazine that Joe Christmas reads in *Light in August*, the dime novels that the Tall Convict reads in "The Old Man," and the spicy pulp stories that Harry Wilbourne writes in *Wild Palms*. Seemingly, Yoknapatawpha County isn't the cultural vacuum that Garrett claims, and neither is Faulkner's fiction.[91] In fact, as Joseph Blotner has mentioned, much of Faulkner's fiction is downright steeped in pulp fiction. Indeed, Faulkner published the story "Christmas Tree," in the flapperish magazine *College Life* (his name appearing on the cover alongside pulp author Cornell Woolrich's), and "An Error In Chemistry" in *Ellery Queen's Mystery Magazine*. Yet there is little critical examination of such accessible and popular aspects of an author who is known for his inscrutability. Likewise, scant attention has been paid to the history of Faulkner's paperback career throughout the 1940s. Despite the prevalent literary history, Faulkner was, at times, not only available in mass market editions, but quite popular as well. Just as critics have overlooked this, others, including Garrett, have commented on the influence that Hollywood and the movies had upon Faulkner, illustrating once again the studied ignorance of a literary pulp existence/influence in literary modernism. Likewise, few authors have examined the popular manifestations/use

---

[90] See Garrett in Abadie and Fowler's *Faulkner and Popular Culture*.
[91] It is telling, of course, that the fiction that predominately invades Yoknapatawpha is pulp fiction, a fact that Faulkner himself discusses in a 1929 letter to his publisher when stating that the magazine store in Oxford, Mississippi "carries nothing that has not either a woman in her underclothes or someone shooting someone else with a pistol on the cover" (quoted by Blotner in *Faulkner and Popular Culture*, 13).

of Faulkner's work *within* popular culture—the recent exception would be studies of the Faulkner figure in the Coen Brother's *Barton Fink* or the mention of *Wild Palms* in Godard's *Breathless*, neither of which are "popular" films.[92] Faulkner relied upon the pulps within his fiction, and, in at least one instance (more if you include Faulkner's stories in *Ellery Queen* and *College Life*), the pulps relied upon Faulkner.

In the September 1935 issue of *Snappy Magazine*, a decidedly spicy pulp, the "Torrid Tomes" book review section reports that: "Recommended to torridity seekers: the episode in William Faulkner's *Pylon* when the lady parachute jumper makes advances to the man pilot five thousand feet up." One would expect a magazine dedicated to a soft-porn audience to cite Faulkner's *Sanctuary*, rather than the relatively staid *Pylon* (and perhaps they had in an earlier issue), for *Sanctuary* is the obvious example of Faulkner at his most sensational (and long derided as such by critics). Tellingly, it was also Faulkner's one hardback book that remained in print through the sparse years before his winning of the Nobel in 1950. This is a curious fact considering that since the early 1950s Faulkner has been considered "the American Joyce" in academia. Faulkner himself tried to distance himself from *Sanctuary* in a later introduction to the book (one that supports critics who discount Faulkner's popular fiction as flawed or less worthy of study), which stated that the book was "a cheap idea," and "deliberately conceived to make money." George Garrett, in the above-mentioned essay, contends that it was the last time Faulkner would attempt such, a statement that ignores popular aspects in many later books. Leslie Fiedler, among others, has placed *Sanctuary* in its hard-boiled pulp milieu, calling it, like the later hard-boiled fiction of Mickey Spillane, an anti-detective story.[93] And, under scrutiny, the parallels between *Sanctuary* and specific hardboiled works are readily apparent. Both Fiedler and Walter Wenska, have found aspects of plot and characterization from Hammett short stories in *Sanctuary*, specifically from four stories published in *Black Mask* in 1928 and which eventually became *The Dain Curse*.[94] Wenska has compiled a detailed comparison of *Sanctuary*'s plot turns, characterizations, and scenarios to those in Hammett's work, as well as other works such as Burnett's *Little Ceaser* and stories by Max Brand. (It is worth noting that both Hammett and Brand were drinking companions of Faulkner.) The aspects that both Hammett's and Faulkner's work share, such as kidnapped and errant debutantes held at a bootleggers hideout, were common enough to be pulp tropes, but Wenska believes that there are too many

---

[92] See Kawin in Abadie, as well as his edited *Faulkner's MGM Screenplays* (Knoxville: University of Tennessee, 1992).

[93] See also Scott Yarbrough's unpublished dissertation, "The Mean Streets of Jefferson: Faulkner's Intersection with Pulp Fiction" (University of Alabama, 1996).

[94] Wenska, "'There's a man with a gun over there': Faulkner's hijacking of masculine popular culture," in *The Faulkner Journal*, Vol. 15, Issue 1 (Orlando: Fall 1999/2000), 2, 35–60, 44–49); "Black Lives," "The Hollow Temple," "Black Honeymoon," and "Black Riddle." Wenska points out that these latter stories were on the stands at the time Faulkner was writing *Sanctuary*.

specific shared components for it to be coincidental. Whether this is true or not, I think that it is safe to say that Faulkner looked to the pulps as a model for salability at a time when his career was floundering, both critically and economically.

Fieldler's analogy of *Sanctuary* as ur-Spillane is telling, for Signet, the paperback publisher of Faulkner in the late 1940s and 1950s was likewise the publisher of Spillane. As André Schifflin points out in his memoir and outline of modern publishing, "The jackets of these paperbacks were uniformly lurid. If you did not look at the title, you would be hard pressed to know whether what you had in your hand was by Mickey Spillane or William Faulkner."[95]

The figure of Spillane looms large in the history of paperbacks, detective fiction, and postwar literary history. Malcolm Cowley, in *The Literary Situation,* cites him as the worst the paperback has to offer, Mike Hammer as the very embodiment of cultural degeneration. The danger of Spillane's work was its undeniable popularity, selling 13,000,000 books in three years. Raymond Chandler saw Spillane as marking the low point of the hard-boiled form. Hence a comparison between Faulkner and Spillane seems somehow sacrilegious, yet if *Sanctuary* is meta-pornography, as Fieldler labels it—a voyeuristic work that removes the reader from the action—then there is perhaps reason, especially considering how a book is marketed and how an audience is introduced to an author. Don't forget that all of Faulkner's paperbacks from the late 1940s and throughout the 1950s carried the byline "By the Author of *Sanctuary.*" Along these same lines, *Snappy's* meta-underlining, as I called it earlier, of modernist sensationalism in *Pylon* offers us an instance, like that with *Ulysses*, of sensationalism as a space of popular leveling of the high/low extremes, and in the case of Faulkner, all the more poignant for it was that same popular sensationalism that ensured his survival through the 1940s.

Interestingly enough, there is some evidence to support the idea that paperback sensationalism can make a career while breaking a literary reputation. Erskine Caldwell, also published by Signet/NAL, sold more than 25 million paperback reprints of his books between 1945 and 1951. The success of *God's Little Acre* even spawned an entire genre of "backwoods" pulp fiction, including such titles as Jim Thompson's *Cropper's Gal,* P.A. Hooper's *Riverboat Girl,* Peggy Gaddis's *Backwoods Girl* (notice a theme emerging?), John Sanford's *The Old Man's Place*, Ann Petry's *Country Place*, and Hubert Creekmore's *The Chain in the Heart.* Another of this genre also included William Faulkner's brother John and, judging purely from the covers, the genre included Flannery O'Connor's *A Good Man is Hard to Find* and William Faulkner himself (Signet's edition of *Intruder In The Dust* even mistakenly carries a picture of John Faulkner on the back cover). Caldwell's early career and Faulkner's have some parallels—though they diametrically diverge at the same time as (some would say because of) the advent of the paperback. Throughout the 1930s, Caldwell published alongside many modernists in little magazines such as *transition* and earned a literary reputation as a socialist/naturalist author (much like Farrell), yet by the mid-1940s

---

[95] Schiffrin, *The Business of Books* (NY: Verso, 2001), 29.

he had become, along with Spillane, New American Library's best-selling author and subsequently was roasted by elite literary critics. Caldwell, who thought of himself as a people's writer, grasped the popular marketing schemes of NAL; biographers such as Wayne Mixon and Harvey Klevar see this strategy as having a direct influence on his reputation and even his loss of control over his fiction.[96] Later in Caldwell's career he published in men's adventure magazines—the 1950s evolution of masculine adventure pulp—like *Swank, Cavalier*, and *Manhunt*. Whether the movement from *transition* to *Swank* was due to Caldwell's populist ethos, the waning of a populist ethos of the 1930s, his loss of authorial control, the popular acculturation of a style that was formerly thought of as modernist, or due to the influence of pulp marketing upon his reputation, what matters here is that Faulkner, whose many pulp paperbacks were marketed similarly to those of Caldwell, escaped the same fate. Faulkner, obviously, won the Nobel and his "modernist" works, such as *Sound and the Fury*, enjoyed academic attention while his "pulp" novels—those that enjoyed large paperback sales—were almost uniformly ignored by the canonization process.

With this in mind, I would like to examine *Pylon* (see Figure 3.10)—a lesser known and less obviously "pulpish" work than *Sanctuary*—in terms of its own pulp milieu in order to get a grasp upon the often problematic relationship between Faulkner and popular fiction. The novel is the story of traveling barnstormers in post–World War I New Valois (Orleans), far from the world of Yoknapatawpha, which may explain one reason it has been long overlooked by critics. The triad of barnstormers, two men and a woman, attempt to live above or beyond the conventions of normal society—as the unnamed reporter who is fascinated by them states, "Because they aint human like us; they couldn't turn them pylons like they do if they had human blood and senses and they wouldn't want to or dare to if they had human brains. ... crash one and it aint even blood when you haul him out: it's cylinder oil the same as in the crankcase."[97] The three are desperately attempting to get enough money to provide for an expected child—it is unknown which of the two men is the father. Faulkner uses monetary concerns to continually bring the three back to earth (which is figuratively and literally symbolized by the airport recently built by the chairman of the sewage board): getting paid for the races or jumps, being taxed, scrounging for drinks, etc. Roger Shumann, the pilot, eventually dies in a crash because he takes unsafe risks for the prize money.

Traditionally, the book has been regarded as "marred," of a "type" not suited to Faulkner's talents, "strained and ineffectual."[98] For the most part, critical

---

[96] Mixon, *The People's Writer: Erskine Caldwell and the South* (Charlottesvile: U P of Virginia, 1995), 139–140; Klevar, *Erskine Caldwell, A Biography* (Knoxville: U of Tenn P, 1993), 315–316, 343–344;

[97] Faulkner, *Pylon* (NY: Vintage, 1985), 42.

[98] Walter Everett, *Faulkner's Art and Characters* (Woodbury, NY: Barons, 1969), 65; other passages quoted in Macmillan, "*Pylon*: From Short Stories to Major Work," *Mosaic*, Vol. 7 (Fall 1973), 185–212, which gives an excellent overview of the critical history of *Pylon* up to that point.

Fig. 3.10   *Pylon*. Signet, 1951

readings of the book have explored it in terms of the many references to Joyce and Eliot, as Faulkner's novelization of *The Waste Land*, or, alternately, as Faulkner's light novel about aviation written to get his mind off the intricacies of *Absalom, Absalom!* More recently, Marxist critics have examined *Pylon*, with its tensions between earth and air, man and machine, commerce and art, as exemplary of the troublesome simultaneity within Faulkner's work of high and low, popular and elite. Karl Zender sees the whole of *Pylon* as a single-minded exposé on the destructive aspect of the material need for money, hence a Faulknerian criticism of his own indenture to Hollywood—an indenture dependent upon Faulkner's own aviation-themed short stories.[99] Michael Zeitlin, on the other hand, sees *Pylon*'s plot as secondary to the novel's primary goal to describe the "radically transfigured reality" of the South under the violent forces of modernization; hence the novel is Faulkner's own "violent purging of a narrative language into which the commodified stamp of 'the age of mechanical reproduction' has sunk deeply."[100] Both of these readings serve to support the traditional stance of modernism as autonomous, outside of the forms and tensions of mass-audience and production. If we consider Signet's 1951 edition of *Pylon*, the cover of which highlights the *ménage à trois* relationship of the three barnstormers, and, ultimately, the book's pulp milieu then the idea of Faulkner's criticism of popular forms in the book becomes highly ironic. Faulkner's relationship to popular literature was much more complex.

Faulkner's love for aviation is well documented; he often constructed fictions about his wartime experience in the RAF that were as outrageous as any pulp fiction. And, in his short stories, he returned again and again to the figure of the disillusioned pilot or the adventuresome barnstormer. 1927 marks the year that aviation "broke" onto the scene of American popular culture; Charles Lindbergh hopped the Atlantic, "Wings"—the first Academy Award winner—was released to movie theatres, and Elliott Springs wrote the popular *Nocturne Militaire*, a book about the World War I air war. The previous year *Liberty Magazine* had serialized Springs' anonymously edited (and freely sensationalized from a deceased pilot friend's war diary) *War Birds, The Diary of an Unknown Aviator*, an account of air combat over France, and one which, according to Blotner, Faulkner utilized for stories such as "Ad Astra," and which he later would adapt for film for Howard Hawks.[101] By the end of the year, there appeared a whole slew of aviation pulps—a genre that would last well over a decade: *Air Stories, Wings, War Birds, Flying Aces, Aces, Sky Birds, G-8 and His Battle Aces*, etc. By 1929 there were at least 18 "Ted Scott Flying Stories" books published by Grosset and Dunlap, as well as the Lucky Terrill Flying Stories series, and the earlier Air Service Boys series; by 1935, the year *Pylon* was published, the aviation story was firmly entrenched in popular culture. Blotner, for one, hints that such pulps probably fed Faulkner's love for aviation.[102] I would reaffirm this, especially considering that many of these magazines featured news and editorials about air shows and barnstorming races, which not only is the backdrop for *Pylon*, but a hobby that Faulkner was passionate about.

---

[99] See Blotner in Abadie; according to Harrison (p. 29) the studios took notice of Faulkner due to *Sanctuary*'s success, but in Hollywood, many, if not most (five in a row in 1932), of Faulkner's "treatments" dealt with aviation. See Phillips, *Fiction, Film, and Faulkner: The Art of Adaptation* (Knoxville: U of Tennessee P, 1988), 13–25.

[100] Michael Zeitlin, "Faulkner's Pylon: The City in the Age of Mechanical Reproduction," *Canadian Review of American Studies*, Vol. 22, Issue 2 (Fall 1991), 238.

[101] Blotner, 256.

[102] Abadie, 18.

The two most sensational aspects of *Pylon*—Lavernne's seduction of Roger in midair, which the book reviewer for *Snappy* picks up on, and the *ménage à trois* relationship between the three aviators, which the cover of the Signet paperback portrays—are instances that critics read as being symbolic of the barnstormers' bohemian lifestyle and affirmation of life, however fleeting. One of the book's main tensions is the threat posed by the barnstormers' lackadaisical attitude toward conventions such as marriage and, more importantly, money. It follows that sensationalism for Faulkner is symbolically modernist.

Tellingly, as Daniel Singal points out, Faulkner's motivation behind *Pylon* "appear[s] to have been partly financial – dreams of selling the rights to a film studio undoubtedly danced in his head."[103] More specifically, though, Faulkner was attempting to write a novel that would fit into a popular pulp genre *and* be a venue for his modernist tendencies (as I have shown in the last chapter, the two are not mutually exclusive), much along the same lines that he intended *Sanctuary* to have "hard-boiled" appeal. *Pylon*, as Duane MacMillan has shown, was built upon a handful of Faulkner's aviation short stories, and according to Faulkner's letters and publishing history, short stories, like screen writing, were the commercial "necessary evil" that Faulkner wrote for money. Referring to the stories that would eventually become *The Unvanquished*, Faulkner wrote, "As far as I am concerned, while I have to write trash, I don't care who buys it, as long as they pay the best price I can get; doubtless the [Saturday Evening] Post feels the same way about it; anytime that I sacrifice a high price to a lower one it will not be to refrain from antagonizing the Post; it will be to write something better than a pulp series like this."[104]

Susan Donaldson has pointed out that for critics there are two Faulkners: the Magazine Faulkner and the "powerful book," that is, good, Faulkner. Donaldson proposes that in *The Unvanquished*, Faulkner, through the addition of "The Odor of Verbena" and passages to the earlier *Saturday Evening Post* stories, undermined the formulaic pulp conventions that he had been forced into for commercial, magazine acceptance.[105] Yet in such a reading, the borders between the two Faulkner's are still apparent. And though this goes far in allowing for a more complex portrait of Faulkner's cultural position, it is still reductive. As *Pylon* shows, Faulkner's form was both popular and sophisticated. It is true that Faulkner's "pulp" short stories enabled him to, and distracted him from, writing his "serious" novels, it could also be true that they allowed him to write on multiple levels. And on the most pragmatic level, the pulp/popular form aided in the construction of Faulkner's reputation, which complicates our understanding of his traditional position as *the* American elite modernist.

---

[103] Singal, *William Faulkner, The Making of a Modernist* (Chapel Hill: U of North Carolina P, 1997), 192.

[104] Faulkner, *Selected Letters* (NY: Random House, 1977), 84.

[105] See Donaldson in Abadie, as well as Katherine Ann Clark's dissertation "Reconsidering Faulkner's Pulp Series: 'The Unvanquished' as Parody, Not Potboiler" (Emory, 199).

Whereas Pound and Eliot are often clumped together with English or European modernists, Faulkner is unquestionably working within American modernism; in regard to stylistic experimentation, he is second only to Joyce. Yet Faulkner had more titles and sold more copies in the popular paperback form than any other modernist or highbrow author, European or otherwise. And Faulkner's post-1950 position in the canon is unquestionable; hence it is easy to overlook the fact that before 1947, he was uniformly overlooked by the academy. It is understandable that *Pylon* was never considered worthy of study, with its mixture of highbrow allusions and lowbrow form, and the fact that it couldn't be placed on a Yoknapatawpha map. Many contemporary critics considered him a second-rate writer who waffled between hard-boiled sensationalism à la *Sanctuary*, and ungainly stylistics à la *Absalom, Absalom!* Bernard DeVoto, in his anti-modernist diatribe, *The Literary Fallacy* (1943), only mentions Faulkner twice, both in passing, both times misspelling his name, so it would seem that Faulkner wasn't well known enough in 1943 for either DeVoto or his editors at Little, Brown to catch the mistake.[106] One gets the sense from DeVoto that Faulkner wasn't prominent enough to explore. Numerous biographies of Faulkner allow that for almost the entirety of the 1940s, none of his books were in print except *Sanctuary*, at least in hardback. The Faulkner that is taught in schools today is different from the Faulkner of the 1930s and 1940s. His reputation is built upon the canonized works of *The Sound and the Fury, Absalom, Absalom!, As I Lay Dying, The Hamlet,* and *Light in August*. But before this canonization, which carefully overlooks "faulty" texts such as *Pylon, The Wild Palms*, and *Knight's Gambit*, Faulkner can, in a certain sense, be considered a popular writer working off the pulp/sensational medium since he was predominantly read in popular, pulp paperback forms. Again, the fact that this publishing career has been overlooked in academia is an instance of the academic prejudice of form.

It is generally agreed that the reemergence of Faulkner into literary tradition was due to Cowley's edited *Portable Faulkner* in 1947. Cowley's book for the first time brought the breadth of Faulkner's created universe into focus for academia, leading to his academic and critical "re-discovery," but his reputation and serious readership were not established right away, not until after he was awarded the Nobel in 1950. As O.B. Emerson has pointed out, in his study of the early critical reception of Faulkner, "Although Faulkner's reputation was shaping slowly, in the early 1940's it lay a good bit outside published criticism. The books had not sold well."[107] Laurence Schwartz in *Creating Faulkner's Reputation*, examines the steps that led to Faulkner's canonization, and shows that whereas Cowley's book

---

[106] Devoto, *The Literary Fallacy* (Boston: Little, Brown, 1944), 107, 114.

[107] *Faulkner's Early Literary Reputation in America* (Ann Arbor: UMI Research Press, 1984), viii. Emerson, as well as Alan Swallow, believes that much of Faulkner's critical acceptance was due to the Southern Agrarian, New Critical rise to power. Emerson's otherwise thorough study never considers the history of Faulkner's paperback publications, hence illustrating again the academy's prejudice of form.

was important for academia, so was the exposure that Faulkner gained from the Armed Service Edition of *A Rose For Emily and Other Stories* and the many mass-market paperbacks. The rise of the paperback made *some* of Faulkner's books popular, "those with popular, non-serious qualities: sex, violence, intrigue. These sales, however, created the income necessary to keep his novels in print. And, without his novels in print, no revival would have been possible."[108]

Even after the limited economic success of Viking and Cowley's *Portable Faulkner* (only 20,000 in four years compared to *The Portable Hemingway*'s 30,000 in one year), Random House had no plans for an overall reissuing of Faulkner titles. Only *As I Lay Dying* and *The Sound and the Fury* were slated for the Modern Library popular editions. What sustained Faulkner through the decade was the mass-market paperback, which, according to Schwartz, was "the most active publishing arena for Faulkner fiction" in the latter half of the 1940s.[109] Even Cowley overlooked this when he stated in 1966, Faulkner's "seventeen books were effectively out of print and seemed likely to remain in that condition, since there was no public demand for them."[110] Starting with Avon's 1942 edition of *Mosquitoes*, there appeared over the next eight years: the Armed Forces Edition of *A Rose For Emily And Other Stories* circa 1943 or 1944, two editions of *Sanctuary* in 1947 (Penguin 632/Signet 632), numerous editions of *Wild Palms* starting in 1948 (Signet/Penguin 659), *The Old Man*, also in 1948 (Signet 692), *Intruder in the Dust* in 1949 (Signet 743), and *Knight's Gambit* in 1950 (Signet 825). And there would soon appear *Pylon, Sartoris, Requiem for A Nun, Soldier's Pay*, and *The Unvanquished*. Since Faulkner's books were in print, but just as paperbacks, Cowley's use of the term "*effectively* out of print" illustrates his prejudice against the popular form (being in paperback is obviously as bad as being out of print); and his statement "no public demand," despite the hundreds of thousands of copies being sold to a mass-audience, seems to mean that the only "public" worth considering is the elite audience that can afford hardbacks.

By May 1948, Signet had sold 470,000 copies of *Sanctuary* alone. Faulkner made $6,000 in three years on that single edition.[111] The fact that Weybright couldn't lay his hands on even a used copy of *The Wild Palms* for the Signet typesetter to reprint (he eventually had to borrow Random House's autographed presentation copy) illustrates the scarcity of Faulkner's books and how close to oblivion he was before the onslaught of his titles in paperback.[112] These paperbacks not only subsidized Faulkner's writing, but invariable got his name out and built the means through which his later reputation could be facilitated—the audience who bought the *Portable Faulkner* had seen Faulkner's name on the paperbacks of the drugstore rack.

---

[108] Schwartz, *Creating Faulkner's Reputation* (Knoxville, U of Tennessee P, 1988), 4.
[109] Ibid., 56.
[110] Quoted in Schwartz, 9.
[111] Schwartz, 58.
[112] Ibid., 58–59.

Hence, books such as *Sanctuary, Pylon* and *Knight's Gambit* far, far outsold *The Sound and the Fury*, at least until the adoption of Faulkner into the University curriculum. Faulkner's later aristocratic persona and presence in the university (both his books' presence, and his own presence at the University of Virginia) is at odds with the physical marketing of the abundant sensational paperbacks of his works. I would even go so far as to say that it is an effectual counterbalance to such sensationalism. André Schiffrin, writing about paperback marketing techniques in his exposé/memoir of modern publishing, states: "Even though Faulkner was described on all of his paperbacks as the author of *Sanctuary*, a book widely read for its highly charged sexual content, the entirety of his work was, in fact, available [in paperback]. It would be many years before his books would be a staple of college courses, ironically losing most of their popular appeal as they became elevated to the canon."[113] If what Schiffrin says is true about the fall of Faulkner as a popular writer and his rise as a canonical writer, it is due to the change in marketing and the entrance of "quality" publishers into the realm of paperbacks—the advent of college editions. Much the same thing happened when Hemingway won the Nobel: Scribners pulled their reprint licensing in order to publish and make money off their own line of (more expensive, less sensational) paperbacks.[114]

If *Pylon* becomes a diatribe against the taint and pull of economics, where a pilot takes undue risks and flirts with death for monetary gain, as happens when Shumann flies Ord's plane in order to gain money for Laverne's unborn child, then *If I Forget Thee, Jerusalem* takes it farther. As I stated earlier, Faulkner uses the pulp magazine in *Light In August* as a symbol of cultural (and racial) degeneration. In the later *Jerusalem*, the pulp magazine as a symbol is more prominent and complex. It illustrates more than a cultural fear; it shows Faulkner's fear of, if not his own artistic degeneration due to the extremity of writing for the short story and film market, at least his wariness of economic pandering.

If I Forget Thee, Jerusalem (Faulkner's original name for *The Wild Palms*), like *Pylon*, is a novel about extremes: economics versus love, pulp writing versus art, "Old Man" versus "The Wild Palms" story.[115] The "Wild Palms" story line follows the love affair between Charlotte, a married artist, and Harry, a poor medical student, as they "elope" and eschew social pressures and conformity in order to truly live. After a series of moves, each one successively farther from urban civilization, and jobs, each one less and less lucrative, Charlotte gets pregnant and Harry performs an abortion; Charlotte sickens and dies from blood poisoning, Harry is sent to prison without defending himself. Throughout it all, there is such

---

[113] Schiffrin, 29.

[114] See Charles Scribner Jr., *In The Web of Ideas* (NY: Scribners, 1993), 56.

[115] Due to the confusing publishing history, in which the books' two stories were split for different editions, I shall clarify my terminology: I shall refer to the book in general as *If I Forget Thee, Jerusalem*, and the two plot lines as "Wild Palms," and "Old Man." When discussing specific editions, I shall refer to the paperback editions as they were published: *Wild Palms* and *Old Man*.

stress on Harry and Charlotte's finances in contrast to the couple's emotional purity that one waxes as the other wanes.[116] Many critics see connections between *Jerusalem* and Faulkner's popular ties to Hollywood. Vincent Allen King looks beyond the film medium and at the pulpish qualities of Faulkner's work. He writes that Faulkner's "unstated fear is that he would be perceived as (or actually become) a huckster of pulp fictions," hence Faulkner's uses pulp magazines and the act of writing for them as symbols for the degraded side of professional writing, directly opposed to emotional and spiritual truth and purity (as well as to the later image that Faulkner constructed for himself of a Southern aristocrat who happened to write in his spare time).[117] The contrapuntal plot lines of "The Wild Palms" and "Old Man" illustrate two aspects of pulp fiction: the absorption by and effect of pulp fiction upon the reader, and the construction by and effect of pulp fiction on the writer. Pulp fiction is the source of the Tall Convict's pulp bovarism; it leads to his arrest and is the source of his "outrage" and "enraged impotence." Harry writes pulp stories for romance pulps, writing them "complete from the first capital to the last period in one sustained frenzied agonizing rush."[118] His pulp production, which exactly describes the method of many pulp writers (including Faulkner's friend Max Brand), rises again and again in elite literary modernism and criticism as the polar opposite to careful and meritable art (see previous section). Yet all of the production throughout "The Wild Palms" is commercial, from Harry's writing to Charlotte's sculpture—with the single exception of the child who is tellingly aborted, which leads to Charlotte's death and Harry's imprisonment. The couple's love is itself a romantic idealism of the kind that was usually thought of as a product of romantic pulp fiction. Harry and Charlotte both define themselves by their reading: after finding a wallet of money, which will allow him to go away with Charlotte, Harry thinks "*That's it. It's all exactly backward. It should be the books, the people in the books inventing and reading about us,*" (which in itself should tell us that Faulkner is playing off the pulp formula) and Charlotte says, "…the second time I saw you I learned what I had read in books but I had never actually believed: that love and suffering are the same thing and that the value of love is the sum of what you have to pay for it and anytime you get it cheap you have cheated yourself."[119] Even here, Faulkner is equating love with writing and economics. Hence the sacrifices that the two make for their love are, ultimately, all artistic sacrifices; Faulkner, in a sense, damns them to the fate of the fallen pulp-era Caldwell.

But notice that Faulkner's usual fascination with blood, specifically tainted blood that usually involves miscegenation, here deals with more bovarism;

---

[116] For an illustration of this, see the appendix to McHaney's *William Faulkner's Wild Palms: A Study* (Jackson: U P Mississippi, 1975).

[117] Vincent Allen King, "The Wages of Pulp: The Uses and Abuses of Fiction in William Faulkner's The Wild Palms, *Mississippi Quarterly*, Vol. 51, No. 3 (Summer 1998), 512.

[118] Faulkner, *Jerusalem*, 103.

[119] Ibid., 41.

counterpointing both the tall convict and Joe Christmas, Charlotte's blood is poisoned by melodrama. "The Wild Palms" tragedy is the lovers' unsuccessful navigation through popular romantic idealism. The figure of Harry as pulp writer obviously reflects Faulkner's fears of commercialism, and the sensationalism of Harry's stories is the same as the accusation of sensationalism that had been leveled at Faulkner since *Sanctuary*. Faulkner escapes Harry's fate via the book's stylistic contrapuntal story lines and self-reflexivity. Faulkner claimed that he wrote the two story lines in tandem, a chapter of one followed by a chapter of the other; he stressed that the accessible, mythic "Old Man," was the necessary simple (and Western genre) counterpoint to the complexity of "Wild Palms" (complex or ironic romance genre).[120] The counterpoint saves both stories from pulpish sensationalism through complexity by begging the hermeneutics of the two parts' relationship.

How ironic, therefore, that Faulkner agreed to split the two stories and have them published separately: *The Wild Palms* in a Signet popular edition (see Figure 3.11) and then "Old Man" in Cowley's *The Portable Faulkner.* The irony was probably not lost upon Faulkner when the majority, by a large margin, of critical attention was later given to "Old Man," quite apparent in the questions asked in *Faulkner in the University,* rather than the "Wild Palms" story line, even though Faulkner stated that the latter was the initial and primary story.[121] The reason for this must therefore lie in the packaging: "Old Man" had the privilege of academic anthologies and scrutiny, while *The Wild Palms* was confined to the sensationally marketed mass-paperback.

Ultimately, what Faulkner's pulp reliance—symbolic, formulaic, or economic—illustrates is an unavoidable gravitational pull of (at least in critical academia) an unseen presence, huge and submerged, within modernism. A presence that Faulkner uses, yet defines himself against; the fact that his fiction is absorbed materialistically in a popular, sensational form only demonstrates the presence of popular and sensational aspects that already exist, despite any later machinations by either the academy or Faulkner in the academy, to ignore this. Hemingway, as we shall see, likewise felt the need to redefine himself away from pulp sensationalism. Despite the ephemeral material quality of the (increasingly rare) pulp and the paperback, their presence still destabilizes accepted literary hierarchies.

Hemingway and the End of Modernism

> Every summer I went down to Florida on treasure hunts, and there's this great restaurant called the Chesapeake and they had a picture of Hemingway behind the bar. So one day the owner asks if she could have a picture of me to put up there, and she puts one there. One day Hemingway comes in and sees my

---

[120] See Blotner and Gwynn, *Faulkner in the University* (Charlottesville: U of Virginia P, 1959), 8.

[121] Ibid., 171–182.

Fig. 3.11   *Wild Palms*. Penguin; 1948; Signet, 1950

picture, and says 'what's he doing next to me? Either take his down or take mine down,' so they took his down and he never came back to that restaurant.[122]

So states Mickey Spillane.

The idea of Nobel Prize winner Ernest Hemingway's picture hanging next to Spillane's might seem incongruous to some—to Hemingway, definitely. Hemingway is the personification of the lost generation, the arch American modernist. Spillane, on the other hand, is the epitome of junk, often sadistic, popular literature. But if we consider the construction of a writer's public persona, then similarities between these seemingly disparate authors emerge. Both are masters of self-creation, of larger-than-life exploits, and writerly (some would say hyper-masculine or misogynistic) posturing. Hemingway's well-publicized marlin fishing and African hunting parallel Spillane's well-publicized deep sea treasure hunting and jet flying. Of course, we can easily write the above anecdote off as Spillane's characteristic braggadocio (something else the two have in common), or we could write it off as yet another bit of gossip that lends itself to Hemingway's myth, a myth that shows no sign of lessening almost 50 years after his death. But, upon scrutiny, perhaps this bit of gossip isn't so easy to disregard. Hemingway might never have actually walked into that restaurant, but the idea that he would loathe, and even feel threatened by Mickey Spillane isn't so far fetched. Considering the fact that they were two of the most recognizable authors of the early 1950s,

---

[122] Carleson, Michael. Interview with Mickey Spillane. *Crime Times Magazine*. (Harpenden, Eng: Old Castle Books, no date; http://www.crimetime.co.uk/interviews/mickeyspillane.html), Nov. 22, 2003.

"What about Chandler? There's that famous scene where Marlowe throws what's pretty obviously a Mike Hammer book into the garbage

I know. I think it's pretty stupid. Did I tell you the Hemingway story?

No

Hemingway hated me. I outsell him and he was steamed. One day he wrote a story for Bluebook berating me. So I'm going on a big TV show in Chicago and I don't get it, that's sour grapes...I mean if you can't say something nice about someone why say anything at all? So I go on this show and the host says 'did you see what Hemingway said about you in Bluebook?' and I say "Hemingway who?"

That killed him.

Not literally?

Oh boy no. Every summer I went down to Florida on treasure hunts, and there's this great restaurant called the Chesapeake and they had a picture of Hemingway behind the bar. So one day the owner asks if she could have a picture of me to put up there, and she puts one there. One day Hemingway comes in and sees my picture and says 'what's he doing next to me? Either take his down or take mine down, so they took his down and he never came back to that restaurant. (Laughs) I don't like to tell that story cause you're talking about a dead guy can't defend himself...but he was a great reporter, but he got carried away with all the other stuff, the bullfighting...I'm always on the side of the bull, I hope the bull blows the hell out of that crazy guy in the clown suit out there. I don't like to see animals hurt, not deliberately. If they're putting the bull out there, don't stick the things in him first."

comparisons are perhaps inevitable. Competitive spirit is one of Hemingway's elemental personality traits, and there is no doubt that the years of 1945–1955, which marked the height of Hemingway's popular exposure and persona, also paralleled Spillane's, who unquestionably outsold Hemingway by many millions of copies. Spillane, in the 1950s, was possibly America's most popular novelist, selling "in three years over 11,000,000 copies of his first five books," as the blurb on the back of the 1952 third printing of *The Long Wait* states (soon to be updated to 13,000,000).

But perhaps the parallel goes beyond just professional competition and approaches issues of a writer's persona: what happens when fiction, marketing, and life merge? The publishers of Hemingway and Spillane, Scribners and NAL respectively, relied upon the public persona of each author as a selling point, often nurturing the interchangeability between the authors and their characters. Hemingway's characters lived the life their author led, or was it vice versa? Often, with Hemingway more so than any other canonical modern writer, author and fiction become blurred. This is likewise true of Spillane—who even starred as his hard-hitting private dick, Mike Hammer, in *The Girl Hunters* (1963). The back covers of Spillane's books showed him with Borsalino and pistol, much as Hemingway's promotional pictures showed him with hunting vest and shotgun. Of course, the melding of private and public life never tortured Spillane the way it did Hemingway. Even in interviews right up his death in 2006, Spillane seems to gloat on the critics' inability to find any difference between him and his misogynistic, commie-hating heroes.

But the comparison between Hemingway and Spillane goes beyond that of public persona. Hemingway, the author of "The Killers" and *To Have and Have Not*, has been called the father of the hard-boiled voice, and Spillane the endpoint of it, either the worst or best depending upon which side of the cultural line one occupies. More importantly, by the 1950s Hemingway had become something of an icon for both pulp writers and men's pulp magazines, an adoption that Hemingway may well not have relished. Hemingway, always a man of contrast, encapsulated both the early ideal of bohemian modernist artist and the proletariat unpretentious real man. Hence Spillane, as the lowbrow paperback icon of the masses, would have symbolized a personal cultural opposite, yet one in which Hemingway may have seen himself reflected—or, if he didn't his audience surely did. In an interview from a 1953 *Bluebook* magazine (which prompted Spillane's anecdote), the interviewer asks "What do you think of America's latest literary sensation, Mickey Spillane?"

> "'Why ask *me*?'" His deep, rumbling voice was friendly but challenging."

> "'Because you're the man who started this school of writing — tough writing about hard guys.'"

Which Hemingway doesn't take too kindly to. Hemingway goes on to lambaste Spillane, working hard to separate his writing from Spillane's:

[Hemingway:] "The Spillane type wouldn't understand [the idea of bravery in "The Short Happy life of Francis Macomber] if they broke their brains trying. So don't tell me they belong in my school. They belong with the comic books."

[Interviewer:] "When I came into the bar I noticed you were reading a comic book yourself."

[H:] "Sure. But I don't call it literature. Spillane started out as a comic-book writer, and he's still one, to my way of thinking. He even admits it himself. People who read him, don't read me. They couldn't."

[I:] "He's very popular."

[H:]"Naturally. There are lots of scared little bank clerks and office boys. They read stuff like 'I the Jury.' But they couldn't read 'The Old Man and the Sea,' I don't break a man's arm just to hear the bones crack or shoot a woman in the belly when there are lots of better things to do with her. Spillane's violence is for its own sake and means nothing. But if you find violence in good literature, it's only because violence is a natural condition of human life — except for bank clerks and office boys. Don't talk to me about Spillane."

Hemingway's idea that "People who read [Spillane] don't read me, they couldn't" is not really the case: there are numerous paperbacks editions of his work that shared venues, marketing, even cover style with Spillane's. And even more telling is how the two of them were constantly featured in the seedy men's adventure magazines of the day, magazines even lower on the culture scale than the pinups magazines that followed in the wake of *Playboy*. Such magazines were decidedly nonliterary.

But Hemingway's statement about women, that there are "lots of better things to do with them" than shooting them in the belly, does reflect a difference between Spillane and Hemingway's fiction and the marketing of it. If Hemingway is a misogynistic author, which I think is arguable, his misogyny withers in comparison (pun intended) to Spillane's, as reflected in paperback covers: Hemingway's are illustrated with sexual scenes, like the cover of *Across the River and into the Trees* that was supposedly banned in Boston, and Spillane's with scenes of violence (see Figures 3.12 and 3.13).

The idea that Hemingway was either threatened or insulted by a proximity to Spillane may have something to do with Hemingway's relationship with sensationalism, for, in the high-cultural language of the late 1940s and early 1950s, Spillane and literary sensationalism were synonymous. As stated earlier, Cowley, among many others, saw him as the embodiment of paperback culture, as the worst American literature had to offer. But two decades earlier, Hemingway had managed to carefully build his own reputation upon a type of sensationalism, different from Spillane's in that it was marked (and marketed) by a constructed bohemian foundation. By the 1950s, this artistic aura had been replaced by a popular, even pulpish colonization, as in *Bluebook*'s idea that Hemingway was the father of Spillane's school of writing.

Lurid Paperbacks and the Re-Covering of Modernism 211

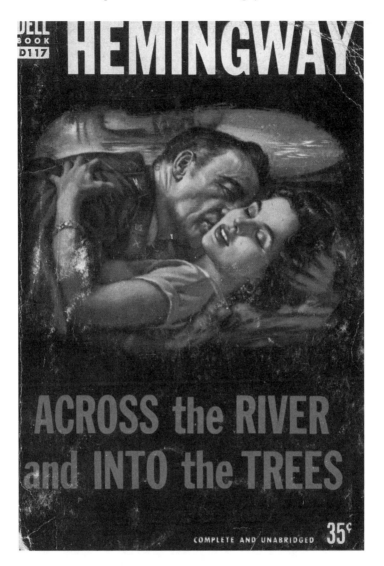

Fig. 3.12   *Across the River and Into the Trees*. Dell, 1953

Much to Hemingway's dislike, critics, from *In Our Time* to *Farewell to Arms*, described Hemingway's writing as "Hard-boiled," a distinctly *popular* catch phrase describing postwar American cynicism, and inextricably linked to pulp magazines and writers.[123] Sheldon Grebstein, in David Madden's *Tough Guy Writers of the Thirties*, cites Hemingway as the progenitor of the Hardboiled School, though

---

[123] For example, Allen Tate's review of *The Sun Also Rises* in *The Nation*; see Myers, ed., *The Critical Heritage*, 93–95.

Fig. 3.13   *One Lonely Night.* Signet, 1952

I think the case is more one of zeitgeist—that both he and the writers of hard-boiled fiction were influenced by both the war and the fiction of the early pulps (Hemingway's juvenilia and early fiction surviving in the Kennedy clearly evinces this pulp influence).[124] But what marks Hemingway's influence is his introduction

---

[124] David Madden, ed., *Tough Guy Writers of the Thirties* (Carbondale: Southern Illinois U, 1968); for Hemingway's early fiction, the only stories that have been republished are those in Peter Griffin's *Along with Youth* (NY: Oxford, 1985).

of proletariat toughness or naturalism of style into the avant-garde. The literati's fascination and use of the term hardboiled and its patronization of hardboiled writers like Hammett by artists such as Dorothy Parker and Gertrude Stein not only marks a reliance upon the pulps as a sexy paradigm (ironic considering that cultural critics also saw them as evidence of the ignorance of the masses), but is indicative of a certain patronizing of the proletariat during the thirties. Hemingway is certainly criticizing this in *To Have and Have Not*.

To Have and Have Not is peculiar in the Hemingway canon. It is his only "Proletariat Novel," his only novel set in the United States, and consistently considered his weakest effort by critics. The fact that the novel itself grew out of a series of short stories (Hemingway, unlike Faulkner, did not see short stories as purely commercial pap) has led many critics to see it as unbalanced and unsuccessful, as well as a failed attempt to be political in reaction to critics calling *Green Hills Of Africa* frivolous.[125] As Toni Knott has pointed out, many critics, including those who saw *To Have and Have Not* as Hemingway's avowal of Marxism and / or disavowal of literary intellectualism, have misread the book's sociopolitical message. Yet Knott herself overlooks how the ambiguous fissure in the book between the first and latter half, between the "haves" and "have-nots," reflects upon Hemingway's own complex stance between popular and elite literature. The reoccurring pattern of Hemingway's use and subsequent disavowal of influences (Anderson, Stein, modernism) points to *To Have and Have Not* as a self-reflexive and even audience-reflexive criticism that utilizes a pulp voice while guiding or warning against its misuse by a parasitic elitist audience.

Richard Gordon, the writer in the book, is an obvious Hemingway-like figure, but one who has lost touch with common humanity: like Hemingway, he lives the vagabond life at the expense of wife and family ("Hills Like White Elephants" a few years on); he uses the conflicts of his surroundings as literary fodder, but does so from a distance—he describes life, but doesn't know how to live it; he writes radical books about labor conflict (what the critics at the time expected Hemingway to do). We can gather that his books are in actuality pretentious or simply romantically radical, since the only real working radical, the Tall Vet, thinks Gordon's books are "shit" and bad enough for him to stop accepting drinks from Gordon. This all comes to a head in Hemingway's "Night Town," Freddy's Bar, filled with scarred and hardened war veterans who serve as counterpoint to Gordon's lack of masculine and lived (i.e., nonvicarious) experience and courage. These vets in Freddy's Bar are anarchy and unchecked violence embodied—the dead debris of the government—literally, as Hemingway saw them (or at least their corpses) after the 1935 hurricane that devastated the upper Keys, which he recounted in an article for *The New Masses*, "Who Murdered the Vets?"[126] One vet in Freddy's Bar, Red, not only takes beatings with no effect, but enjoys them—

---

[125] Toni Knott, *One Man Alone. Hemingway and To Have and Have Not* (Lanham, MA: U P of America, 1999), 11–18.

[126] See Robert Trogdon, *Ernest Hemingway, A Literary Reference* (NY: Carroll & Graf, 2002), 168–171.

"Sometimes it feels good," he grins; other vets are shell-shocked and have no memory. Red could easily have stepped from the pages of a Spillane novel.

The vets are opposites of the writer Gordon, but both are perversions of the Hemingway hero, Harry Morgan. They personify what happens when duty, feelings, and memory are corrupted. The Tall Vet tells Red, the masochistic vet, "First it [the resistance to pain] was an art ... Then it became a pleasure. If things made me sick you'd make me sick, Red."[127] The depiction of Gordon as a fashionable and pretentious writer protects Hemingway from charges of pretence or frivolity himself. Ironically, a vet who Gordon has been buying drinks for, asks "'You haven't got a book [that you've written] with you? ... Pal, I'd like to read one. Did you ever write for *Western Stories*, or *War Aces*? I could read that *War Aces* every day."[128] Gordon and the vets stand as symbols of the dangers that Hemingway needed to avoid—the empty pretence of intellectual and political writings on the one extreme, and the empty violence of the popular pulps on the other.

Hemingway uses the pulps humorously as anathema to Gordon's type of presumably effeminate fiction, yet they, like the vets who read them, are not idealized, except for being exactly that which the intellectuals deride. In Hemingway's world, intellectualism becomes empty without the courage of action. Professor MacWalsey, who lures Gordon's wife away (due as much to Gordon's pretensions as to MacWalsey's own good qualities), is portrayed in a benevolent light due to his own lack of pretence and his ability to live (and drink) among the common Key West Conchs.[129]

Harry Morgan, as the Hemingway hero/man of action, is trapped between the economic extremes of the rich tourists and the empty violence of the vets; he is driven to desperate measures and must take chances for economic gain, which eventually kills him, much like Shumann in *Pylon*. Tellingly, the Cubans who shoot Morgan are driven to violence for political and economic means. Hemingway's montage of the tourists toward the end of the book, which ends in purely economic terms and that critics have cited as being heavy handed and uncharacteristically unsubtle, is Hemingway's depiction of the writer's pitfalls, exactly what *To Have and Have Not* is attempting to negotiate: the pretentious, false literature demanded by the critics on one hand, and the economic pull of the pulps on the other. Likewise the final line of the book advocates a proletariat, workmanlike thriftiness—Hemingway's ethos with and in writing (if not in life)—contrasted with the yacht of yet another tourist arriving in Key West: "A large white yacht was coming into the harbor and seven miles out on the horizon you could see a tanker, small and neat in profile against the blue sea, hugging the reef as she made to the westward to keep from wasting fuel."[130]

---

[127] *To Have and Have Not* (NY: Scribners, 1965), 203.

[128] Ibid., 210.

[129] This reading seemingly parallels the inherent misogyny of the hyper-masculine pulps with that of Hemingway, but that is due to Hemingway's linking masculine sexuality, and mental, moral, and spiritual vigor with purity.

[130] *THAHN*, 262.

Yet if Hemingway is using the dichotomy of Gordon and the symbol of the pulps humorously or ironically in *To Have and Have Not*, that irony is further augmented by the fact that Hemingway, in later life, would himself refuse to be seen alongside the pulp aura of Spillane (although his books were marketed on paperback racks alongside those of Spillane), which, again, may have something to do with the critical reception of *To Have and Have Not*, which treated the book as Hemingway's pulp, and not necessarily good pulp at that.

Sinclair Lewis, in *Newsweek*, lambasted the novel as "puerile slaughter and senile weariness," which would have been redeemed if the violence "were nice exciting killings, as in Mr. Dashiell Hammett."[131] *The Saturday Review of Literature* stated, in not so many words, that the book is "good reading" like a pulp novel, and devoid of any complex characterization or social message: "The story of Harry is so fast and exciting that you read it without caring, at the time, whether it's just a glorified pulp or whether it really says something"—and for that particular reviewer, it didn't.[132] *To Have and Have Not* can be read as an attempt to navigate between the poles of high and low literature, of having and not having. But, ultimately, this navigation fails in the cultural market since Hemingway's criticism in *To Have and Have Not* is misinterpreted, overshadowed by the pulp aspects of the novel, the hard-boiled tone. Much like what happened with Lawrence's criticism of popular and sensational forms, audiences and critics alike overlooked *To Have and Have Not*'s complexities in lieu of the subject and vernacular, foreshadowing what would soon happen to Hemingway's persona.

Hemingway's paperback covers, such as the Bantam *Farewell to Arms* (1949), Perma Book's *To Have and Have Not* (1953), and Dell's *Across the River and into the Trees* (1950), all seem to confirm pulp affinities, as well as mark the apotheosis of Hemingway into a Pulp—rather than a modernist—icon. The diffusion of Hemingway's influence upon popular literature is undeniable: Hemingway changed the face of stylistics and popular literature in a way that Joyce, Eliot, Pound, Dos Passos, Cummings, Faulkner, and Woolf did not. There is a reason why Raymond Chandler has Philip Marlowe call a gun-flunky Hemingway, taking to task the repetitive style and vernacular of, say, "The Killers." It was Hemingway's style that became a mark of excellence for many new popular writers—so much so that his name on the cover of other author's books became a selling point: Avon's 1952 *... Plus Blood in their Veins* states foremost on the cover "The best of its kind since ... Hemingway"; Lion Books' *Lonely Boy Blues* (1956) has another blurb at the top of the front cover stating "Reminds one of Farrell and Hemingway ... startlingly fresh and original"; and Elio Bartolini's *La Signora* (1957), the "frank, sensational Italian novel of a fallen women," is marketed as the "Winner of the Ernest Hemingway Prize"; the paperback covers of Robert Lowry's *The Last Party* and *New York Call Girl* both compared the author to Hemingway. These are just a few of many examples. And in this moment of postwar hyper-masculinity,

---

[131] Quoted in Trogdon, 200.
[132] Ibid., 201.

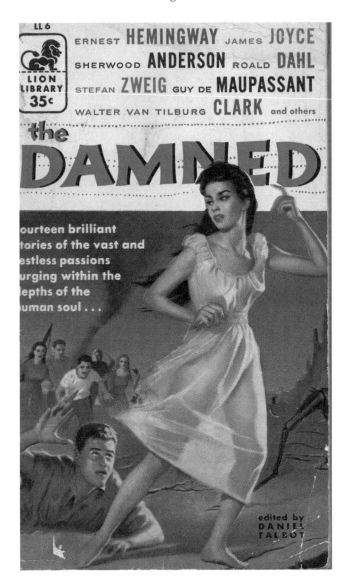

Fig. 3.14   *The Damned.* Lion Library, 1956

Hemingway became something of a pinup for men's magazines—besides the oft-cited *Esquire* articles and stories in *Playboy* there were features and interviews in *Gent* (December 1957), *Bluebook* (July 1953), *Argosy* (September 1958), and men's adventure magazines such as *Man's Magazine*, *Man's True Action*, *Male*, *Man's Illustrated*, and *Conquest*. Each of these instances furthered the popular construction, even caricature, of the Hemingway myth, moving him further and further away from his elite and artistic beginnings. This apotheosis of the fictionalized Hemingway reached its ultimate manifestation after Hemingway's death in the many novels that feature him as the hero: *Toro* (1977), *I Killed Hemingway* (1993), and most recently, *The Crook Factory* (1999); the Hemingway persona was now literally (if not literary) fiction.

Perhaps more ironic is the fact that Hemingway became a means to economic pandering in 1950s paperbacks when his name was used again and again as a literary counterpoint to obvious sensationalism, such as in the paperback anthology *The Damned* (see Figure 3.14), which touted "Fourteen brilliant stories of the vast and restless passions surging within the depths of the human soul..." and Hemingway's name on the cover leading off the list of authors. Other collections shamelessly took advantage of his death to cash in, such as the 1961 edited collection of spy stories that was titled *Hemingway: The Secret Agent's Badge of Courage*. Despite the marketing that made it seem like a new book by Hemingway, his contribution was a one page excerpt from *Men at War*.

There is little wonder that in the mid- to late-1950s, Hemingway returned to an idealized scene of modernism and the foundations of his own reputation by writing *A Moveable Feast*; it was an effort to reverse the move from modernist to masculine/pulp ideal, from Stein to Spillane, as it were. And there is also little wonder, considering this cultural adoption of Hemingway, about his reaction to Spillane's picture hanging alongside his own in a Florida bar. But Hemingway's own relationship to the pulps, as evident in his paperback covers, is perhaps nowhere better illustrated than in a photograph taken in the Finca Vigia in Cuba in 1954. Hemingway, beaming, is being handed the Nobel Prize by the Swedish Ambassador to Cuba. The two are standing in front of a book case, and above them, high up on the shelves, is a line of tawdry paperbacks: *Mystery Ranch, Hit the Saddle, The Sheriff's Son*, and an issue of the 1950s pulp magazine, *Manhunt*, a magazine that regularly featured Mickey Spillane. Of course, one would need a magnifying glass to read these titles, but that is duly appropriate, for within modernist fiction itself can be found traces of the moldy and tattered pulps, if one is willing to look close enough.

Bibliography

Abadie, Anne J. and Doreen Fowler. *Faulkner and Popular Culture*. Jackson: U P of Mississippi, 1990.

Adams, Michael. *The Great Adventure*. Bloomington: Indiana U P, 1990.

Adams, Timothy Dow. *Telling Lies in Modern American Autobiography*. Chapel Hill: U of North Carolina P, 1990.

Adorno, Theodore W. and Max Horkheimer. *Dialect of Enlightenment*. NY: Continuum, 1999.

Allen, Charles, Frederick Hoffman, and Carolyn Ulrich. *The Little Magazine, a History and a Bibliography*. Princeton: Princeton U P, 1947.

Anderson, Margaret. *My Thirty Years War*. NY: Covici, Friede, 1930.

Anglo, Michael. *Penny Dreadfuls*. London: Jupiter, 1977.

Ardis, Ann L. *Modernism and Cultural Conflict, 1880–1922*. NY: Cambridge, 2002.

Armstrong, Tim. *Modernism, Technology and the Body*. NY: Cambridge, 1998.

Arnold, Bruce. *The Scandal of Ulysses*. London: Sinclair Stevenson, 1991.

Ashley, Ellen. *Girl in Overalls*. NY: Dodd, Mead & Co., 1943.

Ashley, Michael. *The Age of the Story Tellers*. New Castle, DE: Oak Knoll Press, 2006.

Attebery, Brian. *Strategies of Fantasy*. Bloomington: Indiana U P, 1992.

Audit Bureau of Circulation, *Publisher's Statements, Periodicals. Period Ending June 30, 1924.*

Bailey, Frankie Y. *Out Of The Woodpile*. NY: Greenwood, 1991.

Baker, Carlos, ed. *Ernest Hemingway, Selected Letters*. NY: Scribners, 1981.

Baker, Houston A. *Modernism and The Harlem Renaissance*. Chicago: U P of Chicago, 1987.

Baldick, Chris. *Criticism and Literary Theory 1890 to the Present*. NY: Longman, 1996.

———. *The Social Mission of English Criticism*. Oxford: Clarendon, 1983.

Balshaw, Maria. *Looking For Harlem: Urban Aesthetics in African American Literature*. London: Pluto Press, 2000.

Beach, Sylvia. *Shakespeare and Co*. NY: Harcourt, 1959.

Benjamin, Andrew, ed. *The Problems of Modernity*. NY: London, 1989.

Ben-Merre, Diana A. and Maureen Murphy, *James Joyce and His Contemporaries*. NY: Greenwood, 1989.

Bennett, Arnold. *Critical Writings of Arnold Bennett*. Samuel Hynes, ed. Lincoln: U of Nebraska P, 1968.

Benstock, Bernard, ed. *Art in Crime Writing*. NY: St. Martin's, 1983.

Benstock, Shari. *Women of the Left Bank, Paris, 1900–1940*. Austin: U of Texas P, 1986.

Benton, Megan. "'Too Many Books': Book Ownership and Cultural Identity in the 1920s." *American Quarterly* 49.2 (1997).
Berg, A. Scott. *Max Perkins*. NY: Dutton, 1978.
Berman, Marshall. *All That is Solid Melts into Air*. NY: Penguin, 1988.
Bloom, Clive. *Cult Fiction: Popular Reading and Pulp Theory*. NY: St Martin's, 1996.
Blotner, Joseph. *Faulkner, A Biography*. NY: Vintage, 1984.
Blotner, Joseph and Frederick L. Gwynn, eds. *Faulkner in the University*. Charlottesville: U of Virginia P, 1959.
Bode, Carl, ed. *The New Mencken Letters*. NY: Dial Press, 1977.
Bonn, Thomas L. *Heavy Traffic and High Culture*. Carbondale, IL: Southern Illinois U P, 1989.
———. *Undercover: an Illustrated History of American Mass Market Paperbacks*. NY: Penguin, 1982.
Bornstein, George. *Material Modernism*. NY: Cambridge, 2001.
———. *Representing Modernist Texts*. Ann Arbor: U of Michigan P, 1991.
Borzoi Press. *The Borzoi 1925*. NY: Knopf, 1925.
Bourdieu, Pierre. *The Field of Cultural Consumption*. NY: Columbia U P, 1993.
Bourke, Joanna. *Dismembering the Male*. Chicago: U of Chicago P, 1996.
Boyer, Paul S. *Purity In Print*. Madison: U Wisconsin P, 2002.
Bradbury, Malcolm and McFarlane, James, eds. *Modernism; A Guide to European Literature, 1890–1930*. London: Penguin, 1991.
Brake, Laurel. "On Print Culture: The State We're In," *Journal of Victorian Culture* (Spring 2001, Vol. 6, Issue 1).
———. *Print in Transition, 1850–1910*. NY: Palgrave, 2001.
Brake, Laurel and Julie Codell, eds. *Encounters in the Victorian Press*. NY: Palgrave, 2005.
Brannon, Julie Sloan. *Who Reads Ulysses?* NY: Routledge, 2003.
Brantlinger, Patrick. *Bread and Circuses*. Ithaca, NY: Cornell, 1983.
Brantlinger, Patrick and James Naremore, eds. *Modernity and Mass Culture*. Bloomington: Indiana U P, 1991.
Breu, Christopher. *Hard-Boiled Masculinities*. Minneapolis, U Minnesota P, 2005.
Brown, Bob. *1450–1950*. NY: Jargon Books, (1959?).
Bruccoli, Matthew J. with assistance of Robert Trogdon. *The Only Thing That Counts: the Ernest Hemingway/Maxwell Perkins Correspondence, 1925–1947*. NY: Scribners, 1996.
Buhle, Paul, Mary Jo Buhl, and Dan Georgakas. *Encyclopedia of the American Left*. NY: Garland, 1990
Burke, Carolyn. *Becoming Modern: The Life of Mina Loy*. NY: Farrar, Straus and Giroux, 1996.
Cahoon, Herbert, and John J. Slocum. *A Bibliography of James Joyce*. New Haven: Yale U P, 1953.
Čapek, Karel. *R.U.R. and The Insect Play*. NY: Oxford, 1961.
———. *War With The Newts*. NY: Berkley, 1971.

Carey, John. *The Intellectuals and the Masses*. Chicago: Academy, 2002.
Caserio, Robert. "Queer Passions, Queer Citizenship: Some Novels about the State of the American Nation 1946–1954," *Modern Fiction Studies* (Vol. 43, No.1, Spring 1997).
Charters, Jimmy and Morrill Cody. *This Must be the Place*. NY: MacMillan, 1989.
Chase, Stuart. *Men and Machines*. NY: MacMillan, 1929.
Cherniak, Warren, Warwick Gould, and Ian Willison, eds. *Modernist Writers and the Marketplace*. NY: St. Martin's, 1996.
Chielens, Edward E., ed. *American Literary Magazines, The Twentieth Century*. Westport: Greenwood, 1992.
Chisholm, Anne. *Nancy Cunard*. NY: Penguin, 1981.
Churchill, Sarah and Adam McKible. *Little Magazines and Modernism: New Approaches*. Hampshire: Ashgate, 2008.
Churchill, Suzanne. *The Little Magazine* Others *and the Renovation of American Poetry*. Hampshire: Ashgate, 2006.
Chwast, Seymour and Steven Heller. *Jackets Required: an Illustrated History of American Book Jacket Design, 1920–1950*. San Francisco: Chronicle, 1995.
Clark, Catherine Anne. "Reconsidering Faulkner's Pulp Series: 'The Unvanquished' as Parody, Not Potboiler." Unpublished Dissertation. Emory U, 1993.
Coates, Robert M. *The Eater of Darkness*. NY: Macauley, 1929.
Cole, John. *Books In Action, the Armed Services Editions*. Washington DC: Library of Congress, 1984.
Conover, Anne. *Caresse Crosby*. Santa Barbara: Capra, 1989.
Conrad, Joseph. *Lord Jim*. NY: Norton, 1996.
———. *Nigger of the 'Narcissus.'* NY: Norton, 1979.
Conroy, Mark. *Modernism and Authority: Strategies of Legitimation in Flaubert and Conrad*. Baltimore: John Hopkins U P, 1985.
Cooper, John Xiros. *Modernism and the Culture of Market Society*. NY: Cambridge U P, 2004.
Cowley, Malcolm. *After the Genteel Tradition*. NY: W.W. Norton, 1937.
———. *Exile's Return*. NY: Viking, 1951.
———. *The Literary Situation*. NY: Viking, 1954.
Coyle, Michael. "With a Plural Vengeance: Modernism as (Flaming) Brand," *Modernist Cultures*, Vol. 1, No. 1, p. 16.
Crider, Allen Billy, ed. *Mass Market Publishing in America*. Boston: G.K. Hall, 1982.
Crosby, Caresse. *The Passionate Years*. NY: Dial, 1953.
Crowninsfield, Francis W. *Manners for the Metropolis*. NY: Arno, 1975.
Curtiss, Thomas Quinn. *The Smart Set*. NY: Applause, 1998.
Daly, Nicholas. *Modernism, Romance and the Fin De Siècle: Popular Culture and British Culture, 1880–1914*. Cambridge: Cambridge U P, 1999.
Damon-Moore Helen. *Magazines For the Millions: Gender and Commerce in the Ladies' Home Journal and the Saturday Evening Post, 1880–1910*. Albany: State University of NY Press, 1994.

Davidson, Lawrence and Frank Robinson. *Pulp Culture: The Art of Fiction Magazines*. Portland: Collectors Press, 1998.
De St Jorre, John. *Venus Bound*. NY: Random House, 1995.
DeForest, Tim. *Storytelling in the Pulps, Comics, and Radio*. Jefferson, NC: McFarland, 2004.
Delany, Samual R. "Racism and Science Fiction." *Dark Matter*. Sheree R. Thomas, ed. NY: Warner, 2000.
Denning, Michael. *Mechanic Accents*. London: Verso, 1987.
Dettmar, Kevin and Stephen Watt. *Marketing Modernisms*. Ann Arbor: U of Michigan P, 1996.
Dettmar, Kevin H., ed. *Rereading the New*. Ann Arbor: U of Michigan P, 1992.
DiBattista, Maria and Lucy McDiarmid. *High and Low Moderns*. NY: Oxford U P, 1996.
Diepeveen, Leonard. *The Difficulties of Modernism*. NY: Routledge, 2003.
Dixon, Robert. *Writing The Colonial Adventure*. Cambridge: Cambridge U P, 1995.
Dolen, Marc. *Modern Lives*. West Lafayette: Purdue U P, 1996.
Dolmetsch, Carl R. *The Smart Set*. NY: Dial Press, 1966.
Douglas, George H. *The Smart Magazines*. Hamden: Archon, 1991.
Drewry, John. *Some Magazines and Magazine Makers*. Boston: Stratford, 1924.
Drown, Eric Mills. *Usable Futures, Disposable Paper: Popular Science, Pulp Science Fiction and Modernization in America, 1908–1937*. Unpublished Dissertation, University of Minnesota, December 2001.
Drucker, Johanna. *The Visible World: Experimental Typography and Modern Art, 1909–1923*. Chicago: U Chicago P, 1994.
———. "Who's Afraid of Visual Culture," *Art Journal* (Vol. 58, No. 4, Winter 1999).
Dryden, Linda. *Joseph Conrad and the Imperial Romance*. NY: St. Martins, 2000.
DuBasky, Mayo. *The Gist of Mencken: Quotations from America's Critic*. Metuchen, NJ: Scarecrow Press, 1990.
Duchting, Hajo. *Edouard Manet: Images of Parisian Life*. NY: Prestel, 1995.
Duffield, Marcus. "The Pulps: Day Dreams for the Masses." *Vanity Fair*. June, 1933.
Dziemianowicz, Stefan R., Martin H. Greenberg, Robert Weinberg, eds. *Hard-Boiled Detectives*. NY: Gramercy, 1992.
Eagleton, Terry. *Literary Theory*. Minnesota: U of Minnesota P, 1983.
Eakin, Paul John. *Fictions in Autobiography*. Princeton: Princeton U P, 1985.
Eberly, Rosa A. *Citizen Critics: Literary Public Spheres*. Urbana: U of Illinois P, 2000.
Ellis, Doug. *Uncovered: The Hidden Art of the Girlie Pulps*. Silver Spring, MD: Adventure House, 2003.
Ellis, Doug. John Locke, John Gunnison, eds. *The Adventure House Guide to the Pulps*. Silver Spring, MD: Adventure House, 2000.
Ellmann, Richard. *James Joyce*. Oxford: Oxford U P, 1983.

Emerson, O.B. *Faulkner's Early Literary Reputation in America*. Ann Arbor: UMI Research Press, 1984.
Erdinast-Vulcan, Daphna. *Joseph Conrad and the Modern Temper*. Oxford: Clarendon, 1991.
Everett, Walter. *Faulkner's Art and Characters*. Woodbury, NY: Barons, 1969.
Eysteinsson, Astrudur. *The Concept of Modernism*. Ithaca: Cornell U P, 1990.
Fabre, Michael. *From Harlem to Paris, Black American Writers in France, 1840–1980*. Urbana: U of Illinois P, 1991.
Fante, John. *Ask the Dust*. Santa Rose: Black Sparrow, 2000.
———. *Wait Until Spring, Bandini*. Santa Rosa: Black Sparrow, 2001.
Faulk, Barry. "Modernism and the Popular: Eliot's Music Halls." *Modernism/Modernity*. 8.4 (2001), 603–621.
Faulkner, William. *If I Forget Thee Jerusalem [The Wild Palms]*. NY: Vintage, 1995.
———. *Absalom, Absalom!* NY: Vintage, 1986.
———. *Light in August*. NY: Vintage, 1972.
———. *The Marionettes*. Charlottesville: U P Virginia, 1977.
———. *Pylon*. NY: Vintage. 1985.
———. *Sanctuary*. NY: Vintage, 1958.
———. *Selected Letters*. Joseph Blotner, ed. NY: Random House, 1977.
Feltes, N.N. *Literary Capital and the Late Victorian Novel*. Madison: U of Wisconsin P, 1993.
Fishbein, Leslie. *Rebels in Bohemia: The Radicals of The Masses, 1911–1917*. Chapel Hill: U North Carolina P, 1982.
Fisher, Rudolph. "The Caucasian Storms Harlem." *American Mercury* 11 (August 1927) 393–398.
Fitch, Noel Riley, ed. *transition: a Paris Anthology*. London: Secker and Warburg, 1990.
Fitch, Noel Riley. *Sylvia Beach and The Lost Generation*. NY: Norton, 1983.
Fitzgerald, F. Scott. *The Great Gatsby*. NY: Scribners, 1953.
Flaubert, Gustave. *Madame Bovary*. NY: Norton, 1965.
Fleishman, Avrom. "Lawrence and Bakhtin: where pluralism ends and dialogism begins." *Rethinking Lawrence*. Keith Brown, ed. Philadelphia: Open University Press, 1990.
Flower, Linda and Christina Haas' "Rhetorical Reading Strategies and the Construction of Reading," *College Composition and Communication* (Vol. 39, No. 2, May 1988) 167–183.
Ford, Hugh. *Published in Paris*. NY: Macmillan, 1975.
Ford, James L.C. *Magazines For The Millions*. Carbondale: Southern Illinois U P, 1969.
Forgue, Guy Y, ed. *Letters of H.L. Mencken*. Boston: Northeastern U P, 1981.
Forter, Greg. *Murdering Masculinities*. NY: New York U P, 2000.
Foster, Hal. "Prosthetic Gods." *Modernism/Modernity*. 4.2 (1997) 5–38.
Foucault, Michel. *Discipline and Punishment*. NY: Vintage, 1995.

———. *Power/Knowledge*. NY: Pantheon, 1980.
———. *The Archeology of Knowledge*. NY: Pantheon, 1972.
———. *The Order of Things*. NY: Vintage, 1994.
Fraser, Keath. "Another Reading of *The Great Gatsby*," *F. Scott Fitzgerald's The Great Gatsby*. Harold Bloom, ed. NY: Chelsea House, 1986.
Fussell, Paul. *The Great War and Modern Memory*. NY: Oxford U P, 2000.
Gardner, Dorothy and Kathrine Sorley Walker. *Raymond Chandler Speaking*. Boston: Houghton Mifflin, 1977.
Garrity, Jane. "Selling Culture to the 'Civilized': Bloomsbury, British *Vogue* and the Marketing of National Identity" *Modernism: Modernity*. 6.2 (1999) 29–58.
Gates, Henry Louis, Jr. *Figures in Black; Words, Signs, and the "Racial" Self*. NY: Oxford U P, 1987.
———. "Dis and Dat: Dialect and the Descent." Dexter Fisher and Robert B. Stepto, eds. *Afro-American Literature: The Reconstruction of Instruction*. NY: MLA, 1979.
Gertzman, Jay. *Bookleggers and Smuthounds*. Philidelphia: U of Pennsylvania P, 1999.
Gikondi, Simon. *Maps of Englishness*. NY: Columbia U P, 1996.
Gilbert, Sandra and Susan Gubar. *No Man's Land: The Place of Women Writers in the Twentieth Century*. New Haven: Yale U P, 1988.
Giles, Steve. *Theorizing Modernism*. NY: Routledge, 1993.
Gillespie, Michael Patrick. "Reading on the Edge of Chaos: *Finnegans Wake* and the Burden of Linearity," *Journal of Modern Literature* (22.2 1999) 359–371.
Gilroy, Paul. *The Black Atlantic: Modernity and Double Consciousness*. Cambridge: Harvard U P, 1993.
Glass, Loren. *Authors Inc.: Literary Celebrity in the Modern United States*. NY: New York U P, 2004.
Goodstone, Tony. *The Pulps*. NY: Chelsea, 1970.
Gosselin, Adrienne. "Beyond the Harlem Renaissance: The Case for Black Modernist Writers." *Modern Language Studies* 26.4 (1996): 37–45.
Gottfried, Roy. *Joyce's Iritis and the Irritated Text*. Gainesville: U P Florida, 1995.
Goulart, Ron. *An Informal History of the Pulp Magazine*. NY: Ace, 1972.
Gresset, Michel and Noel Polk. *Intertextuality in Faulkner*. Jackson: U P of Mississippi, 1985.
Gruber, Frank. *The Pulp Jungle*. LA: Shelbourne Press, 1967.
Guillory, John. *Cultural Capital*. Chicago: U Chicago P, 1993.
Gunnison, John. *Belarski, Pulp Art Masters*. Silver Spring, MD: Adventure House, 2003.
———. *Pulp Fictioneers: Adventures in the Storytelling Business*. Silver Spring, MD: Adventure House, 2004.
Haas, Christina. *Writing Technology: Studies on the Materiality of Literacy*. Mahwah, NJ: Erlbaum, 1996.
Hack, Daniel. "Literary Paupers and Professional Authors" *SEL: Studies In English Literature*: 38.4, 691–713.

Hagemann, E.R. *A Comprehensive Index to Black Mask, 1920–1951*. Bowling Green: Bowling Green U Popular P, 1982.
Haining, Peter. *The Art of Mystery and Detective Stories*. Secaucus: Chartwell, 1977.
———. *The Fantastic Pulps*. NY: Vintage, 1975.
Haldeman-Julius, Emanuel. *The World of Haldeman-Julius*. Albert Mordell, ed. NY: Twayne, 1960.
Hamilton, Sharon. "The First *NYer*? The *Smart Set* Magazine, 1900–1924." *The Serials Librarian*. Vol. 37, No. 2, 1999.
———. "The *Smart Set* Magazine and the Popularization of American Modernism, 1908–1920." Unpublished Dissertation, Dalhousie University, 1999.
Hammett, Dashiell. *The Maltese Falcon*. NY: Vintage, 1992.
Hammond, Paul. *Love Between Men in English Literature*. NY: St. Martin's Press, 1996.
Hanneman, Audre. *Ernest Hemingway: a Comprehensive Bibliography*. Princeton, NJ: Princeton U P, 1967.
Harris, Sharon with Ellen Gruber Garvey, eds. *Blue Pencils and Hidden Hands: Women Editing Periodicals, 1830–1910*. Boston: Northeastern U P, 2004.
Harrison, Robert L. *Aviation Lore in Faulkner*. Philadelphia: John Benjamins Publishing, 1985.
Haslett, Moyra. *Marxist Literary and Cultural Theories*. NY: St. Martin's, 2000.
Haugland, Ann. "Book Propaganda: Edward L. Bernay's 1930 Campaign Against Dollar Books." *Book History* 3 (2000) 231–252.
Haut, Woody. *Neon Noir*. London: Serpent's Tail, 1999.
———. *Pulp Culture: Hardboiled Fiction and the Cold War*. London: Serpent's Tail, 1995.
Haycraft, Howard. *Murder for Pleasure*. NY: Appleton, 1941.
Hemingway, Ernest. *Complete Poems*. Lincoln: U of Nebraska P, 1992.
———. *Dateline, Toronto*. William White, ed. NY: Scribners, 1985.
———. *To Have and Have Not*. NY: Scribners, 1965.
———. *A Moveable Feast*. NY: Scribners, 1964.
———. *The Sun Also Rises*. NY: Scribners, 1954.
———. *The Torrents of Spring*. NY: Scribners, 1998.
Herbst, Josephine. *The Starched Blue Sky of Spain and Other Memoirs*. Boston: Northeastern U P, 1999.
Herr, Cheryl. *Joyce's Anatomy of Culture*. Urbana: Illinois U P, 1986.
Herring, Phillip. *Djuna*. NY: Penguin, 1995.
Hersey, Harold Brainerd. *Pulpwood Editor*. Westport: Greenwood, 1974.
Heyck, T.W. *The Transformation of Intellectual Life in Victorian England*. NY: St. Martin's Press, 1982.
Hill, Wycliffe. *The Plot Genie*. LA: Ernest E. Gagnon Co., 1934.
Hoffman, Frederick J. *The Twenties: American Writing in the Postwar Decade*. NY: Viking, 1955.
Hoffman, Michael and Patrick Murphy. *Critical Essays on American Modernism*. NY: Hall, 1992.

Huggins, Nathan Irvin. *Harlem Renaissance*. London: U P of Oxford, 1973.
Hughes, Langston. *The Big Sea. The Collected Works of Langston Hughes, Vol 13*. Columbia: U of Missouri P, 2002.
Hutchinson, Don. *The Great Pulp Heroes*. Oakville: Mosaic, 1995.
Huxley, Aldous. *Brave New World*. NY: Perennial, 1998.
———. *Ends and Means*. NY: Harper, 1937.
Huyssen, Andreas. *After the Great Divide: Modernism, Mass Culture, Postmodernism*. Bloomington: Indiana U P, 1986.
———. "High and Low in an Expanded Field." *Modernism/Modernity*. Vol. 9, No. 9 (2002) 363–374.
Irvine, Dean. *Editing Modernism: Women and Little Magazine Cultures in Canada*. Toronto: U Toronto P, 2008.
Jacobs, Karen. *The Eye's Mind*. Ithaca: Cornell U P, 2001.
Jaffe, Aaron. *Modernism and the Culture of Celebrity*. NY: Cambridge, 2005.
James Playsted Wood. *Magazines in the United States, Their Social and Economic Influence*. NY: Ronald Press, 1949.
Jameson, Frederic. *The Political Unconscious*. Ithaca: Cornell, 1981.
———. *Signatures of the Visible*. NY: Routledge, 1990.
Jan, Alfred. "Doan, Carstairs, and Ludwig," *Blood 'n' Thunder* (Fall 2006) 16–19.
Janello, Amy and Brennon Jones. *The American Magazine*. NY: Abrams, 1991.
Jenkins, Thomas. "An American 'Classic': Hillman and Cullin's *Mimes of the Courtesans*," *Arethusa* (Vol. 38, 2005) 387–414.
Jones, Robert Kenneth. *The Shudder Pulps*. NY: Plume, 1975.
Joseph, Michael. *The Commercial Side of Literature*. NY: Harper and Brothers, 1926.
Joyce. James. *Dubliners*. NY: Vintage, 1993.
———. *Ulysses*. NY: Vintage, 1986.
Justice, Hilary. "The Necessary Danger: Hemingway and the Problem of Authorship." Unpublished Dissertation, University of Chicago, Department of English. June 2001.
Kain, Richard M. *Fabulous Voyager, James Joyce's Ulysses*. Chicago: Chicago U P, 1947.
Karl. Frederick R. *Modern and Modernism, The Sovereignty of the Artist 1885–1925*. NY: Atheneum, 1988.
Katz, Wendy. *Rider Haggard and the Fiction of Empire*. NY: Cambridge U P, 1987.
Kawin, Bruce. *Faulkner's MGM Screenplays*. Knoxville: University of Tennessee, 1992.
Keeler, Harry Stephen. *I, Chameleon*. Shreveport, LA: Ramble House, 2006.
———. *The Portrait of Jirjohn Cobb*. NY: Dutton, 1940.
Kern, Stephen. *The Culture of Time and Space*. Cambridge, MA: Harvard U P, 1993.
Kershner, R.B. "Framing Rudy and Photography" *Journal of Modern Literature*. Vol. 22, No. 2 (Winter 1998/99) 265–292.
———. *Joyce, Bakhtin, and Popular Literature*. Chapel Hill: U of North Carolina P, 1989.

———. "The Strongest Man in the World: Joyce or Sandow?" *James Joyce Quarterly* 30, no. 4 (Summer/Fall 1993) 667–694.
Kershner, R.B., ed. *Joyce and Popular Culture*. Gainesville: U P of Florida, 1996.
Kery, Patricia Frantz. *Art Deco Graphics*. NY: Abrams, 1986.
Kiernan, V.G. *The Lords Of Human Kind. Blackman, Yellow Man, and White Man in an Age of Empire*. Boston: Little Brown, 1969.
King, Mary C. "Hermeneutics of Suspicion: Nativism, Nationalism, and the Language Question in 'Oxen of the Sun." *James Joyce Quarterly*. 35 (1998): 349–372.
Kirsch, Robert. *Lives, Works & Transformations: A Quarter Century of Book Reviews and Essays*. Santa Barbara: Capra Press, 1978.
Klevar, Harvey L. *Erskine Caldwell, A Biography*. Knoxville: U of Tenn P, 1993.
Knott, Toni D. *One Man Alone. Hemingway and To Have and Have Not*. Lanham, MA: U P of America, 1999.
Knowles, Sebastian. *The Dublin Helix*. Gainesville: U P Florida, 2001.
Kramer, Victor A., ed. *The Harlem Renaissance Re-Examined*. NY: AMS Press, 1987.
Latham, Angela. *Posing a Threat: Flappers, Chorus Girls, and Other Brazen Performers of the American 1920s*. Hanover, NH: Wesleyan U P, 2000.
Latham, Sean. *Am I a Snob? Modernism and the Novel*. Ithaca: Cornell U P, 2003.
Latham, Sean and Robert Scholes. "The Rise of Periodical Studies," *PMLA*, (Vol.121, No. 2), March 2006, 517–531
Lee, Charles. *The Hidden Public*. NY: Doubleday, 1958.
Leff, Leonard. *Hemingway and his Conspirators; Hollywood, Scribner's, and the Making of American Celebrity Culture*. MD: Rowman & Littlefield, 1999.
Leja, Michael. *Looking Askance*. Berkeley: U California P, 2004.
Leonard, Garry. *Advertising and Commodity Culture in Joyce*. Gainesville: U P of Florida, 1998.
Leonard, Garry and Jennifer Wicke, eds. "Joyce and Advertising Issue," *James Joyce Quarterly*. 35 (1998).
Lesser, Robert. *Pulp Art*. NY: Grammercy, 1997.
Levenson, Michael. *A Genealogy of Modernism*. NY: Cambridge U P, 1984.
Leverich, Lyle. *Tom: The Unknown Tennessee Williams*. NY: Crown, 1995.
Levitt, Morton P., ed. *Joyce and the Joyceans*. Syracuse: Syracuse U P, 2002.
Lewis, David Levering. *When Harlem Was In Vogue*. NY: Penguin, 1997.
Locke, Alain. *The New Negro: Voices of the Harlem Renaissance*. NY: Atheneum, 1992.
Locke, John, ed. *Pulpwood Days: Editors You Want To Know*. Castroville, CA: Off-Trail Publications, 2007.
———. *Pulp Fictioneers: Adventures in the Storytelling Business*. Silver Spring, MD: Adventure House, 2004.
Locke, John and John Wooley, eds. *Thrilling Detective Stories*. Silver Spring, MD: Adventure House, 2007.

Lodge, David. "Lawrence, Dostoevzky, Bakhtin: Lawrence and Dialogic Fiction." *Rethinking Lawrence*. Keith Brown, ed. Philadelphia: Open University Press, 1990.

Loeb, Lori Anne. *Consuming Angels*. NY: Oxford U P, 1994.

Loughery, John. *Alias S.S. Van Dine*. NY: Scribners, 1992.

Lucien. *The Mimes of the Courtesans*. NY: Rarity Press, 1932.

Lutz, Tom. *Cosmopolitan Vistas: American Regionalism and Literary Value*. Ithaca: Cornell U P, 2004.

Lyles, William H. *Putting Dell on the Map*. Westport: Greenwood P, 1983.

McAlmon, Robert. *Being Geniuses Together*. NY: Doubleday, 1968.

McCann, Sean. *Gumshoe America: hard-boiled crime fiction and the rise and fall of New Deal liberalism*. Durham: Duke U P, 2000.

McClusky, John Jr. Introduction. *The City of Refuge* by Rudolph Fisher. Columbia: U P of Missouri, 1987.

McCracken, Scott. *Pulp: Reading Popular Fiction*. Manchester: Manchester U P, 1998.

McDonald, Gail. *Learning To Be Modern: Pound, Eliot, and the American University*. Oxford: Clarendon Press, 1993.

McGann, Jerome. *Black Riders: The Visible Language of Modernism*. Princeton, NJ: Princeton U P, 1993.

McGann, Jerome. *The Textual Condition*. Princeton, NJ: Princeton U P, 1991.

McGurl, Mark. "Making 'Literature' of It: Hammett and High Culture." *American Literary History*, Vol. 9, Issue 4 (Winter 1997) 702–717.

McHale, Brian. *Postmodernist Fictions*. NY: Routledge, 1987.

McHaney, Thomas L. *William Faulkner's Wild Palms: A Study*. Jackson: U P Mississippi, 1975.

Mackey, Peter Francis. *Chaos Theory and James Joyce's Everyman*. Gainesville: U P Florida, 1999.

McKible, Adam. *The Space and Place of Modernism: The Russian Revolution, Little Magazines, and New York*. NY: Routledge, 2002.

MacMillan, Duane. "*Pylon*: From Short Stories to Major Work" *Mosaic*, 7 (Fall 1973) 185–212.

MacMullen, Margaret. "Pulps and Confessions." *Harpers Monthly Magazine*. June, 1937.

MacShane, Frank. *The Life of Raymond Chandler*. Boston: G.K. Hall, 1989.

Madden, David, ed. *Proletariat Writers of the Thirties*. Carbondale, IL: Southern Illinois U P, 1968.

———. *Tough Guy Writers of the Thirties*. Carbondale: Southern Illinois U, 1968.

March, Joseph Monclure. *The Wild Party*. London: Picador, 1994.

Marek, Jayne E. *Women Editing Modernism: "Little" Magazines and Literary History*. Lexington: U P of Kentucky, 1995.

Marinetti, Filippo Tommaso. *Selected Writings*. NY: Farrar, Straus and Giroux, 1972.

Marlin, William. *The American Roman Noir*. Athens: U of Georgia P, 1995.
Materer, Timothy, ed. *The Selected Letters of Ezra Pound to John Quinn, 1915–1924*. Durham: Duke U P, 1991.
Meckier, Jerome. "Aldous Huxley, Evelyn Waugh, and Birth Control in *Black Mischief*." *Journal of Modern Literature*. 23.2 (1997) 277–290.
Melnick, Daniel. *Fullness of Dissonance*. Rutherford: Fairleigh Dickenson U P, 1994.
Mencken, H.L. *Mencken's Smart Set Criticism*. William H. Nolte, ed. Ithaca: Cornell U P, 1968.
Mencken, H.L. *My Life as Author and Editor*. NY: Vintage, 1995.
Merritt, A. *The Fox Woman and Other Stories*. NY: Avon, 1977.
Meyers, Jefferey. *Hemingway: the Critical Heritage*. London: Routledge, 1982.
Mierlo, Wim Van. "Reading Joyce In and Out of the Archive." *Joyce Studies Annual* (2002) 32–61.
Mixon, Wayne. *The People's Writer*. Charlottesvile: U P of Virginia, 1995.
Moore-Gilbert, B.J. *Kipling and "Orientalism."* NY: St Martin's, 1986.
Mordell, Albert, ed. *The World of Haldeman-Julius*. NY: Twayne, 1960.
Morrison, Mark. *The Public Face of Modernism: Little Magazines, Audiences, Reception*. Madison: U Wisconsin P, 2000
Moskowitz, Sam. "The Marketing of Stanley G. Weinbaum," *Fantasy Commentator*, Fall 1991, 104–129.
Mott, Frank Luther. *A History of American Magazines, Volume V: Sketches of 21 Magazines 1905–1930*. Cambridge, MA: Harvard U P, 1968.
Muir, Edwin. *We Moderns*. NY: Knopf, 1920.
Mullen, R.D. and Darko Suvin, eds. *Science Fiction Studies*. Boston: Gregg Press, 1976.
Mullin, Katherine. *James Joyce, Sexuality and Social Purity*. NY: Cambridge U P, 2003.
Murphy, Michael. "'One Hundred Percent Bohemian': Pop Decadence and the Aestheticization of Commodity in the Rise of the Slicks." *Marketing and Modernism*. Dettmar and Watt, eds. Ann Arbor: U of Michigan P, 1999.
Myers, Jeffrey, ed. *Ernest Hemingway, the Critical Heritage*. NY: Routledge, 1997.
Nadjer, Zdzislaw. *Conrad in Perspective*. Cambridge: Cambridge U P, 1997.
Nardini, Robert F. "Mencken and the 'Cult of Smartness,'" *Menckeniana*, 84 (Winter 1984) 1–12.
Nelson, James. *Publisher to the Decadents: Leonard Smithers in the Careers of Beardsley, Wilde, Dowson*. University Park, PA: Penn State U P, 2000.
Nevins, Jess. *Pulp Magazine Holdings Directory: Library Collections in North America and Europe*. Jefferson, NC: McFarland, 2007.
Nivens, Francis. "The Wild and Woolly World of Harry Stephen Keeler, part 4" *Journal of Popular Culture* (Vol. 7, No. 1).
Nolan, William F. *The Black Mask Boys*. NY: Mysterious, 1985.
Nolte, William H. *H.L. Mencken, Literary Critic*. Middletown: Wesleyan U P, 1966.

———. *H.L. Mencken's Smart Set Criticism*. Ithaca: Cornell, 1968.
North, Michael. *Camera Works*. Oxford: Oxford U P, 2005.
———. *The Dialect of Modernism*. NY: Oxford U P, 1994.
———. *Reading 1922*. NY: Oxford U P, 1999.
———. "Words in Motion: The Movies, the Readies, and 'the Revolution of the Word." *Modernism/Modernity*. 9.2 (2002) 205–223.
O'Brien, Geoffrey. *Hardboiled America, Lurid Paperbacks and the Masters of Noir*. NY: DeCapo, 1997.
O'Neill, William L. *Echoes of Revolt: The Masses 1911–1917*. Chicago: Quadrangle Books, 1966.
Ohmann, Richard. *Selling Culture*. NY: Verso, 1996.
Osbourne, Peter. "Adorno and the Metaphysics of Modernism: The Problem of a 'Postmodern' Art." Andrew Benjamin, ed. *The Problems of Modernity*. NY: Routledge, 1989.
Osteen, Mark and Martha Woodmansee, eds. *The New Economic Criticism*. NY: Routledge, 1999.
Page, Norvell. "How I Write," *James Van Hise Presents the Pulp Masters*. James Van Hise, ed. Yucca Valley: Midnight Graffiti, [nd 1996?].
Patrick Collier, *Modernism on Fleet Street* Hampshire: Ashgate, 2006.
Pease, Allison. *Modernism, Mass Culture and the Aesthetics of Obscenity*. NY: Cambridge U P, 2000.
Peirce, Constance. "Gertrude Stein and her Thoroughly Modern Protégé," *Modern Fiction Studies* (42.3 1996).
Pendergast, Tom. *Creating the Modern Man: American Magazines and Consumer Culture, 1900–1950*. Columbia: U of Missouri P, 2000.
Peplow, Michael W. *George S. Schuyler*. Boston: Twayne, 1980.
Pepper, Andrew. *The Contemporary American Crime Novel*. Chicago: Fitzroy Dearborn, 2000.
Perelman, S.J. *The Most of the Most*. NY: Modern Library, 2000.
Perloff, Marjorie. *The Futurist Moment*. Chicago: U of Chicago P, 1986.
———. *Postmodern Genres*. Norman: U of Oklahoma P, 1995.
Peterson, Carl. *Each In Its Ordered Place: a Faulkner Collector's Note Book*. Ann Arbor: Ardis, 1975.
Peterson, Theodore. *Magazines in the Twentieth Century*. Urbana: U of Illinois P, 1956.
Petesch, Donald A. *A Spy In The Enemy's Country: The Emergence of Modern Black Literature*. Iowa City: U P of Iowa, 1989.
Philippe, Charles-Louis. *Bubu of Montparnasse*. NY: Berkley, 1957.
Phillips, Gene D. *Fiction, Film, and Faulkner: The Art of Adaptation*. Knoxville: U of Tennessee P, 1988.
Piekarski, Vicki and Jon Tuska, eds. *The Max Brand Companion*. Westport, CT: Greenwood, 1996.
Plimpton, George. *The Writer's Chapbook*. NY: Penguin, 1989.
Pound, Ezra. *The Letters of Ezra Pound*. NY: Harcourt, Brace, 1950.

———. *Pound/the Little Review: The letters of Ezra Pound to Margaret Anderson: the Little Review Correspondence*. Thomas L. Scott, Melvin J. Friedman, eds (with the assistance of Jackson R. Bryer). NY: New Directions, 1988.

Pound, Ezra, et al. *Pound, Thayer, Watson and The Dial: A Story in Letters*. Walter Sutton, ed. Gainesville: U P Florida, 1994.

Pronzini, Bill. *Gun in Cheek*. NY: Mysterious Press, 1997.

Pykett, Lyn. *Engendering Fictions, The English Novel in the Early Twentieth Century*. London: Edward Arnold, 1995.

Quinones, Ricardo J. *Mapping Literary Modernism*. Princeton: Princeton U P, 1985.

Rabinowitz, Paula. *Black & White & Noir: America's Pulp Modernism*. NY: Columbia, 2002.

Radway, Janice. *Reading the Romance*. Chapel Hill, NC: U North Carolina P, 1984.

Rainey, Lawrence. *Institutions of Modernism*. New Haven: Yale U P, 1998.

Reddy, Maureen T. *Traces, Codes, and Clues: Reading Race in Crime Fiction*. New Brunswick: Rutgers U P, 2003.

Rembar, Charles. *The End of Obscenity*. NY: Random House, 1968.

Reynolds, Bruce. *Paris with the Lid Lifted*. NY: A.L. Burt, 1927.

Reynolds, Michael. *Hemingway, the Paris Years*. NY: Norton, 1999.

Reynolds, Quentin. *The Fiction Factory*. NY: Random House, 1955.

Rice, Thomas. *Joyce, Chaos, and Complexity*. Urbana: U of Illinois P, 1997.

Richards, Thomas. *The Commodity Culture of Victorian England*. Stanford, CA: Stanford U P, 1990.

Roberts, Thomas J. *An Aesthetics of Junk Fiction*. Athens: U of Georgia P, 1990.

Rose, Jonathan. *The Intellectual Life of the Working Class*. New Haven: Yale U P, 2001.

Rubin, Joan Shelley. *The Making of Middlebrow Culture*. Chapel Hill: U North Carolina P, 1992.

Ruehlmann, William. *Saint With A Gun, The Unlawful American Private Eye*. NY: New York U P, 1984.

Rutledge, Gregory E. "Futurist Fiction and Fantasy: the Racial Establishment." *Callaloo* 24.1 (2001) 236–252.

Sampson, Robert. *Deadly Excitements: Shadows and Phantoms*. Bowling Green: Popular Press, 1989.

———. *Yesterday's Faces: Volume 1—Glory Figures*. Bowling Green: Popular Press, 1983.

———. *Yesterday's Faces: Volume 2 Strange Days*. Bowling Green: Popular Press, 1983.

———. *Yesterday's Faces: Volume 6 –Violent Lives*. Bowling Green: Popular Press, 1983.

Sannes, G.W. *African 'Primitives': Function and Form in African Masks and Figures,* trans. by King, Margaret. NY: Africana, 1970.

Sawaya, Francesca. *Modern Women, Modern Work*. Philadelphia: U Penn. P, 2004.

Schick, Frank L. *The Paperbound Book in America*. NY: Bowker, 1958.
Schiffrin, André. *The Business of Books*. NY: Verso, 2001.
Schneirov, Matthew. *The Dream of a New Social Order*. NY: Columbia U P, 1994.
Schnitzer, Deborah. *The Pictorial in Modernist Fiction*. Ann Arbor: UMI, 1988.
Scholes, Robert. *Paradoxy of Modernism*. New Haven: Yale UP, 2006.
Schreuders, Piet. *The Book of Paperbacks*. London: Virgin, 1981.
———. *Paperbacks, U.S.A*. San Diego: Blue Dolphin, 1981.
Schuyler, George. *Black Empire*. Boston: Northeastern U P, 1991.
———. *Black No More*. Boston: Northeastern U P, 1989.
Schwartz, Lawrence H. *Creating Faulkner's Reputation*. Knoxville, U of Tennessee P, 1988.
Schwarz, Daniel. *Conrad: The Later Fiction*. London: Macmillan, 1982.
Scott, Bonnie Kime. *Refiguring Modernism: The Women of 1928*. Bloomington: Indiana U P, 1995.
Scribner, Charles Jr. *In the Web of Ideas*. NY: Scribners, 1993.
Scruggs, Charlie. *The Sage in Harlem; H.L. Mencken and the Black Writers of the 1920s*. Baltimore: John Hopkins U P, 1984.
Seebohm, Caroline. *The Man Who Was Vogue; The life and Times of Condé Nast*. NY: Viking, 1982.
Segel, Harold B. *Pinocchio's Progeny: Puppets, Marionettes, Automatons, and Robots in Modernist and Avant-Garde Drama*. Baltimore: John Hopkins, 1995.
Seldes, Gilbert. *The Seven Lively Arts*. NY: Harpers, 1924.
Seltzer, Mark. *Bodies and Machines*. NY: Routledge, 1992.
Server, Lee. *Danger Is My Business: An Illustrated History of the Fabulous Pulp Magazines: 1896–1953*. San Francisco: Chronicle, 1993.
Shaw, Joseph T. *The Hardboiled Omnibus*. NY: Simon and Schuster, 1946.
Sheree, Thomas, ed. *Dark Matter*. NY: Warner, 2000.
Singal, Daniel J. *William Faulkner, The Making of a Modernist*. Chapel Hill: U of North Carolina P, 1997.
Singleton, M. K. *H.L. Mencken and the American Mercury Adventure*. Durham: Duke U P, 1962.
Skenazy, Paul. "Behind the Territory Ahead." *L.A. in Fiction*. David Fine, ed. Albuquerque: U of New Mexico P, 1984.
Smith, Erin. *Hard-Boiled: Working Class Readers and Pulp Magazines*. Philadelphia: Temple U P, 2000.
Soitos, Stephen F. *The Blues Detective, A Study of African American Detective Fiction*. Amherst: U of Massachusetts P, 1996.
Stenerson, Douglas C. *Critical Essays on H.L. Mencken*. Boston: Hall, 1987.
Street, Brian V. *The Savage in Literature*. London: Routledge, 1975.
Sutton, Walter, ed. *Pound, Thayer, Watson, and The Dial; A Story in Letters*. Gainesville: U P Florida, 1994.
Tal, Kali. "'That Just Kills Me' Black Militant Near-Future Fiction." *Social Text*, 20.2 (2002) 65–91.

Tavernier-Courbin, Jaqueline. *Ernest Hemingway's A Moveable Feast: The Making of Myth.* Boston: Northeastern U P, 1991.
Teachout, Terry. *The Skeptic. A Life of H.L. Mencken.* NY: Harper Collins, 2002.
Tebbel, John. *Between Covers.* NY: Oxford U P, 1987.
Tebbel, John and Mary Ellen Zuckerman. *The Magazine in America 1741–1990.* NY: Oxford U P, 1991.
Thompson, Richard Austin. *The Yellow Peril, 1890–1924.* NY: Arno, 1978.
Thurman, Wallace. *Infants of Spring.* NY: Macaulay Company, 1932 (AMS reprint, 1972).
Tratner, Michael. *Modernism and Mass Politics: Joyce, Woolf, Eliot, Yeats.* Stanford: Stanford U P, 1995.
Trogdon, Robert W. *Ernest Hemingway, A Literary Reference.* NY: Carroll & Graf, 2002.
———. *The Lousy Racket: Hemingway, Scribners and the Business of Literature.* Kent: Kent State U P, 2007.
Turner, Catherine. *Marketing Modernism Between the World Wars.* Amherst: U Massachusetts P, 2003.
Tuska, Jon and Vicki Piekarski, eds. *The Max Brand Companion.* Westport, CT: Greenwood Press, 1996.
Valente, Joseph, ed. *Quare Joyce.* Ann Arbor: U of Michigan P, 2000.
Van Ash, Cay and Elizabeth Sax Rohmer. *Master of Villainy, a Biography of Sax Rohmer.* Bowling Green: Bowling Green U P, 1972.
Vanderham, Paul. *James Joyce and Censorship.* NY: New York U P, 1998.
Warner, Harry Jr. *All Our Yesterdays.* Chicago: Advent, 1969.
Watt, Ian. *Conrad in the Nineteenth Century.* Berkeley: U of California P, 1979.
Watts, Cedric. *Coercive Text, An Introduction to Covert Plots.* NJ: Barnes and Noble, 1984.
———. *A Preface to Conrad.* NY: Longman, 1993.
Weinbaum, Stanley G. *A Martian Odyssey and Others.* Reading: Fantasy Press, 1949.
Weir, David. *Decadence and the Making of Modernism.* Amherst: U Massachusetts P, 1995.
Wenska, Walter. "'There's a man with a gun over there': Faulkner's hijacking of masculine popular culture." *The Faulkner Journal.* Orlando: Fall 1999/2000. Vol. 15, Issue 1, 2, 35–60.
Wexler, Joyce Piell. *Who Paid for Modernism?* Fayetteville: U of Arkansas P, 1997.
White, Andrea. *Joseph Conrad and the Adventure Tradition.* Cambridge: Cambridge U P, 1993.
Wicke, Jennifer. *Advertising Fictions: Literature, Advertisement, and Social Reading.* NY: Columbia, 1988.
———. "Appreciation, Depreciation: Modernism's Speculative Bubble," *Modernism / Modernity* (Vol. 8, No. 3) 389–403.
Wicker-Wilson, Carol. "Busting Textual Bodices: Gender, Reading, and the Popular Romance," *The English Journal* (Vol. 88, No. 3, January 1999) 58–59.

Wilson, Edmund. *Axel's Castle*. NY: Scribners, 1948.
Wood, James Playsted. *Magazines in the United States: Their Social and Economic Influence*. NY: Ronald Press, 1949.
Woodmansee, Martha. *The Author, Art, and the Market*. NY: Columbia U P, 1994.
Woods, Paula. *Spooks, Spies, and Private Eyes*. NY: Doubleday, 1995.
Worth, Robert. "*Nigger Heaven* and the Harlem Renaissance." *African American Revue* 29 (3, 1995) 461–473.
Wright, Richard. *Black Boy*. NY: Perennial, 1998.
———. *Native Son*. NY: Perennial, 1998.
Wright, Willard Huntington. *The Man of Promise*. NY: Scribners, 1930.
Wyn, A.A. "Pulp Magazines." *New York Times*. September 4, 1935.
Yarbrough, Scott. "The Mean Streets of Jefferson: Faulkner's Intersection with Pulp Fiction." Unpublished Dissertation, University of Alabama, 1996.
Young, James O. *Black Writers of the Thirties*. Baton Rouge: U P Louisiana State, 1973.
Zeitlin, Michael. "Faulkner's Pylon: The City in the Age of Mechanical Reproduction," *Canadian Review of American Studies*, Fall 91, Vol. 22, Issue 2, 229–240.
Zeitz, Joshua. *Flapper*. NY: Three River's Press, 2006.
Zender, Karl F. *The Crossing of the Ways: William Faulkner, The South, and the Modern World*. New Brunswick: Rutgers, 1989.
Zurier, Rebecca. *Art for The Masses*. Philadelphia: Temple U P, 1988.

Index

10 Story Book, 141, 148
A.L. Burt, 92
Abdullah, Achmed, 3 28, 67
Academia
    And modernism, 6–7, 11–13, 14, 28, 34–8, 50–51, 62, 102, 153–154, 168, 173
    schism between scholarship and theory, 13
Ace High Magazine, 43
Aces, 200
Action Stories Magazine, 43, 136
Action!, 129, 132
Adorno, Theodore and Max Horkheimer, "The Culture Industry," 73, 97–100, 103, 106, 110, 141, 161
Adventure, 65, 75, 105, 118, 179
Ainslee's, 23, 63, 105, 165
Air Stories, 200
Albatross Press, 157, 165, 169
Alger Series (dime novel), 75
Alger, Horatio, 136
All-Stories Love Story, 80
All-story Weekly, 45, 60, 65, 75, 105, 119, 125
Amazing Stories, 114, 128
America's Humor, 148
American Girl, 3
American Mercury, 27, 30, 31, 40, 44, 73, 124, 125
Anderson, Margaret, 28, 42
    My Thirty Year War, 48, 51
Anderson, Sherwood, 28, 33, 36, 67, 156, 168, 213
    Dark Laughter, 30
    Winesburg Ohio, 84, 32
Ardis, Ann, 11
Argosy All-Story, 84
Argosy, 63, 68, 75, 118, 134, 216
Armed Service editions, 153, 168, 203
Armory Show, 47, 118
Armstrong, Tim, 132, 136
Arthur Westbrook Co., 165
Ashley, Ellen; *see* Seifert, Elizabeth

Ashley, Mike, 65
Asimov, Isaac, 114
Astounding Science, 88, 129
Astounding Stories of Super Science, 129
Atlantic Monthly, 65, 104
Audit Bureau of Circulation (A.B.C.), 61–64, 77
Author and Journalist, 11, 142, 144
Autobiography, subjective nature of, 48–51
Avon paperbacks, 155, 165, 203, 215

Bacon, Daisy, 83
Baird, Edwin 26, 65
Bakhtin, Mikhail, 180
Baldick, Chris, 13
Ballantine Books, 166
Bannon, Ann, 194
Bantam Books, 155, 158, 166, 169, 172, 215
Barnes, Djuna, 9, 28, 36, 65, 105
    "Madame Collects Herself," 52
    Nightwood, 51, 52
Bartolini, Elio, 215
Barton Fink (Coen Brothers), 196
Baudelaire, Charles, 7, 174, 185, 186
Beach, Sylvia, 91, 193
    Shakespeare and Company (Memoir), 48
Beardsley, Aubrey, 186–188
Belasco, David, 58n87
Bellem, Robert Leslie, 72, 101
Bellows, George, 118
Benchley, Robert, 168
Benjamin, Walter, 159, 169
Bennett, Arnold, 146, 164, 165
Benstock, Shari, 5, 49
Benton, Megan, 89, 91
Bergson, Henri, 128
Berkley Books, 152
Best Stories, 66
Better Homes and Gardens, 65
Bill Barnes Air Trails, 137
Black Mask Magazine, 3, 28, 42, 43, 78–79, 86, 106–110, 118, 136, 179, 196
Blackwoods Magazine, 65

Blast, 10, 132, 135
Blindman, The, 120
Blish, James, 113–114
Blotner, Joseph, 9, 195, 200
Blue Book Magazine, 45, 63, 79, 118, 179
Blue Review, The, 25
Blue Ribbon Books, 51
Bluebook, 209, 216
Bock, Vera, 156
Bodley head Press, 185
Bogdanov, Alexander, 113
Boni, Charles, 155–157; *see also* Charles Boni Paper Books
Bonn, Charles, 166, 169
Book Clubs, 90
Book of the month club, 97
Books; *see also* Pulps, Paperbacks
  as objects of cultural designation, 89–94, 90–93
  materiality of, 6, 13, 91–92, 129, 155, 157–158, 163, 188–89, 194
  visuality of, 6, 12, 119–120, 158, 159–164, 172–173, 185
Bornstein, George, 61, 173
Bourdieu, Pierre, 3, 69
Boyer, Norman 25
Boyle, Kay, 168
Brackett, Leigh, 98
Brake, Laurel, 10
Brand, Max, 65, 95, 104–105, 196
  Destry Rides Again, 98
Brantlinger, Patrick, 97, 128–129
Breathless (Godard), 196
Breezy Stories, 55, 73, 105
Breu, Christopher, 10, 78
Brief Stories, 52
Brooke, Robert, 168
Brooks, Louise, 55
Broom, 65, 65n105
Broun, Heywood, 112
Brown, Robert Carleton (Bob), 9, 26, 41, 127–129, 131, 135
  Readie machine, 118–121
Bruce, George, 136–137
Buffalo Bill (dime novel), 75
Burke, Kenneth, 113
Burnett, W.R., 196
Burnett, Whit, 190
Burroughs, Edgar Rice, 65, 128, 154

Tarzan of the Apes, 75
Butts, Mary, 5, 36, 195
Byrne, Donn, 26

Cabell, James Branch, 23, 27, 40
Cage, John, 147
Cain, James M., 111, 167
Caldwell, Erskine, 1, 167, 197–198
  God's Little Acre, 167–168, 197
Calverton, V.F., 113
Canby, Henry Seidel, 89, 112
Čapek, Karel, *R.U.R.*, 139
Carey, John, 35, 69, 94, 164, 165
Case, Rathburne, 79
Casebeer, Florence Churchill, 25
Cavalier Magazine, 60, 65, 75, 119, 198
Century Magazine, The, 60
Chandler, Raymond, 9, 98, 100, 106–110, 141, 197, 215
Charles Boni Paper Books, 155–157, 187
Charters, Jimmy, *This Must be the Place*, 51
Checker Books, 166
Churchill, Suzanne, 11
Clayton Publications, 116
Clayton, W.M., 58, 59, 75
Clever Stories, 52
Clive, Henry, 58
Clues Magazine, 116
Coates, Robert M., 65, 105
  Eater of Darkness, 14, 112–113
Co-Ed Campus Comedy, 132
Collector's Publication, 190
College Life, 195
College Stories, 132
Collier, Patrick, 7, 12
Collier's, 23, 75, 104
Colportage, 5
Column, Padraic, 28
Comstock, Anthony, 18, 41
Connely, Cyril, *The Rock Pool*, 186
Conquest, 216
Conrad, 24, 28, 29, 68, 119, 120, 140, 141, 159, 160, 168, 175–179
  Almayer's Folly, 176–177
  Chance, 177
  "End of the Tether," 68
  Heart of Darkness, 65, 94, 139, 167, 179
  Lord Jim, 15, 177–179
  Secret Agent, 128

Youth, 179
Corelli, Marie, 164
Cosmopolitan, 62, 75
Courtroom Stories, 75, 85, 187
Cowley, Malcolm, 12, 21, 35, 74, 113, 151, 154–155, 166, 168, 169, 185, 193, 202–203, 206, 210
    After the Genteel Tradition, 35
    Exile's Return 48, 50–51
Coxe, George Harmon, 98
Crime Mysteries Magazine, 83
Crook Factory, The, 216
Crosby, Caresse, *The Passionate Years*, 48
Crosby, Harry, 26, 118
    Black Sun Press, 91, 185
Crowe, Eugene, 18, 19, 26, 106
Crowley, Alistair, 28, 186
Crowninshield, Frank, 46–48
    Manners for the Metropolis, 47
Cullen, Charles, 186–187
Cullen, Countee, 186
Cultures of Modernism, 5
Cummings, e.e., 137, 215
Cunard, Nancy, 120
    Hours Press, 91
Cupid's Diary, 80
Currie, Enid, 167

Daily Mail, The, 60n94
Daily Worker, The, 114
Daly, Carroll John, 100–101, 106n90, 107
Dan Turner (character), 71–73
Dan Turner, Hollywood Detective Magazine, 72
Davis, Stuart, 118
De Polo, Harold, 28
Debonair, 1, 51
DeBord, Guy, 159
Delany, Samual R., 121
Dell Books, 166, 167, 215
Dell, Floyd 24, 38
Dent, Lester, 100
Der Sturm, 132
Detective (genre); *see* Pulps, Hard-Boiled
Detective Story, 63, 74n11, 75
Dettmar, Kevin, 8, 61
DeVoto, Bernard, 202
Dewey, Thomas, 167
Dial, The, 21, 30–31, 63, 64

Diamond Dick (dime novel), 75
Die Aktion, 132
Diepeveen, Leonard, 13, 35
Dime Detective, 98
Dime Novels, 10, 60n94, 75
Dine, S.S. van (See Wright, Willard Huntington)
Dolan, Marc, 48, 50
Dolmetsch, Carl 22n5
Dos Passos, John, 30, 33, 111, 136, 146, 215
    Big Money, 51
Double Dealer, The, 30, 64n105
Doubleday, 75
Douglas, Aaron, 122
Douglas, George H., 22n5, 26
Dowson, Ernest, 186
Dreiser, Theodore, 38, 41, 105, 113, 167
    The "Genius," 18
    Sister Carrie, 30
Dress Magazine (Condé Nast), 47
Drucker, Joanna, 159, 161
Duchamp, Marcel, 118, 120, 128
Dude, The, 1, 51
Duffield, Marcus, 88, 94
Dynamic Adventure, 132

Eagleton, Terry, 13, 35
Egan, Beresford, 186
Electrical Invention, Science and Experimentation Magazine, 130
Eliot, T.S., 4, 9, 13, 28, 34, 35, 37, 41, 42, 61, 85, 104, 153, 154, 157, 165, 169, 174, 193, 199, 202, 215
    "The Hollow Men," 179
    "Ulysses, Order, Myth," 74n9
    The Waste Land, 9, 35, 62, 179, 194, 199
Ellery Queen Mystery Magazine, 195
Ellis, Douglas, 11, 59n90
Ellison, Harlan, 121
Ellison, Ralph, 167
Ellsworth, Fanny, 83
English Review, The, 24, 39
Escapade, 1
Esquire, 45, 51, 62, 216
Everybody's Magazine, 23, 39, 119
Excitement!, 129
Exciting Stories, 129
Eysteinsson, Astrudar, 13, 35–36

Fallacy of First Appearance, 14, 15,
  66–69, 158
Famous Story Magazine, 66, 68
Fantasy Magazine, 140
Fante, John
  Ask the Dust, 88–89
  Wait Until Spring, Baldrini, 84, 88, 126
Farrell, James T, 111, 120, 167
Fascinating Fiction, 52
Faulkner, John, 197
Faulkner, William, 1, 15, 37, 51, 66, 87,
  105, 109, 137, 142, 145, 153,
  160, 166, 168, 173, 179, 194,
  195–206, 215
  Absalom, Absalom!, 93–94, 199, 202
  "Ad Astra," 200
  As I Lay Dying, 202
  and film, 160
  Hamlet, The, 146, 202
  If I Forget Thee Jerusalem (*Wild Palms*), 204–206
  Intruder in the Dust, 197, 203
  Knight's Gambit, 202, 203, 204
  Light in August, 7, 93, 126, 195, 202
  Mosquitoes, 203
  Old Man, The, (Signet), 203
  "The Old Man," (short story), 167, 175, 195
  Portable Faulkner, 202, 203, 206
  Pylon, 169, `194, 196, 197, 198–201, 203–205, 206
  Requiem for a Nun, 203
  A Rose For Emily (Armed Services Edition), 203
  Sanctuary, 169, 196–197, 201, 202, 203, 204, 206
  Sartoris, 203
  Soldier's Pay, 203
  Sound and Fury, 128, 146, 168, 195, 198, 202, 204
  Unvanquished, The, 201, 203
  Wild Palms (Signet), 7, 194–196, 202, 203, 206
Faust, Frederick Schiller, see Brand, Max
Fawcett Paperbacks, 166, 168
Fearing, Kenneth, 105
Feminism, in pulps, 14, 51–59, 79–83
Ferber, Edna, 166, 194
Fiction Parade Magazine, 3, 66

Fiedler, Leslie, 196–197
Field and Stream, 18, 26
Fighting Aces, 129
Film Fun, 98
Fire!, 122
Fischer, Bruno, 85, 111
Fisher, Rudolph
  "The Caucasian Storms Harlem," 124
  The Conjure Man Dies, 123–124
Fitzgerald, F. Scott, 26, 27, 28, 33, 36, 51,
  54, 86, 153, 168, 179
  "Bernice Bobs Her Hair," 55
  Flappers and Philosophers, 52
  The Great Gatsby, 68, 91–92, 168
  The Great Gatsby (Bantam edition), 169–172
  Tales of the Jazz Age, 52
  This Side of Paradise, 52
Flagg, Francis, see Rice, George Henry
Flapper, The (magazine), 54
Flapper's Experience, 54
Flappers
  as popular modernism, 14, 51–59, 79–83 passim
  in *The Smart Set*, 14, 56–59
Flaubert, Gustave, 179
  "Les Arts et le Commerce," 176
  L'Education Sentimentale, 176
  Madame Bovary, 7, 174–176
Flying Aces, 137, 200
Flynn's Detective Weekly, 52, 84, 125
Football Action, 75
Ford, Ford Madox, 21, 33, 39, 113, 179
  The Good Soldier, 146
Ford, Henry, 94
  fordism, 95, 109
Fortune Press, 186
Forum, 77
Foster, Hal, 132, 135
Foucault, Michel, 13, 37, 68, 102–103
France, Anatole, 28, 68
Frank Merriwell, 75
Frank, Waldo, 112
French Follies, 59
Frey, James, 48
Frost, Robert, 28
Fussell, Paul, 130, 136
Futurian Society, 114
Futurism, 128, 131, 132

G-8 and His Battle Aces, 200
Gaddis, Peggy, 197
Gangland Stories, 79
Gangster Stories, 79
Gargoyle, The, 65
Garrett, George, 195–196
Garvey, Ellen Gruber, 5, 83
Geddes, Donald, 167
Gent, The, 51, 216
Gernsback, Hugo, 112
Ghost Story, 52
Gide, Andre, 109
Girl in Overalls, 81–82
Glick, Carl, 28, 107
Goldberg, Allen, 82
Golden Argosy, The, 60, 74; see also *Argosy*
Golden Book, The, 3, 9, 66–69, 92
Goll, Iwan, 139
Graff, Robert De, 165
Graphic, 166
Gregory, Lady Augusta, 68
Grey Goose, The, 119
Grosset and Dunlap, 51, 66, 91, 92, 166, 167, 200
Gruber, Frank, 98, 100, 104
  Pulp Jungle, 95
Gun Molls Magazine, 75, 80
Gunnison, John, 11

H.D. (Hilda Doolittle), 185
Haggard, H. Rider, 67
Haldeman-Julius, Emanuel, 92, 155
Hall, Radcylffe, 194
Hamilton, Sharon, 21n4, 29, 45
Hammett, Dashiell, 9, 13, 87, 98, 100, 101, 103, 106–110, 141, 196, 213, 215
  Dain Curse, 109, 196
  Glass Key, 101
  Maltese Falcon, 84, 98, 101, 110
  The Thin Man, 92
Hard-Boiled (genre); see Pulps, detective genre in; Pulps, hardboiled, academic penchant for
Harlem Nights (pulp), 122
Harlem Stories, 85
Harlem, 122
Harper's, 60, 65, 77, 88, 97
Harris, Margie, 80
Harris, Sharon, 5, 83

Hawks, Howard, 200
Heatter, Basil, 167
Hecht, Ben, 1, 188
Held, John, 45, 52, 55
Hemingway, Ernest, 13, 14, 15, 27, 29–34, 36, 51, 53, 65, 66, 86, 111, 136, 137, 153, 168, 175, 179, 194, 206–217
  Across the River and into the Trees, 210, 215
  and American Regionalism, 30–34
  Death in the Afternoon, 190
  "A Divine Gesture," 30
  A Farewell to Arms, 91, 168, 211, 215
  Garden of Eden, 188
  Green Hills of Africa, 213
  as hard-boiled, 211–215
  In Our Time, 31, 36
  "The Killers," 209, 215
  Men at War, 216
  A Moveable Feast, 49–50, 216
  relationship to Mencken, 30–34
  The Sun Also Rises, 33–34, 40, 51, 52, 158, 168
  To Have and Have Not, 194, 209, 213–215
  Torrents of Spring, 30–33
  "Who Murdered the Vets?," 213
Hemingway: The Secret Agent's Badge of Courage, 216
Henty, G.A., 136
Herbst, Josephine, 50–51
Herriman, George, 61
Hersey, Harold, 28, 75n14, 79, 86, 101, 122, 187
Heyck, T.W, 42
Hicks, Granville, 113
High (men's magazine), 1
Hilar, Hilaire, 120
Hillman, A.L., 186–187
Himes, Chester, 127, 167
Hoffman, Frederick, 21, 28, 34, 59
Home Brew, 54
Homer, *The Iliad*, 158
Hopalong Cassidy (character), 98
Horkheimer, Max, see Adorno, Theodore
Housman, A.E., 168
Howard, Robert E, 128
Huddleberry, Asa, 112
Huddleston, Sisley, 51

Hughes, Langston, 42
Hughes, Thomas, *Tom Brown's School Days*, 136
Huneker, James, 188
Hurston, Zora Neale 4, 122, 127n158, 159
Hutchinson's Story Magazine, 68
Huxley, Aldous 28, 36, 51, 67, 73, 94–95, 131, 168
   Brave New World, 94–95
   Ends and Means, 94–95, 97
Huysmans, Joris-Karl, 1, 122
Huyssen, Andreas, 6, 28, 69, 74, 175

I Confess, 82
I Killed Hemingway, 216
Illustrated World, 137
Imagismé, 33, 34, 74n11
Isherwood, Christopher, 167

Jack Dempsey's Fight Magazine, 118
Jackson, Charles, 167
James, Henry, 159
Jameson, Frederic, 161, 176, 185
Jem Magazine, 51
Jenkins, Thomas, 187
Jolas, Eugene, 118, 120
Joyce, James, 1, 7, 9, 10, 13, 25, 28, 30, 34, 41, 42, 51, 61, 66, 67, 87, 105, 128, 145, 154, 157, 160, 184–185, 199, 215
   and photography, 160
   Anna Livia Plurabelle, 146
   Chamber Music, 3
   Dubliners, 30, 148, 157, 184
      "Araby," 175
      "The Boarding House," 1–3
      "An Encounter," 84, 126
      "Eveline," 3
      "Little Cloud," 3
      "Two Gallants," 1–2
   Finnegans Wake, 7, 128, 146, 147, 184, 193
      and Chaos Theory, 147–148
      visuality of, 160–161, 164
   Pomes Penyeach, 186
   popular printing history of, 1–3, 67, 157, 162–3, 189, 190–94
   Portrait of the Artist as a Young Man, 160, 167, 193
   Portrait, Signet edition of, 162–163, 190
   Ulysses, 1, 2, 3, 15, 20, 51, 91, 101, 112, 128, 139, 145, 146, 157, 179, 185, 188, 190, 194
      "Calypso," 163
      "Circe," 193
      "Eumaeus," 160
      Gabler Edition, 172, 173, 193
      "Naussicaa," 113
      Pirated Edition, 190
      "Proteus," 163
      Random House Edition, 190–193
      scandal of, 185, 188, 190–194
      "Wandering Rocks," 128, 148
   "Work in Progress" 42

Keeler, Harry Stephen, 15, 101, 141–149
   The Box from Japan, 141
   The Chameleon, 145, 147
   The Green Jade Hand, 142, 146
   The Marceau Case, 146, 147
   The Mysterious Mr. I, 145
   The Portrait of Jirjohn Cobb, 146
   The Riddle of the Traveling Skull, 147
   self-referentiality of, 147–148
   similarities to Joyce, 146–149
   Voice of the Seven Sparrows, 144
Kelmscott Press, 129
Kenner, Hugh, 21, 193
Kent, Rockwell, 156
Kershner, Brandon, 7, 62n100, 160, 184
Kiki (Alice Prin), 52–53
Kirsch, Robert, 152, 166n29
Klevar, Harvey, 198
Knockout Magazine, 118
Knopf, Alfred, Borzoi Press, 91
Knowles, Sebastian, 193
Koestler, Arthur, 167
Krazy Kat, 61

Ladd, Alan, 170
Lady Chatterley's Friends, 184
Lady Chatterley's Husbands, 184
Laity, Cassandra, 185, 188
Lane, Sir Allen, 165
Lanier, Henry Wysham, 66
Lardner, Ring, 61
Lariat Stories, 43
Larsen, Nella, 127n158

Latham, Sean, 10, 164, 165
Lawrence, D.H., 1, 28, 29, 36, 24, 30, 51, 66, 68, 103, 156, 157, 179, 180–184, 188
   Aaron's Rod (Avon), 180
   Lady Chatterley's Lover, 2, 15, 167, 172, 180–181, 188
      Faro Pirated Edition, 184
   The Rainbow, 181
   "The Sisters," 181
   Women in Love, 167, 169, 180
Lending Libraries, 90
Leonard, Garry, 8, 184
Lewis, Sinclair, 33, 105, 215
Lewis, Wyndham, 10, 13, 21, 34, 51, 135, 136, 139, 165, 188
Liberator, The, 64n105
Liberty's Magazine, 59, 200
Life Magazine, 52, 65
Lion Books, 16, 215
Literary Review, The, 105
Little Leather Library, 92
Little Magazines, 8–11, 21, 28–29, 59–65, 114–118, 151, 175; *see also* individual titles
Little Review, the, 8, 20, 21 27, 28, 63, 64
   comparison to *The Smart Set*, 38–42
Live Stories, 25, 63
Live Wire, 105
Liveright, Horace, 30
Locke, Alain, 122
Loeb, Harold, 112
London, Jack, 67
Lone Eagle Magazine, 136
Louys, Pierre, 1, 187
   Cyprian Masques, 186
Love Romances, 83
Love Story, 63, 83
Lovecraft, H.P., 65, 154
Lowell, Amy, 68
Lowry, Robert, 1, 215
Lucian, *The Mimes of the Courtesans*, 186

MacDonald-Wright, Stanton, 23
MacFadden Publishing, 122
Machen, Arthur, 186
Madden, David, 111, 211
Mailer, Norman, 1
Malcolm, Norman, 149

Male Magazine, 216
Man's Illustrated, 216
Man's Magazine, 1, 216
Man's Magazine, 3
Man's True Action, 216
Mandrake Press, 186
Manet, Edouard, 174
Manhunt, 198, 216
Mann, Thomas, 168
Mann, William D'Alton, 22
Mansfield, Katherine, 68, 168
Manutious, Aldus, 164
March, Joseph Moncure, 71
Marinetti, Filipo, 131, 132, 135, 136, 137, 139, 188
Marsh, Reginald, 113
Masses, The, 41, 115–118, 155
Materiality of modernism; *see* Modernism, physical and economic materiality of; modernism, marketing of; modernism, visuality of
Materiality of books; *see* Books, materiality of
Maugham, Somerset, 172
McAlmon, Robert, 112, 120
   Being Geniuses Together, 48, 51
   Three Mountain Press, 91
McCall's, 64
McCann, Sean, 9, 12, 78, 83, 85, 87, 106–110 passim, 116, 179
McClure, S.S., 60
McCoy, Horace, 98, 111, 167
McGann, Jerome, 121, 158, 161–162, 172
McKaye, Claude, 85
McKible, Adam, 11, 61
McMorrow, Will, 87
Mencken, H.L., 3, 14, 17–59, 58, 85, 88, 105, 108, 113, 122, 168
   editorship of *The Smart Set* with Nathan, 14, 18, 23–31
   Hemingway's thoughts on, 32–34
   pulp editing by, 3, 18–19, 42–5, 51–53, 59, 106–107
   relationship to Pound, 27–29, 32
   reputation of, 26–27, 34–40
Mercure de France, 39
Merritt, A.E., 140
   Seven Footprints to Satan, 98
Metropolis (Lang), 139

Michel, John B, (aka Hugh Raymond), 114
Midlands, The, 34
Mierlo, Wim van, 13
Millay, Edna St.Vincent, 105, 194
Miller, Henry, 1
   Tropic of Cancer, 186
Miller, Marvin, 190
Mind (journal), 149
Miracle, 129
Mixon, Wayne, 198
Modern Library, 67, 92
Modern Man Magazine, 1, 49
Modern Monthly, The, 113
Modern Times (Chaplin), 139
Modernism
   authors of found in pulps, 1–4, 9, 14,
      49–52, 65–69, 105, 195–196, 216;
      see also individual authors
   and Decadence, 185–189
   definition and revision of, 4–8, 11,
      13–14, 20–21, 36, 49, 63–65, 69,
      74, 103–104, 173–175, passim, 157
   "Elite Modernism," definition of, 13
   and ephemera, 3, 6–7, 84, 112,
      157–158, 174, 184–185
   instability of, 4, 22, 33, 173, 179–80
   marketing of, 6, 8, 12, 28–9, 33–38,
      42, 48–9, 50, 62, 90–91, 131, 154,
      157, 193, 195, 202–203
   misogyny of, 4–5, 49, 51, 58, 72, 75,
      103. 135, 194
   modernist book production as archaic,
      129, 157, 173
   "Monolithic modernism," definition
      of, 13
   and patronage, 42–45
   physical and economic materiality of,
      6–8, 13, 15, 61, 157, 158, 159, 160,
      163, 176, 183
   popular modernist memoirs, 48–51, 60
   and pornography, 15; 161, 184–191
   relationship to academia, 6–7, 11–13,
      14, 28, 34–38, 50–51, 62, 102,
      153–154, 168, 173
   sensationalism of, 15, 51–59, 157, 169,
      184, 185–94, 196
   and smart magazines, 45–48, 61–65;
      see also Esquire, New Yorker,
      Vanity Fair, Vogue

"Traditional Modernism," definition
   of, 13
visuality of, 15, 119–120, 159–164
Modernism/Modernity, 5
Modernist Journals Project, 10–11, 21
Montayne, C.S., 54
Moore, George, 24
Morris, William, 129
Morrison, Mark, 9, 39, 117, 131
Mosely, Walter, 127
Mott, Frank Luther, 58
Mulford, Clarence, 98
Mullin, Katherine, 185, 192
Mulvey, Laura, 159
Mumford, Lewis, 93–94
Munsey, Frank, 60, 74–75
Munsey's, 60, 75, 119
Murphy, Michael, 51, 62, 64
Murray, John Middleton, 25n13
Myers, Irvine T., 18

N.A.L. (National American Library), 155,
   166, 198, 209
Nash's, 65
Nast, Condé, 39
Nathan, George Jean, 3, 14, 17–59 passim,
   85, 105, 106, 112, 122
   as editor; *see* Mencken.
Nevins, Francis, 141
New Masses, The, 113, 213
New Republic, The, 93
New York Society for the Suppression of
   Vice, 18, 188
New York Times, 77, 88
New Yorker, 45, 52, 71, 72, 113
Newman, Fannie Hodges, 25
Newsweek, 215
Nick Carter Weekly, 75
Nick Carter, 112
Nolan, Phillip Francis, 128
North, Michael, 61, 120–121
North-West Stories, 43
Nugget, 1

O.Henry 23, 59
O' Brien, Edward J, 52
   Dance of the Machines, 95
O'Connor, Flannery, 167, 197
O'Hara, John, 1

O'Neill, Eugene, 28, 68
Obelisk Press, 186
Operator #5, 116
Orwell, George, 167

Page, Norvell, 100
Paperbacks
   history of, 156–157, 164–168
   innate modernism of, 155–157, 173–174
   marketing of, 151–153, 157, 169–173
   modernist authors in, 15, 151–153, 166–173, 194–195, 197–198, 202–204
   reaction against, 154–155, 159, 164, 168
   sensationalism of, 151–154, 159, 166, 168, 169–173, 180–181, 188–189, 210, 215
   visuality of, 15, 159–164
Paris life, 59
Paris Nights, 59
Paris Salons, Cafes, Studios (Huddleston), 51
Paris with the Lid Lifted (Reynolds), 51
Paris, as scene of popular modernism, 14, 51–54, 59,
Parisienne, The, 3, 18, 20, 42, 52, 59, 73, 75, 106, 133
   Sumner's persecution of, 18–20, 58
Parker, Dorothy, 68, 109, 213
Pater, Walter, 119
Patronage, system of, 42
Pearson's Magazine, 65, 119
Pease, Allison, 183, 185, 188, 189
Pelican Books, 169
Penguin Books, 165, 167, 169, 203
Penny Dreadfuls, 60n94
People's Magazine, 63
Pep!, 129, 132
Perelman, S.J., 1, 71–73
Perloff, Marjorie, 131
Petry, Ann, 194, 197
Phantom Lady (Woolrich), 98
Phillipe, Charles-Louis
   Bubu of Montparnasse, 151–153
Picasso, Pablo, 23, 48, 61, 159
Pittsburgh Courier, 123
Playboy, 210, 216
Pleasures of Being Beaten and Other Fleshly Delights, 186–189

Plot Genie, the, 95–97, 145
Pocket Books, 155, 167
Poetry, 28, 32, 65n105, 66
Pohl, Frederick, 114
Polt, Richard, 148
Popular Detective, 116
Popular Library, 165
Popular Magazine, 39, 63, 75, 165
Pornography, under modernism
Pound, Ezra, 4, 9, 13, 20, 21, 24, 25, 27, 28, 29, 30, 34, 36–38, 42, 85, 120, 154, 164, 165, 174, 175, 185, 188, 193, 202, 215
   The Cantos, 94, 129
   intro to *The Natural Philosophy of Love*, 186
   relationship to Mencken, 27–29, 32,
Powell, Dawn, 55, 65, 105, 195
Prejudice of form, 3, 6, 7, 9–12, 20–22, 38, 59–63, 68–69, 83, 153–158 passim
   and the paperback, 155, 15, 159–161 passim, 162, 202, 203; see also Paperbacks, the reaction against
   and the pulps, 62, 83, 85, 93, 124; see also, pulps, critical reaction to
   and *The Smart Set*, 21–22, 38
Press of Classic Lore, 186
Pronzini, Bill, 72
Proust, Marcel 128
Pryzbskewski, Stanlislaw, 18
Pulps
   archiving of, 6, 12, 77
   audience, 78–79, 79–82 passim, 83–87
   and the "cheap book" debate, 89–94
   definition of, 74–75; see also Pulps, history of
   circulation of, 9, 61, 63, 68, 75, 77–78
   critical reaction to, 73, 90–102, 166
   detective genre, 71–72, 78–80, 85, 106–111, 116–117, 130, 131, 135, 141, 141–149
   female editors and writers of, 80, 83
   feminism in, 14, 79–83, 51–59, 79–83
   formulaic aspect of, 73, 84–85, 90–102, 104, 127, 141–149
   as outlet of flapper culture, 51–59, 79–80
   Hard-boiled, academic penchant for, 9–10, 12, 78–79, 79n23, 83, 106, 111
   history of, 41–45, 52–56, 59–61, 74–76

international distribution, 77–78
materiality of, 7, 74, 129
as modernism, 35, 14, 51–59, 73–74,
   86–87 passim, 101–102,
   102–149, 174
racial prejudice in, 83–85, 94, 103,
   107–108 passim, 121
romance genre, 10, 12, 56, 78, 79–83, 130
science fiction genre, 10, 12, 14,
   111–115, 123, 128n160, 128–9
   passim, 131, 149n197
social / political commentary within,
   79–83, 86–87, 105–121
speed as an aspect of, 15, 75–76,
   102–103, 118–121, 127–135
style, as an outlet for male African
   American authors, 121–127
as tool of acculturation, 84, 89
venue for socialism, 110–118
theme of technology and the body in,
   131–140
visuality of, 75, 84
Pyramid Books, 166

Rabinowitz, Paula, 12
Railroad Man's Magazines, 75
Railroad Stories, 129–130
Raine, William McCleod, 167
Rainey, Lawrence, 8, 9, 33, 42, 61, 62, 91, 157
Ranch Romances, 78, 83, 88, 113, 116
Random House, 162, 190, 193, 203
Rapp, William Jourdan, 122
Rarity Press, 186
Reader's Digest, 68
Real Detective Story, 126
Rear Window (Hitchcock), 98
Red Arrow Books, 165
Red Book, 65
Reed, Ishmael, 127
Regionalism, American, 29–34
Remarque, Erich Maria, 137, 167
Reprint magazines, 14, 66–69; *see also*
   Golden Book
Review of Reviews, 66
Reynolds, Bruce, 51
Rice, George Henry, 114
Rickenbacker, Eddie, 132
Roberts, Thomas, 155
Roberts, W. Adolphe, 105

Robots, as a symbol of the mechanization
   of culture, 137–139
Rodman, Selden, 167
Rohmer, Sax, 83
Romance (genre); *see* pulps
Rose, Danis, 172
Rose, Jonathon, 12, 40, 65
Roth, Henry, *Call It Sleep*, 190
Roth, Philip, 84
Roth, Samuel 28, 190
Roving Eye Press, 118
Rubin, Joan Shelley, 40
Russell, Bertrand, 128

Sabitini, Rafael
   Captain Blood, 98
   The Sea Hawk, 98
Sale, Richard, 98
Salinger, J.D., 167
Samples, Ed, 130
Sampson, Robert, 75
Saroyan, William, 190
Sartre, John-Paul, 1
   Intimacy, 154
Sassoon, Siegfried, 136
Saturday Evening Post, 30, 59, 64, 65,
   104, 201
Saturday Review of Literature, 89, 215
Saucy Movie Tales, 98
Saucy Stories, 3, 42, 43, 45, 52, 54, 59, 73,
   75, 106
Savoy, the, 186
Sayers, Dorothy, 149
Scholes, Robert, 4, 10
Schuyler, George, 15, 123–124
   Black Internationale, 123
   Black No More, 123
   "Negro Art Hokum," 123
Schwartz, Laurence, 202–203
Science and Fantasy Stories, 129
Science Fiction, (genre); *see* Pulps
Science Fiction, as venue for socialism,
   112–115
Scientific Detective Monthly, 129
Scott, Bonnie Kime, 4n3, 5, 49
Scribner's Magazine, 11, 60, 63, 66, 68,
   73, 104
Scribners (publisher), 91, 128, 158, 209
Secession, 65n105

Seifert, Elizabeth, 81–82
Seldes, Gilbert, 23, 41, 61
Sennett, Mack, 61
Shadow Magazine, 100, 116
Shadow, the (character), 132
Shaw, George Bernard, 168
Shock, 132
Short Story, 75, 98, 179
Show, 49
Showalter, Elaine, 136, 188
Signet Books, 167, 167, 197, 200, 203
Sky Birds, 200
Sloan, John, 118
Smart magazines, 45–51; see also Vogue, Vanity Fair, The New Yorker, Esquire
Smart Set, The, 3, 14, 17–59, 63, 64, 65, 67, 68, 92, 104, 109, 119, 130, 185, 188
  History of, 22–27, 56–59
  and *The Little Review*, 38–42
  as modernist venue, 20–25, 38–42, 56–58
  as venue for popular modernism, 14, 21–22, 56–58
  pulp authors in, 20, 26, 27–29, 52
  pulp legacy, 58–59
  reputation of, 21, 25–29, 34, 35, 58
Smith, Clark Ashton, 28, 101
Smith, Erin, 9, 12, 78, 83, 86, 115
Smith's Magazine, 105
Smithers, Leonard, 185–186
Snappy Magazine, 190, 196, 197, 201
Snappy Stories, 52–59, 63, 65, 68, 73, 75, 105
Sneddon, Robert W., 52
Socialist Call, 111
Speed, 129
Spicy Adventure, 72
Spicy Detective, 71–73
Spicy Mystery, 72
Spicy Stories, 52
Spicy Western, 72
Spillane, Mickey, 110, 154, 167, 196–197, 198, 206–210, 216
  The Big Kill, 154
  I, The Jury, 210
  The Girl Hunter, 209
  The Long Wait, 209
Sporting Times, 193
Springs, Elliot, 200

Startling Stories, 114
Stearn, Harold, 33
Stein, Gertrude, 23, 26, 85, 87, 109, 112, 120, 146, 154, 159, 190, 195, 213, 216
Stevenson, Robert Louis, 67
Story, 190
Story-Teller, The, 65
Strand, The, 65
Street and Smith, 63, 75, 83, 115, 149, 165
Street and Smith's Complete Magazine, 79
Strindberg, August, 24
Student Writer, The, 144
Sumner, John Saxton, 18, 20, 58
Sure Fire Magazine, 132
Swank, 198
Swineburne, Algernon Charles, 67, 186, 188
Symons, Arthur, 23, 186
Synchromism, 23
Synge, John Millington, 68

Tauchnitz Books, 164
Teasdale, Sara, 26, 38
Telling Tales, 52, 54, 65, 73, 105, 113
Thayer, John Adams, 23, 25, 26
Thompson, Jim, 197
Thurber, James, 112
Thurman, Wallace, 122
  Infants of Spring, 122–123
Time Magazine, 66, 68
Tit-bits, 165
Toomer, Jean, 122
Top Notch, 63, 75, 118, 119
Town Topics, 22
Trade and specialized magazines, 65n106
Transatlantic Review, 49
transition, 49, 105, 118, 119, 197, 198
Trogdon, Robert, 8
Trotter, David, 180
True Confessions, 73
True Detective, 26
True Romances, 78
True Story, 82, 122
Two Worlds, 3

Untermeyer, Loius, 26

Van Loon, H. W., 12, 73
Van Vechten, Carl, 23, 28
  Nigger Heaven, 85

Vanity Fair, 8, 9, 17, 39, 45, 46–48, 61, 62–63, 64, 65, 73, 77, 88, 97, 131, 155
Vico, Giambattista, 128
Viking Press, 67
Visuality
   of *Finnegans Wake*, 160–161
   of Modernism, 6, 15, 119–121, 158, 159–164
   of the book and resistance to it, 6, 12, 119–120, 158, 159–164, 172–173, 185
   of paperbacks, 15, 159–64, 169–173
   of the pulps, 75n14, 184
Vogue Magazine, 46, 61, 62, 64
Vorticism, 33, 34, 74n11, 128

Wall Street Journal, 141
Wallace, Edgar, 87
War Aces, 214
War Birds, 136, 200
War Birds, The Diary of an Unknown Aviator, 200
Warner Publishing, 75
Warner, Eltinge F., 18–20, 106
Weaver, Harriet Shaw, 42
Weinbaum, Stanley, 14, 114–115
Weird Tales, 26, 28, 65, 105, 114
Welles, Orson, 98n69
Wells, H.G., 33, 128n160
West, Nathanael, 36, 111, 159
Western Story, 63, 214
Wexler, Joyce, 181–183
Weybright, Victor, 166
Whitfield, Raoul, 85
Wicke, Jennifer, 5, 7, 8
Wicker-Wilson, Carol, 80, 82
Wild Party, The, (March), 71
Wild West Weekly, 88
Wilde, Oscar, 1, 54, 185, 186
Wilder, Thornton, 156

William Faro Incorporated, 184
Williams, Raymond, 61
Williams, Tennessee, 105, 167
Williams, William Carlos, 85, 120
Wilson, Edmond, 21, 27
Wings [film], 200
Wings! (magazine), 129, 200
Wittgenstein, Ludwig, 149
Wizard, The, 84
Wolfe, Thomas, 167
Wollheim, Donald, 114
Wonder Stories, 114, 130
Wood, James Playsted, 61
Woolf, Virginia, 4, 36, 62, 154, 159, 165, 168, 174, 179, 193, 215
   Between the Acts, 7
   Hogarth Press, 91
   Mrs. Dalloway, 128
   Orlando, 194
   The Years, 153
Woolrich, Cornell, 98, 195
Wright, Frank Lloyd, 71
Wright, Richard, 111, 125, 175
   Black Boy, 84, 125–127
   Native Son, 84, 126
   The Outsider, 127
Wright, Willard Huntington, 22n5, 23–25, 27, 58, 188
Writer's Digest, 11, 83
Wyn, A.A., 71, 87

Yeats, W.B., 24, 68, 128, 185
   Cuala Press, 185
Yellow Book, The, 24
Yorke, C.B., 79–80

Zeppelin Stories, 75, 85, 129
Ziegfield Follies, 61
Zola, Emile, *Nana*, 169, 187